PENGUIN BOOKS

BISMARCK'S WAR

'Chrastil's new book aims to revive the [illegible] and to show, as she states it, how it "transform[illegible] the destinies of Europeans" . . . Elegantly written, marvellously readable . . . *Bismarck's War* is very much worth reading as a lively and effective account of a largely forgotten past conflict' Jonathan Sperber, *The Times Literary Supplement*

'Brings the first "modern" European conflict to life . . . Chrastil's compassionate and thought-provoking history does justice to both sides of this legacy, the great statesman's achievements tempered with their human cost' Camilla Cassidy, *Daily Telegraph*

'Engrossing narrative history . . . The mosaic of glimpses into the human hopes and tragedies of the Franco-Prussian War leaves one thinking long after the last page' Katja Hoyer, *Engelsberg Ideas*

'This is an impressive work, fluent, wide-ranging, vivid in its use of sources, and central to an understanding of Europe's subsequent history' David Crane, *Spectator*

'A fresh and compelling history of the most important European war between Waterloo and World War I. In rich and engaging detail, she shows how it laid much of the foundation for the wars of the twentieth century, even as it was seen at the time, and subsequently remembered, as a relatively conventional conflict. A tour-de-force' David A. Bell, Princeton University

'*Bismarck's War* brings the Franco-Prussian War to life through the words and deeds of participants both on and off the battlefield. Rachel Chrastil's fascinating examination of the conflict compellingly narrates its military and political dimensions, and it puts the war in a global context, emphasizing its human cost and the international response to the humanitarian crisis it created. An engrossing, compassionate, and critical interrogation of a decisive historical event' Carolyn J. Eichner, author of *The Paris Commune*

'Rachel Chrastil colourfully describes how the Franco-Prussian War destroyed the long European peace established after Napoleon's defeat in 1815. Beginning as a midsummer cabinet war between monarchs, one of them Napoleon's nephew, Bismarck's invasion of France bogged down in winter rain and snow, and became a rancorous war of peoples that kindled the inferno of World War I' Geoffrey Wawro, author of *The Franco-Prussian War*

ABOUT THE AUTHOR

Rachel Chrastil is a professor of history at Xavier University and the author of *Organizing for War: France 1870–1914*, *The Siege of Strasbourg* and *How to Be Childless: A History and Philosophy of Life without Children.*

Bismarck's War

The Franco-Prussian War and the Making of Modern Europe

RACHEL CHRASTIL

PENGUIN BOOKS

PENGUIN BOOKS

UK | USA | Canada | Ireland | Australia
India | New Zealand | South Africa

Penguin Books is part of the Penguin Random House group of companies
whose addresses can be found at global.penguinrandomhouse.com

First published by Allen Lane 2023
Published in Penguin Books 2024
001

Typeset by Jouve (UK), Milton Keynes
Printed and bound in Great Britain by Clays Ltd, Elcograf S.p.A.

The authorized representative in the EEA is Penguin Random House Ireland,
Morrison Chambers, 32 Nassau Street, Dublin D02 YH68

A CIP catalogue record for this book is available from the British Library

ISBN: 978–0–141–99161–0

www.greenpenguin.co.uk

For my brother and my sister,
Mike and Liz

Contents

Acknowledgements

Thank you to Simon Winder, for believing in the project and for his generous support along the way. Thank you to Nicolas Bourguinat, Alexandre Dupont, Rebekah Eklund, Colin Foss, Michael Graham, SJ, Colleen Hanycz, Beeto Lyle, Mareike König, David Mengel, the late John Merriman, Odile Roynette, Amy Teitelman, Gilles Vogt and Amy Whipple, for encouragement, support, and opportunities, and to the community of scholars engrossed in this conflict. My thanks and love as always to John Fairfield. My parents and nephew have brought much love to my life. This book is dedicated to my brother and sister, for the perspective they bring to all things.

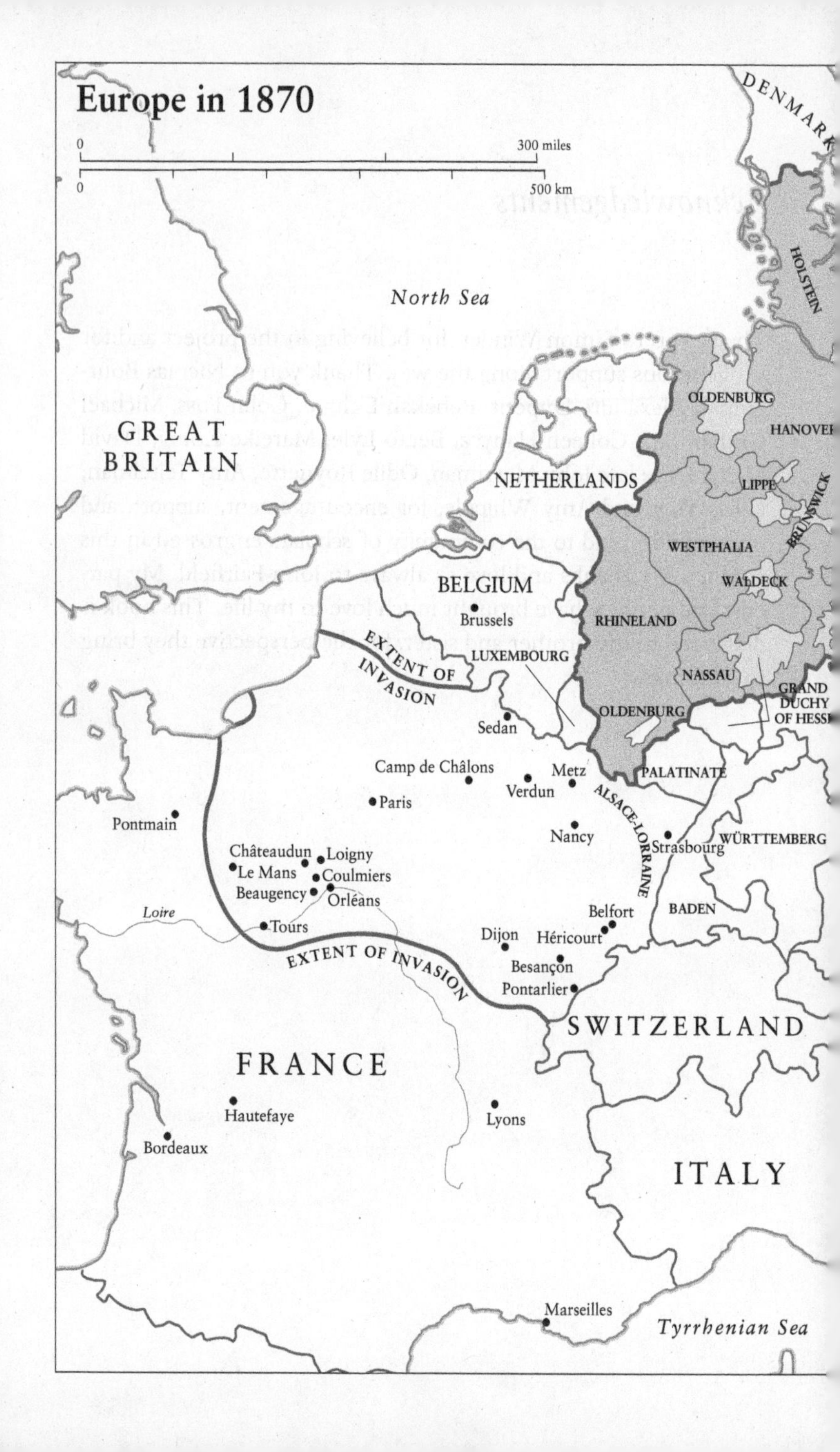
Europe in 1870
0
300 miles
0
500 km
DENMARK
HOLSTEIN
North Sea
OLDENBURG
HANOVER
GREAT
BRITAIN
NETHERLANDS
LIPPE
BRUNSWICK
WESTPHALIA
BELGIUM
WALDECK
Brussels
RHINELAND
EXTENT OF
INVASION
LUXEMBOURG
NASSAU
GRAND
DUCHY
OF HESSE
OLDENBURG
Sedan
Camp de Châlons
Metz
PALATINATE
Verdun
Paris
ALSACE-LORRAINE
Pontmain
Nancy
Strasbourg
WÜRTTEMBERG
Châteaudun
Loigny
Le Mans
Coulmiers
Beaugency
Orléans
Loire
Belfort
BADEN
Tours
Dijon
Héricourt
EXTENT OF INVASION
Besançon
Pontarlier
SWITZERLAND
FRANCE
Hautefaye
Lyons
Bordeaux
ITALY
Marseilles
Tyrrhenian Sea

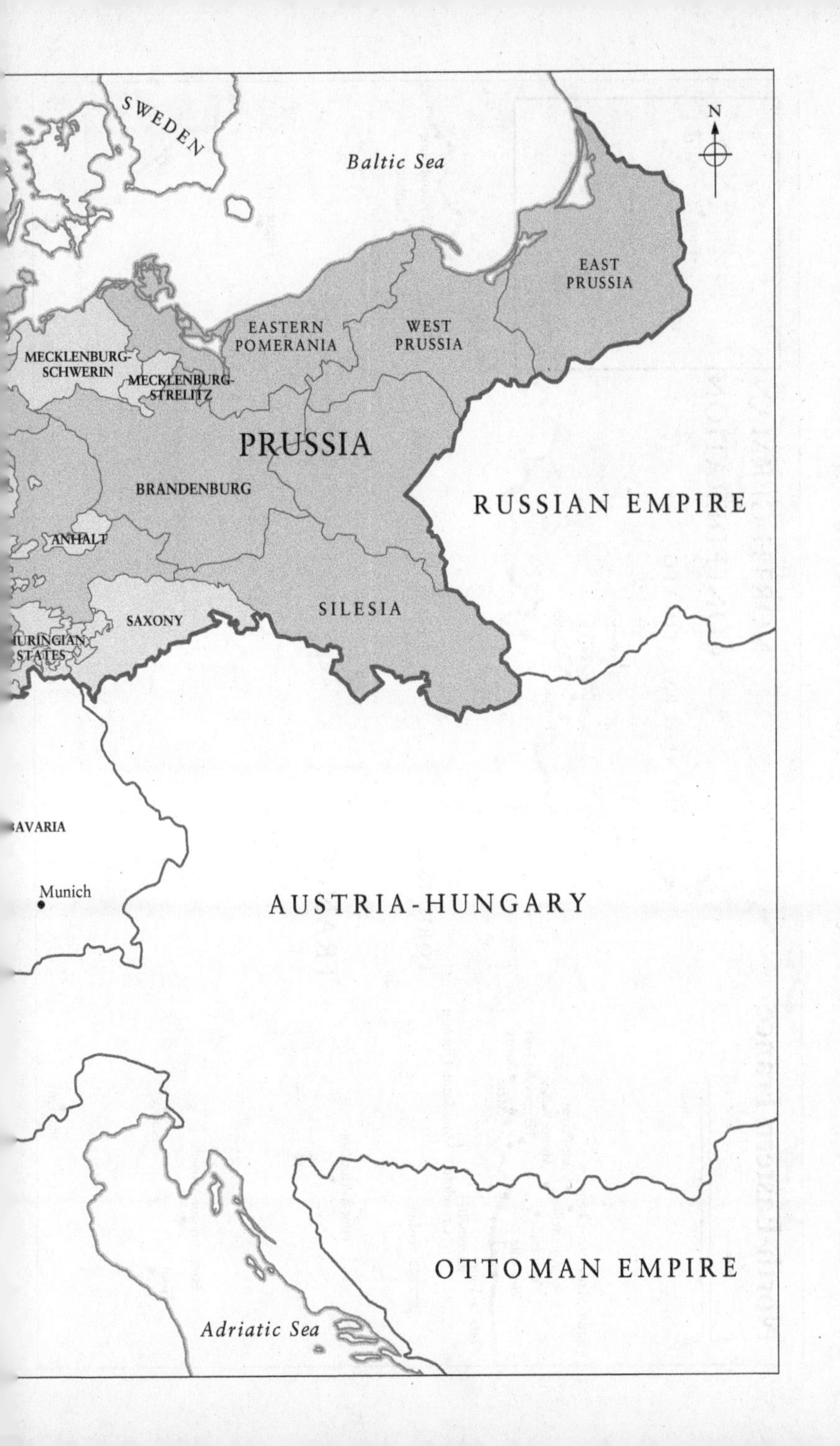

SWEDEN
Baltic Sea
N
EAST PRUSSIA
EASTERN POMERANIA
WEST PRUSSIA
MECKLENBURG-SCHWERIN
MECKLENBURG-STRELITZ
PRUSSIA
BRANDENBURG
RUSSIAN EMPIRE
ANHALT
SAXONY
SILESIA
STATES
AVARIA
Munich
AUSTRIA-HUNGARY
OTTOMAN EMPIRE
Adriatic Sea

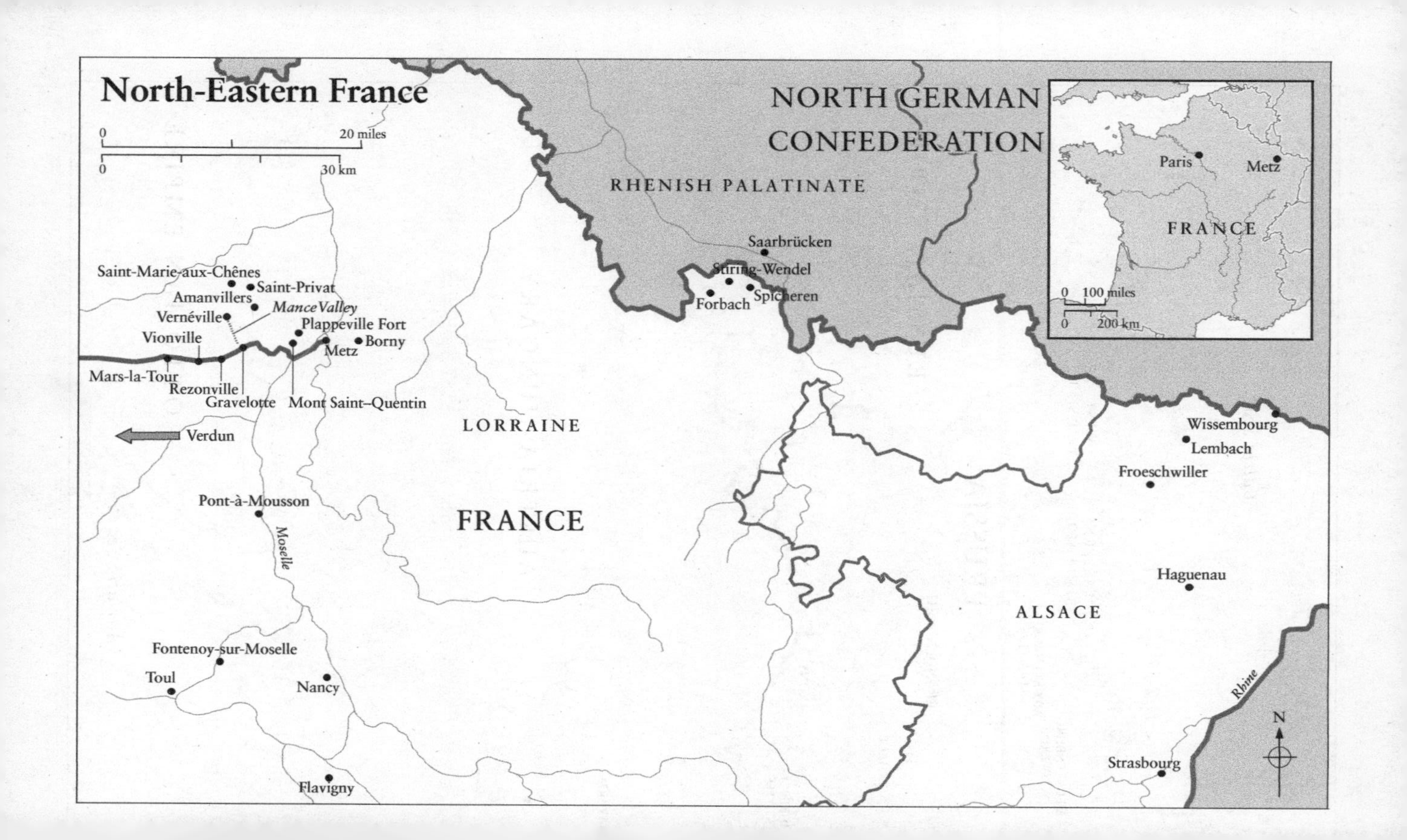
North-Eastern France
0
20 miles
0
30 km
NORTH GERMAN CONFEDERATION
RHENISH PALATINATE
Saarbrücken
Stiring-Wendel
Forbach
Spicheren
Paris
Metz
FRANCE
0 100 miles
0 200 km
Saint-Marie-aux-Chênes
Saint-Privat
Amanvillers
Mance Valley
Vernéville
Plappeville Fort
Vionville
Metz
Borny
Mars-la-Tour
Rezonville
Gravelotte
Mont Saint-Quentin
LORRAINE
Verdun
Wissembourg
Lembach
Froeschwiller
Pont-à-Mousson
FRANCE
Moselle
Haguenau
ALSACE
Fontenoy-sur-Moselle
Toul
Nancy
Rhine
N
Strasbourg
Flavigny

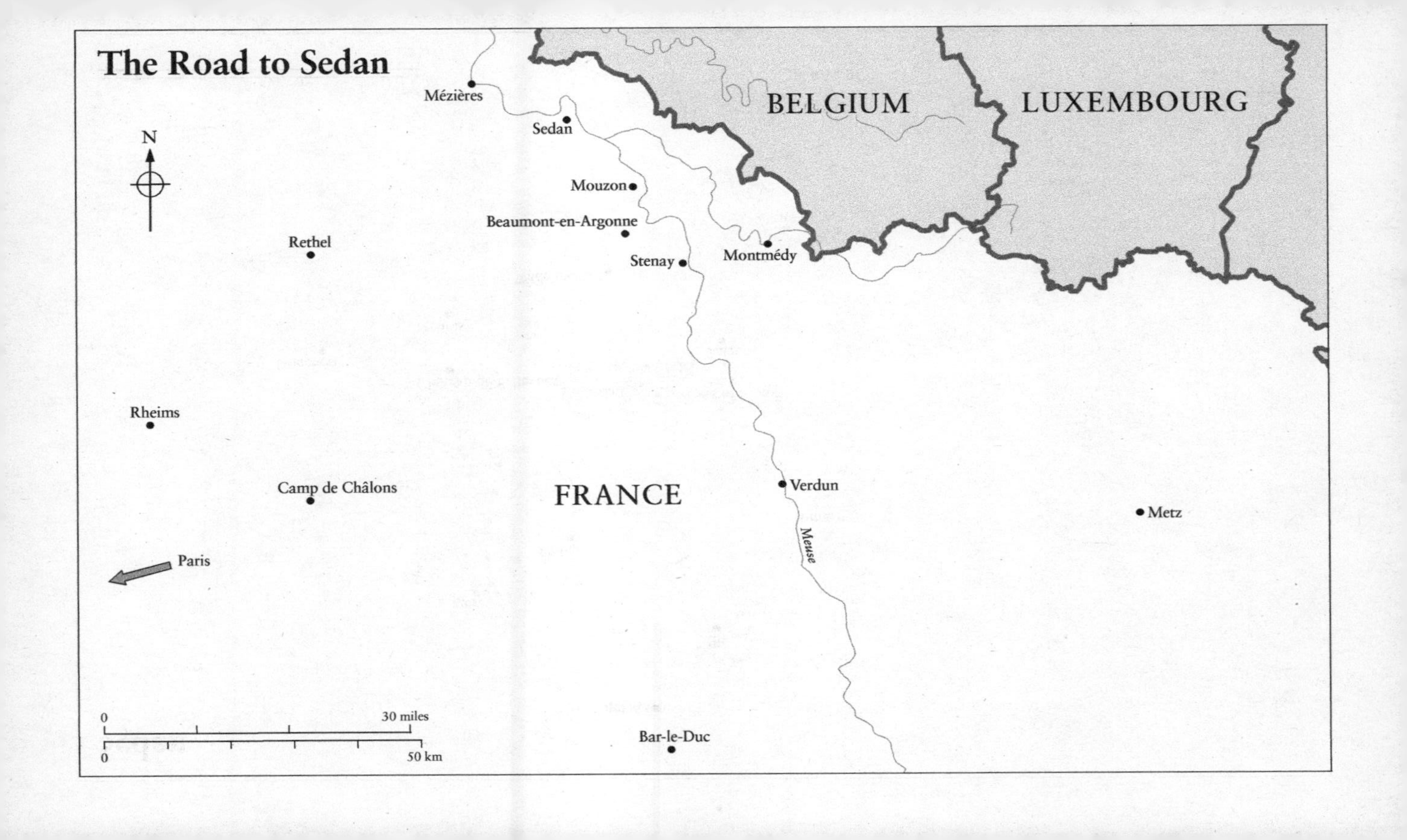
The Road to Sedan
N
Mézières
Sedan
BELGIUM
LUXEMBOURG
Mouzon
Beaumont-en-Argonne
Rethel
Stenay
Montmédy
Rheims
Camp de Châlons
FRANCE
Verdun
Metz
Meuse
Paris
0
30 miles
0
50 km
Bar-le-Duc

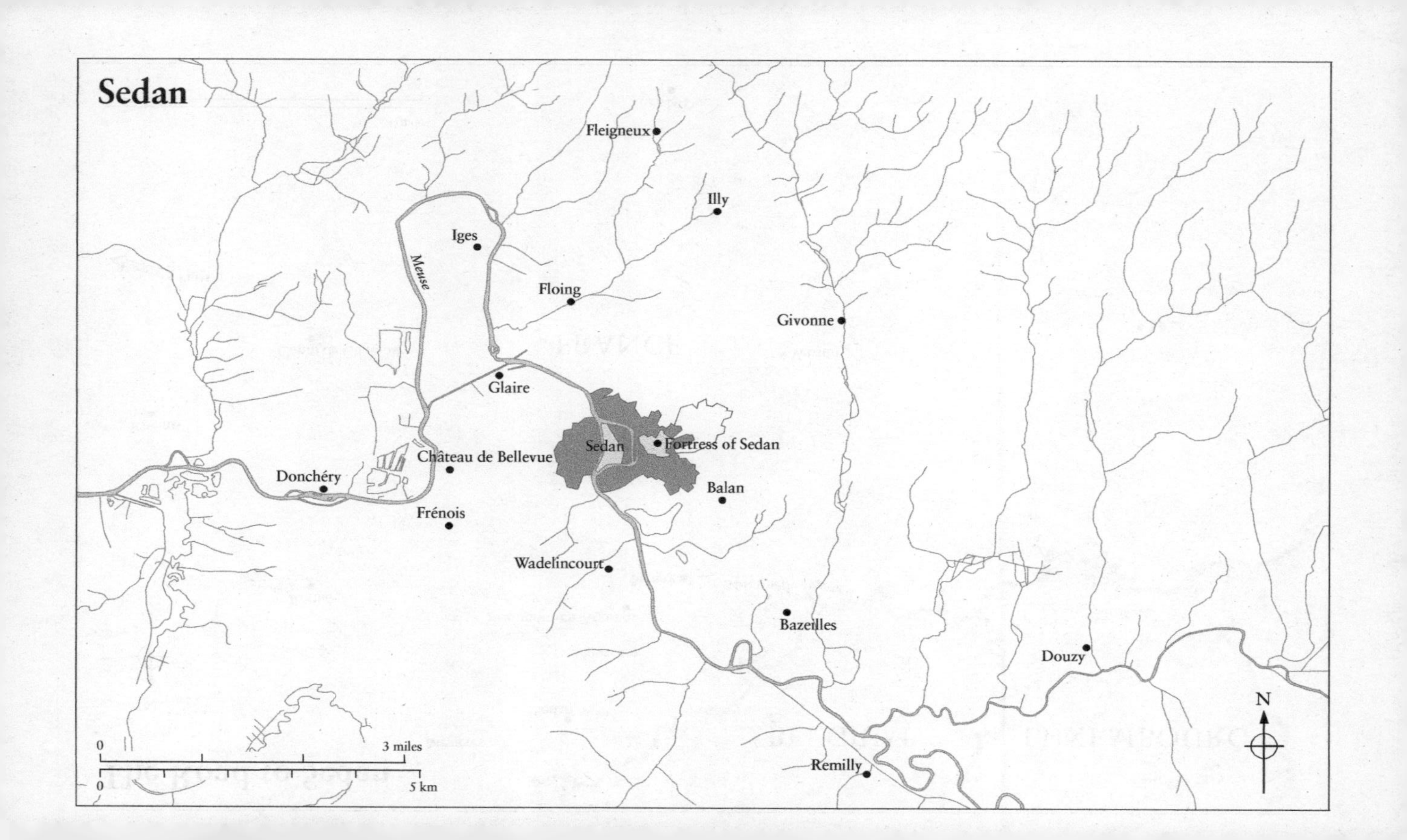
Sedan
Fleigneux
Illy
Iges
Meuse
Floing
Givonne
Glaire
Sedan
Fortress of Sedan
Château de Bellevue
Donchéry
Balan
Frénois
Wadelincourt
Bazeilles
Douzy
Remilly
N
0
3 miles
0
5 km

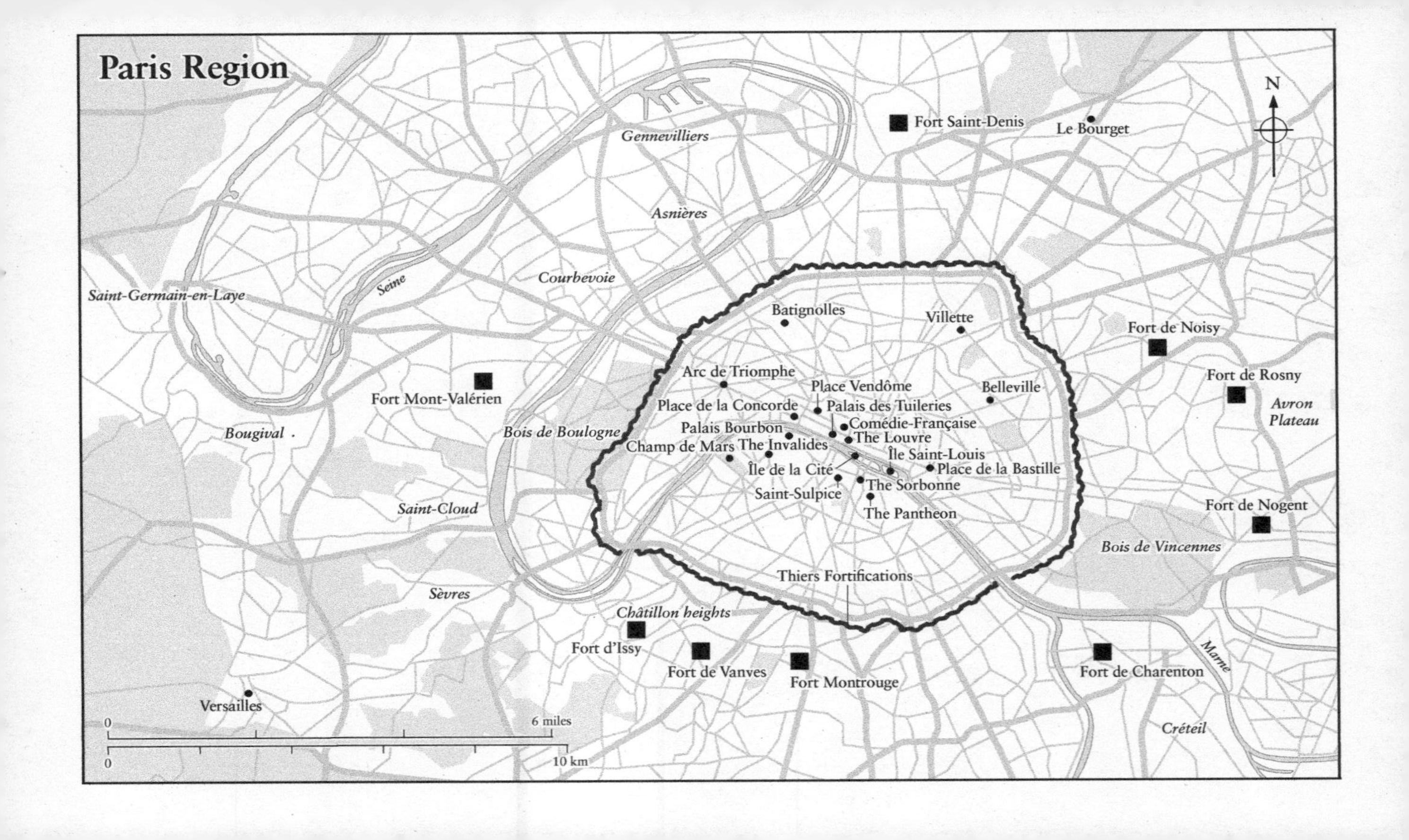
Paris Region
N
Fort Saint-Denis
Le Bourget
Gennevilliers
Asnières
Courbevoie
Seine
Saint-Germain-en-Laye
Batignolles
Villette
Fort de Noisy
Fort de Rosny
Avron Plateau
Fort Mont-Valérien
Arc de Triomphe
Place Vendôme
Belleville
Place de la Concorde
Palais des Tuileries
Comédie-Française
Palais Bourbon
The Louvre
Bois de Boulogne
Bougival
Champ de Mars
The Invalides
Île Saint-Louis
Île de la Cité
Place de la Bastille
The Sorbonne
Saint-Sulpice
The Pantheon
Saint-Cloud
Fort de Nogent
Bois de Vincennes
Thiers Fortifications
Sèvres
Châtillon heights
Fort d'Issy
Fort de Vanves
Fort Montrouge
Fort de Charenton
Marne
Versailles
Créteil
0
6 miles
0
10 km

Introduction

The Franco-Prussian War transformed for ever the destinies of Europeans. It was the largest war in Europe between Waterloo and the Great War. Some two million soldiers took part, and more than 180,000 died. In this conflict, Germany unified, and France laid the groundwork for a lasting republic. It represented the decisive end to French dominance on the continent and the rise of Germany, in one of the most dramatic and one-sided defeats of any modern European army.

In July 1870, France declared war on Prussia, and soon faced a conflict with both the North German Confederation that Prussia dominated and the southern German states of Bavaria, Baden and Württemberg. France entered the war as an empire, headed by Napoleon III. After a series of bloody defeats, culminating at Sedan in early September, Napoleon III was overthrown in favour of a provisional, nominally republican government known as the Government of National Defence. Although the republicans attempted to continue the war, using volunteers to replace the wrecked and captured regular army, they proved to be no more successful than the Empire. Nevertheless, the German forces were now drawn into a six-month conflict that extended over nearly a third of French territory. In January 1871, the united German Empire was declared under Wilhelm I, and, shortly after, the French government finally agreed to an armistice.

This was not a war of angels. It featured nationalistic tribalism, poor leadership, unnecessary physical hardship, and spirals of violence that unfolded across the course of the entire conflict. Mobilized men and their families put their lives and ethical souls at risk for the sake of this dubious conflict. And this is what is so fascinating about the war: without moral clarity about the justness of their cause, individuals and townspeople had to navigate an uncharted landscape of war. Most tried simply to survive, while many strove to make something better than the reality the war presented to them.

We've largely forgotten this crucial war because of the decades of distance between us, the subsequent world wars and the creation of the European Union, which rests on the pragmatic relationship between France and Germany. Neither France nor Germany now includes this conflict among their favoured national histories.

Yet the Franco-Prussian War plays a foundational role in the world wars of the twentieth century. The war of 1870, with its large-scale, mechanized warfare that swept civilians up in a nationalistic conflict, anticipated the motivations, the assumptions and the emotional underpinnings of later conflicts. The line from Sedan to the Western Front was never a predetermined path, and still less complete are the linkages between 1870 and Vichy and National Socialism, yet the Franco-Prussian War provides a bridge from the Napoleonic Wars to the two world wars. It established the daunting challenge of how to face superior defensive weaponry, including long-range rifles, cannon and the early machine gun. It was both an era of global communication through telegraph and one in which orders were shouted on horseback. Armies moved by train yet could be lost to enemy reconnaissance simply by travelling beyond the horizon. The Franco-Prussian War contained novel practices as well. It was the first European conflict in which a nation housed thousands of prisoners of war and in which both parties had signed the Geneva Convention and allowed Red Cross volunteer organizations to care for sick and wounded soldiers. The war also featured the incorporation of colonial forces fighting on European soil and the advent of racialized army stereotypes in European conflict. Furthermore, it demonstrated the challenges of mobilizing a large population of citizen-soldiers over a broad sweep of territory for months at a time. Civilian administration, industry and manpower became disastrously embedded in service to the army.

The Franco-Prussian War also opened new questions about the role of civilians in western wars. The war represented the triumph of universal conscription, war experience and invasion over the civilian claim to peace and normality. Citizen-soldiers contemplated the reality of killing other men and the possibility of being killed. National Guardsmen in Paris tried on the personality of the militarized soldier, while returning home to their families in the evening. The French use of *francs-tireurs*, or guerrilla units, re-opened the question of the appropriate relationship between civilians and soldiers, both in the field and as occupiers.

The war furthermore saw a great expansion in state powers and the ability of government to shape the circumstances of broad swathes of population. Paris became the first modern city to face both wartime shortages and random bombardment. German civilians living in Paris faced the suspicion and ire of French citizens and the French government. At the same time, again and again, individuals, towns and organizations were obliged to fend for themselves, to improvise their reactions to life and death situations for which there had been no state preparation and little guidance. Readers around the world avidly devoured newspaper accounts of the conflict from correspondents on the ground, fuelled by telegrams that could reach across the Atlantic. Newspapers in besieged cities such as Paris, Metz, or Strasbourg, cut off from the outside world, had to manage with scraps of rumours. Citizens formed fire brigades and sought to alleviate the suffering of their fellow countrymen.

The war of 1870 saw the remaking of political relationships both great and small, through violent actions and highly symbolic actions. Political fortunes were made and undone. The German states unified, contrary to centuries-old rivalries, in the fulfilment of German nationalism as a conservative, reactionary force. In France, the declaration of war represented a moment of national unity. Soon after, Napoleon III's Second Empire tumbled to ruins. The fissures in the French Left deepened, while the markers of social status flattened and re-formed under the stresses of invasion. For many, the war demonstrated the continuation of the reactionary peasant against the urban revolutionary. To Karl Marx, the siege of Paris and the Commune that followed were the true harbinger of socialism. To Giuseppe

Garibaldi, the war pitted the Universal Republic against the forces of monarchism and clericalism. To Pope Pius IX, the war spelled the destruction of the temporal power of the Catholic Church.

Finally, the conflict between France and the German states was a war of emotions, from start to finish. Tight-lipped stoicism had no place in the Franco-Prussian War, except maybe for the Prussian Field Marshal Helmuth von Moltke. Memories of the war are replete with tears, outbursts of anger, wounded pride, oratorical flamboyance, pitiable suffering, quixotic charges and the literal bestowing of laurels. All this emotion undergirded a conflict in which impersonal bombardment, long-range rifles and devastating machine guns threatened to dehumanize civilians and soldiers on all sides.

1. *Declaration*

'War! War with France!' On 15 July 1870, the Munich native Dietrich von Lassberg, a twenty-two-year-old officer, thrilled to the announcement that Bavaria would soon join Prussia to fight against Napoleon III's imperial army. His brother Rudolf, also in the army, was delighted at the news too, though Lassberg's 'mother and siblings did not share the joy'.[1] This moment of euphoria, of a Bavarian soldier exulting to fight alongside Prussians instead of against them, encapsulated the power of war to create unity.

The declaration of war represented a key turning point in a long path that, in the end, led to German unification. In the early nineteenth century, Germans seeking the national union of dozens of German states within the German Confederation (established by the Congress of Vienna in 1815) had aligned themselves politically with constitutionalism and liberal democracy, grounding their justification less in a common monarchy than in their German-ness. The dream of a German nation-state had come close to fruition during the revolutionary years of 1848–49, only to be undermined by division on the Left and crushed by reactionaries. In the decades that followed, the conservative Prussian statesman Bismarck threw his weight behind the effort to forge German unification under an authoritarian, Prussian, monarchy, rather than under a liberal democracy as planned by the earlier revolutionaries. In a speech demanding military preparedness at the Budget Committee of the Prussian House of Representatives, he declared, 'The great questions of the time will not be resolved by speeches and majority decisions – that was the great mistake of 1848 and 1849 – but by iron and blood.'[2]

Prussia undertook three wars in quick succession, now known as the Wars of German Unification. At the time, nobody, not even

Bismarck, had a precise plan mapped out. However, the Prussian minister-president shrewdly took advantage of diplomatic situations to play powers both great and small against each other. The wars were less about the direct conquest of territory and more about demonstrating to everyone involved the utility, or even the inevitability, of a Prussia-led unified German state that would heavily influence, but not completely overturn, the delicate balance of the five Great Powers.

First came the war against Denmark over Schleswig-Holstein, duchies that were ruled by the king of Denmark without being incorporated into the Danish kingdom. When the king created a new constitution that directly incorporated Schleswig into the kingdom in 1863 – unlike Holstein, Schleswig included Danish speakers and was not part of the German Confederation – Bismarck objected. He demanded a new constitution, and in 1864 the Danes fought back, assuming that France and Britain would join on their side against Prussia and Austria. The Danes proved friendless and were quickly defeated. The Treaty of Vienna gave Prussia administration of Schleswig, which afforded them the port of Kiel and a military corridor through Holstein, now under the administration of Prussia's tenuous and uneasy ally Austria. Not surprisingly, Prussia and Austria themselves now were headed for war.

That conflict erupted in 1866 and lasted just seven weeks. After securing the neutrality of Italy and France, Prussia marched into Holstein and left the German Confederation. The Confederation – including the states of Hanover, Saxony, Bavaria, Baden and Württemberg – then declared war on Prussia. The Prussians swiftly dispatched the Austrian and other German armies, notably at the crucial battle of Königgrätz. Bismarck ended the conflict quickly – before Moltke could send his troops to Vienna – to avoid intervention from third parties.

In the Treaty of Prague (1866), the dissolved German Confederation was replaced by the North German Confederation, a union of twenty-two states and principalities north of the Main river, with a Reichstag and dominated by Prussia, with King Wilhelm as president (and king of Prussia, of course) and Bismarck as federal chancellor. Bavaria signed a treaty promising to ally itself with Prussia in case France attacked that state, and Prussia annexed Hanover, Frankfurt, Nassau, Hesse-Kassel and Schleswig-Holstein, too. But with Bavaria, Baden, Württemberg and part of the Grand Duchy of Hesse still outside the North German Confederation, it was clear to most observers that Bismarck would seek an opportunity to compel their incorporation, too – not through conquest, but through shared victory.

France provided the most likely target. After 1866, it was clear that, unless savvier leaders took the helm, France and Prussia were heading for conflict. The previous decade had left too many black eyes and bad feelings for Napoleon III to stomach any further ambitions on the part of Prussia. France had been embarrassed in Mexico in the early 1860s in its efforts to replace the Mexican Republic, sidelined in Poland in its struggle for independence from Russia, and brushed off for its neutrality in 1866. Amid that war crisis, Napoleon III had demanded (in vain) that, in return for his not intervening, Prussia allow France to annex Belgium and Luxembourg, a demand that Bismarck used to his advantage four years later.

In the early months of 1870, Napoleon III seemed to have solidified his position after over two decades in power. Louis-Napoleon Bonaparte, the nephew of Emperor Napoleon I, had led France since 1848. He leveraged his name and his claims to support the working class to secure election to the presidency immediately following the revolution of 1848 that had established the Second Republic. On 2 December 1851, he staged a *coup d'état* that dismantled the republic, and one year later he declared himself emperor, heading a regime known as the Second Empire. For years, he enjoyed widespread support among the upper classes and the peasantry, and fostered business and industry, banks and public works. Exports increased, particularly in the metallurgical industry and luxury goods. Entrepreneurs gained access to capital while French investors supported many major construction projects, including railroads and the Suez Canal.

The radical generation of 1848, devastated by Napoleon III's dismantling of the Second Republic, scattered into exile or retreated into private life. Nevertheless, despite Napoleon III's intentions to establish a Bonapartist dynasty, curtail free association and impose censorship, a broad republican culture developed during the Second Empire. Thanks to a strong economy that supported the growth of a middle class of businessmen and professionals, civil society blossomed in the 1850s and 1860s through Freemasonry, the Paris bar, universities, the arts world, as well as through Jewish and Protestant consistories.

Napoleon III maintained universal male suffrage (France was the only European country that could make this claim), while assuring that electors had few real choices. Ministers were responsible to the emperor himself, not to electors, and only the emperor could propose legislation. Napoleon III brought conservatives along by promising social order and by making peace with the Catholic Church.

In the 1860s, Napoleon announced his intention to create a 'liberal empire', in which he aimed to deflate the opposition by co-opting some of their goals. In 1860, France and Britain concluded a liberal trade agreement. Soon, the National Assembly had been granted the right to approve the national budget. Press and labour restrictions were relaxed. In 1868, Napoleon III permitted freedom of assembly, leading to a proliferation of clubs and associations. Rather than dismantle opposition, however, these changes provided additional means for republicans to garner support. Young idealists of 1848, now twenty years older and more experienced, still imagined a future where Frenchmen could freely elect their leaders, though the precise nature of that future remained highly contentious. A few opposition political leaders managed to gain seats in the Corps Législatif.

After an embarrassing 1869 election, the emperor proposed constitutional reforms granting significant power to the legislature. He then called for a plebiscite in May 1870, asking whether voters approved of the liberal reforms that had taken place since 1860. This cunning wording neutralized the ability of voters to express the desire for more radical change. The May 1870 plebiscite therefore passed with a vote of 83 per cent, carried throughout France, except in Paris and Marseilles.

In the summer of 1870, then, Napoleon III's position appeared commanding, yet it was impossible to tell just how strong the opposition had grown. Furthermore, France in early July 1870 had no allies, no formal plans, and no clear military objectives.

The immediate war crisis began with conflict over the succession to the Spanish throne, with the guiding hand of Bismarck assuring that the crisis would support his goal of German unification under a strong monarch. It was Bismarck who encouraged the Spanish to offer the throne to Prince Leopold von Hohenzollern-Sigmaringen, a relative of King Wilhelm. And it was Bismarck, taking advantage of the moment to check French ambition, who made sure that the ensuing dispute between France and Prussia could not be resolved peacefully. Much as they had chafed against Habsburg encirclement in centuries past, the French objected to Prince Leopold's Spanish candidacy as an encirclement that threatened the European balance of power. The candidacy was withdrawn.

Yet, having stoked French public opinion in favour of war, many on the French imperial council did not have enough cover to back down, even if they had wanted to. The French foreign minister, the duc de Gramont, with the support of Napoleon III, pressed for a guarantee from Wilhelm himself, as head of the Hohenzollern family, that no similar future proposal would be made. This was a promise that no sovereign would make. King Wilhelm, in conversation at Ems with the French ambassador to Prussia, Count Benedetti, declined politely. Bismarck edited his response – known as the Ems telegram – to make the king's refusal seem more abrupt and insulting.

In Paris, meanwhile, the minister of war, Edmond Leboeuf, agitated for quick mobilization, and Gramont continued to aggressively seek an opportunity for war. The Council of Ministers decided to call up reserves on 14 July. In the Corps Législatif on the following day, Gramont and Prime Minister Émile Ollivier presented the case for voting in favour of war credits. A few members of the opposition objected, notably Adolphe Thiers. Most, however, followed the tide of public opinion and the convictions of the ministers, and voted to support war credits, 245 to 10. France began to mobilize the next day, and officially declared war on 19 July.

In the days following France's war credits vote, a massive and emotional reworking of allegiances rippled across Europe. In fields and urban squares, through telegraph wires and off printing presses, in public proclamations and private conversations, those caught up in the conflict sorted out their alignments, both chosen and imposed. They learned to become enemies with some; newfound partners with others, or – in the case of non-belligerent countries – to tread a careful line of neutrality. For many in Alsace or in Bavaria, the reconception of their allies as enemies and vice versa was incomplete and jarring.

News of France's vote on war credits reached Berlin on the afternoon of 15 July. An eyewitness reported that the news 'is received with fearful solemnity. Every cheek burns with suppressed indignation. There is resolution too.'[3] A crowd awaited the arrival of the king from Ems, scheduled for 8.40 that evening, around the flag-bedecked train station and along Unter den Linden and Friedrichstrasse. The royal procession finally arrived bearing the king, the crown prince, Bismarck and Moltke. The crown prince announced the war to the crowd, which shouted its approval with hurrahs. One observer noted, 'There can be no doubt, the war henceforward will be popular in this country, and this means much. It means that everybody will act and make sacrifices for the country. It will be war to the knife.'[4]

Placards and handbills printed the mobilizations and were distributed around the city with the expectation that all would voluntarily co-operate. The four main railroads from the Elbe to the Rhine were stopped for private traffic and devoted to the conveyance of troops, so that – according to the plans discussed on 15 July – 240,000 men from the North German Confederation army would stand on the Rhine within five days, followed soon thereafter by reserves. Prussia ordered a general mobilization – not a partial one – from the first day.

By eleven o'clock that evening, 'amazement has changed to joy. A whole city is intoxicated with gladness. Crowds go singing war songs, arm in arm, down the streets. Some shout, some laugh, and some indulge in witticisms.' In mockery of France's role in the diplomatic crisis over the crown of Spain, 'One man takes another by the throat, and cries: "My neighbor's daughter loves your nephew. He will have nothing to do with her; but if you do not declare that he will never marry her, I will knock you down."'[5] Lutheran hymns mixed with patriotic songs. The distance between piety and patriotism nearly vanished.

Across the German states, leaders rushed to show their devotion to the Prussian cause. In the free city of Hamburg, the Chamber of Commerce sent King Wilhelm a telegram expressing devotion to the honour of Germany, news that filled him with 'pride and tranquility'.[6] In Breslau, 'stormy enthusiasm' erupted at the news.[7] In the Grand Duchy of Hesse, part of which had joined the North German Confederation in 1867, the prime minister declared on 20 July that the German frontier had been breached. His call for war credits was warmly approved 'amid cheers for Germany, the King of Prussia, and the Grand Duke'.[8] Even Frankfurt, the seat of the 1848 Confederation parliament that had lost its status as a free imperial city in 1866, now seemed to fully support a united Germany.

Of course, not everyone was convinced of an inevitable victory, though the extent of German opposition is difficult to measure. Popular opinion is not the same as the exuberant public opinion expressed in newspapers when the press was so firmly dominated by the National Liberals, who were pro-unification and heavily influenced by Bismarck. The National Liberal press moved swiftly to clamp down on negative articles regarding the war, so our evidence of German scepticism comes from other sources. Panicked selling of stocks in Berlin betrayed investors' real state of mind. In

Hanover – like Frankfurt, a recent Prussian acquisition – some 'went their own way, grumbling and embittered, out of hatred for Prussia, and even sympathised openly or in secret with the enemy'.[9] At first, the religious press and some sermons saw the war in the traditional religious interpretation: it was God's punishment. The faithful should be penitent. The liberal press declared these sentiments unpatriotic, and this interpretation did not outlast early German victories.

Despite the treaties requiring the south German states to mobilize, there was room enough for doubt in the minds of many observers. South German neutrality remained a real possibility right up to the Ems telegram. Many in Bavaria wondered why they should send their sons to die over a Hohenzollern candidacy for the Spanish throne. The Prussian leadership worried that Napoleon III's threat of a quick invasion of the southern German states would keep them out of the war.

After Ems and the French declaration of war, however, the neutrality party collapsed. Baden was won over easily: the government in Karlsruhe did not want to be occupied by the French, and so the government ordered mobilization immediately. By raising the possibility of a front on France's eastern border, Baden complicated France's ability to anticipate just where German armies might concentrate. The Grand Duchy of Hesse hesitated but soon also joined the coalition. Württemberg quickly turned against the French when the public learned of the Ems dispatch.

Bavaria was the hardest area to convince. Count Otto von Bray-Steinburg, the Bavarian minister of state of the exterior and council president, recognized that if the Bavarians remained neutral, or sided with France and lost, they would be treated harshly by Prussia, whereas if they sided with Prussia and lost, France would still want to maintain Bavarian independence. Bray-Steinburg therefore persuaded King Ludwig to mobilize. It was harder to sway the parliament. Eventually, by 101 to 47, the parliament voted 70 per cent of the requested amount of war credits but refused to declare war, leaving that task to the cabinet. Bavaria went to war without a formal declaration.

The mobilization of Bavaria, Württemberg and Baden clarified the nature and strength of the German position. 'By manifesting a readiness to identify herself with Prussia,' recorded one observer, 'Bavaria has done much to prove that the war, so rashly and unjustifiably provoked, is a war with United Germany. Such is the conviction, and it is a belief which is fully warranted by facts.'[10] Despite these different levels of official enthusiasm, the German states shared in the common burden, sorrows and joys that arose during the course of the conflict, which rapidly built public sentiment in favour of a common German nation. This commonality diminished the particularism, customs and loyalties that until then had divided them.

In Munich, Dietrich von Lassberg busied himself at the barracks assisting with the departure. Lassberg took pride in the work and enjoyed the respect of strangers as he strode the streets of Munich. Arriving reservists were put on parade. Officers were named. Mobilization for these officers signified a moment of validation of the efforts they had made in the army during peacetime. With war imminent, some of them would receive appointments and prepared themselves to be worthy of them. The comings and goings of royalty ranked as a lesser importance. Lassberg does not even mention King Wilhelm's arrival in Munich, and he left for the front before Crown Prince Friedrich Wilhelm arrived.

Lassberg happily accompanied battalions as they made their way out of Munich via train and on foot, including a scorching hot march in new, unbroken boots to Tölz, due south of Munich. Then work in the camp at Tölz. Then a march back. On his travels he stopped to give a young lady a bunch of Alpine roses and edelweiss. He rejoiced as the people of the area blew them kisses and sang songs which lent a jaunty tempo to the morning. Upon returning to Munich, he gave his boots immediately to the cobbler. He had one day off in Munich on 22 July to make his personal parting visits and to let his feet recover.

Reality now set in. Lassberg realized that before him lay 'a big, unknown, perhaps even grim future. It was even possible that I would never see my family again. In the morning we went together to church and commended ourselves to God's protection.'[11] Lassberg's final day at home, 23 July, was difficult 'despite the joy of the advance'. Brother Rudolf left for the barracks at three o'clock that afternoon. They parted with the hopeful '*auf Wiedersehen in Frankreich*'. Lassberg spent the evening with his three youngest siblings, Berta, Franz and Georg (ten, eight and seven years old) to answer their 'funny and laughable questions' about the war, which remained for them, as for Lassberg himself, unimaginable.[12] Lassberg was not concerned that his own family might be affected by invasion, however, or by the diseases soldiers might carry. The next day, his departure from his mother's house at 4.30 in the morning, although 'tearless', was 'quite, quite difficult'.[13] His mother made a cross on his brow, potentially her final blessing. At 6 a.m. Lassberg marched away, singing. His mother and siblings came to the train station to see him off with loud *Hochs* and *Hurras* as they parted. Lassberg did not yet know that he would soon fight in several key battles that shaped the course of Europe for decades to come. In the coming months, he witnessed and participated in acts of violence that he had never thought possible. The war against France soon became not just the adventure of the summer, but the defining year of his life. His family and his country would never be the same.

Not everyone was so pleased about the Bavarian mobilization. Some 360 miles north of Munich, in Potsdam, Crown Prince Friedrich Wilhelm confided to his diary his disappointment at leading the Third Army with its South German contingents. It was, he wrote,

> the most onerous of responsibilities, with these troops so ill-disposed towards us and quite untrained in our school, to have to fight so efficient an adversary, one, moreover, long since prepared against this

War, who will certainly invade South Germany long before those States are likely to be ready with their mobilization.[14]

Like many observers, Friedrich Wilhelm assumed that France would mobilize quickly and undertake the first offensive. He feared that he himself, a hero at the 1866 battle of Königgrätz, would be left out of the chance for glory.

For a week following the declaration of war, the crown prince remained in Potsdam and Berlin. He sang 'Ein feste Burg is unser Gott' at the Potsdam Garrison Church, visited his grandparents' graves on the anniversary of the death of Queen Luise, and prayed at the grave of his son Sigismund, who had died four years earlier at the age of two.

The crown prince marvelled at the enthusiasm for war and the unity across the board that he witnessed or heard report of everywhere, even in southern Germany. He did not hear of, or at least did not record, any reports to the contrary. Instead, he wrote, 'one may truly say that, in the face of wanton provocation of France, all Germany has risen like one man; it will very surely re-establish her unity.'[15] Never before, and certainly not at the declaration of war with Austria in 1866, had he seen this open excitement and enthusiasm. His father the king travelled to Munich on 17 July to solidify the relationship with Bavaria. To Prussia's relief, the crowd greeted him with cheers, respect and uncovered heads. They sang songs of Germany unity, including 'Was ist des deutschen Vaterland'.

Still, the crown prince resented having been given the command of the South Germans, whom he intended to use as a reserve only. With this attitude he prepared to depart for Munich. The feeling of German antipathy – that 'us' versus 'them' meant 'Prussia' versus 'Bavaria' – was mutual. In Schweinfurt, Bavarian peasants cut down their green corn so that it would not be destroyed by the enemy marching through – that is, by the Prussians.

In Paris, demonstrations in favour of the war dominated. The 'Marseillaise' had been outlawed under the Second Empire, but now it was re-authorized and, according to a police report, 'the enthusiasm of France to avenge so many years of humiliations is equal to that which existed eighty years ago to defend our borders' during the invasion of 1792.[16] Senators leaving the Luxembourg Palace were greeted by a crowd of students crying *'Vive l'Empereur!'*, *'Vive la Guerre!'* and *'Á bas la Prusse!'* Deputies and citizens alike cheered Prime Minister Émile Ollivier. Whether at the Bourse, at the residence of the Prussian ambassador, Baron Werther, or at the *hôtel* of Ollivier on Place Vendôme, demonstrators seemed to know where to appear to acclaim the war. Ollivier occasionally stepped onto his balcony to acknowledge the cheers of the crowds. Civilians cheered soldiers as they headed to train stations and bought them drinks, and they went to the Tuileries Palace to await the departure of Napoleon III for the front.

The crowds surged through the boulevards and squares that Napoleon III had spent the past decades building up, stone by stone, into an urban showcase. Under the hand of Baron Georges-Eugène Haussmann, Paris had doubled the length of its thoroughfares and added some 85 miles of new streets, making it easier for commercial traffic to reach rail stations, docks and marketplaces. The streets created monumental vistas, crowned with prominent buildings. The city had gained two massive parks on either side, the Bois de Boulogne and the Bois de Vincennes, along with numerous parks and green spaces inside the city. Underground, an upgraded sewer system paralleled the street above, designed to alleviate cholera outbreaks and the sense of disorder and social unrest associated with disease. Napoleon III had harnessed modern science and bureaucracy to create order and pacify the city.

The rebuilding of Paris pushed less wealthy Parisians out of the city centre and into the peripheral outer districts that had been annexed to the city in 1860, including Grenelle, Vaugirard, Belleville and Montmartre. These communities had their own sense of identity and belonging prior to their annexation, and these ties to place continued and strengthened as they transitioned from independent towns and villages to Parisian outer neighbourhoods. Both the city's working-class people and large-scale factory environments were now separated from the increasingly wealthy and well-heeled inner districts. In this moment of the outbreak of war, reports did not capture dissent, even from these outer districts. Leaders had to personally witness these demonstrations in order to gauge whether they were about to face revolution, and newspapers reported on these events to convey to readers the level of popular support. But the consensus did not last for long.

For now, however, Parisians seemed united behind the cause of war. The *Constitutionnel* published a chilling account of the streets of Paris, of the cries for 'Blood!' in the streets, where 'vast surging crowds, and warlike cries and snatches of the "Marseillaise," the "Chant du Départ," and "Mourir pour la Patrie," are resounding on all sides.'[17] But a young child – wrote the *Constitutionnel* – identified the contradiction in terms embedded in cries of *Vive la Guerre*. If *guerre* means killing, and *vive* means living, the child asked, how can you say, 'Live Death?' The *Constitutionnel* ended with a look to the future: 'Is it out of the mouth of this "babe and suckling" that the philosophy of the twentieth century is foreshadowed?'[18]

Parisians feted soldiers as they arrived at the Gare de l'Est and prepared for departure. On 16 July, the first to depart started to arrive at the train station around two o'clock, a little too early for their 4.15 departure. Civilians convinced them to break ranks and join them for a drink, leading to a certain amount of chaos as soldiers were hoisted up on enthusiastic civilian shoulders and lost track of their equipment. In large provincial cities across France, patriotic demonstrations heralded the departure of soldiers: in Perpignan, Nîmes, Lille, Tarbes, Amiens, Dijon, Le Havre. As trains travelled through towns, townspeople greeted the passing soldiers with bread, beer, and wine. Many across France expressed optimism as they marched off to war.

Few voices spoke in explicit protest. The extreme Left, seeking a democratic republic, voiced its opposition. Legitimists, who sought the restoration of the Bourbon monarchy, were divided over the war and mistrusted the outbursts of patriotism, which recalled the days of revolutionary violence. Moderate republicans stayed quiet. French Protestants, a small minority, expressed dismay at taking up arms against their co-religionists. They vainly pointed to visits from Prussian Protestants during the Exposition of 1867, and the king of Prussia's celebration of Pentecost at the Lutheran Church of the Billettes in Paris.

France enjoyed social stability as the country mobilized, but the economic impact could already be felt. On both sides, the conflict caused a sudden loss of trade. Agricultural products, metal and machines no longer flowed from the German states to France, and French exports to Germany, which thanks to textiles had quintupled during the Second Empire, came to a halt. Industry suffered, though unemployment was attenuated by the fact that so many men were mobilized for war.

For those who worked on the land, the primary concern in July 1870 remained the harvest and fear about what might happen if soldiers passed through. The prefect of the Orne noted that 'everyone is on the task . . . old men, women and children take up the sickle, for there is not a moment to lose.'[19] A long-term drought, hard on peasants since 1868, was also a factor and increased worries and distress. There had been little rain for six months. With lakes almost dry, it was difficult to water and grow crops for animal feed. Peasants resigned themselves to selling off stock at depressed prices.

Along the border with the German states, the declaration of war raised conflicting emotions, particularly in the French region of Alsace that lay along the Rhine as it flowed from the Alps to the North Sea. Since Roman times, the Rhine had served less as a border than a place of connection and a passage for both people and goods. The Alsace region nevertheless had long been a site of contention. Controlled by France since the era of Louis XIV nearly two centuries earlier, it contained many German speakers and Protestants.

Strasbourg lay at the crossroads of this region, a culturally thriving fortress city whose inhabitants did not fall into neat boxes of national identity. Many spoke both French and German or its close cousin, Alsatian. Protestants could be French speakers and Catholics could speak Alsatian. Many Alsatian speakers identified with the revolutionary traditions of France and had themselves participated in the revolution of 1848. They could not imagine themselves under the control of the Prussian monarchy. To complicate matters, people from Baden crossed the border into Alsace on a regular basis to work and live, and intermarriage between Alsatians and Badenese was common.

The news that France had declared war on Prussia therefore brought mixed reactions in Strasbourg. Soldiers and civilians mingled in the squares and in the city's many brasseries. Dr Henri-Étienne Beaunis recalled, 'What enthusiasm and what festivities! . . . The handshakes of men, the smiles of women, the encouragement from all parts.'[20] Some saw the conflict as the continuation of hostilities between Catholics and Protestants. Catholic children in Strasbourg teased Protestants that they would soon take their homes away. Protestants bristled when the local bishop's prayers implied that only Catholics would fight loyally for France. When a Protestant pastor attempted to send New Testaments to soldiers marching for war, police confiscated the tracts and arrested the men involved, claiming that the operation was really a cover for spies sharing sensitive information. 'Tracts', stated the police, really meant '*zouaves*' (a class of light infantrymen) and 'New Testaments' indicated 'cannon'.[21]

Others debated whether to stay or leave. The border city might be safer than the fields outside where battle was believed likely to take place. Yet a fortress city could be besieged, with the inhabitants subjected to starvation, bombardment and sacking. One woman recorded in an anonymous diary her struggles to determine the best course of action for her young children, frustrated that 'there are nevertheless some misfortunes no mortal can anticipate.'[22] After considerable debate, she and her children returned from their summer retreat in the countryside to Strasbourg to try their luck in the protected city. War seemed unimaginable to her, despite the growing presence of French soldiers preparing for combat elsewhere.

She could not fathom that 'all these handsome men [would be] killed or wounded'. After a lifetime of peace, she recorded, 'when you do not know what war is, these ideas cannot come to mind.'[23]

By the end of July, most areas across France had become determined to fight the war, despite their personal struggles, some with simple acceptance, and others with true enthusiasm. By early August, anxiety had given way to open displays of patriotism and militarism. The war between rulers had become a war of nations.

In the frantic month of July, both before and after the declaration of war, France desperately sought allies, while Prussia was determined to keep the other powers out of the conflict. A flurry of diplomatic cables clarified the position of countries across Europe. One by one, powers great and small declared their neutrality, and Bismarck reaped the rewards of years of careful diplomacy. The issues we associate with the start of the Great War were already present in 1870: secret treaties, Belgian neutrality, and America's interest in French democracy. The question is not just why the Great War drew in all the Great Powers, but why the Franco-Prussian War did not.

Declaring neutrality regarding another country was in itself a declaration of strength. Holland, Sweden and Norway had the ability to declare their neutrality, whereas Luxembourg relied on France and Prussia to declare they would respect the tiny country's borders.[24] With so many competing interests and relationships, it was little wonder that wires sometimes crossed. The British Private Secretary's Office in Simla, India, received the following two telegrams. From London on 18 July: 'Announced that Russia joined Prussia.' From London on 19 July: 'Following correction just received from Telegraph Office, Bombay: – Word *rumoured* was omitted yesterday's telegram before words Russia joined Prussia.'[25] Russia confirmed its neutrality within a week. Its interests did not seem to be threatened by the conflict, and Russia had valued Prussian support against the Polish uprising in 1863.

Austria still resented that France had fought alongside Piedmont-Sardinia in 1859 in the Italian province's struggle for independence from the Habsburg Empire. More recently, Austria – through its foreign minister Friedrich von Beust – found the duc de Gramont's remarks in the 8 July Corps Législatif too threatening and France's declaration of war too presumptuous. For any alliance to occur, Prussia needed to appear to be the aggressor, and this did not seem to be the case. In any event, Austria had been militarily crushed by the Prussians only four years before and did not feel able to respond to this potential opportunity for revenge, at least not without a clear sign that France would emerge victorious. Austria declared neutrality on 20 July.

Similarly, Italy did not back Victor Emmanuel's informal statements of support for Napoleon III, not with French soldiers still in Rome protecting the Pope's sovereignty from the Italian state. In Florence, many remembered that Italy had lost Savoy and Nice to France in 1860 and that Prussia had supported Italy in 1866. Napoleon III received, at best, tepid support.

Britain was unlikely to join in active combat, yet the war crisis raised questions about its stance. Since the end of the Crimean War in 1856, Britain had pursued a policy of neutrality and non-intervention in Europe, especially after the death of the prime minister, Palmerston, in 1865. Queen Victoria, who had always maintained an interest in the German states, wanted to intervene in favour of peace. She appealed personally to King Wilhelm, without success. Lord Granville, who had become Secretary of the Foreign Office in early July, was also surprised by the explosive force of the Spanish succession crisis.

The British press split in its position on the war, with *The Times* and the *Daily News* blaming France for the conflict, and the *Standard* and the *Post* laying responsibility at Prussia's door. In Ireland, a 'monster demonstration' took place in Dublin in favour of France and the Fenians.[26]

To one British writer, the whole affair proved nothing but the confirmation of the bankruptcy of authoritarian rule,

> by the fact of two great nations being plunged into war by the headstrong passion of the almost absolute rulers they were foolish

enough to allow to govern them. With a Republican government as a proper representation of the people, the war of 1870, which has disgraced modern civilisation, and called down the wrath of heaven, could never have happened.[27]

Another British observer asked,

How long is Humanity to suffer from these vast national duels, engaged in for no adequate objects and conducing only to the glorification of certain military and political chiefs? How long are the toiling masses of every nation to endure conscription, tyranny, and taxation, in order that soldiers and diplomatists may be enabled to gratify their insane love of glory or exact vengeance for the wounds inflicted on their monstrous vanity?[28]

The British stayed out of the war after Bismarck revealed the secret demand that Napoleon III had made in 1866 for Belgium and Luxembourg. On 25 July, the story broke in *The Times* of a draft treaty dating from 1866 between France and Prussia in which France would support a united Germany under Prussian auspices and excluding Austria in exchange for Prussia's support in the French acquisition of Luxembourg and Belgium. This news raised the possibility that Britain might need to enter the conflict to defend Belgian neutrality.

Two days later, the French *Journal Officiel* acknowledged that some of the topics had been discussed in 1866 but denied that such a treaty had ever been written down. 'Ollivier declares,' reported Reuters, 'that he attaches great value to the confidence and friendship of England and that he always considers the union of France with England most essential to the condition and progress of the world. – He earnestly requests contradictions of the false reports which have been spread by persons desirous of dividing them.'[29]

In August, the British signed a double treaty, one with France and one with Prussia and the North German states, guaranteeing Belgian independence and obliging the British government to intervene militarily if either side invaded the country. Simultaneously, Parliament approved a bill to strengthen naval and military forces by 20,000. However, France bought arms from British suppliers, which the British Cabinet did not prohibit, to Prussia's anger.

News of the conflict travelled to the United States via the transatlantic cable, which had become a feature of communication just four years earlier, in 1866, when a robust and long-lasting cable replaced the short-lived cable first established in 1858. On 15 July itself, the Speaker of the House of Representatives, James G. Blaine, read a dispatch announcing the declaration of war in the House, to the applause of many members. But the French envoy to the United States, Lucien-Anatole Prévost-Paradol, was unable to accept the war. An author, journalist and member of the Académie française, Prévost-Paradol had believed in the possibility of a liberal empire and had therefore accepted his position in Napoleon III's empire despite the disapprobation of his republican colleagues. He shot himself on 19 July and died soon after.

American sentiment at this point favoured the German states. The large number of Germans who had migrated to the United States in the middle of the nineteenth century retained their connection to and interest in their homeland, including through both family and strong commercial ties. In Cincinnati, a city with a substantial population of German immigrants (many of whom came from Bavaria), a mass meeting of Germans expressed enthusiastic sympathy for Prussia. Already by 20 July, in major cities, German societies took subscriptions for the relief of widows and orphans.

Americans also held favourable views of Germans, whom they evaluated in light of their own recent civil conflict. The *New York Post* on 12 August hailed German progress and German greatness, due to internal commerce, compulsory education and a faith in German military training

> whereby all, regardless of rank, wealth, or position, were required, as part of the duty of citizenship, to acquire a military education. If

> the German soldier is to-day a better man than his French antagonist, it is not that he is braver, but that he is better educated; it is because he is like our own northern volunteer, a man, a citizen, defending his home, and knowing and caring wherefore he fights.[30]

Moreover, the figure of Napoleon III was extremely unpopular in the United States. The emperor stood for dynasty as opposed to democracy and nationhood. The press believed that Napoleon was undertaking the war for his personal gain at the expense of the people who would be called to fight and die for the Bonapartes. Although many in the American press felt an affinity for France, they resented the emperor for overthrowing the Second Republic in a *coup d'état* and saw the war as another means for crushing republicanism. They did not closely examine the politics of Bismarck and the Prussian monarchy and remained poorly informed about political controversies in Prussia in the 1860s, in which decentralized aspects of the Prussian military were put under central control. The US press favourably viewed the Prussian system that mobilized citizens instead of professional, hired soldiers. Germany seemed to Americans to be a land of religious freedom and cultural depth, of industry and intelligence.

Furthermore, France had not supported the North during the Civil War, which felt like a rejection of the bonds built with Lafayette during the American war for independence. Support for Napoleon III came almost exclusively from newspapers that had supported the Confederacy. By contrast, Germans had taken out US war bonds, and King Wilhelm and Bismarck had sent the North three telegrams of congratulation. As President Grant lamented in an interview with the *Sun*, 'Not one [telegram] came from Napoleon, who, on the contrary, was attacking us in Mexico' – though Grant appreciated that the Mexican adventure had eaten up supplies that otherwise might have gone to the South.[31]

Whichever way the politics ran, the prospect of war on the Continent also opened some practical possibilities, particularly as the United States struggled to rebuild from its own civil conflict.

President Grant hoped the war would drive Americans abroad back home to advance industry – iron, leather and coal – and allow Americans to compete more favourably with Europe as the war drove up the cost of labour and prices. 'They will no longer be able to make a coat cheaper in Europe than in this country,' he anticipated. 'Our factories will start again. Importations will cease . . . Our breadstuffs and bacon will have to furnish their quartermasters' department indirectly.'[32] Investments, he hoped, would shift from Europe to the United States almost immediately.

The declaration of war raised fears for German civilians living in France. 'An infinity' of Germans lived in Paris in 1870, according to Louis Bamberger's 1867 *Paris Guide*.[33] The 1866 census put the number around 34,000, the largest population of foreigners out of the 2,150,916 total inhabitants of Paris. Recent researchers estimate the number of Germans in Paris to have ranged between 60,000 and 120,000 over the course of the nineteenth century. As many as one in twenty Parisians were German. By contrast, few French had settled in German territories. French statistics state that there were 6,429 French in Prussia, and fewer elsewhere in the North German Confederation, primarily women working as domestic servants, housekeepers, language teachers and governesses.

German immigrants to France came from across the German states, particularly from the south – Bavaria, Baden and Württemberg – and from all backgrounds and social groups, both affluent and impoverished. A street sweeper in Paris was likely to hail from Hesse. Their numbers doubled between 1851 and 1866 while the French population held steady at about 38 million. Germans held the papers and passports of the individual states from which they came, but there was linguistic homogeneity and alliances and treaties that bound them together – the Zollverein (customs union) and the Treaty of Gotha (1851) dealt with the economy, citizenship, naturalization and expulsion. They were often treated as a single group, as 'Germans' or 'the German community' or, more menacingly, 'the German army'. Once the war began, this simplification became more extreme. Along the Rhine, the relationship between neighbouring Alsatians and Badenese suddenly altered. Instead of brothers who worked and lived together, despite Alsace's years of incorporation into France, they now became enemies. Badenese prepared to invade Alsace as parties to a conflict between Prussia and France. Across France, Bavarians, Prussians, Hessians, Badenese and others, whose religious differences, cuisine and accents might have differentiated them, now disappeared. In the eyes of many French, they were all just Germans. Or rather, they were all considered to be Prussians. Unification happened not only in the eyes of the Germans but also in the eyes of the enemy.

As diplomats from Prussia, Saxony and elsewhere pulled out of the French capital, those from the North German Confederation appealed to the US Department of State to protect their citizens. The American ambassador to Paris, Elihu B. Washburne, noted in his memoirs that he had no precedents to follow and viewed the situation as 'very difficult, as well as responsible and embarrassing', for 'no particular rule had ever been laid down under such circumstances'.[34]

In an official announcement on 21 July, the French government allowed Germans to live in France so long as they did not raise trouble. German schools remained open and German-language Protestant services were held. Prussians and their allies would not be allowed into the country without an extraordinary permit. These policies were similar to the ones applied to Russians in Paris during the Crimean War and to Austrians during the war of 1859.

On that same day, however, Washburne wrote to the duc de Gramont to suggest allowing subjects of the North German Confederation to depart. It would be more 'modern and more humane' to permit their departure rather than view these men as 'enemies of war'.[35] Presumably Washburne believed that Germans would be better off at a safe distance from the French population and closer to their native homes and families. Just two days later, on 23 July, Washburne became overwhelmed by the number of German citizens seeking safe-conduct documents so that they could leave

France. The ambassador asked Gramont's advice on how to handle these numbers. In response, the latter now limited the populations of Germans that he would allow to leave. Only women, children and those men who were over the age of forty – and therefore no longer eligible to serve in the army – were given safe-conduct. Regrettably, the order preventing German men aged twenty to forty from leaving was not published. Therefore, many German men headed to the French border only to be turned back into French territory.

Washburne objected to this change in policy. Although Gramont assured him that these German men of service age would be treated fairly and with respect, Washburne believed that Gramont had violated 'all the well-established principles of public law'. The French action, he argued, represented a new step contrary to the law of nations as presented in Emmerich de Vattel's *The Law of Nations* and James Kent's *Commentaries*.[36] Gramont disagreed. He swore that this order would not be accompanied by additional repressive measures. The foreign minister did not plan a blanket arrest of immigrants, as had occurred with Englishmen during the Napoleonic Wars and which later became common practice during the Great War. Furthermore, Gramont cited legitimate concern about German patriotic enthusiasm. The demonstrations widely reported from across German territories fed his fear of these potential expellees swelling the ranks of the German armies.

The legal ground for migrants had shifted. Jurists reasoned in this period that state sovereignty overrode any consideration of individual liberty or international law, which were nascent and flimsy at best. The French state claimed it was free to decide who would stay within its borders, and in a time of war, the nationals of the enemy state constituted a threat. In the past, enemy nationals posed a threat as spies or as smugglers of contraband. Now, for the first time, the threat came from the practice of mass conscription.

As wars increasingly were seen as conflicts between nations rather than between princes or monarchs, it became expected that the nation – that is, male citizens – would fight against the enemy.

While states agreed to grant foreign nationals legal equality when it came to property or personal safety, they did not extend this same equality when it came to the right to remain within their borders in times of international conflict. At this stage, the value of the people's war was so strong that the lawyer and republican opposition leader Léon Gambetta argued that German men of military age must be allowed to depart so that they could honourably engage in the war; patriotism, including German patriotism, overrode national security.

Although Gambetta's view did not prevail, his opposition to Gramont's policy demonstrates the firmly planted belief that a German man would put service to his state over his personal daily interests. In a very short span of time, millions of French and German individuals came to terms with their new wartime alliances and the emotional commitments demanded of them. Next, they prepared to move.

2. *Mobilization*

Mobilization is an immense logistical challenge, a public relations game, and a feat of emotional management. It entails the movement of men as well as the expansion of training facilities, the preparation of weaponry that is currently in storage, and the issuance of equipment following a pre-determined calendar. In 1870 mobilization happened not only to soldiers: it was an event that soldiers and civilians experienced together. For reservists and regulars alike, leaving for war symbolized the opening of horizons and a new and exhilarating experience that they wanted to share. After all, despite the large standing armies, this was a conflict in which civilian-soldiers went to war. Across France and the German states, hundreds of thousands of men prepared for departure.

Departure for where? For the front, for the scene of battle, for the battlefield? None of these terms were technically correct; they departed, rather, for barracks first and from there to villages and farmers' fields, for woods and pastures. No battlefields or fronts yet existed. They would come into being only with the concerted arrival of men who had the intention of asserting their control over a particular segment of land and, more pointedly, of forcing another mass of men on the other side to yield.

Within three weeks, over 304,000 French and 426,000 Germans had gathered on either side of the border. At the end of July, the British diplomat R. B. D. Morier, in Darmstadt, reported back to Lord Granville: 'The present war is one without parallel in the history of civilized nations . . . An entire people has been suddenly called from its daily avocations to take a personal part in a struggle, which promises to be the bloodiest and most deadly on record, and in comparison with which, that of 1866 was mere child's play.'[1]

*

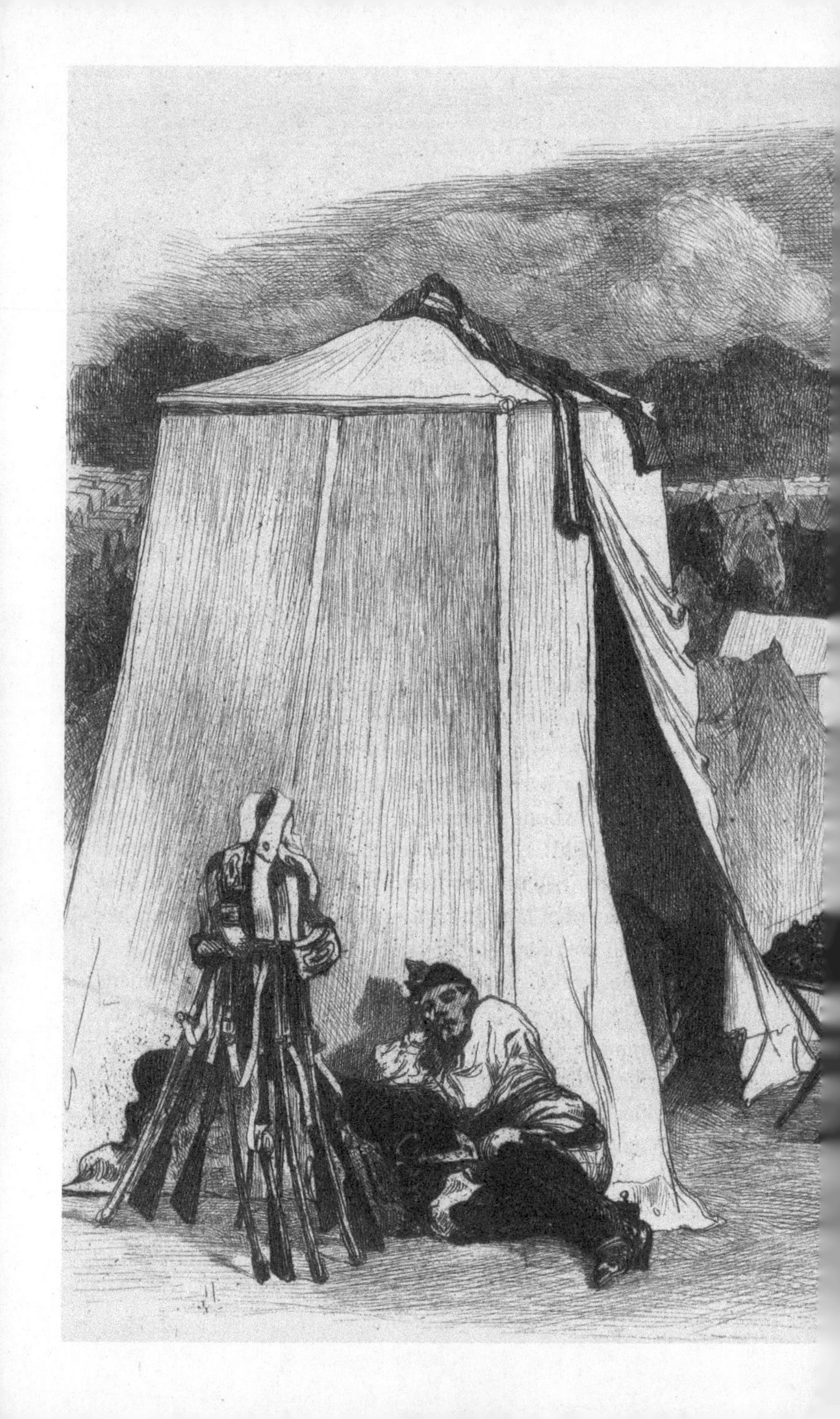

At the outset, neither side had an advantage to mobilization, and Prussia had needed to catch up to France's already superior numbers. Everyone expected France to take the offensive; otherwise, why would France have declared war? The only question remained whether the French would attack via Strasbourg, crossing east into Baden, or head north along the left bank of the Rhine. As it turned out, however, France faced systemic difficulties with moving men into position, especially reservists, and these challenges were exacerbated by a key last-minute change in the army structure and a lack of auxiliary personnel.

On 14 July, General Edmond Leboeuf, the minister of war, declared 'We are ready, very ready!' and supposedly added 'Down to the last gaiter button.'[2] Gaiter buttons are necessary yet showy, and this statement, in quote-ready form, made it all too easy for critics to later accuse the French army of focusing on out-of-date displays rather than on the fundamental needs of the army as it mobilized for war.

Leboeuf planned on five days for dating and sending out prepared call-up slips, then three days for reservists to get to their departmental capitals, then two days for their travel to the regimental depots, followed by five days for men to be equipped and sent to the active areas. On that timetable, the French would be ready for battle by the end of July. The French army counted on its ability to fight hard when it mattered to overcome any deficiencies in leadership at the top and in rear logistics.

In this plan, France did not separate mobilization from concentration, and this lack of distinction created logistical problems up and down the line. Since 1858, France had been divided into six territorial *commandements* known as the *corps d'armée* that followed departmental lines. The leadership structure was based on territory, and leaders only controlled the troops who happened to be stationed in their area. This organization bore no resemblance to a wartime footing in which great units are formed out of elements that come from all over France to muster themselves in strategic areas and are led by new leaders, unknown to their men. If a separation of mobilization and concentration had been adopted, the French regulars and reservists would have assembled within each territorial division and been equipped at that point. Only then would they have been sent to the border.

Instead, soldiers were sent immediately and in smaller groups to the place of concentration, which led to useless movements, dispersion of men, confusion, encumbering of trains, and difficulty in securing equipment, up and down the border region. A 17 July order from the minister of war was indicative of this practice: 'Little by little as the men of the reserve arrive, as soon as you can form a group of about a hundred men or more, if it is possible, they should be directed without delay toward the active battalions under the supervision of an officer or non-commissioned officer.'[3]

This system was aggravated by Napoleon III's last-minute creation of one army instead of the three that had figured in France's plans earlier that year. In spring 1870, Napoleon had begun to favour a project developed by his aide-de-camp General Barthélémy Lebrun in 1868. This project estimated that France would have 490,000 men ready for service, whom Lebrun imagined could be deployed in three armies: one near Lorraine under Marshal Achille Bazaine, a second near Strasbourg under Marshal Patrice de MacMahon, and a third in reserve near the army base at Châlons-sur-Marne under Marshal François-Certain de Canrobert. Mobilization orders had been prepared in advance and only needed the names of the commanders to be added.

This plan put the French on the offensive with the intention of separating the southern German states from the northern ones. It counted on Austria to intervene at some point with an offensive against Prussia and hoped as well for Italy's support, its soldiers passing through Austria via the Tyrol and disrupting Prussia's own potential entry point to France. These vague plans were never fully developed, but they appealed to the French. Not only would the possibility of an offensive align with French notions of the way war should unfold, and give France the advantage of the initiative, but it could potentially drive a wedge between the North German

Confederation and the South German states, perhaps convincing the latter to remain neutral. An early success in this direction might convince Austria and Italy to ally with France and further discourage the South German states. Since spring 1870, the Austrian foreign minister, von Beust, had worked for such a French alliance through his ambassador to Paris, Prince von Metternich. Between 7 and 11 July, France prepared its three armies according to this plan.

On 11 July, however, the emperor announced there would be just one single Army of the Rhine under his command, with Marshall Leboeuf as *Major-Général*. The army and its seven corps now spread across 150 miles between Thionville and Belfort. The emperor aimed to create a more flexible army that could take the offensive more rapidly and, hopefully, convince Austria to join the fray. Instead, this move led to confusion in the mobilization. Whole chains of command had to be redesigned, with cascading disruptions down the line.

Despite the issues occasioned by the creation of a single army, the French ably deployed their regulars to the zone of operations. Many were already stationed near the border, and others moved smoothly from the interior of France to Metz, Châlons, Nancy, Belfort, or Strasbourg.

The challenges arose with the reservists. The recruitment bureau maintained recall orders that only required the addition of a date before being sent out to be delivered to the reservist by the local gendarmerie. However, reservists were required to report to their regimental depots, sometimes hundreds of miles away, without any provisions to help them make this journey. Suddenly, some 163,000 reservists began crisscrossing the country.

In addition, the French lacked detailed maps, and so the routes taken by corps on the march sometimes overlapped or even cut each other off. The confusion was embodied in General Michel's telegram to the Ministry of War on 21 July 1870: 'Am in Belfort; can't find brigade; can't find commanding general; what must I do; don't know where my regiments are.'[4] In addition, the French practice in which the men all camped in the same location, instead of where they were at the side of the road, slowed their progress. They could only march as far as the last-departing men could make in a day, about 7 or 8 miles.

The French army further suffered, as the mobilization revealed, from personnel shortages in auxiliary services. In a memo to Leboeuf on 23 July, Napoleon III noted that the army needed additional auxiliary services, everything from railway construction, telegraphists, army staging systems, military requisition officials, medical services, army postal services, transport for civil engineers, chaplains, printers, interpreters, orderlies, writers, veterinarians, prison camps, kitchens, storehouses, ambulances and hospitals. The emperor understood well the shortcomings the army faced, but 23 July was a bit late. This preparation would have taken months or even years.

The French army had 1,147 doctors and 159 pharmacists – not enough for an army nearing 300,000 men. Nurses were not available, and there were no stretcher-bearers at all. The medical corps fell lower on the priority list versus the artillery and the military transport services in terms of getting horses and wagons. The lack of personnel at mobile hospitals hampered the French ability to conduct sufficient reconnaissance in the early days of mobilization out of concern for triggering a skirmish. As General Frossard informed Bazaine, 'As we have neither materiel nor personnel in the mobile hospitals, our reconnaissance is necessarily made with reserve, and without being aggressive.'[5] Even as late as the battle of Sedan, some army units could not staff these field hospitals.

The soldiers themselves experienced a range of emotions as they set off to fight. Regulars already stationed across France, in Rome and in the colonies had long said their goodbyes and were readily equipped and sent on their way north and east. Their morale remained high. A sergeant recalled that upon leaving the Camp of Châlons on 21 July, happy and smiling soldiers sang the 'Marseillaise' and 'La France guerrière'. General Bourbaki noted the excellent spirit of the Imperial Guard and their general confidence in their future success. Yves-Charles Quentel, a regular from Brittany, was not surprised by his long journey from Quimper to Nevers to be equipped, followed by a second long trek to Forbach. He said his journey was 'most agreeable', despite three days and four nights in a train carriage.[6]

Letters sent back home included details about the crops and animals in the fields, the terrain giving way to mountains, the heat and the climate, the white cows and the vine-covered hills, and the manner and customs of harvest. Of course, many soldiers were illiterate and relied on fellow soldiers to write home on their behalf. The same sentiments, however, could be seen among officers and the upper echelons of the army as well.

Henri Serpollet, a regular soldier, returning from having been stationed in the Rome garrison and joyous to arrive in France to join the fight, wrote:

> If . . . we had to depart for Prussia, be assured that I will do my duty and that you will have no reason to blush about me. Everyone is enflamed, everyone cries out, 'Prussia! Prussia!' Yesterday at the military march, the music played the *Marseillaise*, everyone jumped despite the sixty pounds they had on their backs. I wish you could see it when a new telegram arrives, nobody listens; we all run to the armament . . . we upset the beds, we fight, we roll about, the sergeants try to intervene, we toss them out, discipline is relaxed, we have no more punishments . . . the French soldier leaving for war wants to massacre everyone.[7]

In these early days, soldiers and civilians expressed a deep sense of gratitude and community. Urban soldiers marched alongside rural soldiers. Those who were heading to combat and those who stayed at home felt a common bond. Quentel, a regular in the army since January 1870, wrote to his brothers and sisters back home: 'As we pass through, we're acclaimed. In the countryside, the workers raise their hats and wave their handkerchiefs; the women do the same; in train stations I've seen them cry with emotion.'[8]

The excitement of mobilization could not mask the complex feelings of men heading to war. As he prepared to disembark in Marseilles and set foot again on French soil, Serpollet assured his father, 'Let war not scare you, you know that we will always return with the help of God. I have not lost the good principles that you have inculcated in me; I am both soldier and Christian. I ask you therefore, my dear father, not to forget your child.'[9] As he prepared to leave his depot on 27 July and head toward the Rhine, he placed his trust in God, 'who holds in his hand the lives of men and the fortune of battles'. He received from a nun tokens of piety to wear into combat. Yet he still feared bodily harm, as he confided in a letter a few days later: 'the worst would be to lose some limbs.'[10] For each soldier, mobilization suddenly raised questions about their emotional commitment to kill and be killed for the sake of their country, their national leaders and their fellow soldiers.

At the same time, many reservists resented being called up. They assumed that they had completed their service and grew sullen and disorderly in transit. Many of them had not been trained with the Chassepot rifle and had to learn it on the fly, in the theatre of operations. Only 4,000 French men actually volunteered to enlist in the second half of July.

Each soldier was supposed to carry 75 pounds of equipment, including weapons, ammunition, rations, camping equipment and an extra uniform and pair of boots. It had already been a dry, hot summer, and the oppressive heat continued into August. By the first day of the month, eleven French soldiers had died of heatstroke. Two more committed suicide. It is little wonder that inexperienced soldiers succumbed to the temptation of dumping their packs during long marches in the heat and rain of July and August. French soldiers also removed their leather shakos (caps) whenever possible, at railroad platforms or wherever they could find a square foot. This headwear had been adopted in the 1830s, but the men now refused to wear it. On 30 July the emperor abolished the wearing of the shako in favour of the lighter kepi to head off this lack of discipline.

*

On 17 July the mobilization of the Mobile National Guard began. This body of some 450,000 men had been created just two years earlier and, by law, had never been intended for battle. Instead, the Mobile National Guard was designed to staff back offices, accompany military convoys and provide the military with their civilian skills as locksmiths, bakers, carpenters, butchers, blacksmiths and the like, and thereby free trained soldiers for battle.

The Mobile Guard included married men, in contrast to active-duty soldiers who were obliged to remain single, and so departure became a scene of particular sorrow for men and their wives and children. The prefect of the Orne reported, 'The call of the Mobile Guard caused a certain emotion within families . . . They had been habituated to consider this institution as only being destined to produce a moral effect rather than a real one.'[11] But the law called for the mobilization of young married men, of sons of widows, or heads of workshops. 'When young men came to the price of true sacrifices, to make themselves replacements in the active contingent, they saw that there was neither reprieve nor means to evade the application of the law, complaints arose from all quarters.'[12]

In other words, though they had entered an institution intended to support combat operations, they had not been prepared for the moment of departure, either emotionally or morally. They were left to figure out on their own how to handle this transition, how to act with respect to their families and their home communities, and how to adjust to a new life dependent upon relationships with their fellow soldiers, with their commanders and subordinates, and with the civilian populations that they encountered in transit, day by day.

The army was not ready for them, either. In the rush for general mobilization, the French command could not spare enough personnel to oversee the Mobile Guard and relied instead on civilian prefects or military intendants and territorial commanders to organize the units. Medical authorities did not even have the staff to examine arriving men for their fitness to serve. While the Mobile Guard would not play a large role in the conduct of the war, it provided large numbers of Frenchmen and their families with personal experience of the Second Empire's incompetence.

Moreover, in the scant two years since its creation, the Mobile National Guard had not been inculcated with military discipline. The Parisian units of the Guard proved particularly unruly. They arrived at the training camp at Châlons on 29 July and faced shortages in just about everything, including tents, uniforms and equipment. They turned their encampment into a festival with entertainments and gave Parisian street names to their rows of tents. Some of them refused to perform kitchen duty or garbage detail. Others headed for the cafés of the town of Mourmelon, where they vandalized a statue of the prince imperial. They were joined by certain members of VI Corps, also stationed at Châlons.

The insubordination reached a head on 1 August. At a review, the Mobile Guard from the Seine insulted Canrobert, damaged the imperial eagles and hurled insults against the emperor and Ollivier. Some responded to 'Long Live the Emperor' with '*Un! deux! trois! merde!*'[13] Others cried '*Á Paris!*', indicating that they preferred to overthrow Napoleon III rather than invade Prussia.[14] The incident ended with thirty arrests of men from the Belleville battalion.

Canrobert recommended dispersing these troops to frontier posts, but the fortress commanders did not want them, either. The Paris Mobile Guard stayed in Châlons until late August, when the newly appointed governor of Paris, Louis-Jules Trochu, took them back to Paris. Other battalions of the Mobile Guard were eventually sent to fortresses in Belfort, Toul, Thionville, Strasbourg, Verdun and Sedan.

Republicans repeatedly castigated the imperial government for its distrust of its own people. They cherished the idea that a well-armed citizenry might have contributed to a victory at the outset, or, at the very least, had the salutary effect of inflaming ardour for the nation. Jules Clarétie, who covered the war as a journalist and later served as director of the Théâtre-Français, argued,

> The imperial government has denied the French people any means of combatting not only oppression, but the invasion . . . The Empire,

> out of fear of seeing armed citizens, has thus deprived the country of a free, vigorous, and powerful force. And while citizens, national guards without rifles, saw the enemy arrive at their doorsteps, the authorities, the representatives of the empire were committed to smothering in our hearts the last spark of a patriotic flame.[15]

The slow and unruly mobilization of the Mobile Guard had direct consequences for the French ability to fight in the early crucial battles. If battalions of the Mobile Guard had been in a position to be sent to Lyons, they could have relieved some of the regulars stationed in that city. Those regulars could have joined the rest of VII Corps with MacMahon on Froeschwiller heights. Instead, the regulars awaited other soldiers redeployed from garrison duties, who arrived on 5 August – too late to support MacMahon when he was attacked on 6 August.

Mobilization transformed the German cities and countryside overnight, too. A Parisian reporter in Prussia noted the disappearance of 'every man between the age of twenty and thirty-eight . . . They are all under arms . . . The countryside is deserted. Walls of wheat await the absent scythe, and there are soldiers everywhere one looks!'[16] German civilians suffered from the loss of household earnings. For many families, the absence of the male worker from a household caused immediate economic hardship. Although the wives of soldiers could apply for aid, many were not aware of this assistance, and a robust social welfare system was not yet in place.

Prussia employed novel techniques to integrate their called-up soldiers smoothly into the active army. The state invented the dog tag in 1870, imprinted with a soldier's name, regiment and place of residence. The army also issued twelve postcards with stamps to each soldier, who, unlike most French soldiers, were literate because of more widespread schooling. As Karl Litzmann, a twenty-year-old Prussian Guard lieutenant, boarded his train from Berlin, his mother handed him a letter. It read, 'I am pained by the realization that I may never again hold you in my arms, but far greater than my pain is my joy that you too can fight in this war . . . It is not necessary that you return from the war, only that you do your duty.'[17]

Dietrich von Lassberg and his companions were very glad to leave Munich behind them for the military base at Lechfeld some 40 miles due west of Munich. 'We didn't belong there anymore,' he wrote, 'and could hardly stand to stay in the city any longer.'[18] Life at the Munich barracks also meant isolation: on some days, no newspapers or news at all. Their preparations for war were no longer a drill. Lassberg received notification of his promotion to *Leutnant*. He remained at Lechfeld until 31 July, in anticipation of the victory to come. The very speed and smooth functioning of the mobilization impressed Lassberg and bolstered his faith that the war would come to a speedy conclusion. Perhaps in just four weeks, perhaps in France itself, he would conquer their enemy, and he found joy in the thought. He indicated no fear or anticipation of killing other people. Like other Bavarians, he saw himself as an armed citizen marching off to war to forge a unified nation, and he was thrilled to take part in it.

On 31 July, Lassberg marched to Augsburg and from there took a train to the north-west. According to a fellow Bavarian platoon leader, Josef Krumper, the men were 'packed like sheep' in overheated freight wagons.[19] Officers took the second-class carriages. They arrived at Bruchsal at 6 a.m. and marched 16 miles to Germersheim, on the Rhine, less than 10 miles south of Speyer. It was alternately sunny and rainy, hot and wet, a perfect recipe for blisters and exhaustion. These men, who just days before had been civilians, still stopped to put on their coats when the rain started to fall, slowing the march and putting on display their greenness. They did not have water and so they drank schnapps. They arrived at the French border disorderly, sunburned and blistered. They crossed the Rhine around seven o'clock that evening and prepared to bivouac with about 15,000 men. Lassberg gives no hint of being an outsider in the eyes of the Prussians. Yet Bavaria and the other South German states were under such suspicion that Moltke, the Prussian commander-in-chief, did not allow their officers below the rank of general to have Prussia's high-quality 1:80,000 maps (they were given only 1:250,000-scale maps).

Nor did Lassberg record any concern for how his presence might affect local civilians. Rather, he complained that their wet and dirty potato fields impeded the soldiers' ability to march. Civilians viewed the matter differently. Everyone calculated that France would mobilize more rapidly than Prussia and make a quick strike into either the Rhenish Palatinate or into Baden. A Prussian officer travelling in the Rhenish Palatinate heard everywhere, '*Ei, komme se denn endlich*?' – 'Hey, when will the French get here?'[20] Across the Rhine, Badenese guardsmen dug defensive trenches and destroyed the bridge across the rise at Kehl in anticipation of an imminent French invasion.

Lassberg himself made a second trip to Bavaria and back, to accompany soldiers who were moving west. His brother Rudolf, too, had arrived in Germersheim, but Lassberg could not see him in person. He only managed to send a greeting through a passing officer. On the morning of 4 August, after a night of terrible storms, they arrived at Minfeld, a short march to the French border. Tomorrow, he wrote, 'we hope to come into battle.'[21]

Back in Berlin, Crown Prince Friedrich Wilhelm prepared himself for the reality of departure. The baptism of his daughter Sophie descended into a gloomy occasion, despite the gala dress. All made their farewells to each other, wondering, 'Which of us will come back?'[22] His own departure from his wife and children was almost unbearable. He and his wife, Victoria – the eldest daughter of Queen Victoria – had agreed that they would not have a formal farewell. On the day of his departure, he would leave for the day without any special goodbye. His children, however, understood clearly that their father left for battle, 'but I must not let my thoughts dwell on those moments.'[23] He sent a note to his wife via his four-year-old daughter Viktoria, who left him 'sobbing and crying and would *not* let [him] go'. Friedrich Wilhelm did not explicitly mention his eldest son, eleven-year-old Wilhelm, the future Wilhelm II. The crown prince retained his composure only through 'the thought of sharing the same pang of parting with all my married fellow-countrymen faring to the front'.[24]

The train ride south, however, rewarded Friedrich Wilhelm's pains. At every station – Leipzig, Bamberg, Wittenberg, Altenberg – he was greeted with cheers. 'Who would ever before have dreamed that Bavarians and Saxons would greet a Prussian Prince with tumultuous hurrahs specially emphasizing the Unification of our Country.'[25] In Moosburg, he met King Ludwig II of Bavaria, much changed since they had last met, with his front teeth missing and a nervous manner. Then the crown prince toured Munich, Stuttgart and Ulm, traversing Saxony, Bavaria, Württemberg and Baden in quick succession. Strangers handed him bouquets for his wife, including one featuring the North German Confederation colours in pansies. He felt the responsibility of assuring victory and peace to maintain this sense of unity.

In Friedrich Wilhelm's first encounter with Bavarian soldiers, he tried valiantly to maintain an open mind, but could not quite write out a sentence of praise without adding some dismay: 'The Prussian point of view must be entirely abandoned . . . clumsiness of build and startling corpulence prevail even in the younger class of levies. Still the soldier shows quite a smart bearing, only he does not seem accustomed to be addressed by superiors.'[26] The Bavarian uniform appeared so similar to that of the French that the crown prince considered asking the men to wear a distinguishing armband.

Here, too, however, the sentiment of unity prevailed, as the Bavarians greeted the crown prince as if he were one of their own. 'Indeed,' he reflected, 'I can never again look upon Bavarians and Württembergers as foreigners.'[27] This expression of unity and identification convinced Friedrich Wilhelm that they were ready: 'Men's minds could not be better attuned for all that has yet to be done.'[28] Amid the impersonal call-up cards and railroad timetables, the personal encounter up and down the rail line set the emotional stage.

On the next day, 1 August, Friedrich Wilhelm arrived at Speyer, his new headquarters, content with his tour. Already, dozens of journalists swarmed to his headquarters to seek an interview. The daily newspapers, which became the primary forum for foreign information on the war, sought to attach themselves to armies, and found the Germans to be more hospitable than the French. The crown prince himself officially received Mr Russell of *The Times* and Mr Skinner of the *Daily News*, and allowed them to accompany his army.

In his quieter moments, Friedrich Wilhelm contemplated the approach of the hour of battle:

> Thus then we stand at the beginning of a historical world crisis! I am not despondent, but yet the gravity of the situation makes my heart tremble in view of the battles we shall have to fight, the starting point of which will be an immediate irruption from position on the hills . . . But the point now is to carry out my chosen motto: 'With God, fearlessly and undauntedly to go forward!'[29]

3. *Concentration and Command*

Mobilizing men and moving them toward the likely location of battle presented one set of challenges. In addition, armies needed to ensure their soldiers had the supplies and equipment they needed: weapons, ammunition, food, uniforms, boots, tents and cooking equipment. Moreover, military leaders needed to concentrate all these men and supplies in strategic positions to exploit the enemy's weak points. The successful execution of concentration as a separate step from mobilization differentiated the Prussians from the French.

Concentration required good use of the railroad system and well-arranged marching routes. An infantry division contained about 10,000 men, but in an army corps each division encompassed auxiliary services, cavalry and artillery as well – up to 30,000 men. This large formation could cover about 10–12 miles a day and then required a day to turn from columns into battle formation. As concentration occurs, an increasing mass of men and supplies make use of fewer and fewer roads. The better the plan, the less the risk of error, confusion and last-minute decisions, resulting in a faster and more flexible army. On 2 August, eighteen days after the French voted war credits, the villagers of Saarbrücken in the Rhenish Palatinate became the first witnesses of battle.

On the German side, Helmuth von Moltke, the Chief of the Prussian General Staff, had one main objective: destroy the French army. Moltke was pragmatic about what to achieve and how to achieve it. His plans for mobilization and concentration flowed from his strategic objectives and his adaptations to modern weaponry, communications and railroads. He could be both structured and fluid in how he deployed these operations. Whereas Moltke

PREFECTURE

famously believed that no plan survives contact with the enemy, he also believed that the plan nevertheless must be a good one so that the necessary reaction to the unexpected can be undertaken intelligently and smoothly. Moltke had, furthermore, learned from the experiences of the war against Austria just four years earlier, which gave Prussia and its German allies an incalculable advantage over the French, for whom a large-scale war on its home territory remained a theoretical enterprise.

For Moltke, war and policy were distinct. The army prepared for war, and the government defined the parameters of the conflict. By early 1870, the only military situation that the government defined was a war against France, and one that would have to be decided quickly so that France would be defeated and no potential allies would have time to come to its aid. Moltke thought he could best achieve this goal by concentrating three armies in the Rhenish Palatinate. The Second Army would advance, covered by the First Army to the right that would seek to attack a French flank if possible. The Third Army would meanwhile advance into Alsace on the left and also seek to engage a French flank.

To achieve this aim, Moltke required control over the entire campaign, so that flanking manoeuvres could be set up and then executed. If each of the three armies were to act on its own, he might end up with one long, continuous front unable to outflank and encircle. The continuous front would move forward, but it would be slow and less likely to achieve the policy objectives.

As part of his planning, Moltke needed to address the difficulties raised by the increased firepower and range of rifles and artillery. The state still required short wars, and short wars required taking the offensive. Yet increased firepower meant that the defence would prevail. Moltke responded to this challenge with flank attacks taken at the operational level. Flank attacks were a well-worn tactic that could be of particular use in the early stages of combat when inexperienced soldiers were more likely to panic. To be successful against long-range weapons, the flanking movements would have to be larger and wider. This expansion came at a cost: the larger flanking movement would only make the fog of war and the confusion of animals and men more likely.

To mitigate this situation, Moltke made flanking an operational activity rather than a tactic. He concentrated forces on the field from different locations and aimed them at the enemy's front and flank. In other words, he distinguished between moving to the theatre of war and advancing to contact in the field, separating mobilization from concentration. Flanking operations were also assisted by the new long-range weaponry, which could engage in flanking even if they were behind the main front of engagement, and by the sheer size of armies. Entire corps could be held back the better to shift into a flank attack.

Moltke therefore planned to mobilize and concentrate ten army corps, totalling 330,000 men, in the Rhenish Palatinate. The mobilization plan included details on where troops would be posted at first and then supplied, and information on horses, transport equipment, tools, uniforms. It even indicated who would replace territorial commanders sent to the arena of battle so that the peacetime activities of the reserve army would continue even as the war unfolded.

To pull off this strategy, Moltke required close control over the rail system. Railroads afforded armies consistent movement to the general area where the war would take place. Horses and men arrived at their destination without having been worn out by marching over long distances and could receive new supplies. Railroads could deliver food and supplies and men, allowing armies to stay in the field longer. Railroads also opened the possibility of armies to be rapidly concentrated – at the outset of mobilization, armies could stay separate and therefore more readily supplied, and yet come together quickly.

Railroads were valuable not because trains moved quickly – quite the opposite – but because they travelled systematically, predictably and safely. If planned well, the very slowness allowed for the necessary flexibility in a system with so many moving parts. Men could jump off a train, grab some food or coffee, and hop back on without being left behind. Railroads moved large numbers of forces to several locations that were separated by long distances, then concentrated in the zone of combat.

Prussia's concentration was sufficient, though not perfect. The railway section of the Prussian General Staff could work with the fifty-odd lines – some private, some public, some mixed public–private. The General Staff was able to suspend civilian travel on rails during the mobilization, a large assertion of state power. They practised mobilization during peacetime, touring the concentration areas and the rail facilities, assigning tracks and timetables to specific corps. They determined how many trains and carriages were needed, the location of the freight yards, the direction of each line, and how many soldiers, horses, supplies, transport vehicles and so forth would go on each train.

Moltke's General Staff planned military railroad schedules and carefully selected the marching routes through the Saar valley and into northern Alsace. Six rail routes organized in the North German Confederation could each handle two or three corps in succession – that is, either eighteen trains a day (on the double-track lines) or twelve trains a day on single-track lines. Each corps of 31,000 men moved from bases to disembarkation within 3½ to 5½ days. The Military Transportation Plan was able to schedule the entire army. In the first war-game attempt, in November 1867, they could move the Prussian field army to the west in thirty-two days. By 1870, they had been able to reduce the number of days needed to twenty. In the actual event, Prussia's field force was ready to advance on 3 August, the nineteenth day of mobilization.

Two days after mobilization began, a Prussian officer visiting Moltke reportedly had found the chief of staff relaxing on a sofa reading Sir Walter Scott. The friend asked why Moltke was not rushing about, to which Moltke reportedly replied, 'Why not? Everything is ready. We've only got to press the button.'[1] Minister of War Albrecht von Roon later reportedly remarked that it was the two weeks of his career with the least amount of care and work.

Yet just as the Union armies learned in the American Civil War, dependence on railroads could become a curse when the operation shifted from concentration on a border to the invasion of enemy territory. Rail movement was easily disrupted by unsophisticated methods. As General William T. Sherman declared, 'Railroads are the weakest things in war', vulnerable to a match or a pickaxe. While 'our armies pass across and through the land, the war closes in behind and leaves the same enemy behind'.[2] Moltke planned to circumvent the challenge of a protracted invasion through an early knockout blow.

Still, Moltke feared that a rapid French mobilization would disrupt Prussian concentration in the Rhenish Palatinate. He therefore shifted, on 23 July, to having the three armies detrain on the right bank of the Rhine and then march to their points of concentration. The men had to march 50–80 miles in the hills and over bad roads, with supply convoys to follow.

French supply and concentration did not operate as smoothly. In fact, France had not yet conceptualized concentration as a separate step from mobilization, and so the entire operation unfolded with confusion.

In France, the private Compagnie de l'Est handled the bulk of the work, connecting Paris to Metz and Strasbourg. Nearly 1,200 trains ran between 16 July and 6 August, carrying over 300,000 men, as well as horses, cannon, transport wagons and supplies. The logistics behind such a concentration overwhelmed the French. 'You cannot conceive the difficulty of uniting even 100,000 men,' reported a British journalist from Metz. 'If even 15,000–20,000 arrived each day it would take a week, but even that number is impossible because the cavalry need horses and the artillery need guns. Sometimes thirty wagons roll into the station and, after all the equipment is taken off, just fifty men step down!'[3]

On 29 July, Paul de Ladmirault, commander of IV Corps, telegraphed the minister of war using his most polite yet pointed language:

> I have the honour of requesting you to please be good enough to give the necessary instructions to hasten as much as possible the sending of these reserves, without whom we will be called to cross the border with insufficient numbers. Furthermore, it seems that despite all the recommendations made, men have been sent from the depots without having been provided with necessities for making a campaign. I have the honour of asking you to be good enough to give orders so that reserve contingents do not arrive at their combat battalions unless they have been completely provided with cartridges and camping equipment.[4]

In Metz, the movement of freight dissolved into chaos. The railroad centre at Metz had 8 depots and 4 miles of siding, enough space to unload 310 freight wagons at the same time, and a maximum of 930 in a day. They averaged 775 arrivals per day between 16 July and 15 August, enough to supply the four army corps located within 25 miles of the city. But most wagons were not unloaded and even those supplies that were taken off were not necessarily distributed. Supply trains arrived at Metz but did not depart; they were blocked by troop transport or by incoming supply trains. Railroad dispatchers had to put these wagons somewhere, so they moved them into sidings that did not have facilities for unloading, and so they sat there – the supplies still loaded, the army unfed.

As a result, soldiers arriving at the corps around Metz lacked weapons, ammunition and basic food: bread, coffee, sugar, rice, salt, and even potable water. Pay for the army had not been worked out either, so soldiers did not have cash on hand to acquire revolvers, maps, or additional food. On 1 August a journalist for *L'Étoile Belge* reported from Metz, 'With each passing day, one discovers that one has been deluding oneself to think that French preparations are complete . . . Two thousand wagons block the streets of Metz this morning, mostly hay, straw, and oats that arrived in the night and await a final destination.'[5] Soldiers were sent on the demoralizing task of marching out of the city to stationary trains and carrying supplies back. After the fall of Metz in October, the Germans captured some 16,000 freight cars full of supplies.

Finally, the French lacked horses. During peacetime the French army rented horses out to farmers for budgetary reasons. In some cases, farmers refused to return the horses until the harvest could be completed, or insisted that the army come to them to reclaim the horses, adding to the time and confusion. The French secured 11,000 horses from the gendarmerie (which made it harder for the gendarmerie to mobilize) and had to purchase others, which were often too small or in poor condition. As a result, each cavalry squadron averaged 126 mounted men instead of the 171 stipulated in the regulations. The French cavalry was kept behind the lines – in contrast with the famous Prussian Uhlans who seemed to be on the watch everywhere, gathering reconnaissance. The artillery, too, was short of horses, though they had enough guns and carriages and supply wagons for 396 batteries, but only 17,000 horses of the 51,500 that they needed.

For all these problems, the French did eventually get their equipment and most of the trains did run on time. Almost two-thirds of the lines were double-tracked and the French had a third more rolling stock per mile than Prussia. Still, as a result of these delays, the French were unable to launch an offensive and were forced simply to wait for the enemy in a defensive position.

Napoleon III hoped to use the French navy as part of the war effort. It ranked among the most advanced and efficient in the world, possessing shell-guns, steam power and armour: forty-nine ironclads against Prussia's paltry five. Overall, the French had 470 ships (second only to Britain), ten times the number that Prussia could boast, and Prussia's two naval bases, at Kiel and Wilhelmshaven, were small. Denmark, still humiliated from its defeat in 1864, threatened to join France in an invasion that would advance on Kiel, Hamburg and possibly Hanover. Napoleon III originally planned a landing on the Prussian coast with 9,000 marines and 20,000 reservists. At the outbreak of war, the Channel Fleet, destined for the

Baltic, headed out from Cherbourg on 24 July under Admiral Louis Boüet-Willaumez, while the Mediterranean Fleet under Admiral Fourichon departed from Malta to make the circuitous voyage to the North Sea via the Strait of Gibraltar and Brest.

This planned landing was slowed and stymied by logistics. The Mediterranean Fleet required three weeks to make its way to the North Sea and needed to recall men and draft conscripts in the meantime. Both fleets quickly ran short of coal and therefore slowed their pace. Upon arrival in the north in August, they found that the bays were too shallow for their deep-draught frigates and yet they were still prey to Krupp artillery with a range of 4,000 yards, twice that of their own batteries. Built to challenge Britain on the high seas, Napoleon's navy floundered along Prussia's shallow coastlines. They were in unfamiliar waters with no effective charts, no hope of guidance from German pilots and blocked by submerged mines, chains and cables. Danish support of some 30,000 men would be necessary for the invasion to work, and, after the early French defeats in August, it was clear Denmark's support would not be forthcoming.

Nevertheless, Boüet managed something of a sea blockade until September, though to avoid angering Britain it did not cut off British ships. By the autumn, the blockade was called off as the weather cooled and France faced defeat on its own territory. In the end, France's most important use of its navy was to transport soldiers from Algeria.

When King Wilhelm departed from Berlin on 31 July, his three armies had already gathered in the Rhenish Palatinate. The sudden and intricate movement of men into these three groupings, however, proceeded not only through the careful execution of plans long developed and rehearsed, not only through the co-ordination of railroads, of coal and steel burned and force directed westwards, but also through the steady message, both direct and implied, that this conflict occasioned solemn joy and presaged a strong and glorious future for the German people and their steady royal leaders.

The king was an able commander, effective and informed, but aged seventy-three he became less active in the campaign and depended upon Moltke's advice. He could afford to wait until the end of July to leave Berlin and travel to Mainz. Unlike Napoleon III he did not leave his government behind but rather brought his Civil and Military Cabinets with him to the field, along with experts and officials ready to take over administrative control of occupied territories, and all the attendant spectators, journalists, foreign military attachés, princes and their staff of valets, cooks, grooms and horses.

As he prepared to depart, King Wilhelm seized this moment of symbolic unity. He issued a declaration:

> To my People, – On my departure to-day for the army, to fight with it for Germany's honor and the preservation of our most precious possessions, I wish to grant an amnesty for all political crimes and offences, in recognition of the unanimous uprising of my people at this crisis. I have instructed the Minister of State to submit a decree to me to this effect. My people know with me that the rupture of the peace and the provocation to war did not emanate from our side. But, being challenged, we are resolved, like our forefathers, placing full trust in God, to accept the battle for the defence of the Fatherland.[6]

Some 400 miles to the south-west of Berlin, the king's armies awaited. Together, the First and Second Armies threatened Lorraine and Metz. Prince Friedrich Karl, the king's nephew, commanded the Second Army, which with 134,000 men was the largest of the three armies and included six corps (III, IV, IX, X, XII and Guard) and two cavalry divisions. It was concentrated near Neunkirchen. The Royal Headquarters travelled with the Second Army, in part to keep an eye on Friedrich Karl. The prince was, with Crown Prince Friedrich Wilhelm, the joint victor at the key battle of Königgrätz in 1866 and known to be cautious, reflective and professional, despite his showy nickname 'The Red Prince', for his Hussar uniform.

To the right of the Second Army stood the First Army, composed of 50,000 men (I, VII and VIII Corps), near Wittlich, under Friedrich von Steinmetz. Steinmetz's appointment came as a surprise to those in the know. Born in 1796 and highly distinguished in 1866 – driving back larger Austrian forces at Nachod and then pursuing them fiercely, which helped set up victory at Sadowa – Steinmetz as he aged remained stubborn, impatient and intractable. A staff officer wrote of him, 'His judgment and activity had been affected . . . only his obstinacy remains.'[7] Steinmetz might have been the right commander of the smaller First Army in the event of a major French offensive on the lower Moselle. In the event, however, his refusal to follow orders disrupted Moltke's early plans and almost led to disaster.

To the left of the Second Army was the crown prince's Third Army, situated near Landau and Rastatt in the Rhenish Palatinate, threatening Alsace and Strasbourg. At 125,000 men, the Third Army was almost as large as the Second. It included V and XI Corps as well as two Bavarian Corps and one division each from Baden and Württemberg, and so embodied among its ranks the future of German unity. Friedrich Wilhelm's chief of staff was Karl von Blumenthal, one of Prussia's most competent leaders and fully trusted by Friedrich Wilhelm. The crown prince recognized well that his Third Army was slated for a supporting role. His cousin's central Second Army would undertake the main engagement, with his own Third Army merely attacking a French flank. He himself 'shall hardly be in a position to carry out any great enterprises'.[8] Glory seemed already out of reach.

Moltke purposely left seven divisions behind: one to defend the west coast from a French naval invasion, and the other six (in I, II and VI Corps) to prevent overstretching the railroads and to allow for the divisions to be mobilized later as strategy determined.

The Prussian army in 1870 was three times larger than the one that had fought Austria in 1866. By 3 August, Moltke's three armies stretched along a 100-mile arc between Karlsruhe and Coblenz. They could move in several directions and covered a large space without being so distant as to be unable to assist each other. The arc of the German armies was much broader than the French force concentrating between Metz and Saarbrücken. Furthermore, their superior mobilization logistics meant that they had gathered more men more rapidly than the French, and that the men arrived better rested, better supplied and less frustrated at their situation. Moltke had confidence that he could disrupt any plans the French might have. If the French attempted to invade southern Germany, the Third Army could attack its flank. If they invaded the Rhenish Palatinate, they would meet the Second Army, with the First and the Third ready to protect the Second Army's flanks.

On 30 July, Moltke ordered the Third Army to advance. Already, however, his carefully laid plans were delayed. Blumenthal reported that it was impossible for batteries and supplies to be ready until at least 3 August. He wanted VI Corps to join him before being willing to swing against the French flank. Though Blumenthal did not say so explicitly, his unwillingness to move ahead without VI Corps suggested a lack of trust in the Bavarians. Moltke had to send a special envoy to get the rear echelons sorted out, but without VI Corps. Moltke postponed his forward movement by a few days.

The French command structure meanwhile moved into place. Napoleon III, no great commander even in health – as demonstrated in 1859 – was in constant pain from a gallstone and could barely mount a horse or even think coherently. The emperor now was in the position of shouldering all the accolades of victory and all the scorn of defeat while being wholly inadequate to the task. A single army of 300,000 to 350,000 men would have been unwieldy for the first Napoleon to lead. It posed a real challenge to a man who was simply not up to the job.

The French had not yet adopted the organizational strategy of having a separate individual serve as chief of the General Staff. The *Major-Général* was the closest thing to Moltke's position, and that was Leboeuf. But Leboeuf was also the minister of war, so these functions were combined in one person.

The single French Army of the Rhine comprised eight corps, divided into two wings. The left wing, based in Metz, was the larger. It included II Corps (General Frossard), whose soldiers had been on summer manoeuvres at the Camp of Châlons and who took the forward position, near Saint-Avold. IV Corps (General Ladmirault) stood behind and to the left; these units had come from bases in northern France to Thionville. III Corps (Marshal Bazaine) was in the centre, around Metz; these were units from Paris. V Corps (General de Failly) was on the right, starting at Bitche; these units had come from Lyons and the south-east.

The right wing included two corps: I Corps (Marshal MacMahon) near Strasbourg, which came from Algeria via Marseilles, and VII Corps (General Douay), from south-eastern France and assembling at Belfort, to the right of I Corps. The Imperial Guard (General Bourbaki), the elite corps of the French army, came from garrisons near Paris to Nancy to serve as a first-line reserve force. VI Corps (Marshal Canrobert), coming from west-central France, assembled at the Camp of Châlons as a second-line reserve force.

Napoleon III selected his subordinates from among court favourites who earned their status through the ability to flatter. During peacetime, as Dennis Showalter notes, the emphasis on 'will power and self-assertion' meant that the corps commanders did not develop the habits of deference and taking orders.[9] They were jealous of each other and readily felt how their command appointments conferred status. The culture of the French army was that competence was assumed rather than verified and enhanced.

As the war unfolded, some corps commanders proved more capable than others, and wiser regarding their own strengths and limitations. Overall, however, they were not any better or worse than the Prussian commanders. If they had been under a Moltke instead of under Napoleon III and then MacMahon, they might have done all right. However, in these opening weeks of the war, with their new staff, they had to focus on administration and logistics, which was not the strength of these commanders. Their new subordinates therefore did not have the opportunity to see them at their best and establish mutual trust.

Furthermore, Napoleon III's army did not have a coherent and agreed-upon plan. As of the evening of 27 July, Napoleon III counted on the right wing to swing into Germany through Ratstatt and Germersheim, cut off the South German states, and then head north into Prussia. Canrobert would come in from Châlons and the navy would land at Kiel and Rostock. His commanders had a variety of opinions: MacMahon sent Leboeuf a letter on the 27th requesting a meeting about the role of I Corps; General Charles Frossard wanted an invasion of the Saarland, General Auguste Ducrot advocated for the French to seize Kehl and Landau and cut Prussia off from the South German states. And junior officers met in Metz's *Café Parisien* each evening to talk over the offensive that they hoped to soon undertake.

Upon arrival in Metz on 28 July, however, Napoleon realized how chaotic the French mobilization had been. At this point, the French had gathered some 280,000 men in a thin line stretching 200 miles from Thionville to Belfort. *Turco* and *zouave* regiments from Algeria were just then disembarking at Marseilles, nearly 500 miles away. Even so, Napoleon III's strikingly vague Order of the Day stated: 'Whatever may be the road we take beyond our frontiers, we shall come across the glorious tracks of our fathers. We shall prove worthy of them. All France follows you with its fervent prayers, and the eyes of the world are on you. On our success hangs the fate of liberty and civilisation.'[10] At this point, the Prussians were just starting to move from the Rhine railheads into Prussia's Rhenish provinces and the Rhenish Palatinate. But without a coherent, prepared plan, France was not positioned to quickly concentrate and take advantage of this moment. Reports of the amassing German army, however incomplete, cautioned against invasion rather than pointing to a vulnerability that could be exploited. In a meeting on the evening of the 28th, Napoleon III decided to postpone an invasion of Germany, effectively passing the initiative to the Prussians.

That evening at his headquarters at the Hôtel de l'Europe, the emperor received thirty anonymous letters from soldiers and officers, accusing his generals and marshals of incompetence, greed, or cruelty. Already French morale was low, and the soldiers ascribed delays to incompetence or treason, which only further undermined the emperor's projects. The mood had already settled into dispirited passivity.

Without a larger strategy as guidance, on Frossard's advice, Napoleon III attacked the village of Saarbrücken in the Rhenish Palatinate on 2 August. Six divisions from Bazaine's III Corps and Frossard's II Corps easily captured the village, leaving eighty-three Prussian casualties and eight-six French, including eleven dead. Napoleon III and his son the prince imperial rode up to II Corps on horseback, which was torture to the ailing emperor.

The insignificant victory was highly touted in the French press, which had been starved of information regarding the movement of French troops. The *Journal Officiel* reported on 3 August, 'Our army has taken the offensive, and crossed the frontier and invaded Prussian territory. In spite of the strength of the enemy positions a few of our battalions were enough to capture the heights which dominate Saarbrücken.'[11] The personal popularity of Napoleon III reached its highest point of the war. 'One praises the conduct of the Emperor; confidence is high,' reported the prefect of the Cher.[12]

The British military attaché in Paris saw that the French public did not buy the notion that Saarbrücken was a great victory that, according to the newspaper *France*, 'inaugurated a new epoch of history'. He noted, 'the French have the keenest sense of the ridiculous and cannot help but laugh at this.'[13] It soon became clear that the French had no real objective at Saarbrücken. They did not even attempt to cross the bridges or destroy the telegraph station beyond the river. This small victory proved temporary and was the only battle on German soil during the entire conflict.

Everyone had an opinion about the mobilization, and most agreed that France had failed. The French had over 492,000 trained men available, but only managed to gather 304,208 men along an arc of

200 miles by 6 August, and these men were not well fed or well equipped. Soldiers arrived at their appointed stations with no equipment and no direction. Prussia, by this time, effectively used the rail system to speed 426,000 men to a compact 50-mile point of concentration. Moreover, the North German Confederation and the South German states together could draw on a total of over one million trained men.

These areas of troop concentration did not exist on a blank canvas. They were imposed upon the fields, villages and riverine towns at the historical frontier between the French and Germans, where centuries of peaceful trade and sociability had taken place. Moltke's operational objective of destroying the French army meant that the Germans spread out over a larger territory and thus created more potential for encounters with civilians. Napoleon III's lack of military clarity, too, led to a broad swathe of civilian uncertainty as the threat of large-scale combat loomed.

CHAM

4. *Combat*

Contrary to expectations, Moltke's armies had mobilized faster than the French army. After the brief push at Saarbrücken, the French took up defensive positions that the Germans quickly forced into retreat in three battles: two in Alsace at Wissembourg and Froeschwiller, and one in Lorraine at Spicheren.

By 2 August, Moltke's three armies were ready to move. Between them, he left a gap wide enough for them to manage their supplies and move cleanly, but small enough to eventually come together and prevent escape. Moltke planned for a pocket battle in which his three armies encircled Napoleon III's Army of the Rhine, and he would have liked to have carried this out north of the Saar. The Second Army would receive a French attack, the Third Army would sweep through Alsace and attack the French right, and the First Army under Steinmetz would move down from the Moselle. The adventure at Saarbrücken helped to set the stage for this battle, since Frossard at Saarbrücken could be more readily encircled. However, Moltke's plans to defeat the French army in a battle of encirclement north of the Saar were upended when, instead of continuing the attack, the French simply withdrew from Saarbrücken.

Moltke therefore decided to send the Second Army south into France, toward Spicheren and Forbach, with the intention that the First and Third Armies would engage the French flanks and rear. This too did not work out. Steinmetz, instead of crossing the Saar on the right of the Second Army to cover its flank, on 5 August took the shortest line possible and pushed his own units across the path of the Second Army's march. Moltke now had to disentangle the First and Second Armies.

*

Meanwhile, in Alsace, the Prussian Third Army moved forward. The Third Army was positioned in Baden and the Palatinate, ready to invade France through north-eastern Alsace. On 1 August, the crown prince had crossed the Rhine and concentrated near Maxau and Landau, just 5 miles north of the French border. The Third Army crossed into France on the morning of 4 August.

Once again, the day did not go as planned. The battle at Wissembourg came as a surprise to both sides. MacMahon's four divisions of I Corps were spread over a large square, at Hageunau, Froeschwiller, Lembach and Wissembourg, some 10 miles apart from each other and not readily available to support each other. The division in Wissembourg comprised 8,600 soldiers under the command of Abel Douay, the sixty-one-year-old president of the military academy at St Cyr, and brother of Félix Douay, commander of VII Corps. It was a weak position, but it allowed Douay to seek out badly needed food. French reconnaissance failed to perceive the 80,000 Prussian and Bavarian troops of the Third Army heading their way. Douay's best intelligence came from the subprefect of Wissembourg, a Monsieur Hepp, who warned on 3 August that the Prussians had taken possession of a customs post east of the Lauter. As late as 8 a.m. on 4 August, Douay believed that the Prussians on the Lauter were simply an outpost. In fact, MacMahon had already telegraphed to say that he was planning to move his entire headquarters to Wissembourg.

Rain-soaked Bavarians crossing the Lauter that morning found themselves faced with French Chassepot rifles arrayed across an unbroken line on the slopes above Wissembourg and Altenstadt. These weapons in the hands of experienced riflemen could hit a man some 1,300 yards away, well before the Bavarians had reached the Lauter, at the rate of six to seven shots per minute. The Bavarians also encountered the *mitrailleuse*, which, unlike later models of machine gun, had a fixed position, so it did not spray fire across the field so much as send dozens of balls into a single man. 'One thing is certain,' recalled a Bavarian officer, 'few are wounded by the *mitrailleuse*. If it hits you, you're dead.'[1] The French on the other ends of the rifles were the

First Algerian Tirailleur Regiment, misleadingly known as the *Turcos*, who made use of every defensible wall, ditch, or embankment. It was foggy and damp, with vineyards blocking the path. Bavarians fell without ever seeing the French.

But advance they did, thanks to the superior Prussian and Bavarian artillery, which eventually set the town on fire and dislodged the French riflemen. German artillery could boast well-trained men, accurate cannon and sighting, and projectiles that exploded on impact. The French were starkly outnumbered with no means of protecting their flanks and no reserves. The other divisions of I Corps were too far away to help. Abel Douay himself was killed by a shell at 11 a.m.

Wissembourg soon fell. The French suffered a thousand casualties and a similar number captured. The Bavarians under General Ludwig von der Tann had paid a heavy price too. The Prussians still viewed the Bavarians as undisciplined in the march, unprepared for the war, and too ready to shoot all their ammunition quickly and call it a day. German artillery had won the battle. But the official dispatches on the battle of Wissembourg emphasized the unity of Germans in this first real test. 'The Bavarians have decisively defeated the enemies of Germany,' declared the Prussian *Volkszeitung*. 'The battlefield bears witness to their unwavering fidelity.'[2]

Crown Prince Friedrich Wilhelm was delighted that his men did not break in battle: 'Our fellows behaved just as they always did on peace-time manoeuvres – an observation confirmed quite unreservedly by our Bavarian comrades, and which is certainly as high commendation for the men as it is for our fighting system!'[3] As for the wounded, he reported in his diary that he saw 'dying and severely wounded men spring up by sheer force of will to let me see the joy they felt; many were just able to wave a maimed hand in token of greeting as I passed.'[4]

At Wissembourg, the French and the Germans had their first large-scale encounters with each other. The Germans assumed the worst of the Algerians and were fascinated by their hair and dark skin. The crown prince recorded his every encounter with Algerians in terms of 'veritable savages' engaged in 'villainy' and 'vile tricks'.[5] He never examined how the Algerians might have felt about encountering Germans.

At Wissembourg, too, the first time the Germans took over a French headquarters – that of Abel Douay – they remarked on the poor quality of maps and the too-fancy kitchen wagon and clothes. The crown prince noted Douay's small dog crouched beside his master's corpse. It was also the first time that soldiers came to terms with the violence that they had inflicted on others, unable to drag their eyes away from piles of bodies. Bavarian private Franz Hiller recalled, 'I saw the corpse of a young Frenchman and thought, "what will his parents and family think and say when they learn of his death?" His pack lay ripped open at his side; there was a photograph of him. I took it, and have it to this day.'[6]

That night, following their usual practice, Prussians and Bavarians billeted in houses in Wissembourg. One young Bavarian named Emonts was moved by a woman in tears, nursing her baby. 'After much pleading, we found out that her husband had joined the battle and lay shot at Bitscher Gate. "Oh!" rang out from every mouth. Everyone tried to offer his condolences to the young mother and widow.' After supper, Emonts and his fellow soldiers 'hurried to Bitscher Gate and found here two dead irregulars opposite the position we had occupied in the morning.'[7] Why Emonts and his comrades needed to make this pilgrimage was left unsaid: to witness the dead that they themselves might have killed? to see the dead man who left a widow and child behind? to impress upon themselves the consequences of war – an encounter with a civilian they had not been trained to expect to encounter? After all, King Wilhelm's proclamation to his soldiers before entering France had drawn a bright line between soldiers and civilians: 'We are not waging war against the peaceful inhabitants of the country; rather it is the duty of every honour-loving soldier to spare private property and not to tolerate offence to the good reputation of our army even by individual examples of indiscipline.'[8] Now, after Wissembourg, Emonts and his comrades recognized the consequences of their own actions in war.

The crown prince also grappled with the reality of war the next morning. 'We had to cover a part of yesterday's battlefield,' he wrote, 'the description of which I pass over, because the cruel sight, every time I behold it afresh, grows more and more abhorrent to me.' He spotted the body of a civilian, shot through the forehead, lying in a roadside ditch. To assuage his guilt, he immediately reported that 'Many French soldiers have borrowed civilian clothes, to enable them to escape unrecognized.'[9]

Dietrich von Lassberg, for his part, crossed into France on the next day, 5 August, excited to hear the news of the victory at Wissembourg but a bit angry to have missed out. The town looked sad – no inhabitants to be found, only wounded soldiers and a stray chicken or dog among the damaged houses. He enjoyed his first glimpse of French uniforms on prisoners marching in the other direction. His superior officers reminded the troops not to laugh at or deride the prisoners.

Lassberg soon passed a more sombre sight: a wagon loaded with dead Bavarians, Prussians and French, tossed in as they had been found, 'full of blood, dirt and filth', half-naked and blue from wounds. 'It was a nasty, repellent sight that none of us will ever forget.'[10] That evening, he had to seek firewood, and requisition it, 'meaning we had to take it where we found it . . . I came to this first requisition like a thief.'[11]

Lassberg and his companions awoke early on 6 August, around 3 a.m., after having lain in the rain and mud all night. They were on the march by five o'clock. Soon, to their surprise and delight, they could hear the cannon and thought, *'Heute kommen auch wir dran!'* – 'Today we will also be there!'[12] All morning, they marched closer and closer, and the cannon thunder became more and more clear. And then, the machine gun: 'it is a really eerie sound and, once heard, never to be mistaken again.'[13]

Lassberg was eager to be in the middle of things and did not have to wait long. As he marched through a wood, suddenly Chassepots from afar started destroying the stems and branches around him.

He soon saw the first wounded, and the first dead, from his company. *Leutnant* Emil Ott of the 2nd Infantry Regiment, an old war-school companion, called out to him, 'Greetings, Lassberg! I've been shot in the leg! Farewell and goodbye!'[14]

The wounded cried out for water, but Lassberg could only pause to share the contents of his flasks before moving 'forward, ever forward'.[15] Bullets sprayed through the grapevines and grapevine leaves. Wounded and dead soldiers lay in great numbers on top of each other.

Lassberg's attention focused on wounded French soldiers from Algeria, lying in their own blood. He ascribed treachery to these dying men, rehearsing many of the stereotypes about Algerian soldiers that became part of the ugly commentary of the war. Many were only playing dead, he reported, and shot at Lassberg and his companions after they had carefully stepped away. This was their final act: the men were then immediately shot or bayonetted by angry and bitter German soldiers. An Algerian with a bayonet rushed Lassberg to pierce him through. At the last minute Lassberg noticed him, swerved, and shot him immediately. With a loud cry the man collapsed.

> What a very strange feeling it was for us, that we so suddenly found the much discussed, much praised and much feared African troops together in battle, these Turcos, who seemed to us with their unfamiliar, black, brown and dark yellow faces at first scarcely human, who with an incomprehensible anger and endurance fought to the death and in death still appeared horrible – but once we clashed with them, we knew no fear.[16]

Suddenly, the mood turned. 'We had become, despite a short panic and backward jam of our troops, Lords of the Wood.'[17] Lassberg soon reconnected with his company and battalion. They assembled in the churchyard of a village called Froeschwiller, greeting each other and mourning their losses. Under the light of the flames burning the church, stunned by their victory, the sounds of victory hurrahs in their ears, they came to recognize that they had been part of an unplanned battle.

That night, a broken spyglass and a hole in his backpack gave evidence of the close calls that Lassberg had faced that day unawares. Around him swirled more wounded, more prisoners, more burning buildings.

> So that was our first day of battle! It's not possible to recount the impression, the great impression, that this battle made on me, and really on most of the others; indeed, this evening we cannot have a clear conception of it, we were bodily and spiritually much too excited and not yet collected. What will my family back home think? Through the telegraph they have certainly quick tidings about the battle, but not any news about the losses, about the life and death of Rudolf and me and the wounded in the army. Of Rudolf I also know nothing; tomorrow is his birthday; it would please me to be able to congratulate him on it.[18]

Without realizing it, Lassberg had marched into one of two major battles on 6 August that opened France to invasion: Froeschwiller in Alsace, and Spicheren to the north-west, in Lorraine. Neither battle was planned, and both might have been French victories if they had been able to exploit German weaknesses.

Lassberg's entry into combat on the 6th had followed a day of confusion for the French. On 5 August, the day after Wissembourg and as Lassberg marched into France, Napoleon III – still headquartered in Metz – made another change of organization. He delegated authority to two of his marshals. MacMahon now oversaw I, V and VII Corps, while Bazaine was responsible for II, III and IV Corps. But no new chain of command was created, no staffs were assigned, and Napoleon still issued orders to corps commanders so lines of authority now blurred. Bazaine did not act on his new ambivalent authority, and MacMahon did not have the chance to do anything with V and VII Corps before I Corps was attacked and the marshal was was driven from Alsace.

MacMahon had at Froeschwiller his I Corps, a division from VII Corps and Failly's V Corps coming from Bitche. The latter was slow to arrive after a long march on 5 August and was fearful of leaving the border unguarded. Confusion in the French command wearied French soldiers who had to march from position to position without clarity about what they were intended to achieve. Although they did not go far, the combination of rain and sun exhausted them. Most of VII Corps concentrated further south in the false belief that a German army was gathering in the Black Forest and preparing to attack Belfort. So, MacMahon had 48,000 men on 6 August, instead of the 77,600 he had hoped to marshal. MacMahon's I Corps included six regiments of *zouaves* and *Turcos*, most of whom had come with combat experience in Algeria.

On 6 August, MacMahon sought to strengthen his position at Froeschwiller. Unlike at Wissembourg, the ridge at Froeschwiller provided an excellent defence that allowed the French to maximize their use of the Chassepot rifle. The four villages of Froeschwiller, Elsasshausen, Eberback and Langensoultzbach sat in a semicircle linked by a road that looked down on the valley in which the Sauer flowed and on Woerth, which lay at the juncture of the Sauer and the Sulzbach. The French furthermore dug into trenches and breastworks.

Meanwhile, the 100,000 men of the German Third Army made their way south toward Hagenau and Strasbourg. Blumenthal intended 6 August as a day of rest after a long march and a chance to reorganize supply lines, in preparation to surround and overwhelm MacMahon at Froeschwiller on the 7th.

Instead, the Third Army found itself drawn into battle. In the early morning, outposts of the two armies encountered each other along the Sauerbach. At eight o'clock, patrols of the Prussian V Corps spotted the French on the heights but believed that they were in retreat. They entered the village of Woerth, but French fire from above forced them to retreat. The sound of guns pulled in the II Bavarian Corps through the thickly wooded Sulzbach valley north of Woerth. To the south, French artillery opened fire on the advancing XI Corps and attracted a German artillery response.

Soon after, by 9.30, the commander of the German V Corps arrived – General Hugo von Kirchbach – and, without having received orders from High Command or having been attacked, ordered his men to take Woerth and the heights beyond. Kirchbach sent his entire artillery of sixty Krupp guns into battle. By 10.00, he began to send infantry across the Sauer. At first, French bayonet charges were able to repel the German attacks and push them down the hill and back across the river. This slow engagement made the Germans vulnerable to counterattack, but the French did not take advantage of the opening.

The crown prince and Blumenthal ordered Kirchbach to pull back, but he was already too involved and not inclined to heed the order in any case. By the early afternoon, the crown prince realized that a major battle had been started and hoped to shape it. He sought to create a pincer move in which the French would be caught between the I Bavarian Corps on Kirchbach's right – Lassberg's corps, under General von der Tann – and the Württemberg division on the left. But this move required Kirchbach to delay his attack until he had support on his flanks, and he was unable to do so.

On the right, the mud and the steep and wooded approach delayed the advance until greater numbers of Germans, backed by formidable artillery, could eventually take out the French *mitrailleuse* and dislodge the Chassepots. In any case, Lassberg and his companions undertaking this move on the right had barely slept in two days, and for the morning rations had only received wine. At times, they stayed immobile, refusing to fight, or headed to the rear under the pretext of escorting a prisoner or wounded soldier. The crown prince grew angry at the Bavarians for failing to move forward. 'The Bavarian troops were terribly slow,' he wrote, 'so that I was obliged to say the strongest things to them before, at last, they advanced and attacked properly.'[19]

Some, including Lassberg, took a particular interest in hunting down any Algerian soldiers that came their way, whom they disrespectfully termed the *Schwarzen* – 'the Blacks' – and on whom they projected any fear of dishonourable fighting: ascribing to the Algerians acts such as shooting in the back, killing the wounded and disfiguring the bodies of the dead. After all, it was the defensive tenacity of the Algerians, such as the Second Algerian Tirailleur Regiment, that caused the Bavarians so much trauma that day. The stereotypes of soldiers from Algeria outlasted two future world wars. Yet the Second Tirailleurs won a record number of *Légions d'honneur* at Froeschwiller.

On the left, the pincer move advanced more quickly. XI Corps occupied the village of Morsbronn, succeeded in turning the French right and forced them to retreat. At the centre, growing desperate in the early afternoon, MacMahon sent in the cavalry. They faced novel tactics. In the past, infantry would form squares or hit the ground to avoid the cavalry's sabres and spook their horses. With the breech-loading rifle, however, the tactics changed. Infantry could line up and shoot, more rapidly and with more accuracy, taking down horses and men by the hundreds before they came within even fifty yards of the Prussian lines. Meanwhile, the Bavarians finally succeeded in outflanking the French in the mid-afternoon. By 4 p.m., any French resistance had ended, save for a few units trapped in Froeschwiller, and the Bavarians and Prussians poured into the village. MacMahon pulled back west to Reichshoffen.

Crown Prince Friedrich Wilhelm sent a telegraph to his father, reporting his success. As the firing ceased, 'a deep stillness reigned, as though nothing had happened, while the lovely summer's evening spread its mantle over hill and plain.'[20] He contemplated the historic opportunity to leverage this success toward political unification with the south German states. Meanwhile, German artillerymen inspected a captured *mitrailleuse*, which inspired nervous and bawdy jokes. They had not experienced this intensity of fire at Königgrätz four years earlier.

The crown prince now had the path toward Lorraine open to

him. German casualties were 10,500 killed or wounded, mostly Prussians. French casualties were only a little higher, about 11,000, but, in addition, MacMahon lost 200 officers and 9,000 soldiers as prisoners. In the wake of the battle, French and German doctors worked for three days just to bring wounded soldiers back to their mobile hospitals. It took a week for the villagers of Froeschwiller to bury the dead.

MacMahon reported to Napoleon III: 'I have lost a battle; we have suffered great losses in men and materiel. The retreat is at present in progress, partly on Bitche, partly on Saverne. I shall try to reach this point where I shall reorganize the army.'[21] The French army fell back, beaten and in disarray. MacMahon was cut off from the Army of the Rhine, with Friedrich Wilhelm's Third Army free to either pursue him or head toward Lorraine.

Fifty miles to the north-west, a second battle unfolded on 6 August. By this time, Frossard had withdrawn his II Corps from the hills above Saarbrücken and settled on Spicheren Heights, a commanding bluff overlooking the valley of the Saar and pointing at Saarbrücken just 3 miles to the north and across the border. The heights were steep and rocky, with the eastern slope cut by ravines and covered with woods, while the western slope overlooked a narrow valley through which ran a highway and railroad from Metz to the Rhineland; this is where II Corps had its supply depot. Frossard had managed to pull this supply depot together – it wasn't easy – and he had positioned his men well, with one division on the heights, one holding the valley, and a third in reserve south of Forbach, with the cavalry watching the road west of Forbach to protect the most vulnerable position.

By contrast with MacMahon's army, the French at Spicheren were well concentrated. In addition to the three divisions of II Corps, III Corps' four divisions stood within 15 miles. The French outnumbered the Prussians 54,900 to 42,900. For his part, Moltke did not intend a battle at Spicheren on 6 August any more than he had at Froeschwiller. Steinmetz had moved two of his corps, VII and VIII, toward the Saar – moving due south to Saarbrücken, again in the way of the Second Army. Steinmetz's undisciplined manoeuvre now placed him in a position to blunder into battle. Moltke had still hoped to encircle the French. At first, he had aimed for this encirclement to take place north of the Saar; by 5 August he aimed for this move south of the Saar. The Germans did not know the location of the main French army. They spent the night of 5 August facing in three directions.

The battle started at the initiative of General von Kameke's 14th Division of VII Corps. Here again, the Prussian subordinate officers refused to follow orders: General von Kameke ignored Steinmetz. Instead, his cavalry had spotted French soldiers on Spicheren Heights and assumed that these were the rear guard of the retreating force – they had, indeed, abandoned the hills that they had occupied four days earlier during the incursion at Saarbrücken.

Around noon on 6 August, Kameke ordered the occupation of the Spicheren Heights and advanced six battalions across the Saar, but found them blocked by the French. At the sound of gunfire, more of the First Army and the advance guard of the Second joined the fight.

The French Chassepot again shaped the early stages of the battle by preventing increasingly desperate attacks up the Spicheren Heights. The real threat, however, lay on the French left, in the valley, among the yards and ironworks and slag heaps and rail line passing through Stiring Wendel. For most of the battle, Frossard was able to fight off the attack, but he needed reinforcements. Slow communication and confusion about the extent of the battle delayed movement to assist him. One divisional commander in III Corps, General Metman, had received orders from Frossard, but nobody had told Metman that Bazaine had placed him temporarily under Frossard's command, so he waited to verify the situation before ordering the march. Another divisional commander in III Corps, General Montaudon, had received orders directly from Bazaine, but it had taken two hours for the messenger to reach him.

Germans marched to the battle upon hearing fire; French soldiers did not. And while the Germans arrived slowly, this very slowness made it harder for Frossard to appreciate the number of Germans he faced. As night fell, the French still held steady, with energetic counterattacks and smart positioning. But eventually, with no French reinforcements arriving, the German assaults succeeded. They captured an outwork of the Roterberg – the central height – by 5 p.m. Soon afterward, the appearance of the Prussian 13th Infantry Division under General von der Goltz on the French left threatened the II Corps' rear at Forbach. Around 7 p.m., Frossard had to fall back south. He had received no support from III Corps after all. The divisions in Stiring Wendel withdrew, leaving the houses to burn and their wounded behind. The battle ended with 4,500 Prussian casualties and 2,000 French dead and wounded, plus 2,000 missing or prisoners.

The two battles of 6 August were a French tragedy. The French had fought well, defended well and counter-attacked tenaciously. The Chassepot delivered its promise. But at Froeschwiller, the French were simply outnumbered, and at Spicheren they had been manoeuvred out of position by the continuous arrival of German reinforcements.

The Germans had not fought all that well that day. Their columns dissolved under hard fire from French defensive positions. Yet they had moved quickly and opportunistically, seeking out cracks in the French defence and making the most of them, without ever offering a massed infantry attack. The Prussians were willing to engage without knowing whether they had seized upon an army or a regiment. They were willing to see what happened and to trust that their soldiers would run to the sound of guns. The Prussian way of proceeding threw their enemies, who expected to know in advance the scope of the battles they engaged in, and to encounter a steady attack rather than disconcerting periods of calm as more Prussian units arrived at the scene.

Furthermore, German artillery dislodged the French from their positions and led them to expend their forces on early counterattacks.

With percussion fuses, German shells exploded on impact – unless they burrowed into soft mud – and the gunners were trained for accuracy. (The fact that they were breech-loading did not make a difference. As crews became fatigued, they did not have a faster rate of fire.) Artillery proved decisive as a weapon of offence. Cavalry no longer mattered.

These were battles that the French were supposed to win, the better to encourage neutrals to think twice about supporting Prussia. Now, neither Austria nor Italy nor Denmark could be convinced to side with France. Austria abandoned its half-hearted military preparations by 10 August.

Already, the war had turned in favour of the Germans. Moltke did not have his decisive battle, but he had put France on its heels. At dawn on 6 August, the French believed they would be victorious. By the end of the day, they faced invasion.

5. *Retreat*

In Paris on 5 and 6 August, news arrived of a French victory under MacMahon, prompting the waving of flags and great animation on the boulevards. Crowds gathered at Place Vendôme singing the 'Marseillaise'. But Ollivier's appearance on his balcony on 6 August, pale and sad, made it clear that he had no such news: 'No, there is no announcement of victory. The government owes you the whole truth and will tell you it, good or bad, without reticence. Nothing is compromised. The main part of the army is intact. Have confidence!'[1]

Then, on 7 August, a rainy Sunday, small silent crowds formed to read the posted telegram from Napoleon III, and then dispersed: 'Marshal MacMahon has lost a battle; on the Saar, General Frossard has been obliged to retreat. This retreat is happening in good order. Everything can be recovered.'[2] Great anxiety and disbelief followed. How could the French army allow an invasion? The very word 'invasion' recalled the sombre days of 1815, a time that had seemingly receded into the distant past. After all, the previous invasion of France had taken place as the culmination of two decades of war, first under the revolutionary government and later under Napoleon I. In the fifty years since that time, French civilians had become distant from the site of conflict. Only military personnel, it was believed, would be subject to danger. For generations, the French public became accustomed to reading about war in the newspapers but did not expect it to come to their doorstep. Napoleon III's telegram admitting that his armies were now retreating into the interior elicited public outrage and anger, leading to numerous arrests of individuals shouting seditious cries.

After Wissembourg, Spicheren and Froeschwiller, the government censored news from the front. Anxiety and rumours led to

demoralization, though French citizens did not yet oppose the war. Crowds gathered outside Ollivier's home on the Place Vendôme and demanded that they hear the truth. Still, the rain that immiserated the French soldiers in retreat also kept the streets of Paris relatively quiet. Ollivier put Paris under a state of siege and called up all adult males to serve in one of the two National Guards: the *mobiles* for those under thirty, and the *sédentaires* for those aged thirty to forty.

By 9 August, patience had run out with Ollivier. In the Legislative session, the opposition lambasted him. 'France has been compromised by your imbecility!' cried Jules Favre; 'Come down from there!'[3] Some 10,000–30,000 Parisians demonstrated in front of the Palais Bourbon calling for the overthrow of the empire. Across the country, in Toulon, Marseilles, Montpellier, Le Creusot and Limoges, officials reported anti-imperial incidents.

Ollivier resigned that evening at the request of Empress Eugénie, serving as regent in the emperor's absence. The empress appointed General Charles Cousin-Montauban, known as Count Palikao since 1860 when he had beaten the Manchu army at Pa-li-kiao (Baliqiao) in the Second Opium War, as both President of the Council and minister of war. He was close to the emperor and did not enjoy much public support, and the empress retained authority to direct military affairs to protect the regime. The Corps Législatif opened an extraordinary session on 9 August and met every day that month but could not direct activities in Paris or the provinces. Yet members of the Corps Législatif from across the political spectrum worried about the wartime loss of civil liberties.

For some, despite their opposition to the war when it was declared, the moment called for self-sacrifice and resolution. Léon Gambetta declared, 'in the presence of a nation in arms we too must raise up a nation in arms!'[4] The conscript class of 1870 was called up ahead of schedule and a new war loan of 500 million francs was issued, doubling the initial amount. All veterans under the age of thirty-five were called into active service, whether they were married or not. All this came as bad news in a climate of great anxiety. These efforts reveal the tenuous ground on which the Second Empire now stood. The British ambassador reported on 9 August, just three weeks after the declaration of war, 'If France sustains another defeat, revolution will be inevitable.'[5]

Not all the anxiety and frustration were directed at the emperor. Many loyal to Napoleon III worried about the emperor himself leading his army into battle. This anxiety did not mean despair. On the contrary, it meant that people wanted to take action. Some 36,000 French men volunteered to join the army in August, six times the number of volunteers in the last two weeks of July. Some regions witnessed an increased resentment of republicans as it seemed more and more possible that the end of the empire was approaching. Others felt more hope with the installation of Palikao, with Bazaine leading the Army of the Rhine (as of 12 August) and with Louis-Jules Trochu's appointment as governor of Paris on 17 August. In the Vosges on 1 September, the prefect declared 'the physiognomy of the region [has] changed: people are more assured, they have recovered from the earlier alarms, [they] approach the situation with more calm, confidence, and courage.'[6]

The German advance rippled through the French interior, reaching far beyond the armies themselves. Already by 4 August, the Prefecture of Paris changed course regarding Germans residing in the capital. Rather than encouraging them to leave (except for men of military age), the prefect ordered Germans who wished to stay in Paris to present themselves to the commissariat for their neighbourhood so that they could be issued a permit that allowed them to stay. Two days later, France introduced the requirement of a passport for foreign nationals.

The requirement for passports caused an immediate rush of requests. Since the ambassadors of the German states had pulled out of France, German nationals had to appeal to foreign embassies: Prussians and others from the North German Confederation reported to the American embassy, whereas those from Baden or Bavaria reported to the Swiss and Württembergers to the Russians. The ambassadors worked to prepare passports and secure train tickets east. Germans stood in long lines to put in their names and then waited, either later that day or the next, for the distribution of a packet of passports. An American embassy worker stood on a table outside the embassy to call out the names and then toss the passport in the right direction, trusting the individuals crowded into the street to claim the right one. Within a few days, some 40,000 Germans obtained a passport from the American embassy. Women's nationality was made tricky by the rules of patriarchy. A German woman who married a French man became French and therefore was allowed to remain in the country, while a French woman who had married a German was obliged to leave.

After the two battles of 6 August, Napoleon III commanded a large concentration of soldiers in Lorraine, but had no plan as to what to do next. The movements of the two wings of the French army – under MacMahon and Bazaine – after 6 August had such momentous consequences that it is worth assessing some of the alternatives.

The emperor initially planned to concentrate forces at Saint-Avold – as he learned that Frossard was falling back, he thought, to a strong position at Cadenbronn. From there the French could attack the advancing Germans. On the morning of the 7th, Napoleon boarded a train from his headquarters in Metz east to Saint-Avold to discuss the plan with Bazaine. But before the train departed the station word came that the Germans had captured Forbach and that Frossard could not be found. In a state of dismay, Napoleon instead ordered the entire army back west to Châlons and returned to headquarters.

This scenario, a concentration of 400,000 French to the west at Châlons, would draw the Germans deep into French territory and might break up the German coalition. But this western strategy would also expose large swathes of French territory to German invasion and would also be politically dangerous, as Ollivier pointed out in a telegram on 7 August.

Bazaine now suggested yet another course of action: Napoleon III could order a concentration to the south, in which the five corps around Metz would fall back on Nancy or Langres and join the three corps under MacMahon heading west from Alsace. This move would allow a concentration of the French forces to threaten the German flank as it marched west. The French had time to pull off such a move as Moltke paused his army's advances on 7 August to bring forward Royal Headquarters, to allow the First Army to finally get out of the way of the Second Army, and to give the Third Army a rest after the victory at Froeschwiller. However, this concentration would have left Paris to its own defences, a politically unacceptable situation despite the strength of the capital's fortifications.

In the face of Ollivier's objections to the retreat to Châlons and Bazaine's urging to concentrate at Metz, Napoleon III countermanded his orders on 8 August and ordered a retreat toward Metz. This option posed challenges for MacMahon, because the move involved a flank-march across the front of the German army. Furthermore, the countermanded order caused logistical problems as any change of this magnitude might.

Nevertheless, by 9 August, Bazaine and General Leboeuf had moved the four army corps of the left wing into position 10 miles east of Metz, along the Nied. Following their campaign practices in Africa, their rear-guard cavalry stayed close to the infantry, so they did not have good intelligence about the enemy or significant protection for their own soldiers. Then, realizing that the position was untenable without MacMahon's support, they fell back to the city itself.

Just where was MacMahon? After Froeschwiller, MacMahon's and Failly's soldiers were deeply demoralized as they crossed the Vosges, making a wide arc to the south to avoid any contact with the enemy. Most of the French right wing – MacMahon's I, V and a division of VII Corps – made a long, exhausting retreat from Froeschwiller, first south and then west back to the Camp at Châlons, following the original order of 7 August and avoiding contact with the invading Germans. MacMahon's decision to ignore the call north toward Metz to assist Bazaine remains a striking choice that he never fully explained.

Instead, MacMahon's and Failly's men undertook long marches under five days of heavy rain: V Corps covered 50 miles in under forty-eight hours between 6 and 8 August, and received no rations until the 10th. Eventually they reached Lunéville some 70 miles south-west of Froeschwiller and from there took rail transport on 16 and 17 August, arriving at Châlons on 20 August.

A soldier's letter dating from 8 August captures the long haul:

> Finally, at eleven at night, we have lunch, dinner, and supper . . . Two hours later, we were en route for Sarreguemines. After having gone thirty-four kilometres, we had lunch on the road; at one, we were at Puttelange, after having travelled forty-six kilometres. Many were in distress; stragglers kept arriving until nightfall . . . I entered a pharmacist's to buy some medication for my feet, which had started to suffer . . . I was in deep sleep when I heard a cry to 'look lively' . . . it wasn't anything, just that we were decamping. It was midnight and we had to leave at two. We left at four from Puttelange, we arrived here at noon and have travelled thirty-five kilometres.[7]

The French retreats were both disorganized and demoralizing. For most soldiers, the purpose of these movements seemed wholly unclear. Divisions became entangled because routes were not clearly assigned. Supplies were irregular, forcing soldiers to either go hungry or find food through local requisition or theft. They had often tossed aside their cooking gear and so could not prepare the food that they had. Pouring rain made the retreat miserable and muddy, discouraging soldiers not yet hardened to the campaign.

With MacMahon heading to Châlons and Bazaine to Metz, the two wings of the Army of the Rhine were now completely divided and out of communication. As late as 10 August, it was possible for one soldier to write, 'I don't know what we're doing, but I think we are marching in retreat.'[8] Yet the march solidified the tough reputation of the Army of the Rhine. This army of peasants carried 66 pounds of equipment rapidly over long distances after having fought heroically.

At the same time, a series of other decisions shaped the war's trajectory: Douay stayed in Belfort with the remainder of VII Corps. Canrobert's VI Corps was supposed to return to Paris to form the start of a new army, but on 9 August, on Eugénie's urging, VI Corps was sent to Metz. The infantry arrived just before the railroad line was cut. Back in Paris, on 14 August General Joseph Vinoy was appointed commander of the Paris garrison, called XIII Corps (even though it had previously been named VIII Corps, and no VIII to XI Corps ever materialized). Trochu was sent to Châlons to oversee a new French XII Corps composed mostly of unarmed mobile guardsmen and barely qualifying as a real military unit, a very tenuous corps indeed.

The French command structure groaned under Napoleon III's personal physical pain and debilitating lack of certainty. The emperor, like King Wilhelm, exercised authority over both the armed forces and the state. Upon leaving Paris in July, Napoleon had handed political authority to the Council of Regency under the presidency of Empress Eugénie. It was increasing clear that he was simply no longer capable of commanding the army. Yet after a lifetime in the shadow of his famous uncle and with the patchy record of his previous conflicts, the emperor did not see a way to relinquish command. In the days after 6 August, he became withdrawn and depressed. He could not return to Paris – to do so would spell political defeat – but he could not lead effectively in Metz.

Napoleon decided to take a third route: he would withdraw to Châlons to organize a new army and hand command of the Army of the Rhine to Marshal Achille Bazaine. Bazaine was the best option among Napoleon's top advisers. Leboeuf's star had fallen; on 11 August, the Corps Législatif called for his resignation as Minister of War, and the Council of Regency voted to dismiss him for his role in leading France into war – an unfair decision that laid on Leboeuf's doorstep the mistakes of previous decades. MacMahon was in a weak position after Froeschwiller, while Canrobert was not interested: he knew his limitations and recognized that he was a great corps commander but was not interested in higher strategy.

Bazaine did not look the part, but he was popular as he had risen through the ranks, seemed like a man of the people and possessed physical courage. The chain of command, however, remained hazy. Although Bazaine's command over II, III and IV Corps was confirmed by Imperial Decree on 9 August, it was unclear how much authority he really had. At first, Bazaine was only named commander of something called the Army of Metz. In a bid to demonstrate his own continued but ill-defined power, Napoleon insisted that Bazaine accept General Louis Jarras, who had been Leboeuf's assistant, as his chief of staff. Bazaine just ignored Jarras and kept him in the dark about movements. And Napoleon still hampered Bazaine's command, shaping the plans and expressing his 'desires', which felt a lot like orders to his subordinates. Napoleon appointed Bazaine as commander-in-chief of the Army of the Rhine on 12 August but remained with the Army for four more crucial days in which Bazaine could not exercise real command.

Still, Bazaine might have taken the mantle of leadership more firmly in hand. He did not deliver any operational orders until late on 13 August, when he ordered the four corps near Metz to cross the Moselle away from the Prussians. When General Bourbaki and Leboeuf recommended changes in tactics based on Spicheren and Froeschwiller – such as preventing the French from firing rifles beyond their range – Bazaine did not take up these recommendations. He immersed himself in administrative trivia and failed to destroy bridges on the Moselle as the Prussians surrounded them. After twenty years of authoritarian rule, the power vacuum left by Napoleon III's weakness could not be easily filled and contributed to a general feeling of defeat not warranted by actual French performance in battle.

On the night of 6 August, after the battle of Froeschwiller, Dietrich von Lassberg tossed fitfully in a half-waking, half-sleeping state, his thoughts restless and excited. The young Bavarian had finally realized his hopes of fighting the French in their home territory but had neither victory nor peace in his grasp. The present was more painful, and future more bewilderingly uncertain, than he had expected. At dawn, he crept gratefully out of his tent. Crown Prince Friedrich Wilhelm also struggled to process the emotional toll of the recent battles. 'I am not even yet master of my feelings when I think of these successes,' he wrote, 'but above all when I recall our losses.'[9]

The Germans recovered from the battles within three days – a remarkable feat, considering that during the Napoleonic era armies typically required weeks to re-establish order. Then, over the next five days, they marched through Lorraine to seek a strong position for an encircling offensive. Moltke was able to move some 400,000 men forward in an orderly way despite the poor weather and despite having outstripped his own supply columns. The First and Second Armies moved closely together on a front 22 miles wide. If any single corps engaged in combat, the others would be able to come to their aid. Yet they were dispersed enough to move quickly and requisition supplies effectively.

The march was not perfect. The Germans had a higher proportion of reservists than the French, so many men struggled. For Lassberg and his Bavarian companions, the march proved an endless stream of rain and potatoes. Behind them came legions of non-combatants: telegraph, postal and railroad services; Royal Headquarters, which included the royal household as well as the civil administration brought by Bismarck and Roon so that they could still run Prussia while on campaign; the German princes and their entourages; and the foreign military attachés and the press. The Germans, too, were uncertain of their military objective: their cavalry had lost contact with the French armies, and they had not heard anything from Berlin since 2 August. Only on the 10th did Moltke conclude that the French were retreating in two directions, to Metz and to Châlons.

Still, the Germans were experienced and well staffed, and their routes had been well planned. Soldiers could read maps and knew their locations. By 10 August, the three armies had pivoted toward the west, and four days later, the First and Second Armies had renewed contact with Bazaine near Metz, with the First Army under Steinmetz almost reaching Metz and the Second Army under Prince Friedrich Karl further south near Toul. The Third Army under the crown prince and Blumenthal – except for Prussian and Badenese divisions sent south to besiege Strasbourg – had pushed west through the Vosges to Lunéville and, on 14 August, occupied the open city of Nancy. The First and Second Armies were prepared to attack the French at Metz directly, while the Third Army could support the attack into the French flank and rear.

Crown Prince Friedrich Wilhelm allowed himself to hope for a quick resolution to the conflict. 'I begin to believe,' he confided to his diary, 'that we may yet perhaps be able to keep the harvest festival at home, for I can *not* imagine things can go on much longer here.'[10]

Even before the Germans arrived, French civilian anxiety mounted. In many cases, morale had already been damaged by successive French movements through the area. The prefect of the Meuse reported on 16 August, 'no Prussians in Bar yet, [but the] population [is] in a state of overexcitement that approaches madness.'[11] The subprefect of Provins (Seine-et-Marne) noted on 27 August, 'Great emotion everywhere . . . veritable panic.'[12]

At this point, British reports on the war's violence emphasized that times had changed since the recent past of 1814–15. In a surprising report from Phalsbourg on 15 August and reproduced in the 'War Correspondence' of the *Daily News*, one journalist presented modern warfare as less fearsome than it had been in the past:

> I cannot but think that the whole scene as we advance is a tribute to modern civilization. Here are young girls standing laughing at the cottage doors, not a bit afraid of violence; and we pass after a hundred thousand men, more or less, have gone by along that same road. It would not have been so in the Thirty Years' War. It would

> scarcely have been so some fifty years back. But here it is to-day. The village maidens stand half-shy, half-curious, to see the Prince and his Staff ride on their way; the old people sit basking in the sunshine and shaking their heads over the evil days.[13]

And yet, this same report acknowledged increased tensions between advancing Germans and French civilians:

> The soldiers are not inclined to be harsh, if only they get what they think [they] ought to have, and there is nothing to alarm the inhabitants in the demeanour of their terrible foes. But this difference of language begins to make the everyday intercourse of conquerors and conquered far from smooth. The French accept their ill-luck fairly enough; what they are put out of temper by is being shouted at in strange tongues and shaken by the shoulder [as] if they are dull.[14]

The crown prince reported the same lack of communication. Once soldiers passed from German-speaking areas of Alsace into French-dominant ones, they could not be understood and simply helped themselves to the contents of wine-cellars.

Information of this sort scattered across Europe and the globe via telegram and made its way into the press. At first, the London periodical press did not take the war very seriously, as journalists objected to France's reasons for causing the war and believed it would be over quickly. But once battles were under way in early August, the British press took greater interest. An engraving in the *Illustrated Times* on 6 August depicted a crowd of Londoners surrounding newsboys carrying the latest from France. The weeks of mobilization had created pent-up interest in the war, the newspaper claimed, 'and when newsboys make their appearance in the streets with the morning or evening papers quite a rush takes place upon them, and they are barely able to deal out their wares fast enough to meet the demands.'[15]

The *Illustrated London News* sided with the Germans and praised their discipline and 'military Logic' as well as the 'Appropriateness of motives' in joining the fight. By contrast, the newspaper portrayed the French as frivolous, with an engraving of French soldiers swimming playfully in a river in contrast with Prussians soldiers making a serious assessment of their surroundings. 'Some are getting ready, others frolic' the paper moralized.[16]

Telegrams lent immediacy to the unfolding conflict. News of the battle of Wissembourg, telegraphed from London to India at 10 p.m. on the night of 6 August, reached the Secretary's Office in Simla by the 8th. At times, telegrams from the field feel like bursts of social media. Here's one example sent from London to India on 7 August at 3.30 p.m. It contained more details about the battles of 6 August, drawing on a telegraph that the crown prince had sent on 7 August. Now readers learned that the conflict involved multiple French forces, and that 'two eagles, six *mitrailleuses*, thirty cannons and 4,000 prisoners were captured'. Furthermore, a second battle 'west of Saarbruck' – Spicheren – had led to French retreat with 'many hundred prisoners' as well as heavy Prussian losses, 'especially in Officers'. Moreover, as 'Great excitement prevails in Paris by the circulation of false reports of victory', this telegram claimed better knowledge in London than in Paris itself. Finally, without explanation, 'Government have been forced to promise to communicate every thing.'[17]

At this stage in the war, neither the French nor the German press could be trusted to report on the conflict with much accuracy. British journalists, however, had access to the German military and witnessed the aftermath of battles. Reporters took their duties seriously. The *Daily News* declaimed on 13 August 1870,

> The function discharged by the Correspondent is higher than the office of merely satisfying curiosity, although it includes that. Without the picturesque and ready pens of these gentlemen, we should remain in ignorance of that part of the business of fighting which is ignored in politics, in diplomacy and by historians. Pictures of

> waggon-loads of wounded, of soldiers writhing with pain and thirst, of weeping women fleeing from the cottages amongst which the shells were bursting, tend to make us regard glorious war with feelings altogether distinct from that review and parade temper in which it is placed before the world by romanticists.[18]

The crown prince recognized the strategic importance of maintaining 'numbers of Englishmen at headquarters', and spoke highly of Mr Russell of *The Times* and Mr Skinner of the *Daily News*. Unlike the lazy and apathetic MP and sculptor Lord Ronald Leveson-Gower, Russell and Skinner 'are agreeable and amiable persons, full of the utmost zeal to investigate every detail'. Friedrich Wilhelm directed another authorized observer, Lord Adare, to Strasbourg.[19] Such relationships aimed to keep British opinion and therefore British leadership on friendly terms, even as the Germans moved deeper into French territory.

British public sympathy cut in multiple directions. Parliament was not in session during the entirety of the conflict, and so did not shape public opinion directly. Preachers, however, used the war as a vehicle for their Sunday sermons and printed pamphlets. In Glasgow, Reverend Charles Neilson MacCraig issued his opinion of the war in a sermon to the 10th Argyle Artillery Volunteers. While the United Kingdom should remain neutral, this 'does not imply neutrality in the expression of our sentiments'.[20] France, he declared, bore the full blame for the war. 'See France full of folly and vanity, pride, arrogance, rhodomontade, self-confidence, scornful of peace,' he urged.[21] The French go on and on about how Paris is so historic and beloved, with genius, position, artworks, culture; MacCraig mocked Parisians' fear that Prussia would make Paris 'a playground, a museum of curiosities, a people of valets, something like Rome, less the Pope and the religious prestige'.[22] And it is galling, he continued, that the French were unwilling to sue for peace and blamed others for their own misfortune. After decades of causing European turmoil, 'the thunderbolt she [France] hurled at the head of her neighbour, bursts on her own, and she maddens with rage because on her own head her mischief has been returned home.'[23]

Prussia, MacCraig averred, maintained its dignity in its pursuit of victory: 'No talk, no bluster, all action, the wind-bag of France collapsed, Prussia impregnable.'[24] King Wilhelm was prepared and prudent, as 'prayer, on the wings of pains and promptitude, his armour-bearers, led him on to victory'.[25] Not Moltke but an appropriately Protestant monarch led the victorious cause.

In other words, and not surprisingly for a man of his position, for MacCraig, confessional difference sat at the centre of these reflections. 'Had a Protestant element existed in France,' insisted MacCraig, 'she would not be as she now is.'[26] He traced the root of France's difficulties back to the St Bartholomew's Day massacre of 1572. In a shockingly simplified understanding of the Wars of Religion, MacCraig argued that France had expelled her Protestant population and allowed in the 'revolutionary horrors' of the recent past, as well as the 'present misery, thoughtlessness, frivolity, and gaiety'.[27]

By contrast, Reverend S. Taylor, in a meeting of the Aid to the Wounded in Cambridge, and quoted in *The Times* on 19 August, urged action without favouring one side over the other:

> We should seize the opportunity of showing our sympathy for the brave soldiers who, whether on the French or the Prussian side, have fallen in defence of their country, and in this way we should in the most direct and conclusive manner refute the slander of those who said that our neutrality was synonymous with a selfish indifference to the fate of other nations, and a determination to save our own pockets at all costs.[28]

Taylor's call was heeded. In keeping with the dispositions of the 1864 Geneva Convention, starting in August, the National Society for Aid to the Sick and Wounded in War sent mobile hospitals to the conflict, including volunteer doctors and nurses, with the co-operation of the British government and the Anglo-American

Ambulance. By September, they had sent 110 individuals including 60 surgeons, and £200,000-worth of supplies. Other relief followed suit. This aid may have assuaged a sense of guilt regarding neutrality. In the press as well as in pamphlets, British observers increasingly criticized the policy of neutrality, and those who provided aid, like Taylor, shaped this debate.

To Moltke's surprise, Bazaine – the commander-in-chief with Napoleon III still presiding as emperor – remained on the right bank of the Moselle, east of Metz, on 13 August. The French had nearly 180,000 soldiers at Metz, mostly in a front 7 miles long. They now debated whether to stay or retreat. If they stayed, they could be outflanked and destroyed by Moltke's fast-moving armies. If they left, they faced a challenging retreat that would leave men and materiel behind.

Metz relied on the Paris–Nancy railroad for supplies, and Nancy (33 miles to the south of Metz) had been left open to invasion. Bazaine would need to retreat toward Verdun, 40 miles to the west. The 180,000 French would have to traverse the Moselle at very few crossings along a crowded front, even as their outposts had already encountered the enemy. On the night of 12 August, heavy rains had swept away the pontoon bridges constructed over the previous four days, forcing the army to cram into a front of just 3 miles.

Bazaine compounded these logistical challenges with command flaws. Piqued at having his choice for chief of staff overruled by the emperor, Bazaine did not consult with Jarras. With too little information and authority in that key role, the French were unaware of a bridge at Longeville-les-Metz. Temporary bridges, as they were repaired after the flood, could be accessed only by foot because of the rain-soaked meadows at their approaches. All horses and wagons would therefore be required to pass through the narrow streets of Metz to the two permanent bridges. After crossing the Moselle, the army would converge on one road, with no destination or military objective to pursue.

Bazaine understood these challenges and opposed the move in

private, arguing to the emperor that they should stand their ground. But Napoleon III had received a message from Empress Eugénie reporting that the Germans were already beyond Metz in the south (the crown prince's Third Army) and Friedrich Karl and the Second Army were already cutting to the north to meet the crown prince in Verdun. The French had to move.

Not surprisingly, the French retreat was slow and jammed. Soldiers told to be ready to move at 4.30 a.m. on 14 August were only just crossing the Moselle at 4 p.m. That is when they heard the Prussian cannon. East of the Moselle, the rear of Bazaine's army had been attacked. It was the first of three engagements aimed to halt the French retreat from Metz on 14, 16 and 18 August.

Much like Spicheren and Froeschwiller, the battle of Borny on 14 August was engaged at the initiative of subordinates. This time, General Karl von der Goltz of Dietrich von Zastrow's VII Corps in the First Army took the lead. It was a bold, unauthorized move. The French, with superior numbers and position, held their ground, but they did not counter-attack to crush the German advance, contrary to Leboeuf's advice based on the experience of Spicheren and Froeschwiller. Bazaine was angry that the battle had occurred at all and had no interest in prolonging the retreat with a counterattack. While lacking strategic initiative, Bazaine demonstrated the physical courage that had won him favour by riding calmly around the battlefield even after sustaining an injury in the shoulder from a Prussian shell.

The day ended in stalemate. Inconclusive fighting broke off at nightfall, leaving 4,600 German casualties and 3,900 French. Claude Decaen, who had replaced Bazaine as commander of III Corps for less than two days, was killed. The strategic outcome for the French was more dire: their retreat to Verdun was slowed, while the Prussian Second Army used the opportunity to cross the Moselle south of Metz.

Already, the war rained misery on local peasants. So many refugees had attempted to enter Metz that the gates had been barred. A Saxon lieutenant wrote of the French peasantry near Metz: 'I am shocked by the misery that war brings to the peasants . . . Every village in these parts has been eaten out by successive echelons, leaving the locals with nothing, yet ever more troops arrive needing food.'[29]

After Borny, Bazaine recalled in his memoirs that Lorrainer peasants had immediately descended on the battlefield to seek valuables. As he toured the battlefield on 15 August under a white flag, he observed,

> Knapsacks were emptied out, anything not of value – papers, letters, books, pictures – was scattered about, but all money had disappeared. To steal the ring from a wounded officer, those wretched Lorrainers had cut off his fingers without even bothering to remove the glove . . . I only regretted that as a noncombatant [due to his touring under a white flag] I could not pick up a rifle and shoot those squalid peasants, who were looting every corner of the field not physically occupied by Prussian outposts.[30]

French soldiers saw 14 August as a victory. They had stopped retreating across the Moselle, they had fought together as one army, they had held back the Prussian attack, and they admired the courage of Bazaine. But Bazaine knew he would have to keep moving west, even though he did not feel sufficiently firm in his command to give an order that evening. He waited until ten o'clock the next morning.

Not for the last time, the gulf between the soldiers' perception and their commander's decision created distrust. The retreat on 15 August now followed a single road, which did not divide until reaching Gravelotte 8 miles to the west of Metz. Due to German cavalry raids, supply trains now required armed escorts. Despite the complexity and near impossibility of this retreat, Bazaine did not discuss it with Jarras. By the end of a day of confusion and delay, the French had made it only to the Verdun road.

That evening, Bazaine learned of the threat of a German advance on his left but put off making any orders. In the morning of the 16th at 5.15, Bazaine agreed with General Ladmirault's assessment that the French were so backed up that it would be advisable to postpone movement to be better able to handle an attack. And so, as Napoleon III finally departed Metz for Châlons, Bazaine's army waited.

Meanwhile, during the course of 15 August, the German Second Army had advanced across the Moselle, pivoting to outflank the retreating French and cut them off from Verdun. Moltke finally saw his opportunity for a decisive battle, though he did not yet know quite where and when it would take place. That evening at 6.30 he gave Friedrich Karl vague orders to attack the French on the Metz–Verdun road. Neither Moltke nor Friedrich Karl knew the exact location of the French nor anticipated the slowness of their retreat from Metz. As a result, Friedrich Karl ordered his Second Army too far west, leaving just two right-flank corps, III and X, to face the entire French army on 16 August.

6. *Turning Points*

Bazaine's day of retreat, 15 August, fell on the feast of Saint-Napoleon. This holiday helps us to understand how a sick and weary man could have held the power to lead France into such a precarious situation. The festival originated with Napoleon Bonaparte, who convinced the Vatican to canonize – and almost certainly to invent – a Roman martyr named Neopolis as a patron saint of warriors. The saint's day fell on 15 August, the birthday of Napoleon as well as the Feast of the Assumption, a popular Catholic festival even in areas with less religious practice. Napoleon himself celebrated the holiday between 1806 and 1813.

Napoleon III resurrected this holiday in 1852 to commemorate the First Empire, the principles of 1789, and the emperor himself. 'Our emperor's day', local mayors tended to call it. Despite its dubious origins, the Saint-Napoleon was not only a top-down holiday imposed by the emperor, but also a celebration embraced and embellished by citizens in towns and villages throughout France. Unlike the feast of Saint-Napoleon of the First Empire, which focused exclusively on Napoleon Bonaparte himself in solemn tones and quasi-religious pageantry (borrowing from the turgid Festival of the Supreme Being from the revolutionary Year II), the mid-century Saint-Napoleon feast day was festive, popular and even fun.

The ringing of bells, often the night before, signalled the opening of the festivities. Tricolour flags festooned public squares and hung from private windows. In the morning, local officials dutifully attended a *Te Deum* after High Mass, after which they assisted in the distribution of charity. Local leaders hosted a banquet at which they made toasts to the emperor, the empress and the prince imperial, likely in the presence of a bust of the emperor. They bestowed medals of honour to local citizens, including the Médaille de Sainte-Hélène

to Napoleonic War veterans after 1857. Local associations of veterans, musical groups, charitable organizations, workers' corporations, youth organizations – all these clubs drew French citizens into the festivities. In the evening, citizens lit illuminations in their windows and public squares. If they could afford it, a town held a fireworks display. Otherwise, a bonfire would suffice to extend the festivities into the night with dancing, drinking and shouts of *'Vive l'Empereur! Vive l'Impératrice! Vive le Prince impérial!'*

Saint-Napoleon's Day may have been invented, but for many the sentiment was real: Napoleon III retained popularity and loyalty among millions of French. He fused the image of the sovereign embodiment of the nation with universal suffrage, drawing sovereignty from the people and directly accountable to them. This was a powerful combination. For some, the emperor ensured public order and peace through a strong centralized state; for others, he was the defender of peasants against the nobility. He was charitable to the poor, a defender of the Church, and a champion of the traditional social order. In the 1850s, Napoleon III was feted as a bulwark against anarchy, a successful military leader and a liberator of peoples. In the 1860s, the focus lay on his ability to bring peace and stability. Bonapartists declared that 'everyone was and felt free, because one knew oneself to be protected by a strong and truly popular regime.'[1]

For peasants, the day marked emancipation from patronage and the restoration of national unity under Napoleon III. This devotion had begun with the First Empire and the glory of the first Napoleon. Peasants celebrated the myth of the imperial army that pulled together the French nation and the memory of the Consulate, Empire and even the Hundred Days as extensions of the French Revolution and, especially, of 1793. The Second Empire also brought rural prosperity, including new roads, schools, churches, cemeteries and agricultural societies. Peasants participated in politics, too. They voted in the (uncontested) elections for the Corps Législatif and for municipal councillors. They gave the emperor their votes, and in exchange they expected his concern and generosity. Casting a vote for the emperor's chosen candidates was not (only) the empty and cynical gesture of a sham democracy, but the expression of devotion to the emperor and his dynasty.

The holiday had less sheen in Paris, but in the provinces, local leaders used the day to promote communal solidarity and civility, the use and beautification of public spaces, and nation-building on the local level. Towns competed to show off their amenities and create the most elaborate illuminations, such as candles in the form of a giant 'N' in Bernin (Isère) in 1854.

In their celebratory, popular character, the festivities anticipated the Bastille Day celebrations to come in the Third Republic. They both affirmed the popularity of the emperor and eluded his complete control. The *Te Deum* confined the clergy to a defined and circumscribed role. Religious traditions played an instrumental role – they were not excluded as they later became in the Third Republic, nor were they central as royalists would have preferred.

The festivities also served to allow for positive expression of 'the crowd', an entity long feared since the time of the French Revolution. The holiday proved it was possible to invite masses of unthreatening people into the public sphere for the public good. The Saint-Napoleon provided a common ground on which to cultivate civility and living together despite ideological differences.

That said, Legitimist monarchists never fully supported the holiday. For them, the Second Empire confirmed the travesties of the Revolution: the undermining of traditional social orders and sources of order, the valorization of both the crowd and the individual as opposed to the regimented social hierarchy confirmed by divine revelation. Nor did republicans embrace the Saint-Napoleon. The holiday instead became for republicans the opportunity to demonstrate their opposition to the regime, or at the very least, to convince people to stay at home.

The army, however, frequently played a starring role. After all, the army had helped to overthrow the Second Republic in the *coup d'état* of December 1851 and in the repression in the months that followed. The army stood for many alongside the emperor as the protector of peace and security. 'Long live the army, which has saved us from anarchy' read one banner hung in Brignoles (Var) in early 1852.[2] In garrison towns, military reviews typically took place around noon after the morning's *Te Deum*. Villages celebrated their surviving heroes of the First Empire with toasts and banquets, recalling the glory days of the great Napoleon.

The army's role was enhanced and legitimized in the 1850s by the campaigns in Crimea (1854–55) and Italy (1859). In the Crimean War, the army was transformed from the bastion of domestic order into the means for spreading French glory. The 1855 Saint-Napoleon was overshadowed by the conflict. Many towns pledged to send their charitable funds to the families of soldiers who died or were wounded in Crimea. Moreover, news arriving that very day of French military success led to improvised public celebration and cheering throngs.

This patriotic fervour continued after the fall of Sebastopol in September 1855. Across the country, in towns large and small, citizens clamoured for news and expressed the most ardent joy when France proved victorious. In Rouen, according to the imperial *procureur-général*, 'it is now not only the victory that is popular, it is the war itself.'[3] For others, it was a moment to set aside party difference. In Aix, crowds took to the streets. 'We have to go back to 1814 to witness something on a similar scale,' reported the police commissioner, 'but then the enthusiasm was aristocratic, today it is popular.'[4]

Four years later, after the victory in Italy in support of Italian unification, these patriotic expressions reached their peak. Napoleon III framed this intervention as the liberation of a people, in the tradition of the Napoleonic Wars: 'We are supporting the struggle of a people fighting for its independence, and we shall relieve them of their foreign yoke.'[5] Napoleon III had reached the apogee of his status as a successful warrior, as a new generation of French celebrated military victory and forged a sense of national pride. Despite the failure in Mexico, the French adventure there falling apart in 1867 with the execution of Emperor Maximilian and the forced withdrawal of French troops, the military lustre surrounding Napoleon III remained.

At the same time, the Empire promoted the notion that it stood for peace. *'L'empire, c'est la paix,'* claimed Napoleon III, and many believed it was true. In a speech in Bordeaux in October 1852 he stated:

> Glory may well be transmitted as a heritage, but not war. Did the princes who rightly honored themselves to be the descendants of Louis XIV continue to wage his struggles? War is not made for pleasure, but by necessity; and in these moments of transition where everywhere, alongside so many elements of prosperity, we find so many causes of death, we can say truthfully: 'Woe to he who would be the first in Europe to give the signal of a collision whose consequences would be incalculable!'[6]

In the Parisian Saint-Napoleon celebration in 1857, the fireworks display opened with a large golden 'N' surrounded by the words 'war' and 'peace'. The 1859 celebrations of victory in Italy also marked relief that peace would soon follow. In the 1860s, the political climate changed. Public opinion shifted against war, except in the case of support for intervention on behalf of the Poles. In the 1867 Universal Exposition, a poem celebrated the advent of peace: 'War has fled, and peace reigns on earth / From this end of the earth here to there.'[7] War and peace, glory and stability, were two sides of the same coin.

And so, in 1870, this hot, dry, and anxious August, the celebration of Saint-Napoleon Day was subdued. In towns and villages, local notables heard a *Te Deum*. Some mayors gave talks and processions. Towns were decorated with flags and, at night, illuminations. Localities cancelled their annual games, however – the greased-pole climb, the horseshoe toss and the all-too-significant wheel of fortune.

In Strasbourg, already surrounded by forces from Prussia, Baden and Württemberg, the military commander and prefect jointly called for prayers, redrafting their language carefully: 'On 15 August, after the Te Deum, the Religious Authorities are invited to have public prayers said for the relief of these brave wounded soldiers and for those who ~~have died~~ have gloriously succumbed to the enemy to rest in peace.'[8] They also warned against rumoured protests against the imperial government. 'There are only two possible positions in our current grave circumstances: Friend of France or her enemy.'[9] The festivities were limited: flag, yes; fireworks, no. That night, however, without warning, a few Badenese field artillery sent shells into the city centre, driving down through buildings and killing several civilians. The shells damaged the roof of the building in which Claude Joseph Rouget de Lisle had composed the 'Marseillaise' nearly eighty years earlier. With grim apprehension, many joked that the empire had given them yet one more fireworks display.

Elsewhere, rumours and hostility crystallized into violence and accusations. In the Haut-Rhin, a republican member of the Corps Législatif was attacked. In the Tarn and the Gard, Protestants were accused of supporting Prussia. In Burgundy, it was the clergy under attack for allegedly sending alms to the Germans.

In the town of Albert (Somme), on the eve of the Saint-Napoleon, the Count d'Estourmel – a member of the Opposition in the Corps Législatif – returned to town via train. He was known for having voted against the declaration of war. He stopped by a public house and found a gathering of well-lubricated patriots who did not take kindly to his pessimism about France's chances on the battlefield. Soon a mob of some 600 townspeople threatened, 'Here is the traitor; let us hang him; down with d'Estourmel, down with treason, long live the emperor, long live France.' After several attempts to escape he finally found safety in the railway station. The crowd tried to storm the building but were repulsed. Early the next morning, the count escaped via a freight train.

Far to the south, another young noble was not so lucky. In a sinister turn, a mob in a small village called Hautefaye killed a man called Alain de Monéys, who was accused of the twin evils of being a

Prussian and shouting '*Vive la République!*' On the day after the Saint-Napoleon, 16 August, a mob tortured Monéys for two hours before setting his body on fire.

This strange and violent act unfolded some 400 miles south-west of Metz, in the rural and impoverished department of the Dordogne in the region known as Périgord, at the annual fair. Stereotypes abounded about the poverty and backwardness of peasants of the Périgord, part of the 'Chestnut Belt' in which peasants too often could not access wheat. According to conscription records, men from this region were shorter and less likely to be literate than other French men. About 60 per cent of children attended school and only 36 per cent reported that they could read and write.

Although around 400 individuals lived in the commune of Hautefaye, it was not a community in which everyone knew everyone. About forty-five people lived in the village centre, in fifteen or so houses. Others lived in outlying hamlets and worked on farmland that overlapped with that of other communes. These 'strangers' were not well known to those living in the centre. While some peasants owned land, there was not a class of landowners, professionals, or civil servants, except for the schoolteacher, road mender and postman. The mayor was the village blacksmith, sixty-eight-year-old Bernard Mathieu. The village did not have a town hall or a rural policeman, and lacked civic authorities who might calm a crowd. No village elders had the moral authority to arrest, control or redirect community sentiments.

Peasants in the region despised the nobility. In the Dordogne, since at least the time of the French Revolution, strong anti-noble rhetoric had permeated the region. The rural bourgeoisie encouraged and shaped this resentment, turning the focus away from the nobility's wealth and property (traits that the bourgeoisie shared) and toward their pride and distinctive displays of social standing – their weathervanes, the *fleur de lys* on their coats of arms, the fact that they sat in private pews at Mass. The peasantry hated the clergy as well, and the bourgeoisie encouraged an association of the nobility with the clergy. Thirty-two-year-old Alain de Monéys was part of this nobility, and with over 400 acres, his family was one of the largest landowners in the region. Monéys managed his family estate and served as deputy mayor of the commune. He was short, bald and unmarried, and known, it was said after his tragic death, for politeness and generosity. Unlike the rural bourgeoisie – which by this time was becoming bored with the countryside and was shifting to the towns – nobles like Alain de Monéys were willing to come to the village fairgrounds. However pleasant Alain de Monéys may have been personally, it did not save him from the anger directed at the nobility. His presence at the fair was not enough to make him familiar and part of the group. He remained an outsider.

Most peasants had little love for republicans, either, who came to be associated with the nobles and the clergy as part of a general resentment against the rich. In 1849, the peasants of the Dordogne had voted in large numbers for the socialist-democrats. But they turned against republicans due to the 45-centime tax approved by the government in May 1848. Louis-Napoleon Bonaparte was believed to be the man who would roll back that tax when he was elected as President on 10 December 1848. Republicans further angered peasants with their salary of 25 francs per representative, more than ten times the daily wage of a farm worker during the harvest. With 750 representatives, this seemed to be a considerable sum, the equivalent of paying 10,000 workers. Why pay for hundreds of politicians instead of one sovereign? While there was a republican party in the Dordogne at the end of the Second Empire, for most peasants, republicans appeared to be just one more iteration of their old enemies – the rich.

By contrast, the peasants of Périgord felt devotion and gratitude to Napoleon III. They had erupted in celebration on 10 December 1848, when he was elected President. All the voters of Hautefaye supported his coup in 1851 and the plebiscite of 1852 to re-establish the Empire, and all who voted supported the 8 May 1870 plebiscite on the previous decade's constitutional reforms, with only 8 per cent abstaining. The Empire brought prosperity to the peasants of Hautefaye. They held village festivals. They celebrated Saint-Napoleon on

15 August with fireworks and dances. On election day, despite the lack of real choices among candidates, voters participated in an event that affirmed their support for Napoleon III and their willingness to defend him against his enemies. When the imperial family passed through the region on their way to Bordeaux or Biarritz, peasants cried out *'Vive l'Empereur! Vive l'Impératrice! Vive le Prince impérial!'* They had shouted the same confirmation of imperial support on 15 August 1870.

The violence in Hautefaye on 16 August did not stem from a personal vendetta or a primitive and incomprehensible force. It emerged from a coherent logic: resentment of nobles and republicans merged with fear of the Prussian threat that had become all too real since the army's retreats into French territory after 6 August. The alliance of the nobility, the republicans and the Prussians was a firm belief of peasants in Hautefaye. As in anti-Semitic hatred – in which Jewish people are accused simultaneously of being part of a communist conspiracy and in control of Wall Street – multiple contradictory hatreds were projected onto the same people. They found a scapegoat in Alain de Monéys.

In Hautefaye, the annual fair of 14–16 August, which dated from 1633, coincided with Saint-Napoleon's Day. The fair drew in the wealthier peasantry looking to trade, buy, or sell livestock. The fairgrounds lay on the boundary of two departments, far from the prefecture and with no law enforcement present.

In 1870, by the late afternoon on the last day of the fair, the livestock had been sold (or not), deals had been made, and pride lost or gained depending on the deal. Now was the time, in the cafés and streets of Hautefaye, for joking, drinking and revealing the ways that they'd hidden their animals' flaws from potential buyers. It is likely that the war was a topic of conversation. The prefect had recently reported that the departure of soldiers had been the occasion of great distress. Rumours spread that Prussians had appeared in nearby regions.

Some also rehashed an insulting incident from the day before, on

Saint-Napoleon's Day. Camille de Maillard, a twenty-six-year-old cousin of Monéys and a local Legitimist, had spoken publicly about Napoleon III's limitations and the lack of ammunition. This enraged his listeners, but Maillard managed to escape. When Monéys appeared at the fair the next day, he was asked about the incident. To the anger of many, Monéys refused to accept that Maillard had cried '*Vive la République!*' Monéys rightly doubted that his royalist cousin would support the republic. Monéys himself seems to have truly supported the emperor, and he had recently determined to undo his exemption from military service and enlist. But he misjudged the venom with which his comments would be met.

The crowd swiftly spread the rumour that Monéys himself had cried *Vive la République* and that he was a Prussian. Unlike Maillard, Monéys was unable to escape. Over the course of two hours, Monéys' attackers beat him savagely, with pauses along the way that allowed him brief moments of hope. In the carnival atmosphere turned violent, individuals participated intermittently in the murder. The ringleader was a man called Chambort, a blacksmith from a hamlet in the Charente who did not know the victim or the others. The entire time, the fair continued.

At one point, the crowd approached the presbytery of the curé, named Saint-Pasteur. A young man – ordained in 1864 – he recognized the danger to himself and responded by offering wine and personally pouring it himself, a gesture of civility that may have defused some of the violence. With confidence and cordiality, he demanded toasts in honour of the emperor, the empress and prince imperial. Although Monéys, too, cried repeatedly '*Vive l'Empereur!*' his insistence of his support for Napoleon III failed to put his torture to an end. When Monéys tried to escape into the mayor's house, Mathieu slammed the heavy door in his face.

Following this rejection, the assailants beat Monéys in the blacksmith's shop. One man, François Léonard, a ragpicker, beat Monéys with a heavy hook used for weighing merchandise. He had just learned that his son – a replacement conscript – had been 'blown to bits' in battle.[10] In a final desperate request, Monéys' defenders pleaded for him to be shot rather than for the torturous beatings to continue, to no avail. Instead, the mob forced him to the fairground. The mayor, wearing his sash, followed behind. One last time, Monéys tried to escape, this time by entering a local inn. The innkeeper shut the door on his foot, breaking the victim's ankle. Monéys tried to fight back with a stake. He tried to hide under a wagon. Each time, a member of the crowd dragged him back.

Finally, Monéys fell to the ground and did not get back up. His body was then covered in straw and kindling, trampled underfoot, and then set on fire. The bonfire was lit in the middle of the afternoon, in public view, with the purpose of desecrating and ridiculing the man whose body lay beneath. It is not known whether Monéys was still alive when his assailants lit the match and set the bonfire aflame.

In previous centuries, public torture, execution and the desecration of corpses had served to both exact vengeance and to allow for communal expiation of sin following a criminal act. The wrenching of limbs and dismemberment of bodies allowed the community to regain its sense of wholeness and to reconcile with God. Over time, however, the spectacle of public pain and suffering – of massacre and sacrifice – became severed from the communal need for the sacred. Rather than figuring as a part of the sacred character of everyday life, ritual massacre became merely a site of horror and offence. Mob violence during the revolutionary period clashed with new sensibilities that could not bear to watch. The adoption of the guillotine symbolized a new embrace of a swift execution, ostensibly without suffering.

In the nineteenth century, the infliction of pain and suffering became less and less acceptable. The branding of convicts was outlawed in 1832, the same year that public executions in Paris moved to the outskirts of the city. Anaesthesia began to be administered during surgery from 1846 and the Grammont Law of 1850 outlawed public violence against animals. Furthermore, the dead became increasingly objects of respect, buried in park-like cemeteries.

Mass killing, of course, had not disappeared. The state violently crushed mass political movements in 1831–35, June 1848 and December 1851. The repression of revolutionary movements symbolized a demonstration of power and a restoration of calm, however dearly bought. Thousands of men had died already in the battles of early August 1870. And the violence in Hautefaye differed from previous peasant conflicts. It was not a continuation of bread riots, which ended for good in France in 1868, and it was not related to commune landholdings, gleaning and grazing privileges, or any number of reasons related to the land that might have led violence to erupt in the countryside. The murder was not part of a local vendetta cycle. It was not a protest against the state; the murderers believed they were doing the state's work. There was no playacting or banter as in a carnival. It was instead a means of warding off the fear that had pervaded the countryside that summer and a way to affirm peasant identity. And it was a tragically delusional expression of this fear.

The rest of the country was horrified by the events at Hautefaye. To many observers, the violence underscored the differences already perceived between the deeply rural south-west and the rest of civilized France. On 28 September, *L'Echo de la Dordogne* opined that 'they all have the attitude, faces, and demeanor of poor, uncivilized peasants from the fringes of our *département*, along with the border with Charente and Haute-Vienne.'[11] The mob became an object of fear and distrust whose unbridled actions seemed to come from a subculture that was not fully human.

Arrests began that very night. The defendants were stunned. They believed to the end that they had been acting in the name of the regime and in defence of Napoleon III. The fall of the Empire on 4 September made their situation even more dire. Republicans placed blame for the murder at Hautefaye firmly on the Second Empire for its Caesarean regime that kept peasants in ignorance. The murderers were excluded from the amnesty for political offences since 2 December 1851 that had been extended on 4 September. Four defendants were sentenced to death on 21 December, eight others to hard labour, and seven more to prison terms. Appeals were rejected on 30 January 1871 and the executions set for the following week. The four condemned men were conveyed to Hautefaye to be executed by guillotine on the site of the scene of Monéys' murder. The execution took place on the morning of 6 February in front of a small crowd. Most inhabitants, feeling despised and abandoned by their country, preferred to stay away.

Several hundred miles to the north, the drama around Metz continued, in two large-scale battles on 16 and 18 August. Napoleon III finally left Metz early on the 16th, to meet MacMahon at Châlons. That morning, he sat in silence, despondent and fatalistic, outside the inn at the Point du Jour. He was escorted to Verdun to avoid attack from the Uhlans already patrolling the area, and from Verdun took the train to Châlons.

French fortunes now lay in Bazaine's hands; he was to lead his army to Verdun. Although he would have liked to attack, he could not concentrate his forces enough to do so. The retreat begun on 15 August was still disorganized and followed a single road to Gravelotte. At Gravelotte, the French III Corps – now commanded by Leboeuf, who had replaced Decaen – took the northern branch of the road with IV Corps behind, stuck on the banks of the Moselle back near Metz. The French II and VI Corps and the Imperial Guard took the southern branch. It was this southern branch that was attacked on the morning of the 16th as the French stretched on either side of the road west of Gravelotte that passed through the villages of Rezonville and then Vionville and Mars-la-Tour en route to Verdun. They were caught completely by surprise.

The battle of 16 August – variously known as Rezonville, Vionville, or Mars-la-Tour – was yet another confrontation started by an aggressive subordinate. In this case, it was Constantin von Alvensleben, commander of III Corps under Friedrich Karl, who acted under the belief that he was fulfilling Moltke's plan. When Alvensleben attacked, he thought that he was encountering the French rear with the main army further west. So, he sent 40,000 men against an army of 130,000. While the French II Corps was surprised, it quickly recovered, and the infantry held its ground. If Bazaine had ordered an advance, the French could have pushed Alvensleben's men back. But without such an order, by eleven o'clock the Germans had managed to place artillery along the heights south of Flavigny – a hamlet a little south of the road between Vionville and Rezonville – looking down on the French positions.

When Alvensleben realized that he was facing much of the French army, with the rest a short march away, he determined that his best move was to give the impression that he commanded the strength of the German army. In the assessment of Michael Howard, 'few decisions on the battlefield can have been harder to take, more rapidly taken, and so completely justified.'[12] Alvensleben took Vionville and used his artillery against the French Chassepots.

Still, the Germans could not advance past Flavigny, which was already on fire. The German III Corps was fully engaged, with only X Corps within marching distance to lend support. Friedrich Karl remained back at headquarters in Pont-à-Mousson, unaware until midday of the extent of the French presence. A brilliant French commander might have been able to realize that he could lead the French to victory by striking aggressively on his right, with Leboeuf's III Corps and Ladmirault's IV Corps coming south toward Vionville and Mars-la-Tour.

Instead, the French had Bazaine, who remained as he had always been: a physically courageous leader and excellent company officer, but an incompetent commander. Bazaine focused on protecting his left flank at Rezonville – to maintain communication with Metz – and ignored the possible victory on his right. Furthermore, he missed opportunities to push corps that were not engaged in battle west along the Verdun road and to use his cavalry to help clear his tangled rear, still making its way beyond the Moselle – that is, to advance his objective of continuing west to Verdun.

In truth, it would have taken an unusually gifted general to direct a battle of five corps with 160,000 men that covered an area 6 miles long and 5 deep, on horseback and without means of communication beyond the projection of his unamplified voice. Friedrich Karl did not attempt as much; even after he arrived at Flavigny by 4 p.m., he allowed Alvensleben to continue directing the battle near Rezonville and General Konstantin von Voigts-Rhetz of X Corps to lead the sector before Mars-la-Tour.

The fault lay as well in the French reliance on the chain of command without giving flexibility to subordinates. Leboeuf held back. At noon, he told his staff, that he 'would wait for orders from [Bazaine]' rather than take his own initiative, as a Prussian general would have done.[13]

Alvensleben, for his part, was all too aware of the weakness of his left and feared its collapse against Canrobert's VI Corps' artillery, by this time holding a line north of Vionville. In the early afternoon, Alvensleben called in the cavalry. General Friedrich Wilhelm von Bredow's brigade was the one at hand. Von Bredow knew it was suicidal. He moved slowly to prepare the assault but eventually rode forward around 2 p.m. with six squadrons from the 7th Cuirassiers and the 16th Uhlans. 'Von Bredow's Death Ride' became a legend and for many continued the notion that a desperate cavalry charge could work. In fact, it was perhaps the last time that a calvary charge met with success. Due to the smoke of battle and a depression north of Vionville that hid his advance, von Bredow was able to overrun the French gun line, throwing Canrobert's artillery into chaos. But only 420 out of 800 of his men made it back. (At the end of the day, a French cavalry charge of 8,000 men pushing west under General Legrand was not so successful. It did not break through, and Legrand himself was killed. It was the last great cavalry charge in Europe.)

Still, the Germans were in a difficult position. The French III and IV Corps were now moving in to support VI and II Corps. A division of Ladmirault's IV Corps had arrived from the northern road; if he had attacked, he might have ended the German chances that day. However, he waited for a second division to arrive. That short delay allowed for the long-awaited arrival in turn of the German X

Corps under Voigts-Rhetz. Around 3.30, Voights-Rhetz's X Corps arrived at Mars-la-Tour just as Ladmirault's IV Corps took position a mile north. The ensuing engagement was one of the deadliest of the day, leaving 2,000 of the 4,600 Germans as casualties. Charges and counter-charges left everyone in the same position.

Again, French Chassepots supported the French position. Again, if Ladmirault or Bazaine had ordered a general advance at around five o'clock that evening, the day might have been won. The French showed bravery, exemplified in one report of an officer's sang-froid and heroism:

> A bomb fell on the horse of the colonel, threw them to the ground, both man and horse . . . I believed that my colonel had passed to the other world. But, oh surprise! Now the horse and the colonel got back up without a scratch . . . It was truly miraculous; and when he had caught up with his horse he said: 'My poor beast! You aren't wounded? So much the better. I am quite content. I'd been worried about you.' And he climbed back on the horse as though nothing had happened.[14]

Meanwhile, through the course of the day, the Prussians massed together artillery from various infantry or cavalry brigades in one long line, 2 miles long by the day's end, engaged in massed and crossing fire. Alvensleben's artillery fired over 20,000 rounds that day. The French could not escape. Even as they lay flat on the ground the artillery struck their backs and necks. This artillery allowed the Germans to hold the positions they gained.

The battle sputtered out around 7 p.m. as the sun began to fall. Both sides claimed victory, but no trophies were taken. German infantry had held the positions that they had captured that morning, due to their line of artillery, and had inflicted 13,761 casualties. Two German corps had held off the entire French army. Yet the French also held their positions and had caused 15,780 German casualties.

French soldiers assumed that they would press on the next day to destroy the enemy and then move to Verdun. But the Germans had cut off the road to Verdun via Mars-la-Tour, leaving a single road, which the march experience of 15 August had demonstrated would not be sufficient to move an army of this size. Furthermore, Bazaine would need to reorganize his supply convoys. Frossard's and Canrobert's corps did not receive any supply issues on 16 August, and ammunition was running low. That night at 11 p.m. Bazaine decided – he wrote to the emperor – that he would fall back a bit toward Metz and reorganize, before resuming his movement west.

The French spent 17 August in frustration, marching back toward Metz. Jarras did not have time to develop march tables, compounding the confusion as they encountered their own supply lines. Wounded men were left behind in farms. Due to a lack of transport, and to avoid allowing them to fall into German hands, Bazaine ordered the destruction of supplies in an enormous, dispiriting bonfire.

In response to Napoleon III's telegrams, Bazaine stated that he wanted to resupply and then depart for Verdun in two days' time, but there is not a lot of evidence that he had much of any plan to undertake this move. Overwhelmed by the task before him, Bazaine operated day-to-day and focused on routine tasks rather than on developing a strategic plan.

Meanwhile, Moltke on the evening of 16 August fully realized the strategic possibilities of his position. He determined to push the French as hard as possible north, away from Paris and toward Luxembourg. On the 17th, Steinmetz and his First Army crossed the Moselle just south of Metz and Friedrich Karl moved his entire Second Army north, meeting the III and X Corps on the battlefield from the previous day. The Second Army prepared to pivot north around the First, ready for battle either to the north or east.

Unlike any of the previous battles, the one that unfolded on 18 August was planned and expected. It engaged most of the entirety of the armies on both sides: 188,332 Germans with 732 guns, and 112,800 French with 520 guns. The French started the day along a single line 6 miles long extending from south to north through the villages of Gravelotte, Amanvillers and Saint-Privat. The French left – Frossard's II Corps and Leboeuf's III Corps, with a brigade of V Corps at the very far left – held a strong position. About half a mile east of Gravelotte, the main road from Metz crossed orthogonally a deep ravine, the steep and wooded Mance valley with a line of poplars to the east. The road itself ran through deep cuts including the wall of the farm called Saint-Hubert. Three other farms on the crest east of the ravine had been transformed into French-held strongholds overlooking the Mance valley, with trenches, gun-emplacements and barricades.

Beyond these farms ran a rail line, and beyond that, the French headquarters at Plappeville, 2 miles behind the left wing directly east of Leipzig farm. Bazaine spent most of the day at headquarters directing what he saw as the defence of Amanvillers.

In the centre, just north of II and III Corps, Ladmirault's IV Corps held the open fields around Amanvillers. The wide-open fields provided almost no cover and therefore it was an ideal location for both the Chassepots and the *mitrailleuse* to defend. On the French right, VI Corps at Saint-Privat sat exposed on a hilltop. Bazaine had chosen a different location for the right, placing VI Corps ahead of the line at Vernéville, but acceded to his former superior's request to move to the crest at Saint-Privat, which Canrobert deemed more defensible.

The Germans started the day with an error. Unaware that the French position extended north of Point du Jour, Friedrich Karl ordered the Second Army to march northward from their position between Mars-la-Tour and Rezonville, right in front of the French and through the fields where unburied casualties of 16 August from both sides still lay. He had IX Corps – the Hessian corps – on the right, while on the left, XII Corps (the Saxons corps) and the Guard Corps got tangled up after Friedrich Karl adjusted the order of march; III and X Corps, who had fought just two days earlier, followed in reserve. Friedrich Karl still did not know just where they would attack.

Leboeuf saw the clouds of dust around 9 a.m. and notified Bazaine. The commander had no interest in attacking – such a move would mean leaving his strong positions, and for Bazaine, defence was the order of the day. So, the French did not take advantage of the German mistake. By ten o'clock, Friedrich Karl had a clearer picture of the French position: the battle would take place to the east. However, he did not perceive the entirety of the situation. Repeating the assumption that Alvensleben had made two days earlier, Friedrich Karl believed that he was facing the flank of a rearguard, instead of the full French army. He assumed that the main portion of the French army had already escaped.

The battle began on the German right. At 10.30 Moltke issued the order to attack, just as intelligence arrived of the extent of the French presence. The French extended all the way to Saint-Privat, so the German left could not hope to encircle them. But it was too late: IX Corps, the Hessians under Manstein, were already engaging their artillery in front of Amanvillers, and, after all, German artillery had proved its effectiveness in challenging situations.

Ladmirault's IV Corps responded with artillery fire and the *mitrailleuse*. A German officer later recalled:

> Everywhere, along the whole range, guns sent out flashes and belched forth dense volumes of smoke. A hail of shell and shrapnel, the latter traceable by the little white clouds, looking like balloons, which remained suspended in the air for some time after their bursting, answered the war-like greeting from our side. The grating noise of the *mitrailleuse* was heard above the tumult, drowning the whole roar of battle.[15]

The French used the *mitrailleuse* effectively for the first time. It resembled a cannon mounted on a gun carriage. Inside, however, the *mitrailleuse* contained twenty-five rifle barrels loaded from the breech and fired sequentially by the turn of a crank. These were not yet the machine guns of the Great War. They could not move position quickly, they did not turn, and they did not have a wide spread of fire. Still, with the range of a rifle, they could shoot more rapidly and intensely – three plates of twenty-five bullets per minute. Earlier in the war, the weapon had been deployed alongside artillery, but its range was not far enough to be effective. Now, at Amanvillers, it was placed forward with the infantry, with much more lethal results. Manstein's Hessians and Ladmirault's IV Corps fell into an artillery stalemate all afternoon.

Meanwhile, to the south, the Mance valley became a trap for German soldiers. Upon realizing that he had ordered the attack too soon, Moltke sent Steinmetz a message from the heights south of Flavigny, ordering him to hold back. Steinmetz should have waited until the Saxons near Saint-Privat were positioned to flank the French right so that this distraction on the French left could play a strategic role. It was too late. Steinmetz had already ordered an assault by the infantry from VIII Corps – which Moltke had just removed from Steinmetz's control – and VII Corps under Dietrich von Zastrow. Again, German artillery proved its worth – the VII's artillery deployed 150 guns from noon until night and inflicted serious damage – but did not dislodge the French from their entrenched positions across from Gravelotte.

Steinmetz made a serious attempt to do so around 3 p.m. at the farm of Saint-Hubert, sending fourteen companies rushing into the ravine. He managed to take Saint-Hubert and believed that now he could send the French running back to Metz with another assault. He was mistaken. He sent the infantry and artillery of VII Corps down that same narrow road, with nowhere to disperse or find cover from the French. In short order, the road was choked with men, wagons, casualties, dead horses and damaged guns.

One German observer later recorded:

> Picture to yourself . . . a continuous wall of smoke, out of which the flames of [farms] Point du Jour and Moscou rose up to heaven, a hundred and forty-four guns in action in rear of the valley . . . while in front were masses of infantry, cavalry, and artillery crowding into

> the ravine, some of them pressing on to the front, others falling back under pressure of the enemy's fire as the range got shorter, wounded and unwounded men, infantry in order and in disorder streaming in opposite directions and jumbled together, the echo of the shells as they burst in the wood or above the trees, the whistling of the bullets from either side as they rushed overhead, and over the whole a column of dust which darkened the sun.[16]

It was clear by 5 p.m. that the German assault at the Mance valley had been a complete failure. Once again, if the French had counter-attacked, they might have changed the course of the day. But Bazaine still had no interest in considering such a move. Exhausted and ill-prepared for the responsibility placed upon him, Bazaine was paralysed and unable to take advantage of opportunities. In the afternoon, he left Plappeville. Instead of moving west toward the battle, he headed south-east to check his batteries at Mont Saint-Quentin. So, he gave no instructions to take advantage of the German disorder on the French left.

Yet, Frossard and Leboeuf held their positions. The French disaster came not on their left, but on their right. The battle started slowly in that sector. Once the Germans realized that they faced the centre of the French army and not its flank, Friedrich Karl was cautious and, except for the Guards' artillery, held his corps in check until the arrival of the Saxons around 3 p.m. The Germans then quickly moved French defenders out of Sainte-Marie. One hundred and eighty German guns – from the Guard and the Saxons – now aimed at Saint-Privat, driving the French artillery back. In Saint-Privat, 'the noise of explosions, combined with the horrible cracking of collapsing roofs and crumbling walls, the cries of the wounded mixed with the shrill whistle of bullets and the dull and impetuous shock of the shells and bombs turned the streets of the village into a splendid and horrible hell.'[17]

Thus far, the Second Army had remained restrained as they awaited the Saxons to start their flanking manoeuvre. But then, around 6 p.m., for reasons that remain obscure, the commander of the Guard Corps, Prince Augustus of Württemberg, decided to send in an infantry attack. Maybe he wanted glory; maybe he thought the Saxons were ready to support it; maybe he thought that a moment of silence from the French guns meant that they were moving to a different sector. In any case, he gave the order – without ordering cover from his artillery – and Friedrich Karl approved it. The French Chassepots were ready. It was a massacre. The Prussians suffered 8,000 casualties, nearly as many as Prussia lost at Köninggrätz in 1866, mostly within the first twenty minutes. This charge became infamous for its decimation of the aristocratic Guard Corps with its many royal cousins and relatives. Lieutenant Paul von Hindenburg, later commander of the German Army in the Great War and President of the German Republic, observed that the chaos resulting from this charge hit soldiers 'like a hurricane'.[18]

At six o'clock in the evening of 18 August, the French held firm at every point. But the tide shifted on the French right as the Saxons finally began their flanking movement, forcing Canrobert's VI Corps back to Saint-Privat by seven. By 7.30, a charge of the Prussian Guard and the Saxons – 50,000 men – could not be stopped; the French retreated, some disorderly and some orderly, with hand-to-hand fighting with little quarter for about an hour until the Germans finally held Saint-Privat.

In the centre, Ladmirault's IV Corps continued to hold its ground, but needed reinforcements to help assist Canrobert. He turned to the Imperial Guard, General Bourbaki's force, which lay in reserve on the road south-east of Amanvillers. Bourbaki had been waiting all day for orders: in a curious abdication of authority, Bazaine simply told him to do what he thought best. At 6.15 p.m., officers arrived from Ladmirault at Amanvillers asking for help in his counterattack to relieve Canrobert's VI Corps. Despite some misgivings, Bourbaki agreed to lead a division forward. As he approached Amanvillers, however, Bourbaki could see in the distance that the French VI Corps position at Saint-Privat was falling apart. He turned on his guide and yelled, 'You promised me a victory, now you've got me involved in a rout. You had no right to do that! There was no need to make me leave my magnificent positions for this!'[19] In a rage, Bourbaki turned his division around. The sight of the Imperial Guard apparently in retreat panicked VI Corps in retreat and a section of IV Corps at hand. Ladmirault now found his own right exposed and he had to order a withdrawal.

Meanwhile, the German right underwent a total collapse. At 7 p.m. King Wilhelm, having arrived at Gravelotte from Flavigny, approved Steinmetz's request for a renewal of the attack, erroneously believing that the heights had previously been taken and now were lost. Moltke disagreed but remained silent about it, recognizing the limits to his power. On this order, Steinmetz had Goeben, commander of VIII Corps, attack with his last reserves. The French at Point du Jour fired at point-blank range. The Germans panicked and ran back out of the ravine, through the burning village of Gravelotte, past the king himself, yelling, 'We are lost!' The king cursed them and hit them with the flat of his sword. But they continued back to Rezonville. If the French had attacked, they might have completed the rout of the First Army and cut off the Second Army. Then, the German II Corps, which had arrived late in the day, started to advance. As they moved ahead, they thought they were shooting at the French. Instead, they fired on soldiers from VII and VIII Corps who had remained near Saint-Hubert, difficult to distinguish in silhouette. For the Germans it was an agony of confusion and retreat. Finally, II Corps sounded a ceasefire, and the battle came to an end around 9.30 p.m.

The king and his staff returned slowly to Rezonville. They saw no cause for celebration. The First Army had clearly been deeply shaken, and they had not heard from the Second Army in hours. Only after midnight did the king learn from Friedrich Karl of the French collapse on its right. Despite this news, the slaughter of the day could not allow a feeling of victory. In total the German casualties numbered 20,163. French casualties – incompletely recorded – came to at least 12,273.

As for the French, Bazaine again decided that his soldiers were tired and needed to rest and reorganize. He ordered a fall back on Metz on 19 August to prepare for an eventual movement to Châlons.

The two battles of Rezonville and Gravelotte on 16 and 18 August rank among the most decisive in modern European history yet had been determined by the slimmest of chances. If France had capitalized on Germany's errors and had defeated the invaders, the morale of both the armies, the nations and neutral powers might have changed and tipped the balance, or at least changed the peace terms. Friedrich Karl must bear the blame for misjudging the French position on 16 August – exposing III Corps – and on the 18th for exposing the Second Army as it marched across the French lines. Commanders recklessly threw men directly at the Chassepot, a terrible foreshadowing of the Great War. In both battles, Bazaine failed to win when he had the chance.

The casualty numbers show the close margins of these early battles. The French and Germans suffered nearly equal numbers of dead and wounded at Wissembourg (about 1,600 on each side), at Forbach (4,000 French and 5,000 Germans) and at Froeschwiller (about 11,000 on each side), yet the Germans won all three encounters. In the three battles around Metz, German casualties overall, and on two of the three encounters, exceeded those of the French: at Borny, 5,000 Germans against 3,600 French; 17,000 French and 16,000 Germans at Rezonville; and 20,000 Germans and 12,300 French at Saint-Privat / Gravelotte.

Gravelotte was the last great victory of the old Prussian army, rooted in the age of Friedrich the Great and the Wars of Liberation. Yet artillery carried the day. The Germans hardly saw French soldiers during the battle, only their kepis. Seventy per cent of French casualties resulted from artillery fire, whereas 70 per cent of German casualties were due to Chassepots.

The day after Gravelotte, Bismarck and the American general Philip Sheridan visited the battlefield and witnessed the horrific sight of already decaying bodies. Prussian soldiers spent the day burying the dead in mass graves for some 9,000 men. For many, this memory remained the strongest of the entire war. One soldier recalled decades later, 'The battles, the shooting, the freezing winter bivouacs: all those things I've long since forgotten, but not the interment of the dead at St. Privat; that was so ghastly that it *still* wakes me in the middle of the night.'[20]

7. *The Road to Sedan*

While the Prussians buried the dead after Gravelotte, Bazaine retreated to Metz with some 140,000 men of the Army of the Rhine. The French did not feel defeated. The French VI Corps and the right wing of IV Corps had suffered at Gravelotte, but the others had fought with marked success and were eager to fight again.

Bazaine himself, however, seemed out of touch with reality. A memo from 20 August from Metz declared that 'Our adversaries must now despair of their predicament, for they find themselves overextended everywhere.'[1] Instead of devising a strategy, Bazaine continued to focus on small matters, such as breaches of hygiene. He somehow found the time to play dominoes in the evening.

Within a few days, the retreat to Metz turned into a siege. By 21 August, some 300,000 Prussians had already encircled a 25-mile perimeter around the city, cut the telegraph lines, dug trenches, built ramparts, blocked the road west, torn up railroads and requisitioned food, beverage and livestock. Moltke then reconfigured his three armies into two and left six corps of 120,000 men at Metz under Friedrich Karl. The Prussian was not happy at this assignment. There was no glory in besieging Metz.

In the immediate term, Moltke positioned six corps from the First and Second Armies on the left bank of the Moselle to prevent a breakout toward the west and cement the separation between Bazaine and MacMahon. Soon, however, the troops under Friedrich Karl surrounded Metz. At first, rations were short, billets lacking and hygiene dubious as the Germans encamped near the corpses of soldiers killed in the fields around Gravelotte. Over the weeks, however, the Germans built billets and the wounded in the surrounding villages were sent to Germany, making space for soldiers. More rations and more mail lifted spirits as well.

Already by 24 August, the siege began to pinch and Bazaine's army became dispirited. A French officer noted, 'Our troops need severe discipline; far too many are looters or stragglers, they sneak out of camp and have begun to defy their NCOs, complaining that they lack things: orders, food, wine, or ammunition.'[2] Many regiments lacked officers due to the devastating recent battles.

Nevertheless, if ever there had been a moment for Bazaine to break out, it would have been in the last ten days of August, when fewer Prussians blocked the path of the Army of Metz. On 26 August and on 31 August, Bazaine ordered his men into position. On both days, however, they failed to break out. Just why that is became the subject of intense debate in the years to follow. Was Bazaine treasonous, unimaginative, incompetent, or realistic in the face of overwhelming circumstances? It is difficult to know Bazaine's thoughts, as he left little in writing and, befitting the Napoleonic tradition, he did not discuss his inner thoughts with his generals.

On the 26th, Bazaine positioned his men for a breakout toward the north. Regrettably, the battle was unco-ordinated and poorly planned. While his men awaited the signal to advance, he called a council of war with his generals that afternoon at the château at Grimont. General Soleille painted a bleak picture of his remaining ordnance; he had only enough for one battle, and so a breakout would be of little use. A sortie would only weaken their ability to negotiate an honourable peace. In any case, to what end would they break out? MacMahon's position to the west was completely unknown. The generals did not know about the existence of the Army of Châlons, because Bazaine did not inform them of it until 30 August. Bazaine's generals, who were asked for the first time to discuss strategy, argued for staying put, except for Bourbaki, who was recorded as having agreed with the others but later plausibly claimed that he had argued for breaking out toward the Vosges. Leboeuf was concerned about food, however. Metz was provisioned for a garrison of 20,000 and a civilian population of 70,000, not for the 140,000 men of the army and 12,000 wounded. The advance on 26 August was called off and the men returned to their barracks under a hard rain, now more demoralized than ever.

On 29 August, Bazaine received intelligence from Thionville reporting the positions of the Army of Châlons on the Meuse from two days earlier. It was now clear that MacMahon was on the move and the marshal ordered the provisioning of soldiers with three days' rations. On 30 August, a telegram reached Bazaine from MacMahon himself – sent on the 22nd and eventually secreted into Metz – stating that the Army of Châlons was coming to relieve Metz.

Now, Bazaine's soldiers had reason to believe that they could reach MacMahon. Unlike in previous engagements, they could undertake a surprise attack with superior forces. The sortie of 31 August massed eight divisions with the aim of breaking out to the north-east at Noisseville. But the day was again a failure. Bazaine hesitated until four o'clock in the afternoon to issue the order to advance. This delay allowed Prince Friedrich Karl time to move 60,000 men into the French path and block their advance. Bazaine's lethargy and puzzling delay formed the basis of the later accusations of the marshal's treason. His enemies argued that he could certainly have broken out on 31 August but that he intentionally left MacMahon to be defeated in order to retain the distinction of being the lone commander left on the field. If MacMahon had been victorious, Bazaine could have then, in turn, more easily defeated the armies in his sector.

Another interpretation does not see the reasons for the defeat at Noisseville in Bazaine's politics or his character. To undertake such an immense operation, Bazaine needed twelve hours to effectively deploy. This mass of some 100,000 men was the largest offensive undertaken by the French in the course of the entire war. It was not that Bazaine treasonously hesitated, it was that he was not capable of effectively moving his men into position. The French crossed the Moselle and concentrated on the plateau of Saint-Julien in disorder, and it simply took a long time, about twelve hours. Unfortunately, unlike the Prussians, neither Bazaine nor any of his generals had adequately trained for a battle of such a large scale, and their experiences in Crimea or in Italy did not make up for their lack of study. The French infantry were pushed back by rapid-firing rifles, just as the Prussian Royal Guard had been a few weeks earlier at Saint-Privat. Their officers proved incapable of adapting their tactics to the new reality of massed firepower, a feat only successfully undertaken two months later by the Germans at Le Bourget.

So, what chance of success did the French have? If Bazaine had indeed broken out of Metz, he would have had to cross some 60 miles before linking up with MacMahon – if the information he had received had been accurate, which it was not. MacMahon was not heading directly toward Bazaine on 31 August but had veered north toward Sedan.

It is possible, however, that Bazaine reasoned he could not have successfully out-marched Friedrich Karl, and that his army would secure for France a stronger position intact but besieged than it would if defeated in the field. After all, Bazaine was well aware of the bewildering set of reversals that his soldiers had already experienced despite their strong performances in battle, and the gap between their expectations of how the war would unfold and the reality of their situation. Bazaine likely would have engaged Friedrich Karl in a battle with an uncertain outcome just as MacMahon's army met defeat at Sedan.

In any event, the failure of 31 August, and the 3,000 wounded who now needed all the more water and medical supplies, was cause and consequence of the army's increasing despair. The 'Army of Metz' was all that remained of the imperial army. The only bright spot in this situation was the strong fortifications at Metz. Unlike at Strasbourg, whose outmoded fortifications could be penetrated by a concentrated bombardment, the Metz fortress and its numerous detached forts protected the city well. A relief from MacMahon would have created problems for the Germans besieging Metz, stuck between two forces. Therefore, instead of bombardment, Moltke successfully sought to starve Metz while replenishing his own soldiers via the rail system.

*

At the Camp of Châlons, MacMahon's soldiers included the I Corps, VII Corps and two divisions of V Corps that had retreated 150 miles by foot and by train after Froeschwiller. They were joined by the new XII Corps under Trochu and a few regular units that had arrived from the Spanish border. To these numbers were added several temporary regiments created out of the various soldiers at their regimental depots who were still there after the regulars and most reservists had left in July.

Napoleon III arrived in Châlons on 16 August. The next morning, he held a war council. The emperor now named this random collection of units the Army of Châlons under the command of MacMahon, but with the entire army under Bazaine. What would be its next move? Should it move east toward Metz to support Bazaine or fall back west to Paris, to prepare to meet the German Third Army? Châlons lay in the middle, about 90 miles from either destination. Going to Bazaine's aid meant risking engaging this untrained army and being crushed, but falling back to Paris meant conceding defeat and chancing a political uprising. A third option – to open negotiations to end the war – would almost certainly have led to revolution.

Within two weeks, MacMahon had arrived neither at Metz nor at Paris, but at Sedan, 65 miles north-east of Châlons, pinched against the Belgian border. The tangled story of how he got there – and then suffered an ignominious defeat – unfolded in a series of muddled decisions.

In the 17 August war council, the case for Paris held sway. Napoleon III and his advisers remained unaware that Rezonville had been anything but a victory. The political situation in Paris seemed more pressing than support for Bazaine. Napoleon III's cousin Prince Jerôme-Napoléon took a leading role. He explained that the emperor had left his political leadership behind in July, and now had left his army behind; he needed to recover one or the other. To regain his authority, the prince recommended that Napoleon return to Paris to lead the government and bring MacMahon's army with him. Trochu and the eighteen battalions of *mobiles* were dispatched to help pave the way for the emperor's return to Paris with Trochu as governor of Paris.

That evening, however, Napoleon III received a telegram from Bazaine reporting the true outcome of the battle of Rezonville. Although Bazaine tried to sound confident about the outcome, he nevertheless stated that he needed to fall back to resupply. It was clear now that Moltke's army lay between Châlons and Bazaine.

Meanwhile, in Paris, Eugénie had decided that MacMahon's army should proceed east to relieve Bazaine – either by drawing away the Prussians from Metz or by joining Bazaine on the Meuse to face the First and Second Armies – and had sent such orders to MacMahon on 16 August. When, instead, Trochu arrived in Paris with his *mobiles* in tow, the empress and Palikao were aghast. They had sent the liberal general and the *mobiles* to Châlons precisely to get these dangerous elements out of the capital. The plan for Napoleon III to return to Paris, they believed, spelled political disaster. Palikao pointed out as well that the supply chain could not support the plan for returning the army to Paris. They immediately telegraphed Napoleon. He agreed, reversing his plans from that morning. Reuters reported on 19 August: 'The Emperor Napoleon is reported to have gone to Rheims, and it is rumoured that he is mentally ill. – There are expectations of an early peace.'[3]

So, while Trochu stayed in Paris with the *mobiles*, MacMahon continued to wait. His movements, after all, depended on Bazaine. Bazaine was no help, despite supposedly overseeing the entire army. On 18 August MacMahon received this telegram from the marshal: 'I presume that the minister will have given you orders, your operations being at the moment entirely outside my zone of action.'[4] That same day, Bazaine's aide-de-camp arrived at Châlons with information about Rezonville and Bazaine's intention to head toward Châlons after two days of rest, via a north-west route. The Verdun road was blocked, but Bazaine planned to pass through Briey. The telegraph line was cut between Metz and Châlons shortly thereafter. With a lack of communication and uncertainty concerning Bazaine's position, MacMahon hesitated to move east. He was nevertheless forced to move: on the afternoon of 20 August, German cavalry came within 25 miles of Châlons. It was time to depart. The following day MacMahon and the Army of Châlons set off north-west for Rheims. Napoleon III travelled with MacMahon but exerted little influence during the days that followed. The army comprised 130,000 men and 423 guns, with limited supplies – men had left them back at Froeschwiller – and a shortage of maps.

As the French abandoned the camp and headed toward Rheims, they burned large piles of provisions and forage so that they would not fall into Prussian hands. On the 21st, an enormous plume of smoke rose above the fields of Champagne as the fire consumed tents, sheds, stalls, wagons and all manner of effects, after having been doused with paraffin oil. A long wooden bridge, just over half a mile long, had been built to allow a railroad to arrive at the camp. This bridge also burned, along with the train station.

MacMahon's objective remained in doubt: Paris or Metz? In Paris, the Council of Ministers decided that the political situation required MacMahon to rescue Bazaine from being locked in Metz. There was a chance it could work; Palikao argued that Charles-François Dumouriez had undertaken a similar flanking operation against the invading Prussians in the Argonne, at Valmy in 1792. Eugène Rouher, President of the Senate, travelled to Rheims to give MacMahon this decision.

MacMahon, meanwhile, had determined to return his army to Paris – in part due to their sluggish march that day, and in part due to his conviction that Bazaine could not be rescued. Rouher accepted this argument and began to draft new proclamations.

Just then, a message arrived from Bazaine – which had been sent on 19 August, the day after Gravelotte – in which the commander stated that he was on the march toward the north-west to meet MacMahon. He would pass through Montmédy before turning south again to Sainte-Ménéhoulde and from there to Châlons. MacMahon therefore needed to proceed north and east toward Montmédy to meet him. Meanwhile, the Germans were bearing down on MacMahon along a line from Sainte-Ménéhoulde to Vitry-le-François.

And so, MacMahon decided not to go to Paris after all. On 23 August the Army of Châlons proceeded out of Rheims north-east toward Vouziers. However, it could not move quickly and needed more arms and ammunition almost immediately. The *Intendance* struggled to provision such a large army, spread out and undisciplined, without enough staff or time to distribute supplies at Rheims. A sample of telegrams received in Paris on 23 August alone tells the story: 'Number of *mobiles* presently armed: none.' 'No *mobile* armed with a rifle in the Corrèze.' 'No *mobile* yet armed.' 'Not a rifle, I still am waiting.' '*Mobiles* armed with a rifle: forty out of three thousand.'[5]

Under this pressure, the Army of Châlons veered north again, 18 miles to Rethel, where it could find supplies. This erratic behaviour explains why the German cavalry were unable to track down the French for two days. By the 26th, MacMahon had departed from Rethel and headed east toward the Meuse and Montmédy.

MacMahon's move to help Bazaine was nearly certain to be a disaster. Bazaine never seriously tried to break out of Metz, and the Army of Châlons was not capable of the speed and efficiency required to make any such manoeuvre. MacMahon's army moved slowly, at the pace of new recruits. The men had enough weapons but not enough transport and supplies such as cooking utensils, camping equipment, ambulances and maps. Some lacked shoes. The march toward Montmédy proceeded in a zigzag to deal with the poor roads and to seek provisions.

After Gravelotte, Moltke's three armies briefly reconnected. The crown prince was reunited with his father. 'The King I found well,' he recorded, 'but quite cut up by the frightful losses, the total of which cannot be estimated with anything like certainty, but which threaten to approach the twenty thousand.'[6]

With the armies united, Moltke could reconfigure them to address the next phase of the war. He needed to contain Bazaine and pursue MacMahon, so he rearranged his three armies into two groups by splitting the Second Army in two and conjoining these parts with the First and Third, respectively. At Metz, Moltke left Friedrich Karl with command over much of the Second Army as well as the entire First Army, a combined force of 120,000 men. This arrangement made it easy to remove Steinmetz from his command. The old hand predictably did not accede to answering to Friedrich Karl, and when the general refused to show proper respect to his new commander, he was sent off to Posen.

Moltke then sent two armies west along with royal headquarters: to the left, the Third Army of 180,000 Prussians, Bavarians and Württembergers under Crown Prince Friedrich Wilhelm. This army, arriving from southern Lorraine south-west of Nancy, had not taken part in the three battles around Metz. The crown prince anticipated a decisive battle at Châlons.

On the right, heading toward Verdun, a new Army of the Meuse comprised 120,000 Saxons, cavalry and members of the Prussian Guard from the Second Army. This new force was commanded by Crown Prince Albert of Saxony, forty-three years old, a veteran of 1866 with a successful record at Saint-Privat. The two armies together were more than double the size of MacMahon's Army of Châlons.

Moltke issued orders on 21 August to advance two days later. By the 23rd, Friedrich Karl had completed the encirclement of Metz, and the Army of the Meuse and Third Army moved west. They left besieging forces at Toul and Verdun while the rest of the army – large enough to besiege these cities without breaking stride – continued onward.

Only one problem remained: Moltke did not know what the French had planned. On 24 August, when cavalry patrols discovered the abandoned camp at Châlons, they could not understand the intelligence reporting a move to Rheims. Why would the French move to Rheims when they obviously must be falling back to Paris? The political motivation – the need to relieve Bazaine in order to avoid revolution – did not immediately compel Moltke to change course. He ordered a slight adjustment for the next day, aiming toward Rheims rather than Châlons.

Moltke received confirmatory newspaper reports of a French move to relieve Metz on the evening of 25 August. In *Le Temps* of the 23rd, a Havas agency dispatch stated, 'In this very moment, the army of MacMahon is heading north to go extend a hand east to Bazaine.'[7] Still, the Prussians could not be sure that this information was not a ruse, especially as it ran counter to the common sense that MacMahon should be retreating to Paris.

At a supper at Bar-le-Duc late in the day of 25 August, King Wilhelm, Bismarck, Moltke, the minister of war Roon and Prince Leopold of Bavaria speculated about the reasoning behind the French move. If the uncertain intelligence was correct, then the Germans should turn north to meet them. The decision to pivot the army to the north was risky – it was a large army with a 30-mile front, near a concentrated enemy. In the end, Moltke took a gamble: he believed the reports, and ordered the Army of the Meuse to shift their course to the right, and from there prepare to engage with MacMahon somewhere between Verdun and Varennes. The Third Army turned right as well to the rear and west of MacMahon. Even the corps furthest to the left would wheel toward Sainte-Ménéhoulde and the Argonne Forest. On 26 August, the two German armies undertook this vast pivot. Meanwhile, the 17th Hussars cut the railroad west of Montmédy. The French could no longer escape east to Nancy.

The German march from Metz to Sedan took some 300,000 men across wide swathes of north-eastern France over the course of two weeks. The Germans packed lightly and marched quickly but left indelible marks. They felled thousands of trees for their telegraph lines. Since the Germans did not typically bivouac, they quartered with local inhabitants. And as they moved further away from their own supply lines, they demanded food and drink. They fell into misunderstandings across the language barrier. If the French spoke a language or dialect other than the French that some of the soldiers knew how to speak, mutual distrust quickly escalated into anger.

Those who tried to speak French using a military handbook mangled the pronunciation, and others did not bother to learn French at all. French farmers might find themselves suddenly housing and feeding twenty or forty men at a time, who occupied every room and searched every corner for food. If the French hesitated or refused to serve them, the soldiers took the food anyway.

A Bavarian career officer named Thäter later recalled:

> The men steal, and we look the other way. We have to tolerate *Mundraub* ['mouth robber': theft of food and drink for direct personal consumption], at least under such pressing circumstances. Of course, it is difficult to stop this vice again. The men are like the hunting dog who has once torn into a rabbit.[8]

Others, including a man called Hugo Arnold, did not pretend to have any scruples about taking food from civilians: 'There is no choice, either you or me; that is the relentless maxim in this kind of struggle for existence.'[9] He threatened to burn and plunder farms that refused to yield their goods, and he followed through when tested. A man named Hoesslin reported to his mother on 28 August, 'Here we live like God in France!'[10] To counter this indiscipline, Thäter arranged with his commanders to get orders to requisition food and issued receipts to the farmers whose food he took, but he knew that this action did little to help the civilians and primarily served to keep his own soldiers in line.

Another Bavarian officer, F. Koch-Breuberg, enjoyed the cultivated life with the owner of a champagne factory. He recalled, 'In his house for breakfast we consumed the first rabbit and expressed very different opinions about the quality of this national dish.' And later, after touring the factory and having a tasting, 'What a strange notion I had earlier about the production of champagne . . . That was all so simple and tasted so good.' Finally, Koch-Breuber noted,

> We did not talk politics with Mr Testulat. We did not want to spoil the mood for either him or ourselves, and it was so comfortable in

> his house. I see it still: the dining room with the yellow wooden panelling, the folding table with the lamp over it, and the pretty little sideboard. The desk in the corner was not missing either. That is simply customary in the better bourgeois families in France.[11]

Both sides perhaps were eager to reinforce a class connection and their own good taste, in contrast with the killing outside.

The crown prince also spoke with the rural people along the march. At this point in the war, they were still willing to engage in conversation with him. They did not hesitate to openly blame their own government for the war in what he called 'naiveté', but was perhaps simply self-preservation in refraining from blaming an invading army. Townspeople, by contrast, expressed anxiety over potential social upheaval, 'especially where no troops are stationed, and the workmen are idle'.[12]

Already at this early date, however, Friedrich Wilhelm warned about rumours concerning the formation of *franc-tireur* battalions, which 'must be opposed with all possible earnestness'.[13] As the Germans marched through a succession of villages, they encountered increasingly hostile French civilians. Single shots fired from a house or building 'in a cunning, cowardly fashion' triggered retaliation from the Germans who burned down the house or forced contributions from the surrounding inhabitants.[14]

The German march also included emotion-laden moments of ceremony and levity. The crown prince had the honour of distributing the Iron Cross, the Prussian military decoration dating to the Napoleonic Wars. Friedrich Wilhelm himself felt the weight and privilege of having the 'right as Commander-in-Chief of my Army to bestow this decoration in His Majesty's absence', a right that had previously not been given the 'proper appreciation'. He awarded the Iron Cross to seven officers of various ranks, including General von Blumenthal. The men received the honour with 'tears of joy in their eyes' and disbelief that this decoration, previously seen only in history books, could be in their possession. Major von Hahnke nearly fainted. The crown prince anticipated the 'shouts of jubilation' that would arise when he delivered the Iron Cross to other units.[15] Giving and receiving this honour solidified bonds of reciprocity in the name of national military prowess.

Ordinary soldiers had to settle for somewhat less. On 25 August, the Bavarian troops marched early and long to arrive in the presence of their monarch on the occasion of Ludwig II's twenty-fifth birthday. They joined him in a service of worship followed with three hurrahs. Dietrich von Lassberg, a loyal Bavarian, could not take part, to his great disappointment, because a horse had stepped on his foot and he had to stay in the mobile hospital. Later that day, he also missed the honour of marching past the Prussian king and his retinue. 'That was a frustrating day!' he wrote, missing out on the symbolic honour of being in the presence of royalty.[16] Bavarian soldiers like Lassberg were becoming accustomed to participating in Prussian royal events.

Small incidents became legendary within parts of the German army. Friedrich Wilhelm had a hole in his cloak repaired on the spot by a tailor from the Westphalian Fusilier Regiment no. 37, V Army Corps, to the amusement of the rest of the regiment as they marched past. Another pleasure came from the glee with which the crown prince and his fellows read a letter captured from a French officer. This educated author wrote with brutal frankness to a trusted friend about the lack of supplies and concomitant lack of discipline: 'Everybody, it seems, pilfers, officers of the Staff not excepted; the author had, first his saddlery, and then his horse, his own property, stolen.' The letter spared no criticism of the French leadership, including Napoleon III himself, who burdened the army with his discouragement and lack of judgement. He ended the letter with the Latin phrase *Quem deus vult perdere, prius dementat* ('Whom the gods would destroy they first make mad'). In the crown prince's judgement, 'These utterances are more or less true, but surely accord little with the fanfaronade of the French daily press.'[17]

These moments of lightness provided solace as the Germans approached the hoped-for decisive battle. Under relentless strain, the crown prince recognized the importance of keeping his own mental and physical health for the battle to come.

As German soldiers crossed deeper into French territory, France moved toward expelling German civilians from sensitive areas. In this, as with its earlier decision to prevent German men of military age from leaving the country, France acted without precedent: a large-scale expulsion of foreign nationals who had not committed any offence against their adopted country.

This decision had been brewing since mid-August. On multiple occasions, members of the Corps Législatif presented petitions from French citizens asking for the immediate expulsion of Germans. On 14 August alone, Baron de Barante – a member of the opposition on the centre left – submitted four petitions signed by Parisians. Three days later, republican opposition leader Léon Gambetta presented a petition following an attack on the fire brigade of the neighbourhood of La Villette that was blamed on foreigners.

At the same time, Germans faced increasing hostility and suspicion of being spies. Gangs of men attacked lone individuals. In one case, forty or fifty French confronted a single German. Speaking German in public became a dangerous act. This hostility may also explain the increasing willingness to expel German citizens – it was a way to protect them from the Parisian population. Though they did not mention it explicitly, the Corps Législatif may have been thinking of the September massacres of 1792. The US ambassador Elihu Washburne wrote on 22 August that the decision to expel Germans came 'with the view of both relieving itself from the presence, in the heart of the capital, of some 40,000 Prussians, and at the same time for the purpose of protecting them from the excited population of Paris.'[18]

Just a few weeks earlier, liberal arguments had prevailed: the French defended individual liberties and were willing to view German civilians as autonomous individuals, some of whom might be dangerous and others likely not, rather than as a group with generalized enemy characteristics. Opinions changed rapidly as the

German army advanced. Now, the Corps Législatif was no longer willing to distinguish between good Germans and bad; they all had to go. (The concern might have run the other way, too. At least seventeen Germans fought on the French side during the war, either in the National Guard or in the Foreign Legion.)

On 28 August, the Palikao government announced that it was expelling all Germans, tens of thousands of men, women and children, to beyond the borders of the department of the Seine. The poor and homeless were the first Germans targeted, including the many Hessian street sweepers. Some 40,000 impoverished foreign nationals left the capital, including some 4,000 neutral Swiss. The new Government of National Defence repeated this directive on 5 September.

Washburne tried to alleviate the position of the Germans caught by this policy. He wrote in a letter dated 15 August:

> Since the breaking out of the war no Germans have been able to get work, and the poorer classes have already exhausted the very little they had in store. They are, therefore, to-day without work, without money, without credit, without friends, without bread. Pinched with hunger, terrified by threats of violence, with no means of leaving the country.[19]

Lutheran churches and schools closed, and Protestants of any nationality were accused of spying. Still, the effect on expatriate Germans was limited, if only compared to expulsions that came in later wars. German citizens were not captured and interned. Only those living in Paris and the Seine department, as well as in besieged cities like Strasbourg, were required to leave. Everyone expected Germans to freely return after the war concluded.

Yet this expulsion also crystallized the fear of the enemy within, an anxiety that informed later, more draconian, policies. The situation in Paris set a precedent for large-scale, forced migrations and deportations around the world in the 1880s and beyond. With no international body or agreement to address the treatment of civilians during war (with the exception of those caring for sick and wounded soldiers), the matter of expulsion fell squarely in the hands of sovereign states. People saw foreigners of the enemy side as an internal matter, and not something that could be worked out among combatants. Nothing in the Geneva Convention protected them.

And what about the German side? How did they treat French civilians? It depended on whether the French civilians resided in occupied zones or in Prussian or German territory. Unlike French efforts to cast the war as a conflict between nations, Prussia claimed to view the war as a conflict of armies and therefore promised not to mistreat civilians and their property. At Saint-Avold, in response to the news of the German expulsions, King Wilhelm declared that he would not retaliate, 'as it would be unfair to punish men who belong to a country cursed with a Bonaparte for a sovereign . . . Frenchmen in Germany need not be uneasy. They will, in common with all mankind, be convinced that Germany moves at the head of civilization.'[20] This protection came with a caveat: the Prussians would not harm civilians so long as they did not engage in military activity. Events later proved, however, that retaliation against French civilians who actively resisted German invasion would be harsh and swift.

Within German territories, German leaders did not retaliate against French civilians, in part because the population was so much smaller and largely female. And, of course, the French army was not invading any German states; they had less to worry about regarding French men in their territory, whether compelled to stay or forced to go.

By 27 August, MacMahon recognized that the game was up: he had not heard anything from Bazaine and would not be able to reach him without breaking through at least one Germany army. Instead, he decided to withdraw to Mézières. Palikao strongly objected. He did not realize what MacMahon had figured out, that it was not just a portion of the crown prince of Prussia's army but the entire new

Army of the Meuse that was bearing down on the Army of Châlons and blocking its path east. Palikao rebuked MacMahon with the full support of the Council of Ministers and ordered him to proceed to Metz in two messages sent in the early hours of the 28th. MacMahon, not the type to disobey or resign, no matter how dire the situation, followed orders. That day, the Army of Châlons marched east in the rain, carefully watched by German horsemen on the hills to the south. For their part, the Germans now anticipated a decisive battle at Verdun in the next few days.

On 28 August, a German reserve cavalry patrol captured a certain Lieutenant Georges de Grouchy and, with him, the complete order of battle and march tables. MacMahon's movements were no longer a mystery. Moltke now realized that he had MacMahon in his grasp. Rather than order his two armies to unite on the Meuse, as originally planned, he ordered them to meet at Beaumont-en-Argonne, on the left bank of the Meuse.

Meanwhile, as MacMahon continued east, he sought to cross the Meuse at Stenay. Then he learned that the bridges were blocked. Well aware that the margin of French territory between the Meuse and the Belgian border grew slimmer the further north they marched, MacMahon ordered the march for 29 August to proceed further north to Mouzon. Failly's V Corps, the furthest south of the Army of Châlons, did not receive the orders to shift north – the staff-officer carrying the orders was captured – so it continued east toward Stenay.

Failly's V Corps made contact with part of the Saxon corps on the 29th. After a day of fighting in the Wiseppe valley, the French withdrew, leaving 600 casualties combined on the two sides. Failly pushed his tired soldiers through the dark forest that night, a challenging march. Some of them did not emerge until five o'clock in the morning. As they rested near the village of Beaumont that morning, Failly failed to ensure the establishment of an advance watch.

Late that morning, the IV Prussian Corps and I Bavarian Corps came out of the woods to catch Failly's V Corps by surprise. The French responded quickly to harness horses, take up weapons and flee – along with civilians – north toward Mouzon and the bridges across the Meuse. By 6 p.m. after a steady advance the Germans controlled the plain before Mouzon, with only Failly's infantry on the left bank of the Meuse holding them back to allow the V Corps to cross.

The day was a rout, leaving 3,500 German casualties and 5,700 French. The Germans gathered many supplies, horses, vehicles and prisoners that evening. One Bavarian later recalled, 'The beauty of the scenery, the mildness of the weather, the ludicrous manner in which the enemy had been surprised . . . the certainty of victory, everything in fact combined to produce a lively and joyful advance.'[21] Failly was disgraced for having been caught so completely off guard.

MacMahon's army was now completely cut off from Bazaine and had little chance of retreating to Paris via Mézières. He was surrounded: the crown prince of Saxony and the Army of the Meuse was on the right bank of the river, east of Sedan, and the crown prince of Prussia with the Third Army was approaching Sedan along the western side of the Meuse to block any retreat. Belgium was his only escape route, and this move would require the army to be benignly imprisoned. The strategic implications of the border were not lost on the Germans. If the French crossed the border, noted the crown prince, the result would be either the quick conclusion of the war, or 'an incalculable complication': continued conflict in Belgium and the likely entry of Britain into the war to protect Belgian neutrality and its own interests.[22] That night in Mouzon, his options limited, MacMahon ordered his commanders to fall back to Sedan.

8. *Sedan and Bazeilles*

The old fortress town of Sedan stood just 7 miles from the Belgian border, with fortifications dating from the 1600s. To the south and west, the broad and marshy Meuse valley protected the city. The river ran north-west with higher ground on the left bank and the villages of Bazeilles and Balan beyond the marshes on the right. Then, after passing west through Sedan, the Meuse bent north between Glaire and Floing, and formed a large oxbow around the Iges peninsula before plunging south and then sharply turning west at Donchéry. Beyond Sedan to the north-east lay higher ground.

The small town of Bazeilles, soon to be the site of intense combat, lay 2 miles south-east of Sedan, along the road parallel to the Meuse, where the Givonne flowed south to meet the Meuse. The town comprised 500 houses and 2–3,000 inhabitants. The main road was broad and wide, with houses four or five storeys tall. It was less a rural village than a 'genteel suburb of Sedan, where many of its merchants resided'.[1] To the north of Bazeilles, the villages of La Moncelle, Daigny and Givonne lay along the Givonne river.

When MacMahon's army approached Sedan, rather than stay on the heights south of the Meuse, the French continued across the river and occupied a triangle of high ground north-east of Sedan. MacMahon placed VII Corps in the north, I Corps under General Ducrot in the east along the Givonne, and XII Corps under Lebrun in the south-east, with its right flank at Bazeilles. This latter corps had crossed the Meuse at Mouzon in the night of 29–30 August and did not take part in Failly's disgrace at the battle of Beaumont about 6 miles south. That night, 30–31 August, the French marched north-west along the right bank of the Meuse toward Sedan, tangled up among convoys. In the confusion, the units that MacMahon had assigned to defend Bazeilles were left without provisions.

41

In the middle of the line, just north of Sedan's walls, the V Corps stayed in reserve. Inside Sedan itself, Napoleon III set up his headquarters. The French held in a defensive position; as they intended to march the next day, they did not dig trenches. In previous wars, the Meuse and the fortress could have provided sufficient cover, but not in 1870. Moltke had the forces to encircle MacMahon and pin him within range of the Krupp artillery with no escape except downhill into Sedan. MacMahon knew this danger and did not intend to linger. After all, his aim remained to proceed to Metz. The first day of September would be a day of rest, with the exception of the cavalry, which was ordered to scout the area. Ducrot would have preferred to move 2–3 miles to the north, which might have allowed a retreat to the west, but MacMahon wanted his soldiers to rest after Beaumont.

One significant personnel change set up the events of 1 September. Failly's disgrace on 30 August had been so profound that Minister of War Palikao sent Emmanuel de Wimpffen, the governor of Oran, as a replacement. Furthermore, given Wimpffen's long experience in Africa, he came with the commission to replace MacMahon should anything happen to the commander. This move would prevent Napoleon III himself from taking over.

Meanwhile, the Germans took steps against a French escape to Belgium. The night after Beaumont, Bismarck informed the Belgian government that it should immediately disarm any retreating French; otherwise, the German armies would claim the right to pursue them into Belgian territory. Furthermore, Moltke ordered the Meuse Army – on the right bank of the Meuse and east of Sedan – to march down the right bank and extend its right wing north to the Belgian border, and the Third Army's V and XI Corps north to block a retreat to the west.

As these massive armies converged on Sedan and its suburbs, civilians dreaded the battle to come. Already they had suffered. On 31 August, Dietrich von Lassberg passed through Remilly, which he described as 'a quite pretty, but today deserted and partially burning village'[2] along the Meuse, due south of Bazeilles.

In Bazeilles, the municipality decided to arm firemen and National Guardsmen. On 28 August, they had about forty veterans under the command of a sergeant who had been recently wounded. Hearing that Uhlans had been spotted to the east, these men undertook reconnaissance. Upon arrival in Douzy, an hour's walk due east of Bazeilles, they learned that the mayor had just removed arms there from National Guardsmen out of distrust of these soldiers and fear of retaliation by the Germans if they showed resistance. The contingent from Bazeilles returned home. They no longer planned to take up arms for defence, let alone for attack. Still, according to a local journalist, on 31 August, eight inhabitants of the village – masons and carpenters under the leadership of an officer of the engineers – conveyed barrels of gunpowder to the railroad bridge in order to blow it up. They did not succeed, as they quickly became the targets of German soldiers on the opposite bank of the Meuse.

That evening, along the River Givonne, the Guard Corps and Saxons reached the village of Givonne. On the left bank of the Meuse, the Bavarians and Prussians recognized that if they were to cross the river and attack Bazeilles, they would need to do so under fire. At least they would finally engage the enemy in combat after two weeks on the march. They rushed a bridge that the French were about to blow up. The shells from this brief engagement set the village on fire. The French held on, though, with bayonet charges, and the Germans had to abandon the area at the end of the day on 31 August. Bavarian engineers then built pontoon bridges across the river without incident.

To the south and west, the Third Army had moved quickly along the left bank of the Meuse to Sedan, seized bridges, crossed the river, and occupied the space between Sedan and Paris. Unbeknown to the men of these corps, Moltke aimed for the two German armies to eventually meet north of Sedan to complete the encirclement. 'Now we have them in a mousetrap,' Moltke told the king on the night of 31 August, as he viewed the French camps from the left bank of the Meuse.[3] In Ducrot's summary, 'We are inside a chamber pot, and we shall be shat on.'[4]

All around Sedan that night, soldiers and civilians prepared themselves for the battle to come. In Bazeilles, civilian groups helped to barricade the village, protect their homes from fire, transport wounded soldiers and provide food for French soldiers. Surrounded by a force nearly twice as numerous, soldiers and civilians spent an evening in closeness and ephemeral intimacy, anticipating the events of the next day and uncertain of their own survival.

On 1 September, the day began at 3.30 a.m. By 4.00, General Ludwig von der Tann, commander of the I Bavarian Corps, eager for glory following undistinguished action at Froeschwiller and mindful of the political need for Bavaria to be part of the day's anticipated victory, sent his men across the railroad bridge on the Meuse to Bazeilles. For Lassberg and his companions, this single day at Bazeilles became the central battle of the war that haunted them for the rest of their lives.

At six o'clock in the morning, Florian Kühnhauser's company entered Bazeilles along the main street and did not meet any civilian resistance. Then, they encountered the naval forces of Lebrun's XII Corps from the Army of Châlons: 'From the stone houses on the opposite corner . . . cracked out the first hostile shots. Everyone stopped short.'[5] Lebrun's corps, tucked away in a strong defensive position and armed with their Chassepots, held off the Bavarians, whose shots ricocheted off the stone buildings. The Bavarians suddenly found themselves unprotected in the crossfire. 'In a few minutes,' reported Kühnhauser, 'the entire first half-platoon of the 6th company lay on the ground dead or seriously wounded.'

Kühnhauser and his companions managed to get into a house on a corner. From there, they could gain some cover and divert the French fire, allowing a few men to move forward. These men now broke into a store, which they decided to burn down. The French civilians in the store fled. But at this point, the Bavarians could not move forward. It dawned on Kühnhauser that 'the inhabitants had joined forces with the soldiers, yes, that even women took part in the battle and brazenly brandished shotguns.' These 'deceitful' and 'treacherous' civilians dared to engage in battle against the 'zealous' Bavarians.[6] The French were fighting dirty – so thought the Germans – and could not control themselves, whereas the Bavarians expected a civilized and fair fight against recognizable enemies, in a ritualized battle governed by custom.

Soon, Kühnhauser and his fellow soldiers were ordered to take Bazeilles house by house, in hand-to-hand fighting. They started with a house across the street from where they had taken cover. Heavy fire had come from there and 'Everyone wanted to have his revenge here.'[7] They began to break down doors and to kill with little discrimination. The inexperienced Bavarians encountered a hardened force of long-serving French professionals who were used to fighting in which surrender was not an option.

The most violent acts occurred in the centre of the village on the Grande Rue, near the church square. 'The ground was so furrowed by the bullets,' wrote one observer, 'that you'd swear you were seeing the work of a rake.'[8] For his part, Lassberg trudged through fire, heat and smoke into the main square. He soon engaged in hand-to-hand combat in houses, on the staircases and entryways, in the cellars and rooftops. The flames drove both defenders and attackers out of houses and into the streets or into houses that remained unburned to resume their struggle. Lassberg himself engaged in bitter fighting inside a house until the two beds caught fire. 'This was just a single tableau of the appalling, bitter struggle in burning Bazeilles. It is impossible for me to list all that I saw and experienced.'[9]

Sometimes the Bavarians took prisoners of war. In most cases, surrendering soldiers were treated in accordance with the customs of war. But not all. During the course of combat, contrary to custom, Bavarians executed point-blank the survivors of a company of naval infantry commanded by Captain Maurial in the act of surrender. This convinced French soldiers that they should fight to the death rather than put down their arms – a position that then spiralled as the Germans reciprocated, fighting to the death rather than submitting to a distrusted enemy. Events were also embellished later.

Colonel Le Camus, who at the time was *sous-lieutenant* in the 1st Regiment of the naval infantry, wrote in 1904 that he had seen the Bavarians fake a surrender to shoot men of his own company as they advanced toward the Bavarians, a charge that has not been substantiated. While some soldiers were shot out of hand, there are, however, no reports of a cold-blooded massacre of military prisoners.

Before dawn, Bazeilles was on fire from shellfire and from the deliberate acts of both sides. As dawn broke, Lebrun's XII Corps was holding strong, retaking shops and houses. In the train station, Lassberg tended to the wounded and dying. The Bavarians sought to make the train station a neutral location by displaying a white sheet on which they painted a red cross in blood.

Further north along the Givonne, Saxon advance guards of the Army of the Meuse arrived at the villages of La Moncelle, Daigny and, eventually, as far north as Givonne. The Saxons were seeking to meet up with the Third Army north of Sedan to complete the encirclement. They had been marching with little food for thirteen or fourteen hours a day for several days to complete this *Kesselschlacht*. They met resistance from the French XII Corps, extending along the Givonne from Bazeilles on its right up through La Moncelle and to Daigny, and from Ducrot's I Corps at Daigny.

Meanwhile, the Third Army to the west of Sedan was also heading north. The Prussian XI Corps had massed at Donchéry, due west of Sedan, and prepared to attack the French positions at Floing and Illy, north-west of Sedan. To avoid the oxbow of the Meuse, they marched 6 miles north before heading east, a hard and tense operation as they could hear the distant fighting at Bazeilles. Gebhard von Bismarck of the Prussian 87th Regiment later recalled the nervous strain:

> Suddenly a man stepped out of the company column before me, scrambled up the Meuse embankment and – with backpack, bedroll, and rifle – threw himself into the water below. There was a loud splash, the water closed over him, the rings dissipated, and then

nothing. He never surfaced. The men gaped for a long time; they were nauseated, by this, and by the grinding pressure on their nerves.[10]

Their commanders held a more sanguine view. General Blumenthal, witnessing the troop movements from the heights of Donchéry, was confident in Germany's imminent victory. As they rounded the oxbow, the XI Corps split off south-east to Floing while V Corps climbed to Fleigneux, ready to meet the Guard Corps heading west from the Meuse Army. This Prussian march discipline, painfully executed, made possible the German victory.

In the eastern sector, the French command grappled with the attack at Bazeilles. Then the situation worsened. Around 6 a.m., en route toward Bazeilles, MacMahon was wounded by a shell fragment in the leg that left him unable to walk, let alone mount a horse. Unaware of Wimpffen's commission to succeed him in command, MacMahon appointed General Ducrot as his successor. Ducrot was unprepared for this appointment, as he had not seen MacMahon in several days and had not been apprised of his commander's plans.

Ducrot learned of his appointment at around eight o'clock, just as the Saxons were developing their attack on Daigny, the Guard was about to meet his I Corps' left flank and a shell killed a trusted general commanding the division at Daigny. Ducrot immediately recognized the dire situation of the French: to fight would mean to be destroyed. Fearful that the Germans would seek to envelop his army, Ducrot quickly ordered a retreat toward the west, not realizing that the Germans had advanced on Donchéry. When General Lebrun objected to this plan (in part because his XII Corps was holding its positions well and in part due to the difficult terrain of their retreat), Ducrot argued that the fighting at Bazeilles was a diversion while the Germans surrounded the French flanks, and that the real battle would take place at Illy to the north. Ducrot ordered Lebrun to retreat from Bazeilles at 8 a.m., and Lebrun followed orders and started the retreat.

Then, at around 8.30, Wimpffen arrived and announced that he was in command – and furious. There would be no withdrawing to the west: he knew that the Germans had already arrived in Donchéry and did not believe the French could break through. If anything, the French should move east. For now, Lebrun was to hold on in Bazeilles and await reinforcements from VII Corps so he could eventually take the offensive. 'We need a victory,' Wimpffen retorted to Ducrot. Lebrun countermanded his earlier orders to retreat. Ducrot could not convince Wimpffen to withdraw, warning, 'You will be very lucky, *mon général*, if this evening you even have a retreat!'[11]

By mid-morning the battle was raging everywhere – south-east at Bazeilles, east along the Givonne, and west at Floing and Illy. The Saxons held Daigny by ten o'clock and made contact with Tann's Bavarians. King Wilhelm watched the battle unfold from a hill south of the Meuse above Frénois. He was joined by Moltke, Roon and their staff officers and by Bismarck and the Foreign Office; British, Russian and American military observers; British journalists, including William Russell from *The Times*; and German royalty – Leopold of Bavaria, Wilhelm of Württemberg, the dukes of Schleswig-Holstein and of Saxe-Coburg, grand dukes of Saxe-Weimer and Mecklenburg-Strelitz, and others, all, in the words of Michael Howard, 'watching the remains of their independence dwindling hour by hour as the Prussian, Saxon, and Bavarian guns decimated the French army round Sedan'.[12]

By now the morning mist had burned off to reveal the floodplain around Sedan. Below Wilhelm formed a long line of artillery on the left bank of the Meuse: the II Bavarian Corps between Frénois and Wadelincourt, and to the right at Remilly, the IV Corps' artillery. Beyond the Meuse valley and Sedan proper emerged the line of the Bois de la Garenne, west of Givonne. Further north lay the slopes above Illy and Givonne – now with artillery from the two German armies – with the Ardennes Forest further north still.

In Bazeilles, combat turned ever more brutal. The French soldiers abandoned the village in the early afternoon. Civilians were left to the mercy of German soldiers who themselves felt terrorized by the morning's hand-to-hand fighting. The Germans were also convinced that they had been struggling against large numbers of *francs-tireurs* hidden in the village houses. The number of civilian combatants is difficult to substantiate, but at least some civilians took part in the combat and others helped provide information on the enemy's movements. According to the *Courrier des Ardennes*, German spies had been present on 28 August when the municipality had distributed arms on the Place de la Mairie. The Bavarians also reported seeing armed women, which ran counter to their belief that war was a man's job. Later, a former enlisted man named Weidner, who came from Nuremberg, recorded that 'the poet's aphorism – "women become hyenas there" – proved well-founded, for the aforementioned projectiles were hurled mostly by women, whose faces were consumed by rage. Yes, several had even seized the murder-weapon with their gentle hands and bravely fired.'[13]

And so, the Germans who took Bazeilles on 1 September believed that they had to show strength, establish control and punish those who had resisted. Further adding to the chaos, Bavarian soldiers had been trained to fight in larger units. In Bazeilles, they were left to make decisions on their own without the restraint of their superior officers.

The village was already on fire, and the victors sought to burn down the rest systematically by using paraffin and incendiary cartridges, with the intention of forcing anyone hiding in their houses to flee. Kühnhauser explains the decision to set fire to Bazeilles: 'Things really had to change if we were not all to become victims of this cruel street fighting. That is why orders were given to lay fires in all houses that had been forced open.'[14] Civilians who had taken refuge in their cellars or were otherwise unable to leave their homes were asphyxiated or burned alive. Monsieur Vachelet, his thirteen-year-old daughter Flore and his brother-in-law Antoine Hagnery died in their cellar.

Those who escaped burning buildings found themselves beaten with sabres and clubs, tied up and led to the station where they were kept overnight. A man named Harbulot-Lambert was beaten with a sabre, taken to the Château Legardeur and tied to the post of a staircase by his leg and left arm. Harbulot-Lambert's wife, according to J. Bourgerie, was 'wounded on the forehead with a sabre blow, then led almost naked as far as Dom-le-Ménil, 14 kilometres from Sedan'.[15]

Another woman, eighty-three-year-old Madame Oudart, was forced out of her house by Bavarian soldiers. A café owner named Pierre Liégeois described her predicament: 'She was taken prisoner with us, but she was not able to walk fast enough; the soldiers pushed her and often made her fall down. Each time she fell, the Bavarians stuck her with the point of their bayonets and kicked her to make her get up again.'[16]

In the emotion of the moment, officers did not always follow the correct protocols. In the midst of the fighting, soldiers brought two civilians in the blue shirts of working men to a battalion commander and his officers. Here's the account of one of these officers (named Koch-Breuberg):

> 'Herr Major, they just shot at us!' 'Is that true?' asked the agitated major. He had just buried a good officer. 'Shoot them! On the spot!' he ordered. 'Our people should have killed these men right away,' a calm comrade said to me. Now they actually belong before a court martial.[17]

Some French underwent mock executions or were in fact shot, while others were deliberately wounded. A civilian who emerged from a basement and tried to flee could not escape: 'The villain swore his innocence, even though in his agitation he had kept in his hand the weapon whose barrel was still warm. This scoundrel was made short work of. A countryman of mine raised his weapon – a bang – and he lay in his blood.'[18]

French civilians and Bavarian soldiers both made rapid choices to survive this day. Kühnhauser and his fellow soldiers tried to enter a house but were blocked by a woman holding a child. She swore there were no soldiers there. This may have been true, but it was not the whole story. The Bavarians almost turned away, when they heard a noise and forced their way up the stairs to find only a table with bullets and bullet casings strewn on the floor. Men had escaped across the roofs. A soldier shot after them but missed. 'The woman had achieved her purpose with real woman's cunning,' delaying the Bavarians to allow the men to escape. 'When we came down,' reported Kühnhauser, 'she had disappeared together with the child, luckily for her because the murder of a woman could probably not have been ruled out in this battle-rage.'[19] Kühnhauser felt betrayed by a woman who played on gender stereotypes to achieve her ends. While he did not admit that he would have wanted to kill this woman, he knew that anger at this ploy could lead to murder. Another woman implored Kühnhauser and his companions to allow her to retrieve a few belongings from her house before it, too, burned. 'And even in this bitter fight to the death and although we had already been deceived by a ruse, we granted the request.'[20]

Women were also the victims of rape. Most sources that discussed sexual assault put it to the side, under a cover of modesty. For instance, M. Herbulot-Hubert stated that he saw Madame Leroy led to the station, 'struggling among five or six Bavarians'.[21] In Balan, the village between Bazeilles and Sedan, a Bavarian rifleman named Emonts witnessed the execution of a woman from his perch on a church tower. Through his telescope, he could spot a woman 'who with shotgun in hand, behaved wildly as she was seized by a patrol and forcibly led toward the woods. A circle formed around the apparently wild one. Within it the soldiers worked. After several minutes the circle opened; white clouds of smoke announced an execution.'[22] Were the men obscuring the execution itself, or some mistreatment or sexual assault on the woman during the 'several minutes' in which they 'worked'? Emonts did not say. Age was no protection from acts intended to humiliate and punish enemy women. Henri Entz reported that 'the widow P . . ., aged eighty years, was tied up by soldiers, dragged on the ground and given over to the worst outrages. Another lady C . . . had the same fate.'[23]

*

Elsewhere around Sedan that afternoon, the French command continued to reel under a multi-front attack. While the fire and civilian combat continued in Bazeilles, the Bavarian artillerymen were establishing their guns on the slopes above the village and moving toward Balan. Moving up the Givonne river, the Saxons held Daigny and the Prussian Guard stood above Givonne. To the west of Sedan, from the Third Army, the Silesians of V Corps stood before Flégnieux and Hessians of XI Corps had rounded the Meuse and nearly reached Floing. By midday the artillery encirclement was nearly complete. The Germans deployed 222 guns from Floing to Bazeilles, with a range of over a mile. They fired some 20,000 shells that day, which the French artillery could not hope to match in terms of number or range.

Germans on the front lines did not necessarily recognize the overall strategy, as one account makes clear:

> I was with the commander of the left-wing battery at Illy in the afternoon; he was looking at the French through his telescope and kept shaking his head and muttering; finally he yelled to the nearest lieutenant: 'What the hell is that over there? Shells are exploding *behind* the French guns and they're not ours!' The lieutenant raised his telescope, looked for a while and then shouted back: 'And their right wing and center batteries are limbering up and retreating.' – 'What do you think that signifies?' – 'Fire from behind!' – 'But from whom?' – Slowly it dawned on us: the Prussian Guard artillery, the right wing of the Meuse Army, was now firing from the east, creating a total encirclement of the French. Until this moment, we infantry officers and battery commanders on the front line had been unaware that we were part of an enveloping attack by two entire armies.[24]

The crown prince watched with excitement as the German armies encircled the French 'with mathematical precision' in 'the most daring combination'.[25]

The French had prepared to attack German infantry with their

Chassepots, but the infantry did not come. Unlike at Woerth, Vionville, or Saint-Privat, German infantry held their positions and did not advance. Instead, they let the guns work. This was not a Napoleonic battle in which gun lines laid down frontal fire. Instead, Moltke deployed artillery masses, mobile batteries that converged and then moved on. Officers were empowered to take the initiative, and artillerymen were trained to work efficiently. It was not perfect: the guns did not have great accuracy, and, as they crept forward, they caused friendly-fire casualties. Otherwise, the artillery battle unfolded much as the German commanders had planned since 1866. The French got hammered.

Disagreement and disorganization continued as each French sector suffered from the German artillery and did not have room to escape. The French corps, packed into a triangle, were forced in ever closer. Wimpffen believed he saw an opportunity to break out toward Bazeilles, where he hoped that Lebrun's XII Corps could break through the Bavarians, some of whom were out of ammunition and drinking wine. He enquired whether Douay could send help from VII Corps, and with this assistance assured, he planned for a push east toward Carignan. Wimpffen eventually realized that he would need to act immediately if they were to have any hope of success. He could not wait for help from VII Corps to arrive. Wimpffen gave the order around 1 p.m. and requested that Napoleon III come from Sedan to head the army.

The attempted breakout never materialized. Napoleon knew that Wimpffen's plan was not realistic and refused to head the adventure. Few troops were in position. They simply could not make it there through the fog of war, with messages lost and commanders without maps. Shellfire pinned some down and others were blocked by fires, wagons, horses, bodies. Wimpffen instead managed an attack at Balan, between Sedan and Bazeilles, which drew II Bavarian Corps reinforcements.

Along the road from Sedan to Bazeilles, at the maison Bourgerie on the border between Balan and Bazeilles, a French officer, Lambert, and a handful of men had been holed up since ten in the morning. They continued to fight until around 3 p.m. when they had shot their last cartridge. They were eventually taken prisoner and allowed to live, despite the considerable loss of life sustained in that last stand. Toward the end of the day, General von der Tann rode up to a villa where civilian women and disarmed peasants were being held by officers. Tann declared in French, 'Your emperor has been taken prisoner . . . You are rabble! We're going to shoot you!' In the end, however, Tann did not carry out his threat.[26]

Meanwhile, by 1 p.m., the left flank of VII Corps at Floing was also suffering under German artillery. The French artillery was ruined, and infantry counterattacks could not stop the German advance. In desperation, and unaware that Wimpffen was attempting the same on the east side, Ducrot ordered General Jean Margueritte to send his cavalry to turn back the advancing Germans and help the French attempt to break out toward the west. Margueritte rode out to survey the landscape and was hit by a bullet in the face. He collapsed, with only the strength to point his arm toward enemy lines. '*Vengez-le!*' cried his horrified men as they sped their mounts down the slopes. While they overran the German skirmishing lines, they could not break the formation. A mass of men and horses fell before the Germans. Those who survived regrouped and charged again. From his perch at Frénois, King Wilhelm sighed, '*Ah! Les braves gens!*' at this impotent assault.[27]

By the late afternoon, the Germans had positioned 700 guns, compared with 550 French guns. The French fell back toward Sedan itself in confusion as the various corps converged behind the lines without direction or energy, and as German guns converged from different angles on the same sectors. The crown prince witnessed the utter misery of French infantrymen 'running around unarmed, restless and bewildered' as 'each separate individual betrayed the despair that had seized on all, as they realized that not a chance was left them now to avoid being taken prisoners'.[28] The Germans aimed 200 guns at the Garenne forest alone, as many as the Confederate Army had deployed at Fredericksburg in 1862. The sector fell by late afternoon. Many trapped French soldiers tried to make their way into the fortress of Sedan, through the moat, climbing the walls. The fortress itself held.

In the late afternoon, Lebrun, Douay and Ducrot made their way, separately, back to Sedan to find the emperor and explain the dire situation. Finally, Napoleon III had the white flag hoisted in Sedan. He prepared to send a *parlementaire* to formally request an armistice, but needed the signature of the current commander, General Wimpffen, who was on the road to Balan. When Lebrun found him, Wimpffen insisted on one final assault at Balan, but his men would not follow him. He finally admitted defeat and rode in silence back to the fortress, the road between Sedan and Balan thick with bodies. Napoleon III prepared a letter of surrender to be sent to the Prussian king via General Reille.

The Bavarians cheered when they saw the white flag. They drank champagne out of their metal canteen cups, and had also managed to find beer, though not very good beer, to the amusement of a Prussian officer.

Meanwhile, King Wilhelm, Moltke, Bismarck, the crown prince and the royal retinue learned from Lieutenant von Bronsart of Napoleon III's imminent surrender. They realized for the first time that the emperor had not escaped from Sedan. Unlike the Bavarian infantrymen, King Wilhelm's men could not bring themselves to cheer. 'Each man felt instinctively how inadequate to such a momentous occasion was a mere outburst of cheering of any sort,' recalled the crown prince, 'and that is just our German way, not to give way to noisy demonstrations in matters of grave importance.'[29]

As they awaited the arrival of Reille to deliver the surrender, the king and Crown Prince Friedrich Wilhelm stood with the German princes in a semi-circle behind them, awaiting the general's arrival on the hilltop. The crown prince noted princely jockeying for position, as 'the Grand Duke of Saxe-Weimar endeavored by shifting his position this way and that to get as near as possible to me.'[30]

Finally, Reille arrived with the letter of surrender. King Wilhelm asked the crown prince to read it aloud: 'Monsieur my brother, Not having been able to die among my troops, I must only now place my sword in the hands of Your Majesty. I am the good brother of your Majesty. Napoleon.'[31]

After the king had consulted with Bismarck, Moltke and Friedrich Wilhelm, Bismarck dictated the reply, accepting the surrender. Wilhelm wrote the letter in his own hand on an improvised table made from a couple of straw-bottomed chairs and a sabretache (a type of flat satchel). For the Germans that evening, the moment required both celebration and solemn silence. Some placed lamps and candles in windows. Others hurrahed in joy and celebration. At their campfires, the men sang the Lutheran hymn 'Nun danket alle Gott', 'Now Thank We All Our God'.

The battle of 1 September combined both impersonal artillery and fierce hand-to-hand combat. Casualties included 3,000 French dead, 14,000 wounded and 21,000 taken prisoner, compared with a total of 9,000 German dead, wounded and missing, a four-to-one ratio. Many more French soldiers were soon to be handed over as prisoners. Mobile hospitals staffed by French, Germans and foreign volunteers had sprung up across the area to treat soldiers to the best of their ability. Dietrich von Lassberg, who had spent the day fighting in Bazeilles and now started to grapple with all that he had seen, saw in his Bavarian companions the many and contradictory experiences of that day:

> Calm and serious they stand; with few words these men speak of their deeds and grieve their losses; but in their faces you could observe: bitterness or calm satisfaction, grief and pain; tears standing in many eyes, fiery enthusiasm lighting up others . . . In these brief moments, young soldiers and officers suddenly become warriors![32]

Wimpffen was not happy to negotiate the capitulation, but he was the new commander and had no choice. He faced not only humiliation on the battlefield, but a fundamental insult to himself and his country. Wimpffen and General Henri Pierre de Castelnau of the Imperial Suite arrived at Donchéry to meet with Moltke and

Bismarck. The French sought to be allowed an honourable retreat for the army, with arms and baggage and full military honours, in exchange for the promise not to take up arms against Prussia and its allies. This was too much to ask for such a large army. Bismarck wanted to bring the war to a close and so insisted on its captivity. Wimpffen threatened a renewed attack. Moltke disabused him of the illusion that his 80,000 men could long withstand the now 250,000 or so surrounding Germans.

Wimpffen then argued for generosity to create a lasting peace. Bismarck pointed to France's long record of revolutionary instability, which had disrupted Europe for eighty years and Germany for nearly two centuries. Bismarck cautioned that in a democracy, you could not expect gratitude. In the case of France, 'One can rely on nothing in your country.'[33] Furthermore, the French could not be trusted. They were 'irritable, envious, jealous, and proud to excess. It seems to you that victory is a property reserved for you alone, that the glory of arms is your monopoly.' Germans by contrast were peaceful, he claimed; France had declared war on Germans thirty times in the past two hundred years. Bismarck demanded a buffer of land and fortresses to protect themselves.

Wimpffen countered that France in 1870 was not the same country as it had been under Louis XIV or Napoleon; under Napoleon III, it was a bourgeois country. Not so, replied Bismarck. The French press and the population had thrilled to the declaration of war, and he was determined to march on Paris to teach this population and those journalists a lesson. He concluded, 'The fortune of battle has delivered to us the best soldiers, the best officers of the French army; to voluntarily set them free to risk seeing them march against us again would be madness.'[34]

Bismarck then turned to a key question: did Napoleon surrender himself, or all of France? Was it the army or the state? If the entire nation was surrendering, Bismarck implied, then there might be a different set of terms – better terms – to end the war. Castelnau replied that the emperor surrendered only himself, not the nation. The reply headed off a potential conflict between Bismarck and

Moltke – the latter did not want to soften the terms that would allow the war to end more quickly – but it prolonged the war for many months.

Wimpffen tried again, but Moltke dismissed his attempt by showing the map of the ring of batteries around Sedan. Without an agreement, Moltke bluffed, the bombardment would start again at 9 a.m. (Wimpffen did not realize that the Germans had run out of ammunition). Wimpffen asked for time to consult, and so the truce was prolonged until the next morning.

That night, Lassberg slept soundly, dreaming of the tumult of battle. In the morning, he marched back through Bazeilles, or rather, through its ruins, and witnessed the devastation that he and his companions had wrought. Fires still burned; 37 buildings had been destroyed by shells, 363 had burned down and just 23 were left standing.

> It is now just a big smoky, burning dump full of black smoke and blood; the former streets are covered in the debris of fires, with household utensils, with weapons of all kinds, with dead and charred Bavarians and French; here and there you could see burnt horses or burnt cattle; over everything the flames still cut up into the air, and everywhere you could hear the crash of collapsing walls, here and there a shot cracked.[35]

Thirty-nine civilians had died in Bazeilles. Eight had been asphyxiated in their homes, and thirty-one (thirty men and one woman) had died in or directly after the fighting. Many hundreds more were wounded and dying. As for soldiers, some 5,000 Germans and 2,500 French were casualties at Bazeilles.

Lassberg passed a pile of some 300 corpses jumbled together, 'German and French; European and African', all sharing the same fate at Bazeilles.'[36] This horrifying sight deeply impressed Lassberg, in stark contrast to his earlier appreciation of his fellow warriors:

> This is the dark side of war! It is all well and good to tell soldiers – and we soldiers hear it gladly and even say it ourselves: 'the most beautiful death is death on the battlefield' – but really, the most beautiful dead are not those dead on the battlefield! And how much is left out by the numerous painters of battles, who often give their dead a kind of beautiful and ideal appearance, so that you really seek to put yourself in their place! These beautiful, ideal corpses of soldiers do not exist![37]

Later, Lassberg was joyfully reunited with his brother Rudolf, who had survived the battle unscathed. He witnessed, however, an unsettling parallel scene: another soldier identified his own brother among the dead. The man cried in horror and recognition – 'It's Anton!' – as he all at once learned that his beloved brother had died and witnessed the horrible damage to his body. The man cut a lock of Anton's hair to send home to their mother. Lassberg was so shaken he could barely talk or contain his tears.[38] Only later that day did Lassberg hear the news that Napoleon III had been taken prisoner. At first, he and his companions laughed at this as an absurd joke. When the reality hit, they cheered with joy. In the fighting at Bazeilles, Lassberg – like so many soldiers – was a villain and a hero, a brother and a foe, a Bavarian outsider and a German forger of unity, a warrior stripped of his innocence and a young man unable to own his complicity in unspeakable violence.

Crown Prince Friedrich Wilhelm awoke on the day after Sedan to reflect on a history lesson he had learned as a boy: '*Die Weltgeschichte ist die Weltgericht!*' ('World history shows the world's justice'). For him, this was an unproblematic statement of 'profound truth' captured in the events of the previous day.[39] The rise of Germany and its path toward unification under the Prussian monarchy at the expense of France appeared to Friedrich Wilhelm not only probable but just.

On 2 September, Napoleon and Bismarck met to finalize the terms of surrender at an isolated house outside Sedan where several families and a wine merchant lived. It was chosen precisely because of its isolation and because it fell entirely inside Prussian lines. Napoleon III had set off early in an attempt to make an extraordinary appeal to King Wilhelm but was stopped on the road to Donchéry by Bismarck. Bismarck refused to allow the emperor access to the king until the capitulation was signed. He led Napoleon III to a bench outside a cottage for a good hour of one-sided conversation in German while the emperor sat dispirited on his seat. When Moltke arrived, Napoleon tried to suggest moving the army into Belgium, an option that Moltke flatly refused.

Bismarck now allowed Napoleon a short, awkward audience with the king. The emperor expressed admiration for the army that had just defeated him, especially its artillery. He learned with astonishment that he had not faced the entire German Army, and that seven German corps besieged Metz. Napoleon asked for one favour: to be allowed to enter captivity by passing through Belgium rather than alongside his army, to save him the embarrassment and possible danger of travelling with his men. Bismarck approved this request. Napoleon III spent the following six months in Schloss Wilhelmshöhe near Kassel.

After his conversation with the king, Napoleon III and the crown prince had a brief encounter in which every exchange presented a negotiation of power through politesse. 'When Napoleon saw me,' wrote Friedrich Wilhelm,

> he held out his hand to me; copious tears were running down his cheeks, which he kept wiping away with his hand, as he spoke with the utmost gratitude, evident both in words and manner, of how the King had just expressed himself. I told him it was only natural in every case to meet the unfortunate in a spirit of compassion.

In few words, he established dominance through sympathy. His next question sought to bury Napoleon further in a feeling of impotence – had the emperor been 'able to get anything of a night's rest'? Napoleon replied that 'anxiety for his friends had amid the miseries of a War allowed him little sleep.' This was an admirable parry from an emotionally wounded man, effectively shifting desolation for the war's trajectory from himself to others. If that exchange failed to land its punch, the next one left the crown prince speechless:

> When I then remarked that this War had been of a formidable and very sanguinary character, Napoleon replied, yes, there was no denying that, but it was all the more frightful if one had never wished to have war (*'surtout quand on n'a pas voulu la guerre'*). After that I said nothing for a moment, because I was loath to make any answer and was greatly surprised to hear such a statement from the mouth of Napoleon, the prime originator of the present War.

Whether this surprise was genuine or rehearsed only for his memoirs, the crown prince was consistent in placing blame for the war on the French, and particularly on the emperor and his advisers. Only in the last exchange did Friedrich Wilhelm and Napoleon achieve a kind of parity between men-at-arms, through the contrast with their families: 'Presently I asked after the Empress and the Prince Imperial, of whom, however, he had had no news for a week. On him asking how my wife and children were, I could only give him precisely the same answer.'[40] After the two parties left, a Prussian officer took the chair in which King Wilhelm had earlier sat. He gave a servant woman 3 francs for the chair, although, she later said, she had herself paid 4 francs for it.

At 11 a.m., Wimpffen signed the terms at the Château de Bellevue along the Meuse between Sedan and Donchéry. The army would surrender as prisoners of war with all arms and all materiel, along with the fortress of Sedan. Officers were given the option of freedom if they swore that they would not return to combat; 550 officers took up this offer. Altogether, 83,000 prisoners were taken, on top of the 21,000 captured in battle, along with 1,000 wagons, 6,000 horses and 419 guns.

Sedan became a vast hospital with the white flag of the Red Cross flying atop every church and home, while parades of wounded soldiers processed toward neutral Belgium. The French prisoners were herded into the Iges peninsula, the land surrounded by the Meuse on three sides just to the west of Sedan, for a week with little food and a lot of rain, *le camp de la misère* later dramatized in Émile Zola's *The Debacle*. Eighty-three thousand men and ten thousand horses were kept on six square miles of open grass. Horses dying of wounds and starvation were killed and thrown into the Meuse, adding to the misery and stench. Lebrun reported the conditions on 4 September:

> The troops have little food, they are living today off potatoes that they find in their bivouacs. Indiscipline is great, very great. The most abusive comments are heard everywhere. I traversed the camps a bit and was nevertheless not insulted. I fear excesses and assaults against the officers. Everywhere in the village of Iges, soldiers pillage houses, take away wood, straw, etc. . . . A terrible tableau that I will never forget.[41]

Napoleon III passed through Donchéry on 3 September, to no cheers of *'Vive l'Empereur!'* He wore the *Légion d'honneur* on his chest, his face worn and lined, his waxed moustache still pointed, with tears in his eyes and no sound but the tramp of the horses and their incongruous jingling bells and the intermittent singing of Württemberg soldiers in celebration.

King Wilhelm reported with pride back to Queen Augusta on 3 September:

> When I consider that after one great and successful war I could not expect more glorious things yet to happen during my reign, and now behold this historical act accomplished, then I bow before God, who alone has chosen me, my army, and my allies, to perform what has happened, and has made us the instruments of His will; I can only look upon it in this light, and in humility praise God's guidance and grace.[42]

9. *New Beginnings*

The German victory at Sedan prompted an extraordinary series of reckonings and reconfigurations. The Second Empire fell. A new republic was declared in Paris with the daunting charge of creating new armies and defending the nation while establishing its own legitimacy. The Germans, meanwhile, felt victory in their grasp but could not bring the conflict to a conclusion. They besieged Paris while facing a new threat from south of the Loire. More French towns and villages grappled with an invasion of soldiers who became increasingly frustrated at the ongoing war. The French were defeated, but the war did not end.

As rumours of the outcome at Sedan spread, anxiety rippled across France: 'inhabitants of Cahors recoil', 'city of Angoulême plunged into consternation', 'immense emotion in Saint-Étienne', 'general and deep consternation in Nantes', 'stupor' at Toulon, etc., etc.[1] Many held their breath awaiting news of the mood in Paris. 'It is very important to send me word several times today news of the situation in Paris,' wrote the procurer general of Besançon; 'everyone is preoccupied with it.'[2]

The news of Sedan and Napoleon III's surrender reached Paris in the late afternoon on 3 September via a telegraph from the disgraced emperor to the Ministry of the Interior. Parisian opinion, both within and outside government, seized more on the ramifications for the Empire than for the war effort. In the Corps Législatif that afternoon, Palikao signalled the defeat while underscoring that he had not yet received official word, and Jules Favre called for the supreme command to be conferred on Trochu, the governor of Paris, and for the deputies to proclaim the fall of the Empire. Favre's midnight proposal was 'received in profound silence'.[3] The Corps did not make a decision. At the same hour, the news officially

LA
BLIQUE

BLIQUE
ANCAISE
Rochefort

reached the Tuileries, and the government decided to convene the Corps for the next day.

Meanwhile, the news began to spread, and crowds gathered at the Place de la Concorde and around the Palais Bourbon. The Corps Législatif met in emergency session at 1 a.m. on the morning of 4 September and prepared to establish a provisional government under Trochu. While Napoleon III's ministers hoped to hold on to power through the creation of a 'Council of Regency and National Defence', Jules Favre and the Left saw the moment as their chance to found a new republic. They preferred that this change in government be legally voted for by the Corps Législatif rather than declared in the streets. The chamber again listened to Favre's statement in silence. After a moment of hesitation Count Palikao, whose son had been killed at Sedan, postponed the vote until noon.

The previous evening, leaders of the extreme Left had organized and mobilized for demonstrations in the streets and at the Corps Législatif the next day. There was not a republican plot, but there were many on the Left eager to overthrow the regime that they had despised and resisted since 1851. The news posted early on 4 September confirmed the rumours:

> To the French: A great misfortune has struck the *patrie*; after three days of heroic struggles sustained by the army of Marshal MacMahon against 300,000 enemies, 40,000 men have been taken prisoner. General Wimpffen, who had taken command of the army replacing Marshal MacMahon – seriously wounded – signed a surrender. This cruel reversal does not shake our courage. Paris is now in a state of defence. The country's military forces are organizing; in a few days, a new army will be under the walls of Paris; another army is forming on the banks of the Loire. Your patriotism, your unity, your energy will save France. The Emperor has been made prisoner in the struggle. The government, in agreement with the public authorities, is taking all measures in keeping with the seriousness of these events.[4]

A large crowd of some 100,000 people, perhaps 150,000, took to the streets. Rumours spread that the empress had given orders to blow up the Place de la Concorde and the Corps Législatif if the Left were to triumph. Speakers found their voices to testify to the corruption and illegitimacy of the Second Empire. The wife of a worker, on her husband's arm, cried out, her voice full of indignation, 'You see . . . the butcher of 2 December wants more blood; he hasn't spilled enough! The gendarmes will shoot at us as in 1851. They put a bullet in my head on the boulevard Montmartre; it's still there and I feel it burn today!'[5] The woman had been fourteen at the time and had been shot while returning home from her workshop. As she spoke, people listened and applauded.

Others debated the best form of government to take the Empire's place. Juliette Adam, a member of the inner republican circle, herself gave a speech:

> The Republic is neither a woman nor a divinity whom we must protect from any defilement or that the least stain will soil. The Republic is the greatest sum of courage, intelligence, activity, expansion, that a people can produce . . . The Republic is the result of our best actions, a living composition of our duties, our rights, our largest and most progressive interests. You don't decree a Republic, you make it.[6]

This day of possibility charged the crowd with hope and a belief that the will of the people could overcome any obstacle.

Part of the crowd gathered at the Palais Bourbon, where debate over the fate of the Empire was already under way. Although 5,000 men under General de Caussade were charged with protecting the Palais Boubon, Caussade did not appear ready to maintain order at any price. Around 2.30 in the afternoon, the crowd invaded the Corps Législatif. The deputies of the Left tried to quiet the crowd so that they could continue their session, to no avail. Unable to hold a vote that would undo the Empire, they decided instead to claim the leadership of the crowd. Rather than declare the Republic immediately at the Palais Bourbon, they made their way across the Seine to the Hôtel de Ville, less than 2 miles away. They found leaders of the more extreme Left already at that traditional site of revolutionary proclamation – two members of the Mobile Guard, 'with drawn swords, clamber[ed] up the ornamental chimney, and [sat] themselves in the lap of a marble nymph'.[7]

But the moderates managed to broker an agreement whereby the new government would be led by deputies elected by the Department of the Seine: Paris and the moderate Left now led the new Government of National Defence. General Trochu, upon receiving assurance that the new leaders would uphold religion, property and the family, agreed to join the government as President of the Council. His presence was intended to reassure the provinces with a symbol of order and provide a military presence. Jules Favre led Foreign Affairs, and thirty-two-year-old Léon Gambetta took the Ministry of the Interior. Ernest Picard claimed Finance and Isaac Crémieux, Justice. Émile Kératry became prefect of police. Admiral Martin Fourichon led the navy and the minister of war was General Adolphe Le Flô, sixty-six years old, who as a loyal republican had not actively served in the military since his arrest in 1852 and exile to the island of Jersey. As governor of Paris, Trochu maintained the upper hand on military affairs.

Meanwhile, a crowd arrived at the imperial palace in the Tuileries. As men removed ornamental eagles from the fencing, the gates opened and people flooded toward the palace. An officer with his detachment of guards refused to open the gates to the private garden, but he allowed the National Guard to replace his men in a gesture that gave way to the crowd while saving his honour. Empress Eugénie had already escaped. People wandered with amusement among the albums and toys belonging to the prince imperial, the empty trunks and the empress's unmade bed, all marks of a hasty retreat. Eugénie, after a night at her dentist's house, was smuggled out of Paris and thence to England.

The revolution of 4 September occurred without violence or

riot, and everyone had gone home again by 8 p.m. The next day, the city remained calm.

This revolutionary day left behind immense questions about how the new government would manage the war it had inherited. Many in the crowd had denounced the stupid barbarity of the 'two tyrants' who had made this war and equated the declaration of a new republic with an end to murderous conflicts, while others called on France to fight to the bitter end. Yet France faced the immediate challenge of an invading army bent on completing its victory and annexing French territory. The Government of National Defence (GND) vowed to continue the war. It did not enjoy a Sacred Union, a phrase used in 1914 to claim unity in the name of national defence. No government ever truly enjoys such unity, but in 1870 political bitterness and mistrust remained at the centre of the war effort, and nobody could pretend otherwise. The Second Empire fell because of military defeat, not because it had lost its appeal among many French. The May 1870 plebiscite just a few months earlier had demonstrated Napoleon III's continued support in much of the nation. But in Paris, many rejoiced at the emperor's fall. People sang the 'Marseillaise' and tore down Bonapartist symbols. Édouard Thierry, director of the Comédie-Française, took down imperial insignia displayed in the theatre and replaced them with republican banners that had been created in 1848 to celebrate the founding of the Second Republic. The imperial displays took their place in storage, in case of any future change.

In the immediate term, Trochu and the GND remained in Paris, where they believed the next great battle would occur. The new government was dominated by Parisians, divided by generation and, after twenty years in opposition, inexperienced in conducting the business of running a government. They received no official support from the Corps Législatif.

On 6 September, Favre sent a circular to the chancelleries of Europe declaring France's intention to refuse to yield 'neither a clod of our earth nor a stone of our fortresses'.[8] This position gravely compromised attempts at negotiation. Bismarck had made it clear to Wimpffen after Sedan that no such painless peace would be considered. Yet Favre had some hope for a change in the Prussian's position. The neutral powers were not happy to see how quickly Prussia could advance deep into French territory. They had hoped for an inconclusive end, not the dramatic rise of Prussia. The members of the new French government saw an opportunity to rebuild bridges with the monarchs of Europe and dispatched veteran Orléanist Adolphe Thiers to seek their support. Thiers, born in 1797, had already survived a long and turbulent career, including a key role in the overthrow of the Bourbons in 1830, two brief tenures as prime minister in 1836 and 1840 under King Louis-Philippe, and the publication of an influential multi-volume history of the French Revolution that underscored the need for moderate, liberal government. After Louis-Napoleon's *coup d'état* in 1851, Thiers was arrested and spent over a decade out of politics. After Napoleon III liberalized the Second Empire, Thiers returned to politics in 1863 to represent Paris in the Corps Législatif. Never beloved, Thiers nevertheless earned respect for his long-standing commitment to constitutional monarchy at a time when many European royal families still claimed absolute authority. He was the right man to send to the courts of Europe to seek their aid. Thiers sought to persuade London, Vienna, St Petersburg and Florence that a strong Germany might threaten European equilibrium. This diplomatic effort helped steel Favre for negotiations.

Even as Favre pressed for this hopeful outcome, most in the GND recognized that France would not be able to defeat Prussia, and they did not feel responsible for a war that they believed had been waged against the Bonapartist regime, not against France. Why would they not entertain negotiations with Prussia on the basis of peace without annexation and an honourable armistice? But even this possibility would not be palatable in Paris, where pressure to fight to the death made negotiation a challenge. The GND had only a narrow scope of action.

*

Whether or not Favre's negotiations succeeded, the GND needed the support of the provinces. In the immediate term, the provinces ranged from calm to exuberant over the overthrow of Napoleon III. In Lyons and Marseilles, republicans took power without waiting for Paris. In Nice, Mâcon, Saint-Étienne and Bordeaux, revolts broke out as news from Paris arrived, leading to clashes. A Mobile Guardsman was killed in Mâcon and the prisons emptied in Nice. Red flags flew in Saint-Étienne and Nantes. In Lyons, the extreme Left formed a Committee of Public Safety that declared the republic and called for the arming of all citizens, refusing to recognize the prefect named by Gambetta. It took several days for the new prefect to gather the moderate republicans in hand and assert his authority. In Marseilles, a crowd occupied the Hôtel de Ville on 4 September and the next day took arms from the prefecture. The republican provisional prefect managed to restore order that day, but not before Gambetta characterized the extreme Left as 'traitors' and called on 'good citizens' to maintain calm.[9] The fissures within the Left were clear.

After this initial burst of activity, the GND built its provincial power structures. In each of France's eighty-nine departments, local republican leaders claimed control over key positions. They had been awaiting this moment for a long time. In France's centralized system of government, each department was overseen by a prefect appointed by Napoleon III's central state. After 4 September, republican municipal elected officials stepped in as provisional prefects as they awaited appointments from Gambetta and ensured that imperial functionaries could be held at bay.

For their part, Napoleon III's prefects, subprefects, *conseillers de prefecture* and *trésorier-payeurs généraux* did not resist, as their power had dissipated with the removal of the emperor. But it pained them to step away from their positions at the moment of France's double crisis. As the subprefect of Montluçon (Allier) wrote in his resignation letter,

> After having served the imperial government for fifteen years, I would not know how to betray it on the day it is being tested. Please

> be so good as to replace me immediately. It is painful for me to continue these functions under a government that I do not love. I only keep them at the moment so that I may execute measures that might permit my country to fight against the Prussian invasion and to reconquer the sacred soil of the *patrie*.[10]

Mayors and municipal councils changed as well. Twenty years of administrative power and experience dissolved in two days, just as the country needed to defend itself against an invasion.

Gambetta appointed new prefects within ten days. He replaced Napoleon III's experienced men with local republican leaders who had been in the struggle against the Empire and had developed deep connections. They lacked, however, administrative experience. Two-thirds of Gambetta's new prefects were lawyers, journalists, or professors – men of letters who tended to interpret any administrative slowness as signs of anti-republican conspiracy.

News of Sedan and Napoleon III's surrender travelled rapidly via telegram. It reached India by 9.55 a.m. on 3 September. Londoners celebrated Prussia's triumph over Napoleon and anticipated the consequences. The *Pall Mall Gazette* stated, 'If the Emperor hopes, by a hastily patched-up peace, to find means to transfer the throne to his son, it is the last and greatest delusion of a life of delusions.'[11] William Russell, the *Times* correspondent, rushed from the German HQ overlooking Sedan back to London to see the reaction. He reported that 'people had been petrified, so to speak, with astonishment.'[12]

In the United States, too, telegrams criss-crossed with the joyful news, triggering the firing of salutes, the ringing of bells and processions in the streets. New Yorkers thrilled to learn of Napoleon III's swift defeat, 'leaving him with only the poor refuge of death, a hapless prisoner, sans throne, sans sword, sans friend, sans everything'.[13] German Americans left their workshops to celebrate. The 'Wacht am Rhein' was sung in the Gold Room on Wall Street, 'and a hundred wild brokers danced a weird *can-can* around the fountain in the centre of the Stock Exchange.'[14]

In both Britain and the United States, word of a new French republic complicated this jubilation. Though some doubted that France could succeed in establishing a republic, others rejoiced at the prospect. An American chronicler noted, 'Prussia's strongest supporters abandoned her to her victories and held out their hands to the infant Democracy. The "lost cause" of a Republic was better than a king's magnificent victories. The hatchet raised against Napoleon and Caesarism fell harmless when the young Republic held out her beeseeching [sic] hands.'[15] The United States was the first nation to recognize the new government. Upon receipt of telegraphed news regarding the events of 4 September, President Grant immediately recognized the GND's legitimacy and extended his congratulations on the peaceful declaration of a republic. Ambassador Washburne conveyed this recognition to Favre on 8 September.

German Americans who celebrated the German triumph also hoped for parliamentary representation for their compatriots back home. In early October, a group of German Americans in St Louis sent this message to Bismarck, addressed to the German People:

> Brethren: The struggle which French audacity forced upon you is closing. Marching with your leaders, under the holy banner of the Fatherland, with a bravery unequalled and discipline which can only be obtained by a high civilization, you entered France and your cause was victorious. *We ask that you will make the fortresses which have heretofore menaced you the guards of your border; that you will retain Alsace and Lorraine, of which you were robbed; and demand reimbursement for the expenses of the war.* Let German unity and a full and free representation of the people in parliament be the reward of your bravery.[16]

After Sedan, British observers shifted their generally favourable position with regard to Germany. The announcement of the new French republic was welcome news. Furthermore, rumours of 'the sickening tales of slaughter, the horrible threats of vengeance' had reached Britain as well, leading many to question British neutrality. 'Can it be true (for my own part I can scarcely believe it),' wrote one commentator under the name CIVIS, 'that the great German people are so athirst for revenge that they have commanded their captains and men-of-war to lay waste a whole country with fire and sword, and not to desist, under penalty of disgrace, till they have driven their adversaries to the last stage of desperation?'[17] After Sedan, CIVIS later wrote, England's neutrality became 'shameful' as Germany attempted to extend its victory past an acceptable point, toward the destruction of France. Britain should not tolerate such a conquest of a newly liberated country at the hands of 'men who regard the needle-gun and the *mitrailleuse* as the best exponents of the designs of Providence, and who still maintain, in the presence of an emancipated generation, such worn-out superstitions as the divine right of kings, and the legal irresponsibility of hereditary nobles'.[18] With Napoleon III defeated and deposed, the continuation of the war now raised troubling questions.

Reports came from Berlin of joyful enthusiasm. 'Thousands of people throng the streets,' wrote an anonymous observer, 'moving in ranks with arms linked, singing patriotic songs, shouting, and exhibiting every other sign of enthusiasm.'[19] The crowd assembled before the palace, prompting the queen to appear and address it. Shops closed and Berliners held joyful demonstrations in front of the homes of Bismarck, Moltke and Roon.

For many Germans, the victory at Sedan signalled that the war would soon end and that a united Germany would soon claim swathes of French territory. In the German states, the press gave overwhelming support to the annexation of Alsace and parts of Lorraine. The strong sentiment among German officers and politicians also favoured these annexations. That territory, whose inhabitants tended to be German-speaking and Protestant, could provide a buffer to prevent further French invasion. Even liberals in German territories saw Alsace as part of the German nation, defined as they saw it by the German language. Those who expressed journalistic opposition were arrested and their newspapers seized. Deputy Johann Jakoby, a former radical of the Frankfurt Parliament and long-time critic of Bismarck, was arrested on 20 September after delivering a speech at Königsberg on the 14th against the annexation of Alsace and Lorraine.

The war also provided opportunities to express German unity through peaceful means. On 6 September, from Rheims, the crown prince issued a call for Germans to support wounded soldiers financially through an 'Invalid Fund of Germany', similar to ones established by Prussia in 1864 and 1866, but this time intended to serve men from all of Germany. The call for donations, addressed to 'the hearts of all Germans', stated that 'On the battle-fields of France, the nation has become conscious of its greatness and union, and this gain, sanctified by the blood of many thousands of our warriors, we trust, will keep its binding power for all future time.'[20] This call for donations claimed that Germany already existed and simply awaited discovery and consciousness.

Peace, however, remained elusive. Bismarck was ready to bring the conflict to a close and to reap his territorial gains. He had not wanted to destroy the French Empire altogether, though he had hoped to permanently weaken France and deter a future war. He worked assiduously to avoid foreign intervention, both in terms of diplomacy and the unlikely event of direct military intervention.

Bismarck faced a quandary: with whom should he negotiate? Napoleon III had not abdicated. The Army of the Rhine – bottled up in Metz since mid-August – had sworn an oath to serve the emperor. Napoleon had surrendered himself and his army, but not all of France. Bismarck told the American General Sheridan that he would like to find the prince imperial and place him on the throne. The Government of National Defence claimed to speak for France, but Bismarck did not believe it had sufficient grounding and national support.

This difficulty was no secret. As he passed through Rheims on the march to Paris, Bismarck had an announcement placed in the local newspaper on 11 September:

> The German Government could enter into relations with the Emperor Napoleon, whose Government is the only one recognized hitherto, or with the Regency he appointed; they would also be able to treat with Marshal Bazaine, who has his command from the Emperor. But it is impossible to say what justification the German Government would have in treating with a power which up till now represents only a part of the Left Wing of the former Legislative Assembly.[21]

In the meantime, Moltke did not hesitate to proceed with military solutions. Within hours of signing the surrender at Sedan, Moltke signed orders to march on Paris. The political and symbolic importance of Paris, its revolutionary history and radical present, and its reputation for all that was seedy and sexual in moralistic Lutheran eyes, pointed to Paris as the Germans' next strategic focus.

The advance began on 7 September. The Germans moved quickly and with relative ease, able to spread out and therefore live off requisitions from the inhabitants of the countryside. They advanced on a front over 60 miles wide that moved 10–15 miles per day, engulfing some 800 square miles of villages, farms and fields daily.

Crown Prince Friedrich Wilhelm made his way west via Rheims, drinking Veuve Clicquot champagne and visiting the cathedral while commiserating about the Republic with the local clerics. Along the way, he received the Bavarian Max Joseph Military Order for his victory at Wörth. 'I had hardly heard of the existence of this Order,' he noted, 'which is only conferred for battles won. As we may imagine, this has been a rare event in Bavaria, so at the present moment nobody in that country possesses the decoration in question.'[22] With this dismissal, the crown prince assured himself that the Prussian Iron Cross would remain the higher form of honour.

Royal Headquarters reached Château-Thierry by 15 September. Moltke ordered the encirclement of Paris that day. On the 17th the Army of the Meuse and the Third Army began to surround the capital and cut the railroad to Orléans. The Army of the Meuse occupied the right bank of the Marne and Seine, and the Third Army the left bank. By the 20th, 150,000 men surrounded the city.

On that day, the crown prince and the royal retinue arrived in Versailles, which King Wilhelm soon claimed as his new headquarters.

Versailles was poorly placed from the perspective of communications with Germany. But as the royal entourage expanded, the capacious halls of the palace could accommodate the staff, the many royals and their hangers-on, war correspondents, international military leaders and endless politicians from German states who soon arrived to hammer out the details of a new German Empire. Versailles crawled with royal characters who could be at turns entertaining and ridiculous. The crown prince reported toward the end of September:

> To-day a half-crazy Prince Max of Württemberg turned up to see me, who for years has been taking part in lion-shooting expeditions in Africa. After a breakfast he did ample justice to, and when he had suitably quenched his thirst, he refused to avail himself of my suggestions and went off to roam about recklessly outside the chain of outposts – result he soon got a glancing shot wound on the head.[23]

Meanwhile, after Sedan, Dietrich von Lassberg remained in the area for several days dealing with captured materiel and dead horses. Many German units were charged with securing the rear, repairing rail and telegraph infrastructure, and shepherding French prisoners of war toward Germany. Lassberg's unit conveyed a group of fifty-three prisoners south-east from Sedan, via Bazeilles, to Rouvres, between Verdun and Metz. Many of the French proudly wore medals and decorations. Some tramped ahead indifferently, while others cried with anger and shame. Some of them had fought against the Bavarians at Bazeilles and Balan.

A tall, handsome man particularly caught Lassberg's attention. He was an Algerian soldier, one of the *Turcos* so hated and feared at Wissembourg.

> He spoke not a word, did not look around much, but mostly held his head high and straight ahead. In Bazeilles he suddenly stopped at a

crossroads, looked sharply and attentively at the debris, then softly nodded his head, murmured a word, picked up a stone from the debris and put it in his pocket, and started marching again in the same silence. Perhaps on the day of battle he had fought here, perhaps he had had a particular experience with one of the 'blue devils', as the French frequently call us Bavarians since the battles of Weissenburg and Wörth, and took the stone in remembrance of Bazeilles.[24]

As the day went on, Lassberg and his comrades watched this man with the greatest admiration, especially as Lassberg realized – after two or three hours on the march – that he had been wounded in the leg. The man refused to be carried in a wagon, but accepted Lassberg's offer of bread, schnapps, half a chicken and a cigar. The man thanked Lassberg 'simply and sincerely' by crossing his arm against his chest, and, placing his hand flat against his forehead, making a deep bow. Lassberg imagined that the man found his peace and strength in thinking 'Allah is great and good, Allah will help.'[25] By the end of the day, they had spent sixteen and half hours on their feet in the rain.

For three days, Lassberg and the tall, calm man – a Bavarian and a North African brought together by a conflict to fight on behalf of the powers that they had recently struggled against – marched together. And then, at Étain, the Bavarians handed over the prisoners to a unit of the Prussian *Landwehr*.

In Lassberg's writing, the man was an individual whose personal characteristics won his admiration and praise, far different from his descriptions of the feared and undifferentiated Algerian men he had fought in earlier battles. Lassberg admired this man and tried to imagine his thoughts and experiences, particularly his encounters at Bazeilles. He expressed a far more nuanced view of Algerians than he had previously. Still, Lassberg leaned toward 'noble savage' tropes. His language claimed possession as well as a relationship that the man may not have reciprocated – he referred condescendingly to 'my previously mentioned Turco' and 'my often-mentioned Black friend'.[26] And of course, a basic distinction remained: the man was a prisoner while Lassberg remained free. At war's end, the man would likely return home a subject within the French Empire, whereas Lassberg would march to Munich a citizen in the united German Empire.

Lassberg's final reflection on their parting was, 'What must the poor, good-natured "savage" think about this war under the whites!?'[27] The unnamed man might have asked the same thing about Lassberg: what does this young Bavarian man make of fighting a war on behalf of Prussia? Lassberg himself, identifying himself as white without national or social distinction, did not reflect on this question. He was happy enough to hand over the French prisoners and continue on his way, back west toward Paris. After two weeks of hot, long marches, Lassberg reached Leuville-sur-Orge on 24 September, about 19 miles south of the capital. On 1 October, to his great delight and pride, he received the Iron Cross for his actions at Balan. The fate of the tall, calm man is unknown.

The German encirclement of Paris was a feat in and of itself. A series of fortresses connected by fortifications defended the French capital in a 60-mile circle, 4 miles deep. Preparations for the modern protection of Paris had been under way for fifty years. Most significantly, starting in 1840, the Thiers fortifications were built with an investment of some 140 million francs. North of the city lay the fort at Saint-Denis, with forts at Rosny and Nogent in the east. South-east, just south of the Bois de Vincennes, the fort at Charenton protected the meeting of the Seine and Marne. Then, a line of five forts guarded the south, running from Ivry in the east to Issy at the western end. At the point where the Seine curves north again, Sèvres allowed the passage of people between the city and the outside world. North of Sèvres sat the palace of Saint-Cloud, and further north the fortress of Mont Valérien. In the north-west, hypnotic repeating curves of the Seine provided defences along with long fortifications guarding Courbevoie, Asnières and Gennevilliers. The fortifications around Paris were modern, well provisioned and unbelievably expansive, with 1,300 guns in total and 450 shells in each fortress. Inside this ring, the city was surrounded by a wall some 33 feet high, with 94 bastions and a moat 10 feet wide.

After Spicheren and Froeschwiller, the garrison in Paris had worked to construct redoubts, break up roads, put up obstructions, lay down mines and seal off quarries. Trochu ordered the burning of the forests around Paris on 10 September – Montmorency, Bondy, Mont Valérien and Clamart. The Bois de Boulogne was cut down to stumps. In Seine-et-Oise, a company of *francs-tireurs* was charged with burning down the granges and mills of the department, but in the face of the peasants' opposition they refused. In the end, however, any buildings that prevented the defence of Paris were burned down. The Prussians did the same; on 28 September, they burned some 750 acres of woods that were said to have sheltered companies of *mobiles* or *francs-tireurs*.

As the Germans encircled the city, peasants and inhabitants of suburban towns and villages streamed in, with as much of their furniture as they could transport, along with cabbages and rabbits. The French government tore down their homes and fields to prepare military defensive zones. Meanwhile, city dwellers left. Those who stayed struggled with the uncertainty of when they might next see their loved ones outside.

On 10 September, the republican writer Juliette Adam undertook an audacious visit to her teenaged daughter Alice, whom for safety she had sent to stay with her parents on the Normandy coast. Against the wishes of her husband Edmond, Adam and her maid Julie procured two tickets to Granville despite the crush of people at the train station seeking a way out. 'I struggle, I use the ruses of a savage! Two thousand people at least remained without a seat in the station. We left!'[28] Without concern for taking a place that someone else might need, Adam took the train out of Paris and away from the encircling Germans.

In Adam's train carriage, five men all claimed that they planned to return to Paris the next day. An Orléanist woman repeated again and again her belief that Paris would only hold out for two weeks and the people would meanwhile commit atrocities, and that you must have the courage of your convictions. Adam finally retorted, 'Madame . . . if you have the courage of your convictions, permit me to have the courage of mine. I predict that Paris will hold out for at least two, and perhaps three months, and that it will not commit any horrors. I believe myself authorized to make this prediction, because I am a republican!'[29]

After arriving at Granville, Adam took the omnibus south to Saint-Pair and hurried to the house. She had only a short time to visit, as she had promised her husband that she would return on a train that same day. She had arrived without warning and feared that Alice might be out for a walk along the cliffs. To her delight, however, her parents and Alice all met her at the house. They embraced, they cried, they talked about France. In their forty-five minutes together, 'our patriotic enthusiasm was so great that it conquered our weaknesses and calmed our internal heartbreak.' With so much at stake, Adam had no intention of staying outside Paris, but her return to a city that would soon be under siege weighed unbearably upon them all. Alice told her mother, 'Do not be afraid . . . I will not make you worry about me at such a moment; do your duty and forget me.'[30]

Only five passengers braved the train back to Paris, including a dog. It was not clear that they would be allowed to enter. Eventually, however, they arrived back at Gare Montparnasse, and Adam returned home. She had travelled for twenty-four hours for less than an hour's visit with her beloved family.

On 14 September, Trochu held a military review to celebrate the strength of the Parisian forces. Uniformed soldiers and sailors marched past enthusiastic crowds lining the boulevards along a route from the Place de la Bastille to the Arc de Triomphe. 'At every window of surrounding buildings,' recalled Trochu, 'on the balconies and the terraces there were further ranks of moving heads, of flags, of patriotic emblems. Every voice was shouting, all arms were moving, it was a delirium!'[31] The soldiers included between 85,000 and 90,000 infantry of XIII and XIV Corps, which had been formed by Palikao prior to Sedan, as well as 5,000 cavalry, 16,000 artillery,

6,000 engineers of the engineering corps and 15,000 navy personnel, with more coming in until the city was cut off. The new XIII and XIV Corps were nominally regular forces, but they were almost exclusively untrained conscripts.

In addition, Trochu had ninety battalions in the Mobile Guard, including eighteen Parisian battalions that had returned from Châlons, a total of 105,000 men. Men of military age who had not been conscripted formed the *Garde Mobile*, which served as second-line reserves to the regular army.

The review also featured men from the rapidly expanding Sedentary (i.e., local) National Guard. On 6 September, Minister of the Interior Léon Gambetta had authorized an expansion of the National Guard in Paris from the sixty battalions authorized by the Second Empire. The National Guard was so popular that it expanded to a total of 194 battalions at the end of the month – nearly 300,000 men, many armed with rifles, intended to garrison fortresses and maintain internal order.

The National Guard had originally been created during the French Revolution to keep internal order. National Guard militia units, whose members tended to be the middling sort in wealth and class, were eventually incorporated into the regular army and fought in 1813–14. Napoleon III had abolished the National Guard after his coup of 1851, while maintaining a clause that allowed it to be reformed in time of need, and, in Paris, there were still a few 'old bourgeois battalions' under the Second Empire. Gambetta's expansion welcomed all male citizens and paid 1.50 francs per day, plus 75 centimes to the wives of guardsmen. This wage did not fully compensate for the loss of work (workers might earn 3–6 francs per day) in exchange for patriotic service and to dampen the pain of unemployment, though it did provide an incentive to marry. Republicanism and patriotism drove the Government of National Defence as well as the men who joined up. A decree on 16 September discharged imperial appointees and provided for the election of officers of the National Guard. These units tended, therefore, to embrace workers and foster radical republicanism.

Finally, a number of men joined private volunteer groups, some made up of foreigners – the Légion des Volontaires de France (Poles), the Amis de France (Belgian, Italian and British), the Francs-tireurs de la Presse – and many provincial and suburban groups.

The variety of troops, and the fact that they did not fit a soldierly mould, made the military review all the more moving. The writer and critic Edmond de Goncourt recorded that

> at the sight of those gray beards mingled with beardless chins, those frock coats side by side with smocks, at the sight of those fathers, some of whom were holding by the hand their little girls who had slipped into the ranks, at the sight of this amalgam of working men and tradesmen turned soldiers who were ready to die together, one wondered whether one of those miracles might not occur which come to the help of nations who have faith.[32]

Military men filled the streets of Paris and were warmly welcomed. 'The darling children!' exclaimed Juliette Adam. 'They will undertake with us their apprenticeship of heroism; they will be courageous if we are.'[33]

Despite the personal expressions of faith that these untrained men might turn the French tide, Trochu believed that most of these soldiers were incapable of meeting the Germans in open battle. Only about 100,000 were likely to be effective in a sortie. The service of the Sedentary National Guardsmen in particular was symbolic more than practical. They were revolutionary, they were patriotic and they were drawn by the promise of daily wages and the ability to elect their own officers. However, they had little training and less discipline, and were intended to serve a defensive role in their locality. The tension between Trochu's warranted scepticism and the National Guard's desire to fight the Prussians became a defining issue of the siege.

Trochu had at his disposal General Auguste Ducrot, who had escaped imprisonment after Sedan. Ducrot and Trochu differed in how to best continue the fight; Trochu wanted to minimize futile combat, while Ducrot wanted to attack if at all possible. After his experiences at Sedan, Ducrot preferred to rush into either heroic victory or defeat, whichever it would be. The two disagreed on politics as well. Trochu saw revolution in France as inevitable (even though he was a devout Catholic) and was willing to join the government leadership, while Ducrot supported the Empire and was impatient with Trochu's willingness to placate the far Left. All that said, both Trochu and Ducrot were ready to fight and did not entertain the thought of capitulating in the name of undermining the revolution.

Despite Trochu's misgivings, he allowed Ducrot to lead the most significant action against the German armies during the encirclement of Paris. The heights of Meudon and Châtillon lay just south of the forts of Issy, Vanves and Montrouge, and allowed observation of the French operations in those forts as well as a clear view into the city itself. Although Trochu preferred to concentrate his defences in the forts themselves, he allowed Ducrot to occupy the Châtillon plateau and authorized his command in the sector. On 19 September, Ducrot attacked the flanks of the Germans on the march toward Versailles, but his unprepared soldiers fell apart under shells penetrating the morning fog. The attack was turned back, leaving the Germans to take control of the Châtillon plateau. The following day, the cavalry patrols of the two German armies met at Saint-Germain-en-Laye. The encirclement of Paris was complete.

10. *The Paris Strategy*

Meanwhile, it was not clear that the new Government of National Defence could lead France to a victory, or at least to a better outcome than the Second Empire could. By mid-September, Jules Favre's diplomatic strategy fell apart. Thanks to the intervention of the British embassy, Favre managed to get an audience with Bismarck. On 18–19 September, the two men met at Ferrières, where the Prussian Royal Headquarters was located at the Rothschild palace. Favre believed that Bismarck would be willing to accept a peace, or at least an armistice, given that the war had been started to support the aims of a regime that had now been overthrown, and national elections were now set for 2 October. In addition, Favre demanded that this peace come without any loss of French territory. He was much mistaken.

For Bismarck, France had proven itself to be aggressive decade after decade, regime after regime. The problem ran deeper than the ambitions of a Bonaparte: France itself could not be trusted. The new GND represented by Favre and his claim to give up 'not an inch of our territories' appeared unreasonable. Prussia required a buffer, a frontier that protected its current western territories. Strasbourg and Metz would need to be handed over. Bismarck grew more emotional about his anger at France than Favre expected. The German, after all, was demanding a militarized solution to provide a bulwark against French invasion, when a truly safer alternative would have been to support a peaceful and moderate government that had been accepted by the French people. However, until Bismarck could be assured that French politics could be tamed, he could not offer politics as a counter to the nationalists who wanted Alsace and the military who wanted the fortresses of Metz and Belfort. And perhaps no political solution could have been satisfactory

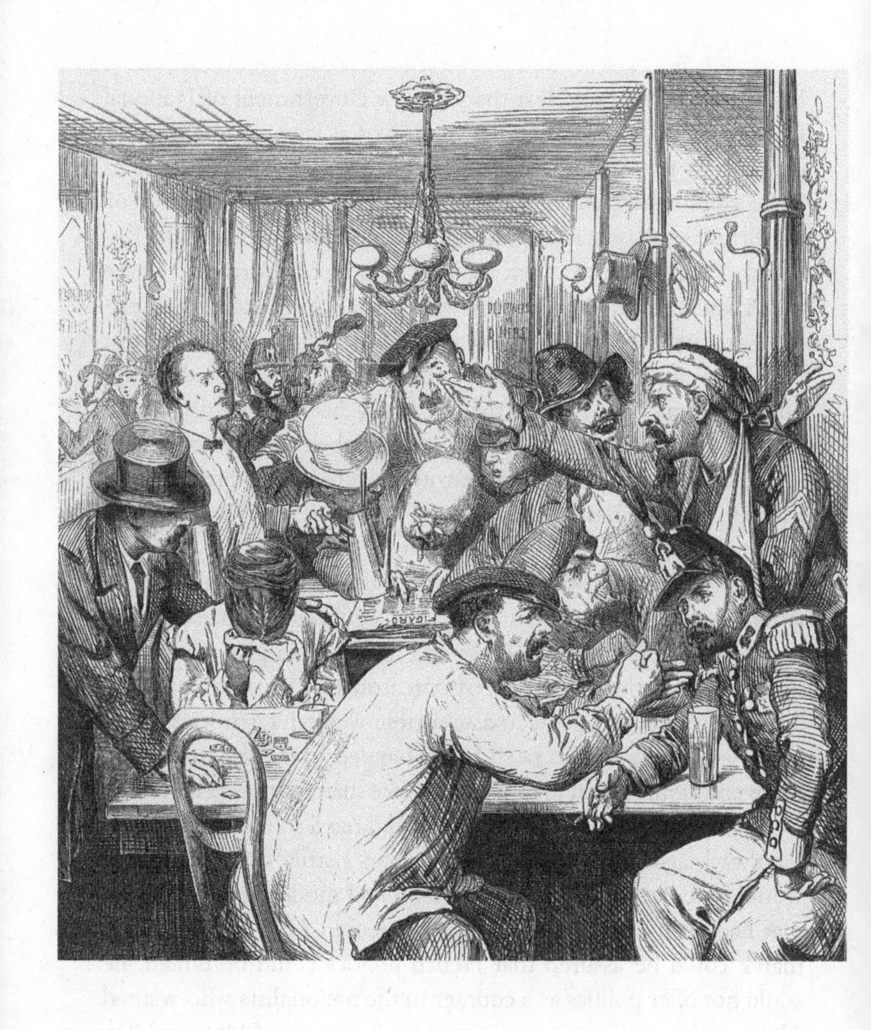
FIGARO

in 1870. In light of Bismarck's demand, Favre abruptly broke off the negotiations. For the next four months, the Government of National Defence continued to insist on seeking an end to the war without loss of territory. A British account of the failed negotiations placed the blame on Paris. They 'will rather bury themselves in ruin. The war will be prosecuted to the bitter end.'[1]

With Paris now encircled, everyone speculated about the Prussians' next move. Many Parisians assumed that the Germans would undertake a direct attack that would be repelled by Paris's defences and superior numbers. Meanwhile, they believed, within a month France would have raised a sufficient army in the provinces to rout the Germans and turn them back.

Victor Hugo, who had returned from exile to Paris, warned of any attempt to storm the city:

> You may take the fortress, you will find the rampart. You may take the rampart, you will find the barricade. You may take the barricade, and then – who knows the resources of patriotism in distress – you will find in the sewers mines of powder, ready to blow whole streets into the air. This will be the terrible sentence you must accept: To take Paris stone by stone, to slaughter Europe on the spot, to kill France in detail; in each street, in each house that great light must be extinguished soul by soul! . . . This city, which yesterday was a Sybaris, to-morrow may be Saragossa.[2]

The Germans shrugged their shoulders at this kind of rhetoric. Moltke knew well that 150,000 men could not hope to take Paris. He had no interest in storming the city and experiencing a Saragossa, a reference to Napoleon I's invasion of Spain. Instead, the Germans awaited either the arrival and instalment of siege guns, or for Paris to starve into surrender.

This solution did not please anybody. Nobody was eager to see German troops undertake the long business of a siege after the joyous victory at Sedan. Bismarck pushed Moltke to move more quickly to bombardment. Meanwhile, the large army would need to be fed and provisioned. Supplies would have to come from Germany, but the two major rail lines had been blockaded by small fortresses and threatened by larger ones still held by the French, even though their defences had not been kept up to date – Lille, Peronne, Soissons, Thionville, Toul, Strasbourg. The lines were blocked due to sabotage and French resistance at Belfort, Langres and Mézières. Trochu also ordered the destruction of roads, farms, villages and livestock to make German provisioning and approaches difficult. The fall of Toul on 23 September assisted the Germans but did not resolve this perennial issue.

Meanwhile, Moltke needed more men to besiege Paris effectively and to counter the new and massive army that the Government of National Defence was building south of the Loire. Despite the overwhelming victory at Sedan, the war had not ended. Moltke had no more opportunities to engage in a large-scale battle and thereby secure victory at the operational level. Instead, he had to split his forces between the siege of Paris, the French efforts to relieve the capital, the siege of Metz and a growing conflict with partisan warriors, the *francs-tireurs*. Moltke hated siege warfare, which would create appalling casualties if truly undertaken. He awaited his opportunity for another large, decisive battle that would crush the French. Meanwhile, he was content to move methodically – much to the frustration of Bismarck, who wanted to end the war as swiftly as possible.

Moltke had only half the number of soldiers that Trochu commanded, when he should have had two or three times the number to carry out an effective siege. He worried that Trochu could potentially mass his soldiers against a Prussian weak point to force a breakthrough. The initial German mobilization had brought highly trained active army formations to fight in the early stages of the war. With 70,000 casualties in battle and 130,000 hospitalized by mid-September, more men were needed. Germany therefore built a new XIII Corps led by the grand duke of Mecklenburg-Schwerin out of the troops that had been held in North Germany to prevent a French landing. Otherwise, German reinforcements would have to depend on the *Landwehr*, the reserves. Although the Roon reforms had sought to limit the use of *Landwehr*, the circumstances now called for their deployment. Four divisions that were built around the *Landwehr* eventually saw action at Strasbourg and Belfort as well as alongside the active army later in the war. Most of it served as rear security and to protect supply lines in occupied France, an ever-expanding territory. By the end of September, a new German railtrack connecting Saarbrücken and Nancy doubled the supply flow to Paris without requiring a passage through Metz.

Paris was now cut off almost entirely from the rest of France. Charles de Freycinet later lamented, 'Paris was going to be besieged like a vulgar stronghold!'[3] Letters and newspapers could no longer leave the city through the usual means. Only a few tenuous lines of communication remained. Gambetta had sent a small delegation of government representatives led by Isaac Crémieux, including Jules Favre, south-west to Tours on 13 September. To maintain contact, and with great secrecy, the government laid a telegraph cable on the bed of the Seine that started operation on 23 September. Unfortunately, it was damaged the next day and dredged up on the 27th by the Germans, who could not decipher the messages and so destroyed the cable.

Unable to communicate by underwater means, Parisians looked to the skies. Balloons had been used during the wars of the Revolution for communication and observation. With the development of coal gas, they became more practical. In the summer of 1870, an inventor named M. Godard encouraged the government to use them. Leboeuf was not interested, but Palikao took them seriously. Once Paris was encircled, the use of balloons became invaluable. The photographer Félix Nadar undertook an experimental flight on 21 September. A test balloon launched out of the city on the 23rd, with the first regular service beginning on the 26th. The hot-air balloons were administered by the Compagnie Nationale Aérostatique, a private company, in co-operation with the French postal service.

For the duration of the siege, two or three times per week a balloon departed from Place Saint-Pierre at the foot of Butte Montmartre carrying out mail, passengers and carrier pigeons, floating out of range of German guns. The pigeons flew back carrying messages that had been typed in columns and shrunk down to fit on microfilm. Gambetta sent fifty-one pigeons to Paris between 9 October and 27 January; forty of them arrived safely, usually within a week. In total, some 10.5 tons of messages left Paris in 65 balloons, along with 164 passengers, 381 pigeons and 5 dogs, and 2.5 million letters on microfilm. While some balloons went astray or fell into German hands, most made their way safely out.

The balloons engendered dramatic images and stories. One story claimed that Félix Nadar had engaged in an aerial gun battle during an attempt to float from Tours to Paris. As he hovered some 10,000 feet above Fort Charenton, it was said, he spotted a second balloon flying a French flag. As they neared, the other balloon opened fire on Nadar and replaced its French flag with a black and white standard. Nadar, whose balloon began to descend rapidly, reportedly managed to stop the hole shot in his balloon, re-ascend, and lob retaliatory fire back at the Prussian balloon, which sank to the earth to be recovered by a detachment of Uhlans.

Despite this effort, balloons and pigeons could not resolve Paris's communication problems. Balloons could not be steered, and so could not be used for a return trip. A new balloon needed to be manufactured to replace each one as it departed. Pigeons could not reliably return, either – only fifty-nine of the pigeons that departed returned to their dovecotes. Trochu ran the war in Paris without consistent communication from Tours or, later, Bordeaux. And pigeons obviously could not carry in food or supplies. Still, with the use of microscopic photography, a single pigeon could carry up to thirty thousand messages. No wonder that the Prussians imported hawks from Saxony to kill pigeons and that Parisians abstained from eating them, despite their growing hunger.

Meanwhile, outposts of the two sides established contact and even friendly relations. At times, Germans allowed French women to seek potatoes in the fields. An official post at the Seine crossing in Sèvres was set up for parley. There, at the call of bugles on either side of the river, a ceasefire would allow officers to exchange news or to pass through for negotiations or to allow neutrals in or out via boat. Bugles notwithstanding, the crossing often came under fire, whether from ignorance or indiscipline. It became known by both sides as the crossing of the Styx.

Outside Paris, a willingness to take up arms against the invaders soon gave way to apprehension. In the immediate aftermath of Sedan, towns and villages throughout the country declared their willingness to fight. For many, post-Sedan brought visions of the Revolutionary Year II and the victory at Valmy that coincided with the declaration of the First Republic in 1792. Urban republicans were galvanized by the moment: 30,500 volunteers signed up in September. In Toulon, the enthusiastic municipal council wrote to the 'citizen-ministers' that 'France is again mistress of herself; that is to say that the *patrie* will be saved as it was in 1792. The commune of Toulon is counting on you as you can count on it. *Vive la République*.'[4]

This enthusiasm did not run deep or last long. Peasants in the Jura, in Burgundy, in the Pyrenees had little interest in joining the fight. The prefect of the Mende reported, 'The torpor of the Lozère country is really impossible to shake.'[5] Outside the urban centres, many French citizens maintained their longstanding loyalties to Napoleon III, even though he was now imprisoned and could not communicate with his followers. The defeat at Sedan had not shaken their faith in the emperor, who had brought stability and prosperity. The evocation of 1792, so invigorating for republicans, reminded many others of the horrors that followed in 1793 – Year II – under the Reign of Terror. Others greeted the new republicans warily. 'If there is not enthusiasm,' wrote the prefect of the Cher, 'it is also right to recognize that there has been no protest anywhere. The new government is uniformly accepted . . . People here are ready for any sacrifice, but they expect [from the Government of National Defence] not circulars and proclamations, but action,

action, and always action.'[6] Newly installed republican leaders came to realize that most French viewed the republic with distrust and that they would have to work with magistrates and municipal councils loyal to the empire.

Further to the Right, monarchists were not numerous enough to pose a threat, although many enjoyed local influence. The danger was greater on the Left. In Lyons, after municipal elections on 15–16 September yielded a radical government, socialist revolutionaries established themselves as leaders of two clubs and briefly occupied the Hôtel de Ville; they declared the abolition of the state and the founding of a Commune. The movement had little support and fell apart quickly.

At the same time, federalist movements – reactions against centralization supported notably by workers – mushroomed, with Marseilles at the epicentre. The federalist Ligue du Midi met on 18 September with delegates from twelve departments calling for radical measures, including a tax on wealth, confiscation of the wealth of 'traitors', the separation of Church and State, suppression of religious schools and freedom of the press. Other political organizations took tentative steps. The Ligue de l'Ouest focused on military objectives while the Ligue du Sud-Ouest had a more classical republican programme. In Nice, separatists sought to overturn the act of annexation that had attached them to France in 1860.

Although none of these movements seriously threatened the Government of National Defence, Gambetta recognized the need to leave Paris and rally the provinces. On 7 October he climbed into a balloon named after the republican revolutionary Armand Barbès and floated out of the capital. Unable to control the direction of his flight, 'thrown like a rubber ball over the walls', Gambetta landed in Montdidier some 60 miles north of Paris and made his way south to Tours two days later.[7] The dramatic episode drew favourable attention to this previously relatively unknown politician.

Gambetta's arrival in Tours in early October gave renewed life to the war effort. He created new armies that soon allowed France to continue to resist the German invasion. In both rural and urban areas, prefects attested to the good morale of the population. While the pace of volunteers slowed – only 17,000 volunteered for armed services in October – the GND raised 94 million francs in domestic war loans at the end of the month.

At Tours, Gambetta issued a confident proclamation:

> We must set all our resources to work – and they are immense. We must shake the countryside from its torpor, guard against stupid panic, increase partisan warfare and, against an enemy so skilled in ambush and surprise, ourselves employ ruses, harass his flanks, surprise his rear – in short inaugurate a national war . . . Tied down and contained by the capital, the Prussians, far from home, anxious, harassed, hunted down by our reawakened people, will be gradually decimated by our arms, by hunger, by natural causes.[8]

Within days of his arrival, Gambetta made two strategic decisions that shifted the course of the war. First, on 10 October, he took control of the Ministry of War, in addition to the Ministry of the Interior, to combine the two portfolios into one unified war effort. Secondly, he appointed Charles de Freycinet, a civilian engineer, as his 'delegate of the Minister with the War Department' – his right-hand man to develop strategy and oversee logistics.

The audacity of these moves is difficult to overestimate. Léon Gambetta, aged thirty-two and with no military and little practical administrative experience, now led France against Bismarck and Moltke, two brilliant and seasoned leaders who had Paris surrounded and had taken up residence at the palace of Versailles. Born in 1838 in Cahors, Gambetta had been a hard worker in school, viewed as 'rather eccentric than intelligent' but 'self-possessed and vehement in tone, fond of solitude, fairly worshipping of his own personal independence, but too precocious and too eminently gifted, perhaps, to be understood by his classmates'. The son of a Genoese grocer and French mother, Gambetta was blinded in his right eye as a youth in an accident at a cutler's workshop. He studied law in Paris, where he became known for his opposition to the Second Empire, then worked for Isaac Crémieux, now minister of justice, 'who gave him his confidence, his friendship, called him his "son" upon all occasions, and predicted for him a brilliant future'.[9] Gambetta advanced rapidly and gained prominence among republicans for his oratory during a controversy over a martyr of the Second Republic, Jean-Baptiste Baudin. He then was elected as a deputy to the Corps Législatif in May 1869 and soon became a prominent orator challenging Prime Minister Ollivier.

Admirers described Gambetta's muscular frame and vigour in his gait, voice and his very hands, 'which seem made for energetic grasping and setting free by turns'. His face, it was said, was 'full of commingled thoughtfulness and audacity, frankness and haughtiness'. Most admired, however, was his ability to balance grand strategy with the small issues. 'His mind is versatile enough to sweep in at one and the same moment the grandest topics and the most minute details.'[10] Freycinet marvelled at Gambetta's intellect and rapid ability to dissect the most challenging situations. How was it, he wondered, that a man without practical administrative experience could so quickly understand the challenges of government and approach them so methodically? 'Eloquence, for M. Gambetta, was not an end in itself, but a means . . . his life was a continuous action . . . He did not waste his time in contemplation.'[11]

Never truly at rest, Gambetta appeared at all moments ready 'to leap upward or to take his flight in the air; in other words, that he is going to speak'. His apartment on rue Bonaparte, the same modest space he had occupied as a student, contained shelves of books and a bust of the revolutionary orator Mirabeau.[12] Gambetta governed with confidence and energy, despite his youth. 'There was authority even in his laugh,' wrote one observer.[13]

Gambetta demanded a rapidity of mobilization that was as vigorous as himself, and this led to both enormous action and comparably large mistakes. His trusted organizer of this effort was Freycinet, a forty-two-year-old civilian engineer without any particular training in military affairs. Freycinet had served the Second Empire as *conseiller général* for the Tarn-et-Garonne and, at the outbreak of war, oversaw the inspection of women and children factory workers for the Ministry of Commerce. After Sedan, as the Prussian noose tightened around Paris, Freycinet felt impotent in his now small role. He wondered, 'Didn't [I] have something better to do? Shouldn't [I] take up national defence? Should I wait patiently until the interruption of communication with the provinces created unbearable leisure? The very thought made me blush. I wanted to do my bit for the common effort.'[14]

So Freycinet wrote a memo to Gambetta regarding an issue he had noticed in the fortifications between Issy and Vanves, followed up by a personal visit. Gambetta was eager to fill the many roles he needed with new republican supporters and dispatched him to serve as prefect of the Tarn-et-Garonne. Freycinet objected; his earlier work on behalf of the Empire would win him few republican friends in Montauban and – unspoken – Montauban was about as far from the action as Freycinet could imagine.

After just a few days at his post, Freycinet presented himself at Tours, where he encountered the lethargy of Crémieux and the delegation of the GND. On 7 October, however, the news of Gambetta's dramatic escape from Paris by balloon electrified Tours. Now the defence would be pursued energetically by a man whose magnetism and leadership impressed all whom he met. Freycinet made sure to secure a personal interview with Gambetta, who acknowledged that the engineer would better serve the national defence in Tours than in Montauban. Gambetta, too, was building the infrastructure of his power as he went, and he needed a right-hand man whom he could trust. He authorized Freycinet to execute operations in the Ministry of War in Gambetta's name, using the title of Delegate. The decree was signed on 11 October and published the next day.

Gambetta and Freycinet continued the work of mobilizing men across unoccupied France. Even with half a million casualties and prisoners from the Army of the Rhine and the Army of Châlons, and 260,000 men defending Paris, France could theoretically deploy over a million men to defend the country. Over the course of the autumn, in a series of decrees, the GND called up an ever-expanding roster of men to serve in either the regular army or in a branch of the National Guard. In addition, the Foreign Legion, previously forbidden by law from serving in metropole France, came from its posting in Algeria. Furthermore, some 350 units of *francs-tireurs*, comprising 60,000 men, volunteered their service.

The regular army expanded to include the classes of 1869 and 1870 (called up one year early) as well as reservists and voluntary enlistments. Between September and January, the GND fielded twelve army corps, an astonishing feat given the circumstances. The quality of these corps, however, varied considerably. The first new corps enrolled after Sedan, the XV and XVI, were formed from the remnants of the regular army, which helps account for their successes around Orléans. The subsequent corps had less training, fewer leaders and sporadic supplies.

The National Guard was raised and equipped by the Ministry of the Interior via the prefects. It was divided into the Sedentary or fixed guard, intended to stay in their locality, which could include men up to the age of sixty, and the mobilized guard that was subject to incorporation into an active campaign and training by the Ministry of War.

On 2 November, the GND made its most sweeping decree yet. It allowed for the possible call-up of all men between the ages of twenty-one and forty, regardless of family status, into the *Garde nationale mobilisée* – that is, to serve alongside the active soldiers, not just as the fixed guard. According to the historian Stéphane Audoin-Rouzeau, 'The principle of universal and obligatory conscription, of the nation in arms, was thus in force.'[15] In theory only those who were infirm or held specific public roles could be exempted.

In practice, however, only men without families aged twenty-one to forty were actually called up; the French lacked the equipment and training capacity to call up all the men who were liable to serve, and even this call-up was not fully realized. Of the 649,000 possible recruits, only 579,000 were actually available (twenty-three departments were occupied and could not send all of their men), fewer than 500,000 were actually remitted to the military authorities, and only 260,000 could be incorporated into their campaign formations before the war ended. Despite the authorization of 2 November, the GND never actually called up married men due to lack of equipment. The war was fought by the young, the single and the childless.

These men fought well and learned as they gained experience. Their success was limited, however, due to the insufficient number of officers to lead them, including a lack of drill officers. Between 4 August and 2 September, out of 158 generals, 16 had been killed and 45 wounded – 38.6 per cent of the total.

To address the leadership gap, Freycinet borrowed a page from the Federal Army during the United States Civil War: he doubled the size of infantry companies, which cut in half the number of officers needed to lead them. A decree of 13 October removed restrictions on promotion, and one from 14 October allowed all soldiers not belonging to the regular army to be grouped together in an auxiliary army attached to the regular army and called the Army of National Defence. This was an important step because it meant that the obligation to defend French territory fell not just on active soldiers. Furthermore, this move allowed the *mobiles*, the *mobilisées*, the *francs-tireurs* and even foreign legionnaires to be appointed to any rank. The Italian Giuseppe Garibaldi and naval officer Admiral Jauréguiberry owed their army commissions to this decree.

Despite these efforts, sometimes the urgency led untrained men – men literally without a day of training – to be sent into battle. Local boys called up to serve found it difficult to adapt to army discipline with their boyhood homes within reach. 'To become soldiers,' wrote the prefect of the Hautes-Pyrénées, 'our Pyrenean *mobiles* need to lose sight of their village steeple.'[16]

The support of these hundreds of thousands of new soldiers required a vast secondary mobilization, all of which was overseen by Freycinet. He faced extraordinary challenges. The Ministry of

War remained disorganized, with only a quarter of its peacetime personnel and no documents in Tours. But Freycinet's precision and detail made him a remarkable administrator. He understood better than the professional soldiers the importance of civilians – scientists, engineers, telegraph operators, doctors, businessmen, architects – to the success of the operation.

Among his first actions, Freycinet ensured that his officers had high-quality maps, and hired civilians to support military doctors, engineers, intendants and back office functions. He gave greater autonomy to the *Intendance* as they sought to supply a new army and diversified the manufacture of key supplies, including of *capsules* for Chassepots. They had been under the manufacture of just one man in Bourges. As the enemy approached Orléans, the manufacture moved to Toulouse and Freycinet charged others to create additional factories in Bayonne, Bordeaux and Toulon. Freycinet furthermore founded eleven new regional military camps for the instruction and concentration of the mobilized National Guard, from Montpellier to Saint-Omer.

Women's combat service in these armies was not considered, although some women did nevertheless manage to serve. Their role in the army as suppliers, called *vivandières*, had been long established. Since the late 1600s, the French state had officially licensed soldiers to serve as *vivandiers*, and their wives often did the work of seeking food, tobacco and alcohol while their husbands were on the march or in combat. They remained essential to the French armies of Louis XIV in the Netherlands, to the expansive Revolutionary and Napoleonic Wars – when they gained the right to hold contracts with the army in their own names, not just that of their husbands, and were increasingly called *cantinières* – and to France's empire-building conquest of Algeria. They travelled to Italy under Napoleon III and continued their service through the entirety of the Franco-Prussian War. *Cantinières* were not officially considered to be soldiers and did not have the right to a soldier's pension. Yet they experienced war alongside regular soldiers, whether in battle at Gravelotte, besieged in Metz, captured after Sedan, or serving in the new armies raised by the Government of National Defence. They tended to the wounded, brought desperately needed supplies, and sometimes fought. They were killed, wounded and captured.

Nevertheless, some individual women did fight alongside men, just as they had in the American Civil War and throughout French history. A Parisian woman named Victorine Rouchy reported, 'Several days later a grand revue took place on the Esplanade of the Invalides; I was invited and presented officially to the 17th battalion and to the 7th company, of which I was part at the time. That's how I obtained a combat post.'[17]

On 10 October, the journalist Félix Belly proposed the foundation of uniformed, armed companies of women, which he dubbed the 'Amazones de la Seine', as part of the Sedentary National Guard. Like male members of the Sedentary National Guard, they would be paid 1.50 francs daily and have no combat role. An American observer, Nathan Sheppard, reported that Belly received fifteen thousand applications, while Belly himself later said the number was fifteen hundred. The interested women tended to be *femmes du peuple*, cooks, laundresses, some shop workers and seamstresses, women accustomed to hard work, strong and older (said to be at least twenty-five). In any case, the government had no intention of creating this battalion, and the project came to an end, an object of derision or curiosity.

One woman's soldiering life was celebrated and reported above all others. Antoinette 'Tony' Lix was born in Colmar in 1839. Throughout her life, Lix combined the qualities associated with femininity with the ability to fight when necessary. She was raised by her father, who supported education for girls and taught his daughter how to use a rifle by the age of ten. Yet Lix also learned to care for others. She spent six years in Poland as a governess and tutor. When the Polish insurrection against Russia broke out in 1863, Lix joined the fight disguised as a man. Her experiences in Poland encouraged her support for freedom and, as she wrote, 'developed in me a powerful and strong love [for France]'.[18] She returned to her native country in the late 1860s, where she immediately began caring for victims of the cholera outbreak in Lille and founded a Société des dames de charité in the Vosges. During the Franco-Prussian War, Lix became part of a group of *francs-tireurs* from the Vosges and later served as a nurse.

For Giuseppe Garibaldi, hero of the Italian Risorgimento, the conflict now took a new dimension: the fight for the universal republic against the forces of monarchism and clericalism. It was bigger than the ambitions of Napoleon III and Bismarck. War had driven Austria and the Pope from Italy – and the continuation of this epic struggle would lead to the liberation of all peoples from feudalism.

Garibaldi arrived in Tours in October to offer his aid to the GND; he was sent to the Vosges to organize irregular soldiers in that region. By mid-November, he and his forces began co-ordinated raids that created enough trouble to distract the Germans and divert resources. Garibaldi's extravagantly uniformed men knew the local geography and, armed with occasional artillery pieces, managed to harass outposts and supply columns, blow up bridges and even send three locomotives into the Meuse.

In response, the Germans took civilians hostage and charged contributions. They sent columns of lumbering *Landwehr* after the partisans, to little avail. Eventually, 18,000 men served under Garibaldi and another 20,000 reported to local committees of public safety in the Côte d'Or. The Garibaldians at Dijon – that is, *francs-tireurs* under Garibaldi and his two sons, Menotti and Ricciotti – were seen to be more menacing and professional than the French *francs-tireurs* due to their experience in the wars of Italian unification. Their defence of Dijon earned the respect of the German commander, who granted amnesty, did not issue reprisals and demanded only a damage deposit of 500,000 francs, to be returned if the inhabitants of Dijon behaved well.

Gambetta's strategy, in the words of the author George Sand, boiled down to a faith in civilian authority. 'The regular army is destroyed, demoralized, lost; it will not save us. It's the *civilian element* that will bring us victory, it is the improvised citizen-soldier that we must summon and encourage.'[19]

Sand deeply distrusted this strategy. 'You can improvise soldiers in a threatened location and mobilize them to a certain degree', but to make them carry the burden of an entire campaign was 'a dream, and experience has already proved it'.[20] A new insurgency along the lines of the Vendée region against the Revolutionary Terror could not stop the Prussian army. 'Can willpower give us cannon?'[21] Sand reported that Gambetta was known to be a remarkable orator, a man of action, will and perseverance. Some saw in Gambetta the man who could save France. 'But isn't the task beyond the strength of a single man?' asked Sand. 'And could this young man know about warfare, which is, they say, a science that is lost upon us?'[22]

The political landscape proved challenging as well. Would the republic really be able to buy enough time in the provinces? In many localities, it was not difficult to mobilize reservists and recruits; they had got the harvest in and they recognized the value of being fed by the army in the winter. In the Aude, republican army recruits sang for Marianne, the personification of the Republic, as they marched:

Boulen la Marianne,	We want Marianne,
La boulen, mai l'ouren,	We want her and soon'll have her,
Gambetta lou borgne	The one-eyed Gambetta
Sara lou presiden	Will be our president[23]

In other areas, the departure of troops became the occasion for demonstrations and had the effect of alienating the country from the GND. In the Creuse, George Sand reported despair at the calling up of the mobilized National Guard on 12 October. Family members cried in the streets to see their loved ones go. The physical examination was an abomination, she said, in which men with physical infirmities, who were blind in one eye or who suffered from skin diseases or mental illness were deemed good for service.

Sand was not optimistic about the success of an army composed of such men.

In this, the Prussian crown prince agreed. He thought little of the French plans to mobilize its citizens:

> I shudder to think how so many unlucky Gardes Mobiles and Gardes Nationales must meet our well-drilled, triumphant troops. No doubt a good proportion of them are moved by patriotic enthusiasm, but that does not make them into trained soldiers; rather they will become the useless tools of the obstinate and deluded politicians who sit round a table making resolutions, without ever coming within sight of war, and drive these hordes to the place of slaughter.[24]

The Germans were ideologically opposed to the *levée en masse*: it refused to accept the French defeat at Sedan in conventional warfare; it engaged in activities deemed treacherous – ambush, street-fighting, sharp-shooting, sometimes with female participants; and it was associated with republicanism and Parisian revolution.

The tension between military authorities and the faith placed in the *mobiles* played out in Sand's characterization of the war of words in the press:

> 'The *mobiles* are brave.'
> 'No, the *mobiles* weaken everywhere.'
> 'But no, it's the regular troops who waver.'
> 'No, I tell you, they are the ones who hold on!'[25]

Not surprisingly, Gambetta and Freycinet, two civilians placing France's future in the hands of untrained men, grated on the professional military that they now led. General d'Aurelle de Paladines chafed at Freycinet's leadership: 'He was to offend [the Army] daily by his harshness, his demeanor, his haughty words, and his complete ignorance of hierarchical principles which he had anyhow determined to tread under foot.'[26] Yet these same senior officers had led France to the disasters of the early part of the war. Senior officers therefore were compelled to obey Gambetta and his trusted administrator, even when they issued orders that long-serving generals opposed.

The Loire flows from the Cévennes to the Atlantic along an expansive curve that forms a natural line of defence. It runs north-west for some 300 miles before it reaches Orléans, the city at its northernmost point, 70 miles south of Paris. The river then bends south-west to Tours and from there expands west toward the Bay of Biscay on the Atlantic. If not for the political importance of Paris, it would be obvious from a purely military perspective that French armies should pull behind the Loire if their initial defences have failed.

Instead, Gambetta and Freycinet took it on faith that the outcome of the war depended upon the relief of Paris and, more crudely, upon the food supply in Paris. Nobody in Tours ever seriously questioned this strategic focus. It seemed obvious that the strategy was to march on the capital as directly and quickly as possible. All of the armies raised were intended for this purpose.

The strategy depended on the numerical superiority of poorly trained men and irregular forces. By late autumn, hundreds of thousands of men concentrated in a vast arc beyond the reach of Moltke's forces: in the Loire valley, in the north around Lille, and in the east in the Vosges. Throughout the autumn and winter, Gambetta and Freycinet urged breakouts from Paris that would be supported by offensives in the provinces intended to distract and wear down the Germans and possibly come to the aid of the Parisians. Just maybe, they believed, the republic could stall long enough to wear down the overstretched Germans and force them to negotiate a peace that did not involve the loss of territory.

With Paris as the focus of the French efforts, the GND lost the element of surprise. The moments of uncertainty about the location of the enemy army that characterized the early stages of the war now faded away. It was quite clear to everyone that the Germans surrounded Paris and that the French would direct their efforts toward the relief of the city through the victory of regular soldiers in a few great battles near the capital. The GND might have fared better by focusing on the German supply lines, but this strategy was pursued too late. Yet it would have been equally fraught to abandon Paris.

Tours itself was not a great choice as a second capital. True, it had good railroad connections and was protected by the Loire. But it did not have any particular military value and accordingly had not been fortified prior to the war. The French armies of the Loire therefore had to stay close at hand to protect the government, instead of pursuing the Germans.

While the Germans continued the slow work of besieging Paris, Moltke also contended with the provincial relief armies. North of Orléans, the French XV Corps was coalescing under General de la Motte-Rouge and started moving forward on 5 October. Moltke had to address this threat, even though it was not quite clear what XV Corps was doing. In early October, he sent General Ludwig von der Tann with his Bavarian I Corps, a Prussian division of XI Corps and a few Prussian cavalry divisions from Paris toward Orléans to push back any French. If the new armies could not come to fruition, the Germans might be able to persuade France to surrender.

Tann's Bavarians did not have a great reputation. They had seen little action except at Bazeilles, and Tann himself was considered to be too cautious. Nevertheless, Tann attacked on 10 October with 28,000 men. After a day of non-stop gunfire against French troops who had not eaten for two days, the Germans advanced into Orléans at midnight on the 11th. Tann ordered the city to pay an indemnity of 1.5 million francs.

Dietrich von Lassberg participated in the fighting around Orléans and wore his Iron Cross as he marched in victory into the city, proud that his Bavarians were the first Germans in Orléans. He wondered what the French inhabitants made of Germans soldiers singing 'Die Wacht am Rhein' at the foot of the statue of Joan of Arc. 'It was such a beautiful moment that cannot be described; you have to have been there to understand it.'[27] A moment of peace, of comradely celebration, of German unity? Lassberg does not say. In Versailles, the crown prince was pleased to hear that 'the Bavarian Infantry fought very well, when they were in close touch with ours.'[28]

Gambetta was furious and wanted La Motte-Rouge court-martialled. He was persuaded against this, but nevertheless replaced the general with Louis d'Aurelle de Paladines. Aurelle de Paladines had most recently served as the commandant in Marseilles but had been forced out and fled the city under pressure from republican crowds. Just a month after the fall of the Second Empire, the new Government of National Defence had experienced its first major setback.

11. *Choices*

In the late morning of 18 October, Prussian cavalry advanced north-west on the route d'Orléans toward Châteaudun, a small city of some 7,000 inhabitants. Soon to follow came 12,000 Prussians with 24 cannon. By noon, the Germans had met fierce resistance in Châteaudun from *francs-tireurs*, members of the National Guard and *mobiles*. Combat continued through the afternoon as shells and incendiary bombs landed on the city. The fighting centred on the square in front of the Hôtel de Ville, where the mayor and municipal councillors spent the day putting out fires.

As night fell, much of the city burned from the day's bombardment. Frustrated by the day's combat, the Germans set fire to the rest. They engaged in brutal house-to-house combat similar to that seen in Bazeilles six weeks earlier. The fighting lasted until 3 a.m. when the Prussians took the final remaining houses and occupied the Hôtel de Ville. In the days that followed, Châteaudun and its people were required to provide cash payments and hostages as retribution and to guard against further resistance.

Châteaudun became an emblem of the tragedy of resistance and a warning to other towns. Throughout the autumn, more and more French civilians had to grapple with Germans in their homes, farms and towns. The Germans had no truck with resistance, especially if civilians were involved. Yet there was no agreement on how French civilians should interact with German soldiers, or how they might prepare for this encounter. Mayors and civic leaders had to manage their local National Guard and partisan *francs-tireurs*, while placating the invading Germans in an ever-changing landscape of war.

The catastrophe at Sedan, coupled with the declaration of a new republic and the vastly extended scope of the German presence in

France, shifted the terms of civilian engagement with the war. Many came into contact with the invasion and occupation for the first time.

By the end of October, German forces had extended into the Oise, all of the Seine-et-Oise, the western edges of the Eure and most of the Eure-et-Loir. They had taken Orléans and were close to Besançon and Belfort. More than twenty departments were occupied, either entirely or in part. Eventually, 'like an oil stain', all or part of thirty departments came under German control, covering a third of French territory.[1] Perhaps a quarter of the population saw German troops marching through their towns and villages during the autumn and winter of 1870–71.

The Prussians created General Governments based in Alsace-Lorraine, Lorraine (Nancy), Rheims and Versailles. In Alsace-Lorraine, the General Government was intended to prepare for annexation and to assure security and administration in the other three areas, using French functionaries at times, too. Lieutenant General Friedrich Alexander von Bismarck-Bohlen, a distant relative of the minister-president, oversaw the General Government in Alsace-Lorraine. Even as the war continued, he installed Prussian administrative personnel, implemented new structures of *arrondissements* and municipalities, introduced the Prussian penal code and recruited a judiciary to enforce it, installed new scholarly rectors and academic leadership, and closed French-language newspapers.

German-occupied territories lost touch with the rest of France. The mayor of a small town in Seine-et-Marne complained at the end of December that 'the population remains in ignorance of the decrees and the order of the government that do not reach them.'[2] In November, a clergyman in a small commune in Eure-et-Loir wrote, 'Each commune is a prison that nothing enters, from which nothing leaves, without the permission of the Prussians.'[3]

The German presence in a given locality was not always so stark or permanent. Moltke did not have enough soldiers to leave a thick presence in all the towns and villages of France. Germans might enter a town and stay for a few days, then move on, leaving the town to recover until the next wave passed through.

The areas of German presence were therefore discontinuous and often scattered, especially at the margins where Germans gathered requisitions to send back to the soldiers encircling Paris. Until the armistice in January, there was no fixed or firm border between occupied and unoccupied France. It was porous and malleable, more like a shape-shifting dotted line.

Rumours and uncertainty intensified as the autumn wore on. It was very difficult for anybody to have good information about anything, and wishful thinking or deepest fears drove misinformation. From Nohant, George Sand recorded the hopes of local villagers: 'One day we have killed in one fell swoop three hundred thousand Prussians; another time, the king of Prussia has been taken prisoner.'[4]

The summer of 1870 had already been one of heat, disease (including the illness of Sand's own son and two grandchildren), wildfires, wolves and storms. As the invasion continued, Sand felt a numbness and inability to peer into the future: 'We fall into the unknown, we enter into the phase of days without a day after; we have the feeling of those condemned to death who aimlessly await the day of execution, and who are ready to get it over with because they are no longer interested in anything.'[5]

Yet for Sand, the war remained a distant shadow, almost unbelievable, as her account of waking up in the countryside in mid-September attests. 'As I open my windows,' she wrote,

> breathing in the freshness of the morning and the profound silence of a countryside still basically quiet, I ask myself if all that I have suffered for the last six weeks is not a dream. Could it be that this blue morning, this renewed verdure after a torrid summer, these pink clouds that climb in the sky, these rays of gold that pierce the branches, could be the dawn of a day happy and pure? Is it possible that the heroes of our battlefields suffer a thousand deaths at this moment, and that Paris perhaps already hears the growl of the

> German cannon around its walls? No, it can't be. I have had a nightmare, a fever has unchained its phantoms upon me, it has broken me. I get up, all is as before. The grape-pickers pass by, the cocks crow, the sun extends its carpets of light across the grass, children laugh along the pathway. – Horror! Here are the wounded coming back, conscripts who depart: woe is me, I did not dream!'[6]

For many civilians, however, the nightmare of war now arrived unambiguously on their doorstep. Without clear guidance from the government or the military and little practical knowledge, they improvised strategies for survival. While much of France had been occupied following the Napoleonic Wars, that period lay too far in the past for most French to remember. For most in 1870, the experience of occupation was new and unexpected, and was accompanied by violence believed to be out of proportion with nineteenth-century norms. While most encounters between civilians and German soldiers were brief and peaceful, the undercurrent of physical threat and the actual use of violence became mutually scarring and demoralizing during that rainy and cold autumn. Individuals and families had to make decisions about their strategies for survival. Yet many sought ways to serve their fellow citizens and to slough off the burden of victimhood through salutary volunteerism. Women and men took action to help their fellow citizens in this time of dire need.

Men who were not conscripted had to choose whether or not to fight. For all the men called up to serve in the army, a large contingent of older or married men remained at home in their farms, villages and communities. They could volunteer for the National Guard or, if they had experience as riflemen, they could join a unit of the *francs-tireurs*.

Print media predominantly encouraged men to join the fight. The editors of *L'Avenir National* urged every man to fight 'for his life, for his hearth, for his wife, for his children'.[7] General Auguste Ducrot, second-in-command during the siege of Paris, directed weary soldiers to think about 'your ruined families, your sisters, your wives, your desolate mothers!' for inspiration.[8] In drawings in the illustrated magazine *Le Charivari*, caricaturist Cham (Count Amédée-Charles Henri de Noé) portrayed women shaming their husbands and boyfriends into joining. In one sketch, a bourgeois woman chides her dandified friend:

> 'Arthur! How are you, *ma chère*?'
> 'What do you mean, *ma chère*? Aren't I a man?'
> 'No, or else you'd be at the front.'[9]

Despite these exhortations, the decision to fight was not easy. If men went to battle, they left their families without protection and without their major source of income. George Sand's son Maurice did not join the republican army because he dreaded leaving his wife, children and mother to the Prussians. When the Vineuil family of the Oise saw a group of refugees passing, young Robert believed the men were cowards for fleeing in front of the Prussians. His older sister Berthe disagreed; she responded to Robert, 'if you had a wife and children, maybe you would also flee to save them.'[10] Either way, women were cast in the role of passive victims in need of protection.

Families furthermore had to decide whether women, children and the elderly would be best protected at home or away from battle zones. As the Prussian army swept into France, and increasingly larger areas were occupied or under threat of attack, refugees fled in front of the advancing troops. More and more, as the Germans approached Paris, they found that villages had been abandoned with the animals gone and wells blocked. It was not easy to become a refugee. Berthe related to her brother André her encounter with a young woman from a village outside Bar-le-Duc:

> Her child had been born six weeks before, in one of the carts; she does not know what has become of her husband. He did not want

> to leave their little house, but he insisted that she depart with the neighbours. Since then, she has not had any word from him, and since he was not the type to let anyone take his property without defending it, she imagines that he must have been shot.[11]

Despair and insecurity were unfortunately the fate of many women touched by the war.

Women on the road felt isolated and at risk more than usual during the war. George Sand related the fears of her travelling companion Léonie about their trip from Nohant (Indre) to Saint-Loup (Creuse), undertaken to protect Sand's grandchildren from a smallpox outbreak. Léonie confided, 'Nowadays [during the war] you have black ideas that you never had before. You imagine that every man who appears must be a spy who is planning our ruin.' Sand agreed that she too had had those thoughts during their journeys through evening fog.[12] Madame de Vineuil's sister, Madame de Thieulin, fled her chateau in Eure-et-Loir with her husband. On the road, Prussian soldiers stopped their carriage and accompanied them on part of their trip. Despite Madame de Thieulin's fears that 'they would condemn us to the shadows', the travellers arrived at their destination unharmed.[13]

In the wealthy and respectable Vineuil family, Monsieur and Madame decided that Monsieur would join his oldest son, engineer Maurice, in Paris to work on building fortifications. Younger son André served as a soldier, while Madame and Berthe remained at home with *les petits*. When Berthe questioned this decision, her father responded, 'Paris will probably be under siege. We would rather not choose a besieged city to enclose women and children.'[14] Berthe did not ask further.

Seventeen-year-old Lucille Le Verrier, whose brothers and father took part in the National Guard before Sedan, believed the gender divide unfair, but resigned herself to it. She found it 'distressing to only be a woman, to be unable to spill our blood like men . . . to take our part in the great national trial. We are left to suffer in our hearts.'[15] Le Verrier quickly internalized the expectation that she should be a mother. She wrote to her friend, 'I am happy to be so young: I will see Prussia crushed in its turn, and perhaps by us, for this generation of young girls will inspire in their children a hatred and a terrible desire for revenge.'[16] Both Berthe de Vineuil and Le Verrier learned, through the war experience, the proscribed and prescribed roles for upper-class women.

Civilian women also performed extraordinary acts of daring. Stories of women helping men across enemy territory or delivering precious letters abound. A rumour spread about a young woman who disguised herself as a peasant in order to sneak into Paris on foot to smuggle in letters. The Vineuil family secretly supplied a French soldier with food while also quartering Prussians.

The story of twenty-two-year-old Juliette Dodu epitomized female courage during the war. At the outbreak of war, Dodu lived with her widowed mother in Pithiviers (Loiret), where she worked at the Bureau des Postes et Télégraphes. When the Prussians cut the telegraph lines, Dodu re-established contact with Orléans, sending the French intercepted Prussian messages that warned the French army of an attack. Dodu was eventually caught and condemned to death by the Prussians but was saved when the war ended.

Dodu, a young, single woman working in a white-collar job who put her skills to use in a particularly daring and proactive manner, may not have been a typical French woman, but she was certainly appreciated. In honour of her service, Dodu received a military medal in 1877, and the *Croix de Chevalier de la Légion d'honneur* in 1878. During the extreme circumstances of war, women showed themselves capable of daring and skill. In many ways, women proved 'in hospitals, in workshops, in *cantines*', as Hermione Quinet wrote, 'that one can contribute to defence in ways other than carrying a rifle'.[17]

Many women and men stayed put, whether to defend and protect their homes and farms, out of a commitment to places and communities, or due to a lack of resources and no alternatives.

Those who stayed faced difficult choices when the Germans

came to town. The Germans expected no resistance, and compliance with their demands for requisitions. The French had to weigh up whether armed resistance – in the form of the National Guard or partisan *francs-tireurs* – was worth the cost of retributions. Beyond the question of whether or not to fight, they had to determine what preparations to undertake once the Germans entered their area. Finally, they navigated endless demands for requisitions.

The Empire had not given local authorities guidance on how to deal with these questions – one of its many omissions. Gambetta issued orders on 6–7 September that enjoined prefects to organize the defence of their departments against the invasion through local defence committees, including the mobilization of firefighters, the National Guard, forest officials and customs agents. Then, on 14 October, Gambetta issued a 'state of war' decree for all areas within 60 miles of the enemy. In those areas, military committees could set up roadblocks, demolish buildings, or build fieldworks. They could remove crops and livestock – either sending the animals out of the area or destroying them with the promise to repay the owners later. Those who could not fight could be evacuated. Local notables, including mayors, priests and schoolteachers, were empowered to help carry out these orders.

In all of these determinations, male civilian leaders – prefects, mayors, municipal councillors – played key roles. They were the intermediaries between civilians and both the German invaders and the many branches of the French army, and thus trod a careful line between reining in civilian resistance that might trigger disproportionate retributions and appearing overly accommodating to the invading army. Their tools were limited to their abilities to proclaim, persuade and cajole, to negotiate and communicate.

In addition, ordinary civilian men and women who did not hold political office organized efforts to mitigate the war's damage. Priests, schoolteachers, journalists and women of means worked with energy and creativity. While women were excluded from holding office and from most professions, they nevertheless created opportunities to serve.

For both men and women, service in the war effort tended to be framed as mitigation of the damage of war, rather than as action that would lead to a French victory. They couched their work as helping the unfortunate victims of war. As for themselves, they tried to avoid the label of victim, and instead they shifted it onto others.

As mayors anticipated the approach of German forces, the distinction between the French National Guard and the *francs-tireurs* became a matter of life and death. The National Guard was raised and equipped by the Ministry of the Interior via the prefects. The sedentary arm of the National Guard was intended to stay in its locality and could include men up to the age of sixty. The Germans acknowledged the National Guard as an official, uniformed branch of the French armed services, and recognized its right to defend towns and to enjoy the respect accorded to honourable soldiers.

The *francs-tireurs*, composed of experienced riflemen who operated as guerrilla fighters, were a different matter altogether. The *francs-tireurs* gained an outsized reputation from the events of 1870–71, despite – or perhaps because of – their ambiguous role in the French army. They were not a new phenomenon. Partisan warfare had been extensive against Napoleon I, including for and against the Prussian army during the Wars of Liberation. Prussia also had experience fighting small numbers of partisans in 1866 (in Bohemia, Moravia and Upper Silesia).

In 1870, however, Prussia did not expect partisan warfare because it was assumed the war would be over quickly and peace swiftly negotiated. The Second Empire, wary of arming civilians who might be hostile to the empire, did not draw on guerrilla fighters as part of the French strategy. After Sedan, however, the GND authorized the creation of *francs-tireurs* units, paid by the Ministry of War. By the war's end there were 300 units with 57,600 men, including foreigners and, occasionally, women, often with outlandish uniforms, hats and jackets, or no uniform at all. In Strasbourg, seventy-year-old Frédéric Piton tried to enlist in an early, makeshift unit but found to his disappointment that the others were 'young men unknown to me who were mostly interested in the question of Tyrolean hats and armbands with hunting horns'.[18] Piton left discouraged, without signing up.

Yet after the initial flush of excitement surrounding the formation of *franc-tireur* units, by 11 September the GND clearly focused its efforts elsewhere. The *francs-tireurs* were dwarfed by the regulars, the *mobiles* and the National Guard. Gambetta wanted organized, uniformed soldiers in his republican armies, and therefore progressively incorporated the *francs-tireurs* into the regular military organization. By 29 September, they were subject to the same discipline as the *mobiles*. Then, on 14 October, they were incorporated into the auxiliary army, which was fused to the regular army. On 4 November, *franc-tireur* units were attached to various army corps or to military divisions, and so followed regular military authority. In mid-January, Gambetta discontinued the formation of any new corps, and they were dissolved shortly after the armistice.

From the outset, the Germans made their opposition to the *francs-tireurs* clear. Despite their official authorization by the French GND, the Germans viewed these units as unlawful guerrilla fighters who could be treated without mercy. Furthermore, according to the Germans, the presence of *francs-tireurs* could lead to retributions against entire towns, which would be assumed to be abetting their activities. Not only that, but the Germans also considered any individual sharpshooter to fall into the same category as the loosely organized *francs-tireurs*.

The Germans' view of *francs-tireurs* reflected a fundamental difference in their assessment of civilian engagement in war. By contrast to the French admiration for the *levée en masse*, the Prussians expected the French to uphold a rigid distinction between civilians and soldiers. An invasion can be resisted by uniformed soldiers, but not by armed civilians. Once the Germans rode into a town, the invasion swiftly became occupation, which should be accepted by a pacified population. The Germans did not distinguish between individual snipers and recognized units of partisans – both were outlaws. An 1867 Prussian decree had established the death penalty as a response to armed civilians. In instructions issued on 25 July 1870, the Prussians claimed occupation as soon as their army was present, even prior to the establishment of an effective administration. On 12 September the governor general of Alsace-Lorraine, Bismarck-Bohlen, reasserted these proscriptions on civilian resistance.

Moltke expressed his disdain for this strategy in a letter to his brother from late October:

> The [Republican] government still tries, by means of lying reports and patriotic phrases, to rouse the unfortunate population of the provinces to a new resistance, to put down which will entail the destruction of whole towns. Then, too, the nagging of the *francs-tireurs* has to be paid for by bloody reprisals, and the war puts on a more violent character. It is bad enough that armies have sometimes to be set to butcher one another; there is no necessity for setting whole nations against each other – that is not progress, but rather a return to barbarism. How little can even the *levée en masse* of a nation, even so brave as this one, do against a never so small but well-trained division of troops![19]

Moltke saw the National Guard as legitimate and the *francs-tireurs* as illegitimate barbarians who could be summarily shot and who brought punishment to the surrounding community.

On 22 September, General von der Tann, commander of the I Bavarian Corps, posted the following notice in the Seine-et-Oise:

> Because several murders have been committed by *francs-tireurs* who are living in the woods, I order the following: 1) Every individual found inside the woods or in the thicket must be regarded as a *franc-tireur*. 2) High contributions shall be imposed on those communities that have not denounced the presence of such individuals within their territory. 3) In certain cases, municipal authorities shall be condemned.[20]

Tann believed that *francs-tireurs* lurked behind every tree, and his proclamation reflected and codified the culture of suspicion among the German troops. Bavarian soldiers now confiscated all firearms, even if they were antiques. In retaliation for partisan warfare, they took hostages, burned houses and shot civilians, sometimes following formal courts martial, and sometimes without trial. On the night of 7–8 October, for example, the town of Ablis, near Orléans, was razed and its male inhabitants killed in reprisal for an attack by *francs-tireurs*.

The fear and hatred aroused by *francs-tireurs* far outstripped the numbers of Germans they actually killed: about a thousand soldiers by the end of the war, less than 4 per cent of the German total who died of combat wounds. It was the months on constant alert, the fear of possibly being shot from afar, the isolation of the rear guards being harassed that created the outsized hatred of the *franc-tireur*. The cutting of a telegraph wire was easy to do and hard to interpret: an isolated villager or an approaching army? The uncertainty heightened German anxieties. Compounding the issue, more and more German civilians were active in France as railroad workers – 3,500 by the war's end – and not surprisingly, they were distressed when shot at by other civilians.

Retribution could come swiftly. During his visit to Sedan in November, a British observer named J. W. McMichael reported:

> As we were dressing, we saw a melancholy procession pass under our window. Ten or twelve country waggons, without springs, were bringing into the Ambulance [mobile field hospital] about eighty poor fellows who had just been wounded in an engagement with francs-tireurs, some few miles from Sedan. Lying in the straw and jolting over the stones, they presented a sight sickening to behold. A detachment of Prussian Infantry, preceded by Uhlans, left shortly afterwards in pursuit of the francs-tireurs, and my friend suggested that we should follow them, but we mutually agreed that 'discretion was the better part of valour.'[21]

It was also said – by a French account – that *francs-tireurs* along the Seine not far from Troyes had killed wounded enemy soldiers whom they had captured, and thrown their bodies into the Seine – in blatant disregard for the Geneva Convention. As a reprisal, the Germans burned several hundred buildings and homes in the neighbouring villages of Conflans-sur-Seine and of Marcilly-sur-Seine. Inhabitants of Marcilly just barely escaped being burned alive in the church.

The *francs-tireurs* undertook sabotage by attacking convoys or pulling up rails. They did not have the co-ordination, nor the explosives, to inflict major damage on bridges and tunnels, but some units helped with tactical reconnaissance, intelligence, or the harassment of enemy outposts. German calvary raids damaged as many bridges and viaducts as did French partisans – sixty-eight in total, half damaged by each side, at a total cost of 33 million francs. German soldiers tended to blame partisans for all disrupted train service and supply shortages, though much of the blame rested on the jams caused by single tracks without enough sidings and ramps.

Around Orléans, *francs-tireurs* not only cut telegraph lines but transposed them, so that messages went randomly to unpredictable locations and the source of the problem could not be easily identified. *Franc-tireur* units were less active along the main lines of the German communications, where the Germans could swiftly retaliate, and local authorities were quick to discourage such action. On the margins of the German occupation, with fewer patrols – in the Vosges mountains, along the further reaches of the Oise and the Seine – the *francs-tireurs* operated regularly. To counter these actions and protect supplies and communication lines, Moltke had to employ some 105,000 troops.

To avoid retaliation, most civilians wanted nothing to do with guerrilla warfare and sought to co-operate with the German invaders. In the Ardennes, peasants who had tried to resist saw their villages burned, and this example dissuaded others. When news of the burning of other villages arrived, many peasants turned in their arms to the local authorities. Most French people wanted to harvest their crops, tend to their animals and protect their families. They wanted to survive the war and longed for peace. Across towns and villages, local leaders posted proclamations urging citizens to stay calm and resist the temptation to rise up against the Germans. Mayors often sought to disarm and rein in anyone who wanted to cause trouble. In addition, mayors tended to disarm the National Guard as German troops arrived. Why bother destroying a bridge if the Prussians could just march to the next one? Such sabotage only harmed the local inhabitants. The subprefect of the Andelys tried to dissuade *francs-tireurs* from acting; the death of a half-dozen Prussians did not compensate for the burning of a village.

In Pontoise (Seine-et-Oise), inhabitants feared that the presence of *mobiles* in their town would lead to reprisals, and so they encouraged soldiers to leave. In Nogent-sur-Seine, as in other locations, the inhabitants were eager to prevent trouble by welcoming the Uhlans. The postal director in the Aube wrote with despair on 13 September that some inhabitants offered the Uhlans the 'best of their fruits, sweets, wine and eau de vie'.[22] In town after town, the same scenes were repeated: the parade of peasants bringing cartloads of furniture and animals; the transformation of public spaces into depots for cows, supplies and suburban refugees; the hasty displacement of precious items – manuscripts, paintings, furniture – into cellars. Then they awaited the arrival of the German invaders.

Not every locality laid down its arms. In some cases, the National Guard actively resisted the invasion and even left the city walls to meet the invaders: at Epinal (Vosges) in September, at Rouen (Seine-Inférieure) in October. At Boynes (Loiret), they barricaded the approaches of the initial patrols, and in Gisors (Eure) the National Guard pushed back forty Prussians on 7 October.

In other places, the defence became more aggressive. At Saint-Quentin (Aisne) on 8 October, a combined force of National Guardsmen, firemen and *francs-tireurs*, with the encouragement of the prefect and likely with the assistance of local inhabitants, pushed back the Germans at a cost of some fifteen casualties. (In a second German offensive later that month, the inhabitants let the Prussians enter the city.) Other examples occurred in Roan (Vosges), Epernon (Eure-et-Loir), Nogent-sur-Seine (Aube), in which twenty-five inhabitants died, and in Dijon (Côte-d'Or), where the National Guard fought alongside the regulars and the *mobiles*.

The events at Châteaudun on 18 October, then, were not entirely out of keeping with the actions of other towns, but nevertheless came as a shock and a warning. Châteaudun showed how the actions of just one day could have terrible consequences.

Most of the small city and its fortress rested on a peninsular cliff at the edge of the Beauce plateau. The cliff protected approaches from the west and south, and from the north, too. Down a steep plunge from the heights ran the two branches of the Loir, with floodplains in between. Only the *faubourg* Saint-Jean lay in the lower city along the road of the same name, heading north away from the fortress, across the Loir and north toward Brou.

The city was most accessible from the east, on roads from Chartres, Orléans and Angoulême. The central square in the upper city united these three approaches from the north-east, the south-east, and east from the rail station. The straight and symmetrical streets dated from 1723, when the entire city had been reconstructed after a fire. In the middle of the surprisingly large and grand square stood an ornate neo-Renaissance fountain. This fountain, the work of the sculptor Gaullier and inaugurated just ten years earlier, provided the upper town with water pumped up from the Loir, the result of a new water turbine installed among the water mills in 1855. The fountain featured four central round-arch windows and a separate element with Ionic columns in a circle, a little gazebo, supporting a dome atop of which was a phoenix, a symbol of the town's revival after the 1723 fire. The Hôtel de Ville sat on the square's west side.

The events of October were not the first that Châteaudun had seen of the war. Troops had passed through the train station on their way north-east. Sick and wounded soldiers had returned, bringing tales of their battles and of the ineptitude of their leaders. The inhabitants of Châteaudun had organized for them food and a hospital.

Then, in early October, a detachment of 700 *francs-tireurs* rode toward the town. This unit came from a battalion that had departed from Paris on 9 September in a semi-uniform of black trousers, a blue belt and an American cap. Some 1,200 or more volunteers in 8 companies – students, soldiers, artists, workers, veterans and young recruits – had volunteered to fight for France's liberation. Following the egalitarian ethos of the *francs-tireurs*, the soldiers had voted to replace their commander, named Arohnsonn, in favour of Ernest de Lipowski. Moustachioed and dashing, Lipowski was born in Strasbourg in 1843 to a family of Polish origins and had studied at Saint-Cyr.

After marches and counter-marches through the month of September, the *francs-tireurs* arrived in Châteaudun. At first, they received a warm welcome from the municipality. But the loyalties of the mayor, Ernest Lumière, who had been elected to his post on 2 October, lay with the town rather than with the unproven *francs-tireurs*. On 12 October at ten o'clock in the evening, the subprefect of Châteaudun suddenly arrived at the Hôtel de Ville to convey the news that the enemy had taken Orléans and that a detachment of some 600 to 1,000 were heading to Châteaudun that very night. They were only 15 miles away in Tournoisis, suggesting a force of some 12,000 to 15,000 men to come.

At this news, Lipowski proclaimed that, while he was prepared to fight to the bitter end, they should not try to defend the town – they would be overwhelmed – and the commander of two squadrons of hussars agreed. The council declared shortly thereafter that the city would not be defended, to prevent the town from being destroyed and pillaged 'with no gain for the general defence of the country'.[23] This decision was to be transmitted by the subprefect back to the commanders. Meanwhile, the National Guard was asked to return their arms.

The *francs-tireurs* regarded the council's decision as a betrayal.

Lipowski changed his mind and on 13 October committed to fighting to the last extremity and 'completely disavowed the disarmament of the National Guard of Châteaudun'.[24] During the frigid night of the 13th, Lipowski oversaw the construction of barricades throughout the city. The following day, Mayor Lumière called for 'concorde' and declared that the municipality saw its 'duty as refraining from any discussion or justification of its acts that has any aim other than the interests of the city'.[25] The next day, after the prefect criticized the disarmament of the National Guard, the council gave the arms back and the troops returned.

Later accounts of the days leading up to the battle at Châteaudun obsessed over who was where and when, and whether or not they had arms. The mayor carefully explained that he had received no warning or declaration of war from the approaching army, thus positioning the Germans as unlawful aggressors, yet the town had been well aware of the German movements and could prepare ahead of time. Units moved from town to town seeking authorization and claiming legitimacy. Authority, it seems, was up for grabs. Prefects, mayors and municipal councillors had to fend for themselves and make up their own rules. As readily visible fires blazed in Varize and Civry, the people of Châteaudun erected twenty-eight barricades throughout the town. The barricades – if we can believe the 1883 painting by Félix Philippoteaux – consisted of bricks, casks, crates, bundles of sticks and straw. They provided minimal cover against rifles and cannon.

On the morning of 18 October, Châteaudun was defended by some 700 *francs-tireurs* under Lipowski and a company from Nantes, as well as members of the National Guard, *mobiles* from the Loir-et-Cher and from the Gers, and the squadrons of hussars: a total of about 1,200 men all together.

At 11.30, the tocsin sounded, calling soldiers to the barricades. To the east of the town, General Ludwig von Wittich's forces appeared with 12,000 Prussians, 24 cannon and 2 howitzers. Around noon, seven cannon fired at the train station. Combat began. The Prussians wanted control over the rail line and pushed the *francs-tireurs* behind the barricades. Soon, the entire town was encircled by Prussians, and it was impossible to escape.

The bombardment continued throughout the afternoon, from 12.30 to 6.30 p.m., at a rate of some ten projectiles per minute. Cannon positioned in a field east of the train station or south of town could reach targets a mile away, including the far edge of the mossy, turreted chateau walls and several points along rue Saint-Jean heading north-west out of town, a main but narrow road with flat-faced houses packed tight up against each other. Buildings collapsed as they were hit by shells and incendiary bombs.

By evening, the French fell back toward the central square as the Prussians advanced. At some point, Lipowski ordered the retreat of his men from the square: moving toward the north-west, descending the heights, crossing two branches of the Loir and then departing via the Saint-Jean neighbourhood. While accounts agree on this retreat, they differ on the timing. According to Lipowski's own report, he left around 10.30 or 11.00 p.m. Lipowski also noted that the infantry soldiers were 'very young' and 'did not hold' and were liable to 'retreat at the least serious attack'.[26] The National Guard commander, Testanière, placed Lipowski's retreat much earlier, around 6 p.m., well before the National Guard stopped resisting at around 10 p.m. One commentator drily stated of Lipowski's account that 'the author does not explain in a satisfactory manner his premature retreat.'[27]

But the resistance continued. Marie-Julienne Jarrethout, a fifty-three-year-old *cantinière-hospitalière* who had joined the first battalion of *francs-tireurs* along with her husband and two adult sons, engaged in combat. Donning the dress of a man, she fought, distributed munitions and assisted with the wounded. Some Germans emerged on the square and advanced to the fountain. On the orders of Captain Ledeuil, who remained behind after Lipowski's retreat, the *francs-tireurs* who remained in the city advanced at the sound of the 'Marseillaise'. A terrible night battle commenced. Three times the enemy was pushed back on rue de Chartres (now rue Jean Moulin – heading north-east) and rue d'Orléans (now rue de la République). Flames arched overhead and bodies covered the ground. The French undertook one more counterattack and temporarily pushed the enemy back again. They could not hold. The final French soldiers withdrew discretely via *faubourg* Saint-Jean.

Mayor Lumière himself stayed at his post at the Hôtel de Ville, on the main square, from noon until 11 p.m., accompanied by a municipal councillor. The two men spent the day literally putting out fires. The other councillors were absent or fighting in the National Guard. Lumière expected the Prussians to seek him out at the Hôtel de Ville, but instead they had gone to his house and elsewhere in town, 'anywhere other than at the mayor's office'.[28] He was frustrated that he was not able to confront or negotiate or greet the Prussians on his official turf. When he finally returned home, he was greeted with shots but managed to escape.

Around 9 p.m., von Wittich ordered his men to take the town by assault, house by house. German soldiers ransacked the homes and buildings between the railway station and the central square – doors were forced open, windows breached, homes pillaged and their inhabitants brutalized or forced to flee. All buildings were set on fire, whether or not the inhabitants were still inside. The French would only leave a house when it caught fire.

One observer described well-organized incendiary groups of Germans in sections of sixty or eighty men, half in the streets to keep an eye out for snipers, and the others in squadrons of fifteen to twenty, the first entering homes, pillaging anything of value, and then the second squadron entering to set homes alight in ten places at once. One often-repeated story described a sixty-six-year-old man who was forced to bring the Germans a lit candle and watch as the soldiers set fire to his bed curtains. He then was obliged, at bayonet point, to bring the soldiers to a store of fodder – which they burned – and then was taken prisoner. In another version, two elderly inhabitants were forced to set fire to their own curtains.

Long after the fighting had ended, reported the mayor, civilians were killed in their beds and the wounded thrown into the flames. The Hôtel du Grand Monarque was made to serve dinner to seventy soldiers, but despite the pleading of its director, Madame Sénéchal, von Wittich then refused to spare the building. This harsh combat lasted until three in the morning, when the Germans took the last houses and occupied the Hôtel de Ville. The desolation and destruction were almost indescribable. Thousands fled west or north-west throughout the night while firemen tried in vain to douse the flames.

That night, the Germans set up camp around the town, on the hills of Bellevue and of Saint-Jean on the right bank of the Loir, sending signals from their camps into the town.

The next day, a hundred civilians of all ages and conditions were taken prisoner and led off to Germany. The mayor reported 30 killed and 40 wounded during the fighting, 235 houses completely destroyed, and 12 inhabitants who died in the fires. A combatant named Paul Montarlot related the burial of twenty-six National Guardsmen and *francs-tireurs*, including 'ten who are entirely charred and almost without human form'.[29] Observers compared the ruins of Châteaudun to Pompeii.

That day, with the municipal council and the subprefect, Lumière and his colleagues were forced to

> submit to exigencies and exactions of the most difficult and humiliating sort. At three o'clock in the evening, we were summoned under the most violent threats to provide, at six o'clock, a war contribution of 200,000 francs that we were able to reduce to 52,000 francs, a sum still exorbitant for our half-destroyed and deserted city. The humiliations of that day were crueller than that of the bombardment.[30]

The Prussian army left Châteaudun on 20 October at 4 a.m., leaving behind only ruins and ashes. In the days to follow, the suffering continued. The Germans took local notables hostage as a guard against further resistance. One of the hostages, named M. Renoult, a father and a gardener from the Saint-Jean neighbourhood, was killed on the 23rd. It was reported that he had accidentally pushed a

Bavarian soldier in an argument over a piece of bread, though his hands were tied behind his back. Renoult was beaten, condemned to death, and had his nose and ears cut off and eyes blinded, before facing a firing squad. He was buried in a shallow grave, and later disinterred after the occupation ended in March.

The remaining houses were used to quarter German soldiers. One of the inhabitants described the Saxons staying in his house charitably: 'My fifteen Saxons were at heart some pretty good devils. Most of them hastened to tell me that they were married, fathers of families, impatient for a peace that would return them home, and I saw them caress with real emotion young children whose age awoke in them some sweet remembrance.'[31] During the four months to follow, soldiers passed through several times and the inhabitants were obliged to quarter Bavarian soldiers through a bitter, hard winter.

Following a report issued by the Châteaudun municipal commission, the government in Tours swiftly authorized 100,000 francs to assist the town in rebuilding, in light of its meritorious defence against the Prussians. Trochu asked the mayor of Paris to rename a street, prompting the rechristening of rue du Cardinal-Fesch in the 9th *arrondissement* as rue du Châteaudun. Theatrical performances in Paris were organized to celebrate and raise funds for the unfortunate town. Poetry and song were devoted to the heroism of Châteaudun. On Victor Hugo's suggestion a cannon was renamed in the city's honour.

Despite this outpouring of support for Châteaudun, other towns were not willing to follow in its footsteps. In Chartres, inhabitants had prepared to defend the city against the invading Germans, but when they heard about Châteaudun, the mayor offered them the keys to the city.

Châteaudun was just one of dozens of towns and villages forced to navigate the demands of German invaders and occupiers. Hundreds of thousands of German soldiers came in close contact with French civilians who were, on the whole, not used to interacting with soldiers. Prussian military culture typically kept soldiers in contact with civilians, whereas French military culture siloed its professional soldiers in separate barracks and, during the war, set up in camps outside towns. French civilians, excepting those in fortress cities, had less experience of soldiers in their towns and houses. As the German armies marched deeper into France, they depended more and more on requisitions of food, drink and forage, through a principle of requisition established after 1866.

After Sedan, General Philip Sheridan, a victor in the Union Army during the US Civil War, reportedly advised Moltke, 'The proper strategy consists in inflicting as telling blows as possible on the enemy's army, and then in causing the inhabitants so much suffering that they must long for peace, and force the government to demand it. The people must be left nothing but their eyes to weep with over the war.'[32]

For the most part, however, through September, French civilians and German soldiers managed the situation with relatively few incidents. Most accounts of those early months involve a German soldier playing with children or buying drinks or asking for a match. German conscripts had been civilians at home with their own children and taverns just a few weeks earlier. Violent acts against civilians were punished through official courts martial. Most observers viewed the invading Germans as disciplined and serious. They had much better supply systems and staffing than previous armies had enjoyed, which lessened their desperation when seeking requisitions. Families like the Vineuils were required to quarter German soldiers and horses. Madame de Vineuil, alone with her children, felt she had to comply, although she refused to speak German with the soldiers. 'My task is not to simplify theirs,' she told Berthe.[33]

As the autumn wore on, however, requisitions became harsher and less restrained. As in Châteaudun, the Prussians authorized destroying buildings, taking hostages and levying contributions as a punishment on any locality that failed to disarm its population. The Germans demanded requisitions of firewood, bread, meat, fat, coffee, tobacco and alcohol, as well as oats, hay and straw for the horses. And just what constituted 'firewood' when a peasant's home, fences and barns were constructed of combustible material?

One soldier, named Rindfleisch, recalled the shift.

> At first we were forbidden, with the severest penalties, to burn vine-posts in bivouacs, and woe to him who used unthreshed corn for his palliasse! Child-like innocence! Now no one asks whether you are using garden fences or the doors of houses or waggons for fuel, and only scrupulous idealists like ourselves care whether a hurriedly abandoned fire will catch the straw nearby and then one's host's roof; no Frenchman can any longer lay claim to property or means of livelihood.[34]

Requisitions became steeper and more common as the German supply lines grew more tenuous and stretched. Even with rail lines in place, the Germans often had to transport food, animals and ammunition over 30 miles by road. Soldiers resorted to foraging and often to pillaging and bullying the peasants and townspeople. Even if Germans thought they were following good codes of behaviour, requisitioning was of course not welcome. When they paid in coin, their cash was not of much use to peasants who needed their grain for food. Nor did the Germans always bother to ascertain the proprietor of the animal in question. The practice of allowing animals to forage widely made their ownership unimportant to a hungry German seeing a chicken wandering down a lane.

Encounters in the countryside tended to be harder as peasants and villagers were more isolated and self-sufficient than townspeople and there was less chance for a French official to help sort out the friction. Soldiers were young, immature and armed. As Sand wrote (in this instance, speaking of French requisitions), 'families are abandoned to the protection of God, no men, no rifles, no horses. They are requisitioning everything.'[35] These interactions happened on a farm-by-farm basis, direct and unmediated. In the Eure-et-Loir, war damages from fire and destruction amounted to 500 francs per inhabitant in some communes.

Local officials also responded to the German tactic of taking hostages either as punishment for resistance or as a preventative measure. Often the Germans took local leaders hostage, typically the mayor or his deputies, or even the local priest. A village in the Seine-et-Oise which lent support to the *francs-tireurs* had fifty inhabitants taken hostage and threatened with execution. In the Aube, hostages were put on trains to prevent the sabotage of rail lines. On 27 October, the civil commissioner of the General Government of Rheims, Prince Karl von Hohenlohe, ordered respected local inhabitants to accompany trains on their travels and that they be placed on the train in such a way as to make their presence known, to avoid any attacks or damage to the train or the tracks. Inhabitants protested against this 'useless' and 'barbaric' requirement, but they complied.[36]

The Germans also used cash contributions as a mechanism for requisition and punishment. In these cases, the local mayor and municipal leaders played a key role in mediating between townspeople and occupier. The municipal commission of Soissons published a statement on 28 October addressing the town's citizens after a shot fired in the middle of the night wounded a German sentry in the hand:

> Until now the population of Soissons has showed itself to be calm. And we have good reason to count on it continuing to understand the situation and the duties that it imposes. Nevertheless, a wrongdoer that we do not believe to be from our city has indulged tonight in an act of hostility toward a Prussian sentry. These facts are not only condemnable, they can lead to reprisals and to harshness that everyone must ward off. We have too much confidence in the loyalty of our fellow citizens and the sentiment of duty that animates them to doubt for an instant their assistance and their efforts to prevent in the future the renewal of such an act.[37]

This message elicited strong responses. The *Moniteur de Tours* called the members of the municipal commission the 'assistants and spokespeople of the enemies of France', whereas the *Progrès de l'Aisne* agreed that 'Our duty is to wage war against enemies but not to assassinate them' and praised the 'courageous' and 'concerned' leadership of Soissons.[38] The municipal commission of Soissons countered, 'We aren't the police for the enemy. We are acting for the town of which we are the administrators and representatives.'[39] Yet this statement demonstrates the ambiguity and difficulty of municipal leadership under invasion. Did they not also act in the interest of the occupiers?

Increasingly, the Germans imposed cash contributions and penalties for such actions. The rules of the game were well understood. The Prussians knew that they asked far more than a town or village could provide – as in Châteaudun – to set a high bar against which mayors would try to negotiate, to maximize the amount obtained in the end. Mayors prolonged negotiations as long as they could. In this strategy the mayors often had to go it alone, because the central French government and the prefects could not officially endorse foot-dragging. Furthermore, mayors had to figure out whether they would pay these requisitions by drawing on the cash already in reserve in anticipation of French taxes, or through subscription, or by loans – free or forced, with or without interest. They couched these requests in the spirit of patriotism.

In Épinal, for example, the mayor negotiated the initial demand of 500,000 francs down to 100,000 francs. He then, on 18 October, asked the citizens to pay their 1870 taxes and to pay in advance three-fifths of their 1871 taxes. The announcement ended, 'the Mayor counts on the public-spiritedness and patriotism of his fellow citizens' to accomplish this task without delay.[40]

This strategy engendered debates over the true definition of patriotism. The mayor of Saint-Dié (Vosges) delivered a frustrated speech on 31 December, under occupation, at a rocky meeting dividing up the local requisition burden. 'Here and now,' he stated,

> we recognize that the true patriots are not always those who criticize and constantly go on about . . . never paying, neither their

> money nor their person . . . but rather those who, in a sincere disinterestedness and by true affection for their fellow citizens, are resigned to undergo for them and to make others accept measures against which their hearts protest and their dignity revolts, but to which they submit in order to not attract greater evils upon the thousands of beings who are entrusted to them.[41]

Those who insisted on continuing their protest, he declared, could take up arms, march to the local Prussian leadership in Épinal – and suffer the consequences.

Over the course of the autumn and winter, the spiral of terror and reprisals intensified. As early as 25 August, forty-nine disarmed Mobile Guardsmen were massacred by German guards at Passavant (Marne). Even as the war continued, those enmeshed in the conflict wondered about how it shaped themselves and the soldiers around them. For George Sand, 'to make a man an excellent combat machine, you have to remove a part of what makes him a man.'[42] The formation of soldiers, in and of itself, dehumanized men. 'No more heroes; everything is machine gun.'[43] Don't ask 'who has the most courage . . . ask who has the most bullets'.[44] The war symbolized a step back for civilization and the decline of civilized men to 'the most moronic citizens of the world', representing the 'bronze age'.[45] This war is nothing more than an 'exchange of projectiles more or less numerous, [that] have greater or lesser reach, that paralyses individual merit, renders null the conscience and the will of the soldier'.[46]

Soldiers observed the change in themselves as the war dragged on. A Bavarian named Hugo Arnold at first was sympathetic to courts martial for French civilians. But later in the war he wrote, 'In the face of the burning fanaticism of the French . . . mercy was not merely an absurdity, but rather a crime. Against the enemy, especially against one who places himself outside the law [*Recht*], only one principle can be applied: An eye for an eye [and] a tooth for a tooth!'[47]

Another Bavarian, named Karl Tanera, recalled an episode during the Loire campaign in late September in which he, two NCOs, a bugler and forty-five riflemen were ordered to 'roam the woodlands; turn out, capture, and shoot armed civilians; requisition livestock and turn it over to the nearest troops; make ourselves, that is, the German uniform, visible in even the most obscure areas; and do everything that increases the security of the army against treacherous raids.'[48] They engaged not only in punishment but in the arbitrary harassment of civilians. They executed one man, but they spared a mayor whom they threatened to kill because he had lied about the presence of weapons in his town; Tanera was not sure whether he had the right to execute this mayor. In Fontenay-Saint-Père (Seine-et-Oise), German soldiers not only burned down several homes but also – according to one source – took hold of a fireman, threw him on a pyre and burned him half alive.

Vengeance, too, played a role. On 18 October, a Bavarian named Hoesslin reported in a letter to his brother, 'We have bloodily revenged our many friends and comrades.' Three days later, Hoesslin told his mother that all of his friends had been killed: 'I could have shed bloody tears over the tragedy of my friends and almost felt joy at falling enemy soldiers, for my torn heart craved revenge.'[49] By 1 November, thirty-four of the original fifty-two soldiers in his unit had been killed or wounded, or had fallen ill. Hoesslin himself was killed on 2 December.

French soldiers also pillaged the homes of their fellow citizens. After all, the French armies remained woefully undersupplied, missing tents, boots and even trousers. Over the course of the winter, there were hundreds of complaints about French soldiers from the Mobile Guard and the National Guard damaging French homes, pillaging for food, and stealing or burning linen, doors, furniture and rugs. In a few cases, *francs-tireurs* were blamed for having burned down farms or mills as they were about to fall into the hands of the Germans. Many suburbs of Paris burned in the course of conquest and reconquest, causing widespread devastation: Gentilly, Montrouge, Garches, Le Bourget, Mesly, Champigny, Villemomble, Asnières,

Courbevoie, Levallois-Perret, Neuilly-sur-Seine. And others – Chevilly-Larue and L'Häy-les-Roses – were burned by the French.

Crown prince Friedrich Wilhelm also wrestled with the moral consequences of the conflict for himself and his soldiers: 'Despite all victories and our improved prospects resulting from them, I ask myself every day how the present mangling of each other like wild beasts, contrary to all Christian precepts of virtue and morality that are preached day by day and looked upon as characteristics of our age, can still be possible.' He shied away, though:

> But I must *not* let my thoughts rest on these contradictions; otherwise I might almost go mad over it all, seeing that, placed as I am in the midst of the fray, I am bound to be planning ever new ways of destroying my adversaries, all the quicker to make an end of the miseries of war.[50]

He did not refuse the role into which he had been placed, to use violent means for the sake of national aims. Instead, the crown prince rolled along with his army. In his reflections on the battle of Sedan, he noted his pride that the Bavarians spoke well of him. He expressed no concerns about the fighting at Bazeilles other than a remark that Tann was 'staunch as his sword, but must curb his fiery temper'.[51]

As the conflict deepened, French and Germans alike began to characterize the war as a conflict of nations in which the actions of the other side justified the intensification of brutality. The librarian Auguste Castan of Besançon noted the 'inflated rumours around the town, digging an abyss of hate between two nations that have no reason to hate each other'.[52] Each side believed they were defending civilization against barbarians.

Newspapers in Germany emphasized the hazards facing Germans living in France. Although the plight of such Germans paled compared to French civilian suffering, it was used to heighten the nationalized interpretation of the war. A journalist for the pro-Prussian *Christenbote* (a Protestant newspaper in Württemberg) imagined that if France had invaded,

> our towns and villages would have been plundered, battered down and burnt, because these enemies do not show any respect for divine or human law. We shiver at the mere thought of the horrible devastation that would have hit us, the countless victims of the sword, flames, hunger, and diseases, which our rough, cruel enemies, denying civilization, would have inflicted upon us. All of us could be killed or driven from our burnt town and bereaved of all our possessions.[53]

Newspapers particularly emphasized the fate awaiting German wives, sisters and daughters if the French had invaded, particularly at the hands of the *Turcos*: 'Whoever got to see these *turcos*, thanked God from the bottom of his heart that we did not get these men as victorious enemies in our country,' wrote the *Christenbote*.[54]

But George Sand, like many others, decried Germany's militaristic turn at the expense, she believed, 'of the savants, of the philosophers and artists, Germany of Goethe and Beethoven! What a fall, what shame!'[55] She was disappointed in Germany for taking revenge on France 'as though the half-century that has passed [since Napoleon] had not initiated the law of progress and the notion of solidarity'.[56] The Prussian influence now dominated smaller German states to the detriment of all. 'In this war,' she wrote, 'you are not for us Badenese, Bavarians, Wurttembergeois, but forever, in the reprobation of the present and the legend of the future, Prussians!'[57]

In Strasbourg, as the young historian Rodolphe Reuss witnessed the destruction of the city's great library in a fire caused by Prussian bombardment, he experienced a powerful new emotion of anger and resentment boiling up within himself. 'We felt our voice break off in sobs and, in our heart, we felt rise one of those furious national hatreds believed to have been now forgotten and that will not be snuffed out anytime soon.'[58] Reuss had long believed himself to be a cosmopolitan who looked beyond national borders, but the war had hardened him. 'If they are barbarians, let us treat them as barbarians: they will only reap what they have sown!'[59]

The feeling was mutual. Hoesslin also reported his disdain for

> the indescribable immorality of the French performances. No wonder a people that from youth onwards seeks its amusement in the vulgar cannot resist a people with a nobler attitude toward life. Religiosity and discipline, which for a good soldier are absolutely essential, must, by such a decline in moral standards, be lacking in the French soldier.[60]

Some Germans even called the war a 'racial war' or *Rassenkrieg*, a Social Darwinist term for a struggle for existence between two peoples.[61]

By the end of October, the strain of continued sacrifice became difficult to bear. Train services remained disrupted, and food and other supplies were hard to come by. 'All the sacrifices are demanded at the same time,' complained George Sand. 'Will we have the joy of having suffered for the deliverance of the *patrie*? . . . If it were thus, no one would complain; but if nothing is used, if the present state is prolonged, we will march toward an inevitable catastrophe, and our poor Paris will be forced to surrender.'[62]

Still, while Germans engaged in harsh reprisals, the Franco-Prussian War saw mostly action against property, not people, and nothing like what happened in the Vendée during the French Revolution, Spain during the Napoleonic Wars, or the border states and South during the US Civil War. If France had engaged in an all-out partisan war, the conflict would have become even more miserable. Instead, Gambetta focused on the relief of Paris, and for that he required an army prepared for an open battle. While he undertook this work, civilians in French towns and villages grappled with relentlessly difficult choices.

12. *Under Siege*

In Metz, meanwhile, soldiers and civilians still awaited relief. Since 19 August, following the battle of Gravelotte, Bazaine and some 152,000 soldiers and 70,000 civilians had remained immobile inside the city walls. Cut off from the rest of France, they missed the events of the previous two months: the battle of Sedan, the fall of the Second Empire, the tumultuous rise of the Government of National Defence, the encirclement of Paris and the fall of Orléans, the combat at Châteaudun, and the spread of invasion across the vast French north-east. Rumours of these developments arrived late and incomplete. In mid-October an officer noted that 'we are completely unaware of what is happening in France'.[1]

It took nearly a week for Metz to learn of the battle of Sedan. At first, hearing reports of soldiers marching eastward on 6 September and crossing the Moselle, Bazaine believed that the Prussians were on the run. Soon, however, he realized that these were unarmed French soldiers: prisoners from Sedan heading into German territory. The news was confirmed when Friedrich Karl authorized an exchange of prisoners to ensure that Bazaine received a full account of the scale of the disaster at Sedan.

As commander of the Army of Metz, Bazaine was the only representative of the Second Empire still in a position of authority, and he had sworn an oath of allegiance to Napoleon III. Bazaine had no love for the republicans or Trochu and recognized that he had no future under the new regime. By contrast, under a restored Napoleon III or the prince imperial, Bazaine might have a chance at holding a leadership position. Empress Eugénie remained a force whose agreement mattered. She and Bazaine did not like each other, but, given their reversals of fortune, they both thought they

might need each other. Furthermore, Bismarck treated Napoleon III as a visiting monarch rather than as a prisoner of war in part as a way to help pull Bazaine away from supporting the GND.

During the siege of Metz, Bazaine did not officially recognize the new government. The best he could muster came in his Order of the Day on 16 September: 'Our military obligations towards the country remain the same. Let us then continue to serve her with devotion and the same energy, defending her land against the foreigner, the social order against evil passions.'[2] It is hard to know just what the marshal meant by this final phrase. Was the defence of the 'social order' a statement of defiance against the Government of National Defence or an expression of concern against further revolutionary action? In any case, Bazaine and Gambetta had little contact and did not strategize about how to co-ordinate or work with each other's forces. Bazaine's army had not declared its loyalty to the new republic and so its trustworthiness remained in doubt, even as the siege of Metz unfolded. Bazaine could continue to hold out, he could surrender at any moment, or, many worried, he could fight his way out in order to defeat the republic.

In the years following 1870, it became an article of faith among republicans that Bazaine's actions constituted treason and contributed to the defeat of France. Given his real options, however, the question bears less on the outcome of the war and more on Bazaine's personal honour. To republican leaders, it was obvious that the commander should attempt to break out of Metz. To Bazaine, the matter was less clear. His men grew more tired, hungry and despondent by the day, in large part due to Bazaine's own decision to retreat to Metz after Gravelotte. Rations had been cut on 4 September, and by the end of the month hunger had become more apparent. On 23 September, 200 French soldiers died trying to fight forward to gather potatoes. Rationing policies led to conflicts with civilians. Soldiers kept busy with routines – issuing rations, inspections and so forth – but to what end? In August, it was difficult enough to imagine that Bazaine could expect to outmarch Friedrich

Karl and meet up with MacMahon's Army of Châlons. After Sedan, it was even less clear what his next step would be: assist Paris? Create a distraction to wear down the Germans? Muster enough strength to meet one of Moltke's armies in battle? It was little wonder – though extremely demoralizing – that Bazaine postponed and cancelled planned sorties in September.

Bazaine did not receive any quarter from his dispirited troops. Fairly or not, many believed that they should attempt a sortie. On 25 September, Bazaine received an anonymous note under his door from 'a soldier of the Army of the Rhine' protesting against his poor leadership. 'You are aware,' the letter began,

> of the rumors coursing through the army with regard to your inaction in the face of the enemy over the past twenty-two days . . . This inaction has ruined our cavalry and will soon ruin our artillery, which will reduce the army to impotence. The tragedy at Sedan and the army's continued ignorance as to the plans of its generals makes it susceptible to the rumor that it is being prepared for delivery, *pieds et poings* [bound hand and foot], to the enemy. And yet the enemy outside is inferior to us in every way; you must be aware of that fact. Surrender the army to the enemy when you have 130,000 elite troops in hand? It is unthinkable.[3]

Bazaine twice attempted to negotiate a peace with Bismarck via intermediaries without the knowledge or support of Gambetta. This fact alone could explain the animosity of the GND and of republicans against the commander. Furthermore, it could be that Bazaine actively sought a position for himself in a restored Bonapartist regime. Or it could be that he simply wanted to conclude an honourable peace that neither Napoleon III nor the GND was willing to contemplate.

The first attempt came with the aid of Edmond Régnier, a businessman and staunch defender of the Empire who managed to take a role in high diplomacy. Régnier was able to gain access to Bismarck thanks to his acquaintance with the prince imperial. For his part, Bismarck took the opportunity to pursue a negotiated peace, since talks with Favre were stalled. He knew a helpful pawn when he saw one. Régnier explained his plan to persuade the commanders of Metz and Strasbourg to capitulate in the name of the emperor. The empress would then summon members of the former government – under the protection of these armies – to convene and negotiate a peace. Bazaine himself, in some tellings of this intrigue, would be named at this government's head. Régnier arrived in Metz on 23 September and met in secret with Bazaine. Bazaine then sent General Charles Bourbaki, disguised as a Red Cross doctor, to England to pursue negotiations with Empress Eugénie in Hastings. But Eugénie had no interest in this scheme or in giving Bazaine a leading role. Bazaine, after all, had shown his incompetence during the campaign around Metz and she had no particular interest in his success. She denied knowing anything about the affair and stated that she would not do anything to undermine the Government of National Defence.

The most important outcome of this episode proved to be the release of Bourbaki from Metz. Upon his attempt to return, Bourbaki was temporarily not allowed back into the city. His pass had been misdated, and at first the Prussians foolishly upheld the wrong date. By the time Moltke ordered his subordinates to allow Bourbaki back into Metz, where he would be less dangerous, the French general had already left to serve the GND.

By this time, the seasons had turned from hot to unremittingly cold and rainy. Food in Metz came at a premium: 'horseflesh one franc per pound, beef six francs, bacon eight francs, potatoes one franc, sugar and salt each six francs, eggs seventy-five centimes . . . and milk two francs the litre.'[4] Rumours of merchants hoarding food abounded, and children suffered and died from increased dysentery and diarrhoea exacerbated by malnourishment.

The German armies were not doing so well, either. By the first week of October, 15 per cent of the Meuse Army was sick either due to complications from their wounds or due to flu, dysentery and typhoid fever. Bavarian II Corps suffered in particular – half its men were sick, more than six times its battle losses.

The villas and gardens surrounding Metz had been cleared by the French and now featured just the stumps of trees and the foundations of houses. Visitors to the area a scant week after the end of the siege reported the devastation surrounding Metz:

> Here too we saw traces of the encampment of its late besiegers. Thousands of bags of corn, and many casks of biscuits, some under cover, and others soaked with rain, were on either side the rail, while the scene was varied by the carcasses of dead horses and the remains of camp fires. The country here showed a striking contrast to that near Sedan; it was utterly wasted and down-trodden, the fields and roads being a mass of mud and scarcely distinguishable from each other.[5]

The surrounding villages, caught between the two sides, suffered as well. During the course of the siege, the village of Peltre saw ninety of its one hundred houses, along with the church, burned to the ground. An observer piecing together conflicting accounts of this destruction believed that the village had been 'occupied first by the Prussians, whom the French drove out by shelling it; the latter then used it as a point from which to make sorties, till one night the Prussians set fire to it, burning the poor creatures out of house and home.'[6]

The French crisis compounded on 7 October when Bazaine sent foraging parties out along the Moselle. Two thousand men were killed. On 10 October, Bazaine held a second council of war. His generals had little hope that a sortie was possible. Only Leboeuf suggested one more battle. Metz had only ten more days of flour rations – perhaps eighteen if they cut bread back by two-fifths. General Grégoire Coffinières, the Metz garrison commandant, reported that 19,000 sick and wounded clogged the hospitals, with mounting cases of typhus and smallpox. The council of war decided to hold out until all supplies were used up, in order to pin down the 200,000 besieging Germans rather than allow them to contribute to the Loire effort, and to make one last attempt at a negotiated surrender.

Following this council of war, Bazaine sent his aide-de-camp, General Napoleon Boyer, to Versailles. Bismarck received Boyer at the palace on 14 October. Boyer proposed that Bismarck permit the Army of Metz to withdraw to southern France or Algeria, allowing the Prussians to capture Paris, end the war and defeat the republicans. Prussia would then deliver France over to Bazaine's army (fortified with 140,000 returning prisoners of war), who could then sweep away the republicans and establish a conservative government that would create a lasting peace.

Bismarck may have wanted to pursue this plan, but the crown prince did not trust Bazaine's intentions and Moltke was not interested. Instead, Moltke insisted upon the straightforward capitulation of the army and surrender of the fortress. Furthermore, the Germans were not so sure that the empress and regency council would accept the terms that the German public demanded, and, even if they did, would France? To conclude such terms, they needed to discuss the proposal with the empress, but time was running short for Metz.

Boyer returned to Metz on 17 October for further discussion the next day with the council of war. The plan seemed dubious – would the soldiers go along with supporting the Empire, or just go home? – but it was the best they could do without admitting complete defeat. Boyer, therefore, left for London on 19 October and arrived at Eugénie's new residence at Chislehurst on the 22nd. Eugénie wanted to know what these peace terms were that the Germans were demanding. The Prussian Embassy revealed that they had not decided yet. So Eugénie would have to sign a blank cheque, which she refused to do, and King Wilhelm would not go further without her firm guarantee. The negotiations came to an end.

By late October, the army could no longer provide food for its soldiers, and on 20 October civilians received only 10 ounces of bread per day. Horsemeat rations increased from ½ pound to ¾ pound in early October, but Metz had little salt to make it palatable. One soldier – Yves-Charles Quentel of Brittany, whom we met at the time of mobilization – later wrote in a letter back home, 'I saw some companions eat in one meal the rations made for five days.' At the end of the siege, he went four days without bread, only horsemeat and a little flour.[7] Captain Sonnois wrote on 24 October that his soldiers had eaten their final remaining rations. 'They tell us that tomorrow we will have 200 grams [less than half a pound] of biscuits and afterwards . . . nothing!'[8] Soldiers searched for potatoes in fields or tried to surrender to the Germans. Only 540 horses were still alive. It was time to capitulate.

The Prussians demanded the surrender of the fortress, the imprisonment of the army, and the intact handover of all materiel of war. The council of war accepted the terms on 26 October. The terms aroused indignation. The fact that Bazaine agreed to hand over materiel as well as the colours – that he declined to spike the guns and ruin the powder – seemed like another shameful action, another instance of treason. The *Indépendant de la Moselle* published an editorial on the 28th that recalled how in 1815, after the fall of Paris, the city of Metz had specially constructed a bridge over the Moselle outside the city so that Metz would not have the shame of the allied army passing through its city gates. The editorial also evoked 1792 and the fight for liberty and the rights of man. 'It is not *we* who capitulate,' the paper claimed.[9]

As the last straw, Bazaine refused Prussia's offer to allow his soldiers to march out with their arms in hand, with bands playing and with their officers leading them. He claimed to refuse because of the weather, and later said he doubted the soldiers could have done so with discipline in arms in front of the Prussians. It seems, however, that the real reason for denying his soldiers this honour was that Bazaine could not himself bear to see his troops after having been nearly invisible to them through much of the siege. On 29 October, in a cold rain, the army of 133,000 men and 600 guns surrendered. Men and officers separated that day, with officers allowed to return to Metz without Prussian guards, and soldiers going into Prussian captivity. French soldiers spent 29–31 October cooking and eating as captives of Prussia near Metz. Then they were loaded into boxcars and sent east to Germany. With the fall of Metz, all of Napoleon III's original forces had been killed, captured, or wounded. The scale of defeat was unprecedented in modern Europe. Now only two regular army regiments remained at large: the 35th and the 42nd regiments had been garrisoned in Rome before the war and had finally returned to France to serve a new regime, leaving Rome in the hands of Italian forces.

The population bitterly resented Bazaine for capitulating. But on 31 October, the editors of the *Indépendant de la Moselle* realized the need to call for calm.

> Be calm, dear fellow citizens, be calm, and still be calm, and always be calm, support this trial with courage; no foolish attempts, no unreasonable demonstrations. Have the dignity that becomes us at the present moment: repress in the depths of the heart certain opinions; not cursing those who are *within* our walls but those who are *without*. *They* are to blame. Again, once more, tranquillity and order – no aggressions – no acts of violence.[10]

As for Bazaine himself, the last of Napoleon III's commanders was allowed to hand himself over to the Germans. He arrived too early, however, and had to spend the day inside a suburban villa awaiting capture, in a humiliating and rain-drenched posture of cowardice.

The French reaction was swift and full of pain. With the fall of Metz, the return of Napoleon III was now utterly impossible and his supporters saw this clearly. Captain Claude Lombard expressed his reaction to the sight of the French flag replaced by that of Prussia:

> Day of mourning and desolation. All is over. Poor France! An army of 100,000 men pushed to its knees, without making a final effort . . .

> Dear national colours! Symbols of valiance and glory, reminder of our grandeur, of our victory, of our military honours, here you are trodden on the ground, dragged through the mud, and in your place on our forts and citadels fly enemy colours. Oh! Shame! If our fathers rose from their graves, what would they say to their descendants? Bastardized generation that was unable to defend the doorstep of the fatherland and could not chase the enemy from its foyer.[11]

For Lombard, the surrender brought profound desolation. Others gave a more bellicose response, such as the five or six thousand people who demonstrated in Angers on 2 November, bringing an address to the prefect that ended, 'No armistice! No peace! No elections! To arms!'[12] For radicals and revolutionaries, the fall of Metz demanded a call for authoritarian measures, including the creation of committees of public safety. Renewed revolutionary attempts arose in the Midi: in Lyons and Nice on 3 November, in Saint-Étienne on 31 October and in Valence on 30 October. None of these movements went anywhere. The most serious disturbance occurred in Marseilles on 2 November, but even there the city was calm by the following day. When the Government of National Defence disagreed with more extreme measures, this radical faction viewed the GND as at best weak and defeatist, and at worst complicit in Bazaine's alleged treason.

Gambetta's proclamation of 30 October fanned the flames of suspicion against Bazaine. 'Such a crime,' he declared, 'goes beyond even the punishments of justice . . . The Army of France, stripped of its national character, is swallowed up, despite the heroism of the soldiers, by the treason of its leaders, in the disasters of the fatherland.'[13] With this statement Gambetta committed the rhetorical error of lumping all imperial officers together as though they were all to blame for Metz, including those who continued to serve the GND. This proclamation was disseminated and repeated by local authorities. The crown prince of Prussia called it a 'pitiful production full of high-sounding, bombastic phrases à la Victor Hugo'.[14]

Can we blame Bazaine? Not for the capitulation itself. By that point there was not much that could be done, and a breakout would have served little purpose after Sedan. But he did fail to adequately pursue plans for a breakout in August, especially during those crucial days when he had reason to believe that MacMahon was heading his way. He also failed to support the Government of National Defence, to co-ordinate with it and serve it. He might also have ruthlessly rationed food and supplies from the beginning so that Metz could hang on as long as possible. If Metz had held out a few more weeks into mid-November, perhaps Moltke would have been forced to send forces from Paris to the Army of the Loire, which might have allowed Trochu's sortie from Paris (discussed on page 335) a better chance. This commitment from Metz would not have changed the course of the war but might have made the defeat less complete. Alternatively, a smarter or more devious commander might have successfully plotted to restore the Empire. Bazaine's focus on minutiae instead of strategy is a caution to other leaders in a crisis. In the campaign around Metz, his vacillation and incompetence, second only to that of Napoleon III himself, helped to create the circumstances that brought the Second Empire to its ignominious conclusion.

Meanwhile, across north-eastern France, a constellation of fortress cities came under siege. These cities often protected rail lines, making it difficult for the Germans to have multiple supply lines to support their expanding operations. Three rail lines crossed the border between France and the German states, at Saarbrücken, Wissembourg and Strasbourg. Control over these lines would help to determine Germany's success in bringing the conflict to a conclusion.

The southern line ran through Strasbourg, Mulhouse, Belfort, Vesoul, Langres and Chaumont. With Belfort holding out for the long haul, this line was not useful to the Germans. The northern line was blocked, too, by fortresses at Metz, Thionville, Montmédy and Mézières. It only became available to the Germans after the fall of Mézières on 2 January. The middle line, which passed west from

Frouard (just north of Nancy) to Toul, Bar-le-Duc, Châlons-sur-Marne, Château-Thierry and thence to Paris, had similar disruptions but proved more readily useable once Toul fell on 25 September. Nevertheless, this route was disrupted by a major act of sabotage by retreating regular French soldiers. In late September, they planted half a dozen mines in a tunnel near Nanteuil-sur-Marne. The explosion filled the tunnel with tons of sand, causing damage that was impossible to repair. The Germans needed to construct a separate railroad loop, which did not open until 22 November. Meanwhile, the Third Army outside Paris had to transport supplies over 30 miles of roads from the last usable station at Château-Thierry.

Capturing French fortresses therefore became an important part of Germany's war operations. In most cases, it was not a difficult task. With few exceptions, including Belfort, the fortresses were outdated, and their guns did not match those of the Germans. They did not have good shelters and sometimes lacked disciplined soldiers. The Germans just needed some time and to concentrate their forces. That said, fortresses were a distraction that required troops and made them unavailable for use elsewhere.

Those inside a besieged city found themselves treated as pawns in this struggle. Civilians and their suffering were integral to the siege and to its outcome, and they strained to advocate either to resist or to surrender. Strongholds varied in their willingness to hold out, based on their commanding officer, their garrison, their defences, and civilian pressure. One young man in Toul wrote on 23 September, 'The population, a model of bravery, preferred to be crushed under the ruins rather than surrender.'[15] Toul fell on 25 September.

In Strasbourg, civilian leaders struggled to defend inhabitants while protecting their city's honour. The city had come under siege in early August following the battles of Wissembourg and Froeschwiller in northern Alsace. Its importance lay in its symbolism as the leading city of Alsace rather than its military significance. By contrast with Metz, in which Bazaine became the central figure whose actions dominated accounts, the siege of Strasbourg had no one leading character. The locus of activity lay with a cast of civilians whose energetic work on behalf of their city elicited admiration. As the siege wore on, they found themselves immersed in increasingly difficult choices to balance their civic and national pride against their own survival.

The military features of the siege set the stage for these activities. In Strasbourg, by contrast with well-defended Paris and Metz, the Prussian aim was to blast into the fortifications and create a practicable breach that the Germans could assault in an attempt to force a surrender. If they failed to break through the walls, they could then use hunger as a weapon. The suffering of civilians – men, women and children – lay at the heart of this strategy. Both the French and the Prussians anticipated that the siege of Strasbourg would unfold largely as such events had for centuries. Army commanders communicated through intermediaries who conveyed highly formalized messages to each other. The besieging army constructed a series of entrenched parallels to protect its approach to the city and its flanks from enemy fire as it brought its artillery into place.

Strasbourg came under the command of sixty-eight-year-old General Jean-Jacques Alexis Uhrich, a retired general who had served in France's many mid-century conflicts, from Spain to Algeria to the Crimea and Italy. For the first time, however, he served in France to defend his own country. Straightforward and loyal, Uhrich strove to serve the French well, but he had few tools with which to innovate.

Until 17 August the German Badenese division stood alone around Strasbourg, awaiting Prussian reinforcements. On 14 August, Moltke appointed Prussian Lieutenant General August von Werder as the commander of the besieging army. A veteran of the battle of Königgrätz, Werder enjoyed the favour of Crown Prince Friedrich Wilhelm. He had been sent to Strasbourg after the victory at Froeschwiller with simple directions from Moltke: 'The mission of Your Excellency is to render yourself master of this place as quickly as possible.'[16]

Uhrich knew that he had to follow French military regulations regarding siege warfare, which stated that 'military law condemns with the death penalty and military degradation the commander . . . who capitulates without having forced the enemy to pass through the slow and successive stages of sieges, and without having repulsed at least one assault through practicable breaches.'[17] In a proclamation of 10 August, Uhrich went a significant step further, by declaring that Strasbourg would not surrender 'so long as there remains a soldier, a hunk of bread, a cartridge'.[18] Uhrich later regretted this hard-line stance, but it set him apart from the morally questionable Bazaine.

Strasbourg's fortifications dated from the 1680s. Like those of so many of France's fortresses, they were designed by Sébastien Le Prestre de Vauban, who helped Louis XIV secure his new borders following France's annexation of much of Alsace. With its massive proportions, vast storage capacity for both food and ammunition, and elaborate outcroppings and lunettes, the Strasbourg fortress had been the height of rationality and technology in the seventeenth century.

The walls around Strasbourg were shaped like an isosceles triangle laid on its side, with the military esplanade and the pentagonal citadel located at the eastern point heading toward the Rhine. There were two openings for the Ill river to the south-west and the north-east, protected by fortifications and towers. Vauban had decided to place the citadel on the eastern side in order to defend the French army against resentful citizens as well as against the Holy Roman Empire. This decision left the north-west corner of the city vulnerable. Despite the presence of two forts on the western side, the west – and particularly the north-west – remained a weak spot that the Prussians exploited. Seven gates provided entry to the city. In addition, the rail line penetrated the walls, with the station just inside them on the western edge. Despite recommendations to update the fortress in the 1860s, no repairs or maintenance work had been performed.

By 1870, the fortress was outdated in comparison with modern artillery. Although the French maintained superiority in terms of their rifles and the new machine gun, the Prussians had developed the best artillery with the steel Krupp cannon. The Krupp cannon could fire more quickly and further than the French bronze front-loading cannon, which dated from 1859. While the French could handle shot weighing four and twelve pounds, the Prussian shot weighed up to twenty-four pounds. The Krupp was also far more accurate and could be fired twice as fast. The Prussians used a variety of projectiles, including solid shot, shells filled with gunpowder, and shells with shrapnel. In addition, the Prussians used percussion fuses that exploded on impact, rather than the time-fuses used by the French that were pre-set to explode at 1,200 metres (¾ mile) or 2,700 metres (1½ miles). From 2½ miles away, the Prussians could inflict a great deal of damage. Finally, in this siege the Prussians employed the tactic of indirect fire. They calculated the angles of their fire and therefore could use artillery while under cover rather than expose themselves to sight their targets visually. It was much more difficult for the French defenders to counter artillery under these circumstances.

The rivers and canals around Strasbourg provided water for engineered flooding as an extra measure of protection, but Uhrich hesitated to order this flooding due to the civilian houses and gardens covering the fortification slopes. This delay gave the Germans the chance to approach for reconnaissance more easily and begin their bombardment.

By mid-August, the French garrison consisted of only 17,000 men, including Mobile Guardsmen, National Guardsmen, firemen, customs officials and sailors. They faced 40,000 Germans. Pleas for reinforcements went unheeded; they were needed elsewhere. Strasbourg's best hope was its massive earthworks. To blast through them, the Prussian artillery had to draw close so that they could aim low. They faced 250 French cannon and many accurate rifles on the ramparts. And so, creating a practicable breach would take time.

Civilians readied themselves for this siege by creating fire brigades that met every evening in local taverns to patrol the streets looking for fires. They brought their own pumps and uniforms and operated by candlelight as the gas had been turned off to prevent explosions. Starting on 15 August, Saint-Napoleon's Day, the Germans lobbed shells into the city every evening as they slowly manoeuvred into place during the day. For the Germans, this was a period of painstaking, boring investment. For civilians inside, it was nightly horror. Over the course of forty-four nights, from 15 August to 27 September, a projectile fell on the city of Strasbourg every twenty seconds. This random, impersonal bombardment shook civilians to their bones. The anonymous mother who had previously debated whether or not to spend the war in Strasbourg now shepherded her young children, Émile and Marie, into the cellar every night to face the possibility of being buried alive. She set up makeshift beds and screens for privacy from the neighbours as three families washed and ate together. Her children slept with shoes on in case they needed to make a sudden escape. Her house caught fire three times, each time saved by volunteer firefighters. The anxiety sometimes became unbearable. 'Fear is not reasonable,' she recorded; 'it catches you in spite of yourself. It is a contagious evil.'[19]

Civilians had not expected the relentlessness of bombardment. The journalist Paul Raymond-Signouret described the horror of the experience:

> A flash illuminates a point, then a long silence that lasts 3, 4, 5, 10 seconds . . . during which one sees the gleaming streaks traced in the night by the fuses . . . then, suddenly, the dull noise of the [cannon's] detonation, which arrives almost at the same time as the striding shudder of the air under the effort of this heavy mass; then again, but almost instantaneously, the detonation . . . of the projectile itself, which has just burst as it hit an obstacle, and whose mass or fragments have destroyed some section of a wall, or massacred some human creature, perhaps a relative, perhaps a friend.[20]

Rich and poor, old and young, all were subject to the possibility of violent death in their beds. Three hundred civilians died from injuries sustained during the bombardment, mostly adult men who were more likely to be out in the streets. Many civilians believed that such treatment broke the laws of war. In reality, however, civilians were entitled to no such protection according to the scant international agreements governing the exercise of war at the time.

To the Germans, however, the siege moved far too slowly. Impatient for results, Werder decided to attempt to force the city to surrender by using heavy bombardment on the centre for three days, from 24 to 27 August. This strategy unmistakably targeted civilians rather than military fortifications. Prior to unleashing this bombardment, he asked Uhrich to surrender and denied the French commander's request to allow women and children to depart. After all, Werder's strategy relied on their suffering. Instead of aiming to create a breach in the walls, Werder hoped that civilian outcry in the face of intense, deliberate bombardment would convince Uhrich to surrender. During this period, Prussian mud-caked artillery units served in 24-hour shifts, in which they fired 400 shots per gun. 'It is a very burdensome and also dangerous task,' recorded the German journalist Julius von Wickede, 'but the brave artillerymen perform it with delight and joyful sacrifice.'[21]

The night of 24 August proved to be the most destructive of the entire siege. The Protestant New Church and its school and library caught fire. The pastor and his daughter, Elise Reichard, vacated the wounded from the Red Cross hospital hosted in the complex. A bucket chain worked all night in vain to save the structure. By the morning, the last roof tile fell, and the dome collapsed with its silver bell. Reichard lamented, 'It will no longer call us to church on Sundays, nor will its bright voice mix with the ringing of its sister at the cathedral to honour the Lord!'[22]

The loss of the New Church library particularly traumatized Strasbourg's cultural elite. A place of learning since the Reformation and the second largest library in France, it housed a collection of early printed books and illuminated manuscripts, notably the twelfth-century *Hortus deliciarum* (*Garden of Delights*) of Abbess Herrad of Landsberg. For a city that claimed Gutenberg as their own, the loss of a library, with every page now a cinder, meant the destruction of culture and identity. For Rodolphe Reuss, a historian who taught at the New Church's school, the loss could not be repaired. 'Thinking of our beautiful Library,' he wrote, 'of so many work projects for the future destroyed by these Vandals the Prussians, I began to cry with rage: it was one of the saddest moments of my existence.'[23] Civilization itself seemed to be under siege.

In the morning, Werder sent Uhrich a message asking for surrender. Uhrich responded, 'My walls remain standing, and I cannot dream of rendering a place that honour and the interests of France command me to defend to the last extremity.'[24] A local historian, Frédéric Piton, noted that, despite their suffering, the citizens of Strasbourg refused to capitulate: 'in every group filling the streets, the firm resolution dominates that they will not let themselves be knocked down; they will resist to the end.'[25] The bishop of Strasbourg, seventy-six-year-old André Raess, with Uhrich's permission, tried to negotiate with Werder, but walked away empty handed. Raess compared himself to Pope Leo I, who successfully stopped the Huns: 'I am not Saint-Leo, but I found worse than Attila.'[26] That night, the bombardment continued. This time, Strasbourg's magnificent cathedral caught fire. As the copper roof burned, it cast green and blue flames that haunted the lacy stonework of the façade. The gargoyles spewed out molten lead. In the flickering light, the spire seemed to grow to a grotesque height. Although the cathedral did not collapse, the sight of this fire caused Bishop Raess to fall gravely ill.

Municipal leaders began to wonder if it was time to surrender, but Uhrich knew he was bound by military law to hold out until the Germans had created a practicable breach in the defences. Meanwhile, after failing to break the city through heavy bombardment, Werder turned to regular siege methods, following the rules and traditions of siege warfare with a focus on the fortifications. The first parallel was completed on the night of 29–30 August north of the Pierre Gate, about 700 feet north-west of the walls. On 1

September, the Germans began a second parallel about 300 feet closer, cutting through Sainte-Hélène's Cemetery.

Despite the encroaching Germans, civilians inside Strasbourg found ways to carry on. The pastor of the New Church preached from the burned-out shell of this house of worship, with no roof overhead, no altar or pulpit, the floor still warm from the flames. Burials took place in a local garden since the cemetery was no longer available. Now that the intense period of bombardment had passed, some civilians experienced the regular siege as a period of relative relief. The journalist Auguste Schneegans wrote, 'So terrible had been the terrors of the first days that the disasters of the days to follow seemed like mere accidents.'[27] Societies such as the Freemasons continued to meet. Social calls to family and friends, too, continued at a regular pace. 'Never so many visits as during this siege,' recorded Reuss, 'and to say and hear everywhere the same thing!'[28] Everyone wanted to check in to see if anyone had died or been wounded overnight.

At the end of August, the Orléanist mayor, Théodore Humann, recognized that his municipal council had largely dispersed and no longer held the confidence of the inhabitants. Humann called for nominations to a municipal commission that had greater standing in the community, including moderate republicans who had been active in 1848 or in the opposition to the Second Empire. These new leaders included Auguste Schneegans; Antoine Zopff, who had already distinguished himself as an organizer of the Red Cross; and Émile Küss, a doctor who had been a local leader of the republicans in 1848 but remained at the margins of politics under Napoleon III. On the news of this municipal commission on 30 August, inhabitants of Strasbourg demonstrated in Place Gutenberg demanding that it investigate and report to the people via posters 'the real state of things'.[29] The military leadership under Uhrich could not be trusted to share information about food supply or military strength, and the municipal commission was invited to step over military regulations to keep the army accountable to the people. Unlike in Metz, where trust of the military under Bazaine also ran extremely low, the local government in Strasbourg had higher standing with the citizenry. Uhrich of course was not swayed by this request to divulge the army's situation to the general public.

The municipal commission therefore focused on finding shelter for the newly homeless, and providing unemployment and food relief and hospitals. It opened public buildings to house those whose homes had burned down, including the covered market, the slaughterhouse and the Imperial Palace. Workers filled the theatres and the elderly stayed in schoolhouses. Zopff established an Extraordinary Communal Workshop to place unemployed workers in workshops, as firefighters, or as city employees charged with clearing debris and horse cadavers. He also set up *restaurants populaires* to serve free meals of dry legumes, bread and wine or coffee. These establishments, and the privately funded *cuisines économiques* that offered slightly better fare at a low cost, helped keep the peace as well as ward off starvation. Strasbourg never experienced the club radicalism of Paris or other cities.

Throughout the regular siege, Werder and Uhrich occasionally negotiated the departure of individual civilians. Rodolphe Reuss and his family received news that they had been granted a safe-conduct over lunch on 2 September. 'Great emotion!' the teacher recorded in his diary: 'Papa does not want to leave, Aunt Elise insists, Hélène [Reuss's sister] yells and cries. Stormy deliberation.'[30] Just as Juliette Adam refused to leave Paris in its time of distress, the Reuss family was torn between staying as resisters and accepting the path of the refugee. Furthermore, the safe-conduct only provided passage through the German lines. Once they left Strasbourg, nobody could tell whether they would find food or shelter. The external situation was completely unknown: nobody realized that, on that very day, Napoleon III had surrendered himself and his army outside Sedan. In the end, Reuss's father, mother, grandmother, sister, four female cousins and two female servants departed. Reuss himself 'did not dream of leaving, and *maman* did not insist too much'.[31]

He and his uncles and a single female servant stayed behind. After the family packed into a carriage and passed through the gates, Reuss lingered over a cigar in his father's study wondering if they would ever meet again.

Similarly, the anonymous mother who had suffered anxiety over the fate of her children Émile and Marie managed to procure a safe-conduct out of the city. Now, the uncertainty of what she would find outside, far from her husband, presented new challenges. She nevertheless took responsibility for leading her two children out of the city. In a memoir written to her children, she recorded leaving the city gates: 'Your father, seeing the door close on us, was the happiest of mortals. Alas, it was not the same for me, seeing myself outside, alone, without supports, and your father in that hell, not knowing if I [would] see him again one day . . . All my courage abandoned me . . . I no longer had the strength to think.'[32] Still, the woman navigated the challenge of Prussian guards who questioned the validity of her pass and threatened to turn her back for having taken the wrong route. Her spirits lifted as she made her way onward. After weeks of travelling by carriage, boat and train, and despite both of her children falling ill, she made her way to her parents' home in Colmar.

Outside, the Germans slowly inched their cannon closer to Strasbourg. Crown Prince Friedrich Wilhelm, writing from Versailles, eagerly awaited the city's surrender. 'The maddest part of the whole business is,' he wrote, 'that desiring to make that town German and gain it over to ourselves, we must first reduce it to ashes to attain our object. But what else is left for the besiegers to do?'[33]

In early September, visiting Swiss dignitaries brought official confirmation that Napoleon III had surrendered, and a new republic had been declared in Paris. Municipal leaders hastened to appoint new republican leaders to replace the imperial ones. They selected Émile Küss as the new mayor. Küss was willing to compromise to protect his fellow citizens. On 18 September, he and forty-five municipal leaders decided to petition Uhrich to capitulate. They believed that they and the city had done their duty, and that surrender would be honourable and would spare the city from the consequences of an assault. Schneegans later explained,

> To bury oneself under ruins and bury with oneself 60,000 men, women, and children is certainly marvellously heroic, and if this sacrifice were useful to the *patrie* and could save the country, it would absolutely be demanded of each and every one; but if this heroism is purely in vain it becomes reprehensible, and those who impose it on a population assume responsibility for all the uselessly spilled blood.[34]

In this view, holding out was not noble but foolish given the context. Rather than follow the principle of fighting to the death, the municipal leaders reasoned that the city had done enough and could suffer far worse if they continued to resist. They accepted that they were civilians charged with the welfare of their people, not soldiers bound to die for a cause, and as good republicans they claimed the right to influence the course of events.

Uhrich did not accept any of this reasoning, bound as he was to uphold military duty to fight until the Germans had created a practicable breach in the defences. Loyal to the army, whether commanded by Napoleon III or the Government of National Defence, Uhrich overcame his own personal feelings about the matter and the suffering that he was party to creating. 'Believe me,' he told the municipal leaders, 'no one feels more deeply than me the misfortunes caused to the city of Strasbourg; but I am not free to follow the fervour of my heart. Military law dominates me, and it is my honour to obey loyally.'[35]

One final unexpected element surprised the city: the arrival of Edmond Valentin, the new prefect of the Bas-Rhin sent by the new republic to replace the imperial prefect. Valentin had spent decades in exile rather than live under Napoleon III. Unlike Küss, who had established a medical practice and lived quietly in Strasbourg, Valentin had become a republican freethinker who volunteered in the military and later taught military history in Woolwich. Unlike Uhrich and the municipal leaders, Valentin did not see any way out of the siege other than to fight to the death. Valentin's daring arrival took him swimming through canals, crawling through fields, and using disguise and his English-language skills to sneak through the Prussian lines. These heroics won some admiration among the people of Strasbourg, but Valentin did not convince the authorities to hold out beyond military necessity. Schneegans was annoyed that when Valentin arrived, 'we suddenly saw reappear that same system of [falsely] comforting telegrams that for a month had worn out our patience.'[36] Most civilians had no interest in Valentin's reckless stance. For his part, Uhrich no longer believed that the city should keep fighting to the last soldier, hunk of bread and cartridge.

On the night of 11–12 September, the Prussians constructed their third parallel. From this position, they could destroy the outermost French artillery and take lunettes 53 and 52. The primary wall was now vulnerable to direct attack from close range. Uhrich continued to reject German calls for surrender until a breach had opened in bastion 11 on 27 September. His officers reported that an assault could occur in as soon as a few hours. Instead of waiting for such an assault, as the regulations stipulated, Uhrich, with the support of his defence council, decided to surrender. The white flag was hoisted atop the cathedral at five o'clock in the afternoon of the 27th. While Uhrich undoubtedly saved lives with this decision, he was reprimanded by a post-war military inquest. Frédéric Piton, who saw the flag raised from his attic, recognized that all was lost: the suffering of the previous six weeks had been for nothing. Municipal leaders expressed their anger. 'We cried tears of rage and sadness,' wrote Schneegans. 'Our fate had been decided! We, who had not wanted this war, we became its first victims!'[37] An outraged crowd gathered on Place Gutenberg to demand further resistance, but even Valentin admitted it was all over.

At two o'clock in the morning on 28 September, representatives of Uhrich and Werder signed the capitulation agreement in a boxcar in Koenigshoffen. The next morning, the people of Strasbourg came under German occupation. Those who had hoped for a new French republic found themselves under the Prussian monarchy. While Uhrich and his officers were offered honourable release, some 17,000 French soldiers became prisoners of war. Mayor Küss now mediated between the German occupiers and the civilians of Strasbourg, whose bitter disappointment could not be disguised as disorderly French soldiers marched out of the city and into captivity. Küss called on inhabitants to maintain the peace and avoid reprisals. In this, he was successful. That evening, Reuss found himself compelled to drink a glass of wine with eight Prussians.

News of Strasbourg's fall reached Crown Prince Friedrich Wilhelm on his morning ride in the grounds of Versailles, to his great relief. Berlin's *Volks-Zeitung* soon reported 'the crown of German cities is today one pearl richer. Strasbourg is ours.'[38] Although the annexation was not official until the end of the war, the German occupiers of Strasbourg took immediate steps to normalize German control. 'Die Wacht am Rhein' played in the square in front of the cathedral, and by 2 October the black and white flag of Prussia flew alongside the red, black and white flag of the North German Confederation. Strasbourg began the task of clearing its streets and reopening shops. The Germans did not impose a war indemnity or march through the city streets, but instead exacted a symbolic price: a Protestant service in the Church of Saint-Thomas on 30 September, the anniversary of Strasbourg's capture by France in 1681. Hundreds of Prussian soldiers packed into the church. In the front pews, Mayor Küss and Protestant municipal leaders, including Schneegans, sat alongside Werder and his officers.

The occupation of Strasbourg between the fall of the city and its formal annexation on 1 March 1871 proceeded with relative calm. Two fatalities are recorded, each involving French men who had reportedly threatened German soldiers in the city streets during the early days of the occupation. Frédéric Piton soon quartered ten German soldiers in his house. Although every windowpane had been broken during the siege, the soldiers seemed to find the accommodation pleasant enough. Piton appreciated that their presence shielded him from any looting. 'They are polite,' Piton wrote of his lodgers, 'they don't ask for much, and to judge from their conversation, would prefer to go home rather than hold down Strasbourg . . . I don't detect any hatred or animosity toward our country.'[39]

With between 8,000 and 10,000 now homeless and hundreds wounded, the civilians of Strasbourg struggled to recover from the six-week siege. A man who had spent several days buried in his cellar recorded,

> I had entered without a grey hair, today I am completely white; I had aged in four days more than twenty years. As for my shops, everything is burned. I had worked for ten years to be able to give my family modest comfort; I had envisioned for my wife and for myself a happy, carefree old age; today everything must start over again: I envision on the horizon only misery for our old age.[40]

As the ruins were cleared, the remains of entire families were discovered.

Even as the war continued elsewhere, German war tourists soon inundated the city, particularly from neighbouring Baden. The French inhabitants resented their callous curiosity, treating their ruined city as a tourist attraction and paying to enter the damaged citadel (the Prussians gave the proceeds to the city). Piton was disappointed in 'the malicious joy, the cynical arrogance . . . I didn't hear a single expression of pity or sympathy.'[41] The warm relationship that previously existed between Alsatians and Badenese had now been severed, just as they became part of the same unified country.

Due to Strasbourg's dramatic circumstances, an unprecedented flood of financial aid – nearly half a million francs – soon arrived from across western Europe and the United States in a show of support for civilian victims that had not occurred during the Crimean War or the American Civil War. These funds were distributed to those who had lost their homes or family members by the Strasbourg Aid Committee for the Victims of the Bombardment.

Rebuilding Strasbourg became a priority during the occupation, particularly the rebuilding of the religious and cultural edifices that had been so damaged during the period of intense bombardment. In the years to come, the German government reimbursed the city for almost three-quarters of the costs incurred during the siege, including the quartering of German soldiers, and provided the equivalent of over 50 million francs to rebuild the city's streets and buildings. The Germans established a new university and a library whose collection of over half a million books was, for over three decades prior to the Great War, the largest in the world. The struggle of civilians in the midst of the siege was forgotten as Strasbourg re-emerged as a German city.

13. *Autumn in Paris*

As Metz and Strasbourg fell, the siege of Paris had just begun. The state of siege trapped Parisians together at the same moment that the new Government of National Defence opened up new political freedoms, particularly regarding speech, assembly and the press. In September and October, it seemed possible that a new social order might be at hand, with the National Guardsman emerging as a heroic figure in the defence of Paris. Prior to the war, many Parisians had undergone a process of reinvention as they moved from the country to the capital city. They now reinvented themselves again as the heroic defenders of a besieged city. Not for the last time, the City of Paris lived up to its motto, *Fluctuat nec mergitur* – 'Tossed by the waves, but does not sink'.

By late September, service in the National Guard had become common for Parisian men. Soldiers now populated the streets, walking to and from their daily duty on the ramparts. The army did not have tents or barracks to house these soldiers. Most of the men therefore returned home at night in a curious daily commute from the ramparts to the domestic hearth. National Guard battalions were organized by the *arrondissement*, not citywide, so they were local in character and tied to their neighbourhoods.

Soldiers from the provinces were also billeted in Parisian apartments and houses. In addition, lodgings and cellars were requisitioned to store ammunition and supplies. Étienne Arago, the mayor of Paris, announced this arrangement on 7 September:

> Dear fellow citizens, The Mobile Guard from the provinces is speeding to aid the defense of the great City. You will welcome as brothers these brave children of France who are coming to share your dangers. They need shelter: you will open to them your residences.

Each mobile guardsman will receive a housing voucher delivered by the mayor indicating the name and the address of the inhabitant at whose home he will present himself.[1]

Daily routines were overturned. Familiar Parisian spaces now became the scene of disorienting sights: displaced rural people hauling carts down the Champs-Elysées, the enrolment of volunteers in the square in front of the Panthéon. Areas of leisure and glamour became spaces of utility and violence.

Yet public spaces retained a curiously domestic and civilian character. Soldiers washed their clothes in the fountain at Place Pigalle and shaved in the Tuileries gardens. The ramparts became living spaces. Conversely, spaces typically reserved for civilians became militarized. Hotels, theatres and department stores were turned into hospitals. The Louvre converted its Grande Galerie into an armament shop. Train stations were also repurposed: Parisians ground flour in the Gare du Nord and manufactured balloons in the Gare d'Orléans. Semaphore stations, including the Arc de Triomphe, the Panthéon, the fort of Mont Valérien and the heights of Montmartre, signalled across the city.

The Opera House of Charles Garnier, the ornament of the Second Empire, now became a water reservoir. Fearful that the Prussians would cut off Paris's aqueducts, Garnier drilled open the concrete layer on which the foundations of the Opera House had been built, revealing a vast well of water that pooled down from Montmartre. This bizarre amalgam of chthonic flood and opera house later inspired Gaston Leroux's *Phantom of the Opera*.

Parisians – both those who served on the ramparts and those who did not – soon fell into the wartime tension between high anxiety and pervasive boredom. They waited with hope and dread for something to happen, with each day similar to the one that had just passed, but a little darker and with less food. There was little that anyone could do to alleviate the siege, and to many the loss of agency felt debilitating.

The streets emptied at night. As of 9 September, the provisional police prefect, Émile de Kératry, announced the closing of all theatres: 'Considering that the country is in mourning and that the opening of theatres stands in contradiction with the general attitude of the Parisian population.'[2] Public establishments, including cafés, were ordered to close at 10.30. As Fulbert Dumonteil lamented, 'Sparta goes to bed at the time that Babylon woke up.'[3] The unique posture of the *flâneur* – the knowing dandy strolling up the boulevards and observing the scene through a lens of studied boredom – fell apart during a time when everyone was already either bored or in crisis, everyone was watching everyone else and citizen-soldiers roamed the streets.

Paradoxically, with the ordinary entertainments shut down, the city itself became a spectacle, with new sights to see on the ramparts, at encampments, at the long food lines. Juliette Adam wrote that 'Paris, since its imprisonment, lives on its boulevards.'[4] An anonymous diarist described on 3 October: 'The very different aspect of these formerly charming places doesn't seem at all sad, since despite the devastation the whole area is full of animation and the curious crowds abound, armed with lorgnettes to try and see the Prussians.'[5] Artists depicted boulevard life as a space where unaccompanied women could now move freely, without sexualized connotations. It was a golden age of the postal service, of neighbourhood bonds, boulevard life and political ferment.

Parisians turned to the written word for consolation and to make sense, day by day, of their experiences. During the siege, Parisians published 860 new non-periodical books and the number of newspapers doubled. Most publications were penned by unknown authors, though Victor Hugo's *Les Chatîments* (*Castigations*) was an exception that gained a huge audience.

Tiny printers became the motor of these publications, in part because of the removal of most regulations, but also because Paris itself contained only 7 per cent of the nation's printers, as the city was too crowded to house large, steam-powered presses. Printers in Paris were small, niche operations, such as the one described by the journalist and engineer Maxime Vuillaume and owned by a woman known as Mother Gaittet:

> I can still see [. . .] the cobblestone courtyard covered with all sorts of equipment, hand carts, outdated furniture and tools. In a corner, a little boutique stuffed with printed papers, behind which a cobbler pounded on shoes. Through a gray door, there was the printing press, where the owner quickly arrived, a tall, graying woman eternally wearing a blue fustian dress, and perpetually followed by a large, jaundiced greyhound, its snout thinning in old age.[6]

These smaller organizations picked up the demand for books and pamphlets by and for the besieged: political manifestos, accounts of fighting on the ramparts, political poetry and siege diaries. The Law of 11 May 1868 had already loosened restrictions on publications, allowing pamphlet-makers like Gaittet to publish. Once the GND abolished censorship and the *caution*, a one-time tax on new periodicals, Parisians enjoyed a rare moment of complete editorial freedom with regard to their political opinions.

Newspapers were problematic to publish but ardently read. Due to a paper shortage during the siege, newspapers were shorter (often just one sheet) or published on a smaller paper size. They had little to report on events outside the city walls. As they competed for attention at newspaper kiosks, they often printed unsubstantiated rumours. This led to such misinformation as the *Petit Journal*'s 5 September edition proclaiming 'VICTOIRE DE SEDAN'. The newspaper never retracted the story. It simply got buried in the ongoing rush of news.

Parisians also engaged in more personal writing in the form of diaries. This daily meditation allowed citizens to make the tedium and uncertainty bearable and to give some order to the undifferentiated days. With the outcome of the siege unknown and the national context largely absent, diarists could not plot the arc of their writing, but rather remained stuck in the present, like some latter-day chroniclers recording a repetitive litany of breaking news and unresolved rumours.[7]

Parisians created an astonishing amount of new and inventive art despite the adjustments that artists were obliged to make under siege conditions and often in service as soldiers in the National Guard. Three new characters appear in the art of the siege: the new soldier (who became the star of cultural representation); the besieged woman honourably seeking provisions or being bombarded; and the displaced rural person, who tended to symbolize disorder and need. Édouard Manet, a staunch republican and friend of Gambetta, joined a National Guard battalion from Batignolles and managed to complete two paintings during the siege, both grim landscapes of snow-bedecked Parisian neighbourhoods.

The painter Gustave Courbet was selected to head a government commission to protect national works of art during the war. Although best known now for his alleged role in destroying the Vendôme Column during the Commune, during the siege Courbet focused on art preservation and good administration through democratic procedure. Versailles sent fifty-seven works of art – largely painting and sculpture – to the Louvre for safekeeping; Saint-Cloud, the Trianon, the Elysée Palace and the Tuileries Garden acted similarly. The Louvre curatorial staff placed the packed artworks in basements or under the vaults of rooms and stairways, and stacked sandbags in the windows. As the German cannon came into place, however, Courbet did not think these measures would offer sufficient protection.

Courbet also spoke out against the Germans. In a speech directed at German soldiers, including artists whom he knew to have republican views, he made his politics plain: 'Until Sedan you even did us a favor . . . But now that you have settled the score with Bonaparte, what business do you have with the Republic? You want to put the Republic in chains? Poor fools! You put the cord around your own neck.'[8]

Despite the French effort to expel German nationals, between 5,000 and 9,000 Germans remained in the capital during the siege. Those who did not feel a kinship to Germany, or whose family members were French, decided to take the risk of living clandestinely in Paris. In some families, only the man departed while his wife and children remained.

Some German domestic servants stayed under the protection of their employers – though they were sometimes later denounced, put on the street, and imprisoned, deprived of their liberty often to protect them from harassment by Parisians. Fifty-two Bavarian women were held in the prison of Saint-Lazare at the war's end. Afterwards, the Swiss embassy freed the Bavarian women in Saint-Lazare, in small groups, to avoid attracting the attention of Parisians.

Germans were not allowed ration cards during the siege. The American ambassador, Washburne, counted 3,000 Germans that he assisted with food, money and firewood during the winter of 1870–71. Others did not seek help as they feared discovery. They spent months in hiding. On 9 January, one of Washburne's employees arrived at the domicile of a German family with five children. They were out of food and, to stay warm, had burned all their furniture, including their beds. The employee left some wood, wine, chocolate and sugar. The war did not end for almost three more weeks.

Some foreign nationals sought French citizenship in the midst of war. The Government of National Defence claimed the right of the Ministry of Justice to oversee this process on 12 September. On 26 October, a decree made it possible for foreigners who had taken part in the war to seek naturalization, a process simplified by a decree on 19 November. Many of these were men who had married French women. Others simply did not want to be the enemy during the course of the war. One woman, Rose Leib, had lived in Paris for twenty years and ran a laundry service. She made an official request to remain in Paris for the duration of the war. She produced a letter in her favour signed by nine of her neighbours. Her only enemy, she wrote, was a rival in the laundry business, whom she feared would denounce her to the authorities. Good personal relations could exist and outweigh the general hysteria regarding Germans in Paris. Unfortunately, we do not know the outcome of her request.

The French who oversaw naturalization requests tended to be strict and see Germans of all origins as Prussian. And yet, others in the same office took a different perspective. 'What an incorrigible Germanophobe you are,' wrote one superior with regard to his staff member's rejection of a dossier. The dossier in question was the request for naturalization from one Jean Furterer, aged fifty-one, originally from Württemberg, who had been living in Paris for twenty-six years and was married to a French woman. His papers were in perfect order, he already had received his residency permission, and he had included a letter of recommendation from Étienne Arago, the mayor of Paris.[9]

With the fall of Napoleon III, long-standing hopes for remaking French social relations and political power seemed within reach. The social democracy espoused in 1848, long under duress, seemed on the cusp of reality. On 4 September, the worker movement had pushed for the immediate election of municipal councils, the abolition of the prefecture of police, the election and accountability of magistrates, total freedom of the press, freedom of association, the abolition of the budget to support religion, the end to political imprisonment, and the arming of all citizens. Soon Parisian radicals formed vigilance committees in each *arrondissement*, who sent delegates to a central committee.

At first, these committees supported the GND, but the legitimacy of the provisional government remained in doubt pending national elections to a constituent assembly. Over the question of elections, Gambetta left himself open to the criticism that he led without legitimacy and posed the threat of creating a new dictatorship. On 8 September, the GND set the date for national elections to a constituent assembly for 16 October. Still, Gambetta rightly feared that such an election would in fact demonstrate that he did not enjoy deep and widespread national support.

Indeed, by mid-September, the slow pace and moderation of the GND began to grate on the vigilance committees. Would this new republic really be any different from the Second Empire? Then, on

16 September, to assist with Favre's forthcoming negotiations with Bismarck, the GND moved the election earlier, to 2 October, and at the same time, the municipal elections were set for 25 September. The earlier date for national elections disappointed republicans both inside Paris and the prefects outside, who recognized that it might swing the vote for a conservative peace. Furthermore, from the perspective of the radicals, the purge of imperial men from the government had not been complete enough, while military preparations moved too slowly. The extreme Left furthermore deemed Orléanist Adolphe Thiers' mission to meet with royal leaders abroad to be counter-revolutionary.

As the month wore on, Parisian critics of the GND gained momentum. News of Favre's failure at Ferrières and of the complete encirclement of Paris arrived at the same time, exacerbating these tensions. By 22 September, the central committee published demands with a strikingly more radical tone calling for 'the triumph of the European revolution', the 'abolition of misery' and the establishment of a 'sovereign commune, revolutionarily operationalizing the defeat of the enemy and then facilitating the harmony of interests and the direct government of citizens by themselves'.[10] The press on the Left excoriated the GND for seeking to negotiate with the enemy. The central committee began to sit permanently.

After Favre's failure to come to an agreement on 19–20 September, quick elections no longer seemed particularly helpful to securing a favourable peace. In Paris itself, the municipal elections planned for September threatened the possibility of an elected Parisian government that would operate in parallel with the GND or seek to subvert it. Both national and municipal elections were postponed indefinitely on 24 September. The members of the Delegation of Tours contested this decision and, on 1 October, called for elections on the 16th. But when Gambetta arrived in Tours on 9 October, he again adjourned the elections, and that was that.

Parisians found both solace and fuel for their anger in neighbourhood clubs that arose across the city and met frequently, sometimes nightly. The clubs directed their resentment against the GND, which they blamed for inaction, military failures and inability to supply the city. The National Guard battalions, by contrast, were called to represent the neighbourhoods' will to continue the fight in a democratic show of arms. The fact that the GND claimed the mantle of republicanism only made their prevarication on elections harder to take.

These siege-time meetings built on the recent 'meeting movement' that had begun in the final years of the Second Empire. In 1868, Napoleon III had the Corps Législatif pass a law allowing electoral assemblies and non-political meetings. Meeting organizers now simply had to notify the prefecture of police, rather than receive permission to hold such a meeting. Meetings quickly grew popular, with 776 meetings in Paris between June 1868 and April 1870, especially in the peripheral *arrondissements*.

The meeting movement was all the stronger in areas of Paris that had been recently annexed to the city – including Belleville, La Villette, Montmartre and Batignolles – in which everyday life was more likely to be structured by neighbourhood ties than by craft. These neighbourhoods were already the place for informal interaction, and the advent of the public meeting movement made this political collective identity clear. Any radical, socialist revolutionaries used this opportunity to spread their messages. As club meetings became more confrontational, the police dissolved them. Twenty per cent of meetings in the outer *arrondissements* ended in this way. Those attending the meetings learned to see the state and its police – not the capitalist order – as the primary enemy.

During the siege, then, people attended these clubs night after night because they often had pre-existing neighbourhood bonds that became even stronger through the crucible of the siege. Liberalization in the final years of the Second Empire allowed social protest to emerge and solidify, much more strongly and angrily than Napoleon III had anticipated – and certainly more strongly than republicans believed could possibly be directed toward them. National Guard battalions, too, were believed to reflect the character of the neighbourhood from which they were recruited; more so than the city as a whole. Speakers in clubs used neighbourhood rivalry to spur action and commitment: 'There are other *quartiers* where they have more energy than in Belleville ("It's true! We are soft!"), where they are determined, this very evening, to march on the Hôtel de Ville. Are we going to let ourselves be outdone by La Villette or Montmartre? ("No! No!")'[11] Parisians had relatively fewer contacts with individuals from other neighbourhoods, and when they did find others similarly fed up with the government, club speakers used that information to stir up their own neighbours against the central state.

Over time, some Parisian radicals became more militant. They began to demonstrate in front of the statue of Strasbourg on Place de la Concorde, at the Louvre, or at the Hôtel de Ville, seeking the removal of any government functionary with a connection to the monarchy, the distribution of Chassepots to the people, or calling for municipal elections. On 5 October, Gustave Flourens, elected by five battalions of the National Guard, led a force of some eight to ten thousand armed men from Belleville down to the Hôtel de Ville to demand municipal elections, mass war against the enemy and authoritarian powers of requisition. A demonstration on 8 October organized by the central committee targeted members of the GND with chants of 'Down with the *capitulards*! Down with traitors!' While both of these revolutionary moments failed, they demonstrated the extreme Left's ability to mobilize quickly.

To critics of the GND, the administration of 4 September grew increasingly 'burlesque and derisory'.[12] The press from the Left attacked the GND, calling for a Commune, a *levée en masse*, a Committee of Public Safety. The GND did not want to suppress the press – Favre opposed Picard's suggestion – but the newspapers did make it difficult to govern. Still, Favre did not want to face the political consequences of quashing the free press, nor did he want to follow the Second Empire. The challenges of a free press came fast and sharp in the crisis of war.

On 11 October, Edmond Adam, Juliette Adam's husband, was named prefect of police, and the couple moved into the prefecture. Edmond struggled with the tension between press freedom and squelching rumours. On 15 October, *La Vérité* recklessly claimed that a red republic had been established in Lyons, that Crémieux accepted it, that Admiral Fourichon had resigned, that Bazaine had capitulated, and that there had been defeats in both Orléans and Normandy. 'The emotion is terrible, the consternation general,' wrote Juliette Adam. The government decided not to suppress the newspaper but ordered Edmond Adam to arrest the journalist. Juliette recorded her consternation. '[Edmond] Adam asks Jules Favre to point to the law that seems to authorize an arrest of this kind. It is a law on posters! M. Portalis is arrested. I regret this act, which I find arbitrary.'[13]

Meanwhile, National Guardsmen became increasingly dissatisfied with standing guard on the ramparts. Despite their lack of training and discipline and the poor quality of their equipment, the National Guard felt prepared to face the enemy. After all, Trochu had 400,000 men and good armaments from the city's factories against 236,000 Germans spread thinly around a mammoth perimeter of 50 miles. Why not attack the German lines? They were told repeatedly that they were excellent, but nevertheless not trusted in battle. This frustration led to the persistent story told in the streets and in the clubs that the GND was defeatist, especially within the radical north-east *arrondissements*.

Under this pressure, Trochu surveyed his possible next moves with increasing trepidation. The encounter at Châtillon on 19 September had confirmed Trochu's belief that the French could not handle an open battle against the disciplined and well-trained Germans. He prepared to defend Paris against an expected attack. Nevertheless, he allowed Vinoy, the Paris garrison commander, to attempt an 'offensive reconnaissance' to the south on 30 September. (Trochu did not connect such an attack to an overall French strategy.) With 20,000 men protected by guns at Bicêtre and Ivry, Vinoy attacked the villages of L'Hay, Chevilly and Thiaïs, but was driven back as the artillery failed to make a dent in the German defences.

On 13 October, Vinoy undertook another offensive reconnaissance in the south with seven battalions against the villages of Clamart, Châtillon and Bagneux, while to the west French fortress guns at Mont Valérien opened fire and destroyed the palace at Saint-Cloud. While the French were more cautious and skilled by this time, they nevertheless were pushed back by Bavarian guns on the plateau of Châtillon. They lost 400 casualties but also took 200 prisoners. This relative success made the French call more strongly for an attack.

Trochu now recognized that he needed to co-ordinate any attack with action on the Loire. Yet, an attempt to break out to the south seemed like a bad idea – the Germans were strong there. But to the west? The multiple folds of the Seine created an obstacle, yet the river also prevented the Germans from establishing strong defences. So, the French planned for a breakout of 40,000 men under the support of guns at Mont Valérien and the Seine flotilla, with the aim of heading toward Rouen to create a connection with the Loire armies by sea. This plan had obvious flaws, but it was as good a plan as any at this point. Trochu and Ducrot planned this sortie in secrecy, but in the streets and cafés the rumour spread of 'le Plan Trochu'.

Before launching the attack, Ducrot decided to attempt a smaller engagement in the sector to test the German defences and build French morale, and, if possible, to nab some territory to assist with the main launch. The attempt at Buzenval on 21 October involved 8,000 men. They were pushed back, but the men fought well and remained steady. Trochu and Ducrot therefore planned for the main attack to occur in mid-November. But although they submitted the plan to Gambetta, it never won the minister's full support.

At the end of October, however, events moved beyond Trochu's control. First came the disappointment at Le Bourget. This village lay to the north-east of Paris, directly east from Saint-Denis and outside the French line of forts and fortifications. On the night of

27 October, a unit of *francs-tireurs* under General Carrey de Bellemare located in Saint-Denis fought across the fields to take Le Bourget. This was a rare victory, celebrated in the press – and one that Trochu neither authorized nor expected. Bellemare demanded more troops, but Trochu had no strategic interest in Le Bourget. The Germans for their part were not particularly interested in fighting to recapture it. At this point, they just wanted to be home for Christmas and not be one of the last ones killed in this war.

Nevertheless, the Prussian Guard counter-attacked on 30 October after having shelled the village. They proceeded to use novel tactics that, for the first time in military history, allowed for infantry to approach a stronghold defended by long-range breech-loading rapid-fire rifles. They broke into smaller units, widely spaced, using as much cover as possible. They offered smaller targets, not shoulder-to-shoulder in a mass, and advanced in quick spurts followed by rest and cover. Furthermore, they were encouraged to take the initiative to shoot rather than to await a formal moment of attack. These tactics made it challenging for the French to mow them down as they had at Saint-Privat. Now, the Germans could advance despite the defensive Chassepots and guns of the French forts; they retook Le Bourget. In Paris, the exaggerated sense of victory gave way to crushing defeat. The Prussians' innovative tactics were largely forgotten.

The defeat at Le Bourget hit the battalions at Batignolles particularly hard. Édouard Manet wrote to his wife Suzanne, who had left the city, 'Batignolles is in a state of desolation. It was *mobiles* from Batignolles who were at le Bourget; they were almost all taken prisoner.'[14]

That same day, Adolphe Thiers returned from his failed attempt to persuade European rulers to support the French in pursuing a negotiated armistice. The tsar did not want to support a republican regime, and instead sought to take advantage of French disorder to reject the Black Sea clauses in the Treaty of Paris that had ended the Crimean War. Victor Emmanuel, following the departure of the

French garrisons, used the opportunity to take control of Rome. Britain, too, could not be persuaded, although it was ambivalent in its joy at German victory over the long-standing enemy of France: fears of an overly strong Germany were starting to grow. Vienna had no interest in supporting France after Sedan. The French would have to fight alone.

With this happy news in hand, Bismarck allowed Thiers into Paris via 'the Styx' to confirm French terms. Thiers counselled the Government of National Defence to accept Bismarck's terms, including the loss of territory. Trochu was willing, but only if elections were held that included voters in Alsace and Lorraine and only if Paris could have the chance to receive supplies. Thiers knew that Bismarck would never support Paris's resupply, but Trochu insisted. It was not a surprise to anyone, then, that Thiers' report at Versailles on 31 October did not go anywhere. Furthermore, the news that the GND had been seeking to conclude an armistice angered those who still believed that France could win in the field.

Then a third blow fell. That same morning, reports of the fall of Metz reached Paris. For those still confident in France's chances, the news of Metz hit like a second Sedan.

This series of crushing blows proved too much for revolutionaries in Paris. On the afternoon of the 31st, delegates of the twenty *arrondissements* met at Place de la Concorde and marched on the Hôtel de Ville, calling for the removal of provisional president Louis-Jules Trochu and the declaration of a Commune of Paris. Seasoned revolutionaries, notably the followers of Auguste Blanqui, Félix Pyat and Charles Delescluz, used the moment to bolster their long-term plans for revolution. In Belleville, National Guardsmen headed toward the centre of Paris. According to Juliette Adam, groups of women cried out, 'All men must go down! No armistice! Better to blow up Paris than to surrender!'[15]

In the confusion in front of the Hôtel de Ville, rumours spread that there would be a *levée en masse*, that elections had been declared for the next day, that a Commune had been declared. Multiple lists of new government leaders circulated. A detachment of the

National Guard broke into the room where the Ministry was meeting and declared the government overthrown. The ministers present found themselves prisoners.

But the revolutionaries, it seems, had not made plans for what to do next. In the hours of confusion and oratory that followed, Trochu and several ministers escaped with the help of a battalion of the National Guard. Ducrot sought a military intervention, but Trochu insisted that the action be undertaken by friendly battalions of the National Guard under the command of Jules Ferry, then prefect of the Department of the Seine.

That evening, Ferry opted to negotiate rather than attempt a dangerous direct attack. By this time, the rebels wanted to get out alive and with dignity rather than press a revolution. Even before Trochu and Ducrot arrived at the Hôtel de Ville in the early hours of 1 November, it was all over. The insurgents had departed.

That night, the GND announced that a referendum on whether the GND should stay in power would be held in two days' time on 3 November, in Paris alone. But instead of holding elections for a new municipal council, the GND authorized only the election of the *arrondissement* mayors, a move that rankled with radicals seeking municipal autonomy. At stake was whether Napoleon III's centralization of power, particularly his control over municipal councils, would continue under the new regime. Napoleon III's prefects frequently dissolved municipal councils that they deemed problematic until voters and local republican leaders were worn down. The emperor had prevented Paris and Lyons from electing their municipal leaders altogether: the minister of the interior appointed their councils and mayors. The GND's refusal to hold national elections and elections to municipal councils continued to frustrate the Left.

Nevertheless, the calculation worked. The 'no' vote received support from only 14 per cent of Parisian electors – men over the age of twenty-one – losing to the 'yes' vote 557,996 to 61,638. The Left was soundly defeated, despite a few victories in the elections of *arrondissement* mayors on 5 and 7 November. An anonymous diarist presented a common sentiment in his account of 3 November:

> I'm doing everything in my power to exercise my rights as a citizen in order to give my vote to the present government, which, given the circumstances we find ourselves in, is the only permissible one, the only one capable of getting us out of the situation and, I would add, it is also the most honourable one, the only one for which moderate and level-headed citizens should vote and in which my political thoughts and esteem are invested.[16]

Still, the vote is telling: the 'no' vote concentrated in the outer *arrondissements*, notably the 18th (20–30%), the 19th (20–30%), the 11th (30%+) and especially the 20th, where it received over 50 per cent of the vote. Including an estimate adding women and young men under twenty-one, and the abstentions of the most radical who refused to vote, Paris was home to maybe 100,000 radicals.

After 31 October, the Left in Paris was shown to be weak and small, but unbowed. Edmond Adam was replaced as prefect of police. Gambetta had taken power in hand at Tours, but Trochu wavered for two days over whether to arrest the leaders of the 31 October insurrection. Political dissent continued, shortages worsened, and social divisions continued to widen. Even the crown prince of Prussia saw the vote as no better than 'a comedy staged with tricky scenic effects worthy of the Napoleons'.[17]

Thiers attempted another round of negotiations with Bismarck on 1–5 November. Backed by Favre and others, he demanded the resupplying of Paris following the events of 31 October, which Bismarck refused unless compensated with the surrender of a fort. On 5 November, Thiers met with Ducrot and Favre at Sèvres to try to convince them to accept the German terms (Trochu sent Ducrot as his representative; due to the recent unrest, he did not want to leave the city or allow Thiers to enter). Ducrot refused to surrender. Like many Parisians with very different politics, he foresaw honour and victory through a long slog into the winter. Many Parisians agreed. The idea of seeking peace without victory seemed an unimaginable affront. In her record of 11 November, Juliette Adam shared the indignation of the majority of the Parisian press: 'What humiliation! What shame! What! With six hundred thousand men, we will accept a surrender?'[18] Peace became further out of reach.

In the provinces, the will to fight was not so clear. From Saint-Loup, George Sand despaired, 'The armistice is rejected, it is war to the death. Let us prepare to die.'[19] Sand had not seen such miserable and bedraggled soldiers since 1839 in the mountains of Catalonia. Their horses were skin and bones from head to tail, and the men themselves 'half naked', having been deprived of food and munitions.[20] 'For two days we are without news of our Army of the Loire. Has it been destroyed? We are not sure that it ever existed!'[21] As the snow fell in early November, the ground was white, but the trees still held sombre, dying leaves.

For all the turmoil inside Paris, the Germans in Versailles had grown bored and impatient. After three months of constant movement, King Wilhelm and his inner circle settled in for what turned into a dispiritingly long winter. The royal entourage sent for furs and warm clothing as the temperature fell and the war failed to come to an end. Wilhelm grew depressed and felt the strain of each challenging decision. Age and responsibilities took their toll. Moltke had turned seventy on 26 October. Roon and King Wilhelm were both in their seventies. Roon's son had been killed at Sedan. Moltke and Roon came into conflict as Moltke demanded more and more men and materiel from the minister of war. And almost everyone disliked Bismarck, offended by his reservist's uniform and his claim to authority over military matters.

The most serious conflict arose with regard to the bombardment of Paris. Moltke and Roon did not think that a bombardment would be necessary – at least not at the outset. Moltke thought that food shortages would lead to a quick capitulation. After all, the Germans believed Paris had supplies for only six weeks – that is, through to the end of October. Furthermore, he realized that a bombardment might simply waste ammunition and alienate the people, without leading to surrender, as had occurred in Strasbourg. It also posed technical difficulties and required a lengthy investment.

For all these reasons, Moltke continued to focus on surrounding Paris for an extended siege. His soldiers could find billets in abandoned suburban villages. He established elaborate telegraphing from the rear to the front. Even the outposts were strong and difficult to damage. Moltke was, moreover, willing to send his troops deeper into France to meet the gathering threat of new French armies.

By contrast, Bismarck urged a rapid and punitive bombardment that would force the GND to surrender. He protested that the military men were dragging the war into the centre of France unnecessarily and publicly criticized the delay in bombarding Paris. For many in Germany, the bombardment of Paris would be vengeance for France's centuries of misdeeds and its moral decay. The German press, encouraged by Bismarck, called for the bombardment of civilian areas, not just fortifications.

Bismarck believed that the bombardment was purposely delayed out of misplaced scruples 'fostered by the Crown Prince and through him by the Princess Victoria and her English friends'. He wrote to his wife on 28 October:

> There hangs over this whole affair an intrigue contrived by women, archbishops and professors . . . Meanwhile the men freeze and fall ill, the war is dragging on, the neutrals waste time discussing it with us, while the time passes and France is arming herself with hundreds of thousands of guns from England and America . . . All this so that certain people may be praised for saving 'civilization'.[22]

For his part, the crown prince found the clamour for bombardment distressing:

> I regret to hear from Berlin that people grow more and more bloodthirsty, burning with impatience to see the bombardment of Paris begin at last; nay, that many wish to have some of the forts stormed, deeming it would be more honourable for our arms to capture Paris downright and take the city in due accordance with all the scientific

rules of siege warfare than to force it to surrender by mere starvation. It is verily a bad business when the laity, safe at home in well-warmed rooms and sitting round a table, presumes to give judgment on questions which they know nothing about and do not understand.[23]

In the end, however, the crown prince acquiesced to preparing the bombardment in the interest of achieving peace: 'Yet surely it is the very first thing prescribed to aim at winning with the greatest possible successes with the smallest possible sacrifices of men, and this is the object I set before myself, for by now we have quite enough bloody victories to show.'[24]

14. *Generosity*

In November 1870, J. W. McMichael and his friend Thomas Ironmonger set off to see for themselves the consequences of the war on ordinary civilians. The pair left Bridgnorth – west of Birmingham on the River Severn – on 2 November and travelled via train to Oxford, London and Dover and thence by boat to Belgium, with landfall in Ostend and arrival in Brussels by the morning of 3 November. Through a series of high-placed connections in Brussels, they received honorary membership in the Belgian Red Cross, which allowed them to travel through Belgium and Luxembourg at half fare, and free travel in Germany and France. They promised to provide the amount they saved in relief of the villagers of Balan. They also received the brassard of the Red Cross to wear on their arms in case of need. Many in Brussels had connections with people in Metz and addressed letters that they hoped McMichael and his companion might be able to bring to their loved ones.

McMichael and his companion engaged in war tourism, travelling to the sites of battles and of national humiliations that were no longer the site of active engagement, but where the civilians left behind testified to ongoing distress. They visited Sedan, Bazeilles, Balan and Metz, with stops at both the humble house where Bismarck and Napoleon III had discussed the terms of capitulation and the château where the surrender was signed. At each location, they encountered witnesses whose level of charm and intelligence they never failed to note, and who shared tales of deprivation and brushes with the emperor. They made modest charitable contributions and brought news of the ongoing war back home.

McMichael's travels highlight a sense of obligation that civilians felt to intervene in the Franco-Prussian War. In neutral countries as well as in the belligerent nations, many civilians sought to ameliorate

Champigni. Decembre 1870

IN DE
A. Lançon

the suffering of both civilians and soldiers, and to transcend at least for a time the nationalistic character of the war.

As conditions for French civilians deteriorated, British civilian calls for an end to the conflict became more insistent but did not sway the foreign secretary, Lord Granville, from his policy of non-intervention and no alliances. Samuel Lobb, a thirty-seven-year-old journalist who published in the *Daily Examiner* under the name of CIVIS, increasingly called on the British government to intervene on behalf of French civilians, with particular concern for the plight of Parisians. He wrote shortly after Thiers visited Granville, suggesting that the visit helped to sway public opinion in Britain: 'If no considerations of mercy or humanity can restrain King Wilhelm from an act of Vandalism which will make his name a bye-word to posterity, if he is determined to make the French people drain the bitter cup to its last dregs, Europe ought not to look on in silence.'[1] Lobb appealed not only to the government but also to 'all Englishmen who have the true welfare of their country at heart, and who desire to see England hold a place in the councils of civilised nations worthy of her great renown' in his fruitless campaign to encourage British statesmen to bring the war to an end.[2]

While many in Paris sought to continue the conflict, other French were eager for the war to end. This sentiment spread as the winter deepened and more regions came in direct contact with German invaders. Already in October, the newspaper *Pays* estimated the cost of the war to France – mobilization, lost battles, requisitions, property damage, business loss of income, harvests – at 12 billion francs. Some began to wonder if continuing the war was worth it.

Civilians had precious few resources to petition for peace. Julia Durand-Dassier and her sister-in-law, Madame Monod, both married to Protestant pastors, tried to leverage their religious bonds to seek peace. They wrote to the queen of Hanover, asking her to use her influence to end the fratricide between 'two brotherly peoples'.[3] The queen responded on 5 November with the gentle resignation of female impotence, which masked the lack of influence that Hanover could exert on Prussia's actions. 'Alas! If it had been given women to act in favour of a peace so necessary to humanity, these efforts would have already been crowned with success . . . Let us ask God to put an end to it as soon as possible.'[4]

The most concerted effort for peace came from Countess Valérie de Gasparin of Geneva. On 9 September, Gasparin published an appeal entitled 'Guerre à la Guerre' in the Protestant newspaper *l'Espérance*. Using the military metaphor of the *levée*, Gasparin asked women of both nations to rise up and unite in prayer against the destruction of war. 'If we, the mothers, wives, fiancées, and sisters of France and Germany, want peace,' she declared, 'there will be peace.'[5] Like feminists who used motherhood as an argument for women's civil rights, Gasparin blurred the public and the private spheres. Having strong religious or domestic concerns did not automatically relegate women to silence. Thousands of signatures were gathered with the help of articles in Protestant newspapers, sermons and canvassing door-to-door, especially in the south-west of France where more Protestants lived.

The petition raised the same fault-lines between those ready for unconditional peace and those who could not yet contemplate the shame of such an act. The sacrifices had already been too great to accept the conditions that Bismarck was imposing. In Bourdeaux (Drôme), Pastor F. Prunier reported that he had to add these words to the petition to get signatures: '"The peace must have a basis in justice and love of the people," for the women of Bourdeaux do not want peace at any price.'[6]

From her home in neutral Geneva, Gasparin held firmly to the idea of unconditional peace. She responded to critics in the *Évangéliste* on 17 October, 'if there are women in France or elsewhere who find that war is not terrible enough, that there is not enough human flesh pulverized . . . let them withhold their signatures.'[7] The petition gathered 20,782 signatures by 26 November, when it was presented simultaneously to the Government of National Defence in Tours and the Royal Headquarters of the German armies in Versailles. By Christmas, 4,553 new names were added, for a total topping 25,000. There was no response.

McMichael and his companions journeyed from Brussels to Sedan to Metz and back home again across a damaged landscape with uprooted and struggling inhabitants. While the Germans and the French dutifully kept the war out of Belgium, the war had a way of making its way across the border, anyway. Travel from Brussels to Sedan was not as easy as the visitors expected, as the rail line on the French side was occupied by German soldiers who were preparing to besiege Mézières, just 12 miles north-west of Sedan. Instead, they were obliged to take a train to Poix (a little to the east and less direct) and from there take a country stagecoach to Bouillon, on the southern Belgian border just 16 miles from Sedan. The 'galled and bleeding shoulders' of the horses pulling the coach showed that they had not yet adjusted to their harnesses. These horses had been captured by the Prussians from the French at Sedan, and given to the driver by them, 'who were glad to be saved the trouble of shooting them'.[8] So said the driver at least.

In the coach, the travellers encountered a peasant girl named Julie who hailed from Bazeilles. She had left her home in the wake of the battle and had travelled with a wine merchant from Brussels who, like many in that city, had decided to come to Bazeilles to witness its ruins. This man convinced Julie to accompany him back to Brussels, where he said he would employ her as his servant. As it turned out, the merchant's intentions were of 'so questionable a character' that she ran away and took her chances with poverty. She was making her way to Bouillon. The travellers took an interest in her. One of their Belgian colleagues vowed to help her find a position upon his return, and the others agreed to call on her family upon their arrival in Bazeilles.[9]

In Bouillon, they heard the congregation sing a haunting hymn in French, 'The Sigh of the Exile', and were so moved that they requested a copy that they had translated into English. From there, they made their way via omnibus in cold and clear weather, but hills proved too much for the new transport technology and they walked a lot of it. Along the way, Belgian detachments kept watch on the border.

From their fellow travellers McMichael and Ironmonger heard stories of Prussian atrocities. One elderly gentleman who had lived twenty years in Bazeilles and now took to the road told tales that McMichael was unwilling to repeat and 'which were, one would hope, exaggerated'. The old man, reported McMichael,

> declared that one poor fellow had his hands and feet severed from his body by some Bavarians, and that he was afterwards thrown into a heap of straw and burned to death. This story we heard again and again, and when at Bazeilles, it was repeated to us most piteously by a woman, who declared herself to be the widow of the poor wretch so treated. That this tale is either capable of contradiction or explanation is possible, but it was certainly generally believed, and good use made of it against the enemy.[10]

For his part, the coachman reported that on the day of the battle, from 9 miles away, he could hear the pounding cannon and the whirr of the machine gun, 'a weapon in which he and all our fellow travellers firmly believed.'[11] He could feel the earth tremor beneath his feet.

At the Château Belle Vue, where the terms of surrender were finalized, the gardener's wife greeted them.

> The old woman, whose intelligence was of rather a low order, told us how, during the battle, she had concealed herself in the cellar; how the Prussians consumed all her provisions, so that, to use her own expression, 'she had hunger till she was dead.' Her devotion to the Emperor was thorough . . . She expressed great satisfaction in having peeled and cooked some potatoes for her royal favourite![12]

Later, en route to Metz, the travellers encountered the hasty graves of German soldiers marked with makeshift crosses. Soldiers whose rapid mobilization and ability to cross long distances by foot or by train had figured so prominently in the first month of the war were now buried on the spot where they had died. On many, a name had been written on a slip of paper and pressed into the cross with sealing wax. Regrettably, all too often, already by November, the names on these crosses had been destroyed by weather or by 'an unfriendly hand'.[13] Outside Sedan, they traversed a pasture with two hundred dead cows, killed by rinderpest, now doused with paraffin to be burned with a horrific stench.

At every turn, McMichael witnessed details that made clear the suffering wrought by the war. About a mile from Sedan, the road passed through a sharp perpendicular cut some 30–40 feet deep. McMichael imagined the terrible loss of life that had occurred in that spot as cavalry racing above failed to see the steep drop and fell to their deaths in the roadway. In Givonne, a French village tucked in a valley, the homes were occupied and damaged following the battle. 'Much wanton damage was done here,' McMichael reported, 'of which the broken windows and doors on either side the road gave abundant evidence.'[14] They later encountered a woman whose fifteen-year-old son had attempted to smuggle four captured French Chassepots into Belgium to sell. The Prussians searched his wagon, discovered the rifles and arrested the boy. He awaited sentence in prison. The mother begged for mercy but was not able to see her son. In Saarlouis, McMichael witnessed French prisoners of war carried east in railroad cattle-cars. In Saarbrücken, the travellers visited the heights on which the prince imperial experienced his supposed 'baptism of fire'. Both Germans and French denounced this supposed moment of glory as a piece of folly and a masquerade. Nearby, bullet marks covered every single building of the iron works of De Wendel and Co. These were all that remained of France's incursion into Prussian territory.

It was through these varied encounters that McMichael told the story of the war and shaped British public opinion back home. In a kaleidoscope of characters and images, the war's damage came into focus, with each inhabitant concentrated on their moment of most intense anguish, adding up to a picture of grief and desolation that cried out for aid.

For McMichael and his companions, Bazeilles became a central site of suffering. Sedan itself held little interest for the travellers. The town seemed 'prostrate and paralysed, and all the ladies testified their view of the situation by wearing deep mourning'.[15] Yet the city itself was not severely damaged, despite the five hundred or so shells that fell upon it during the course of the battle.

Therefore, McMichael and Ironmonger left immediately for Bazeilles, an hour's walk from the centre of Sedan. Along the way, they passed through the village of Balan. One family's farm had been completely burned, leaving only the iron manger behind. A woman pointed dolefully to a pile of lime under which her horse and two cows had been buried. Any projection from a house – waterpipes, shutters, sign-boards – had been pierced with bullets. The town hall had been used as the English hospital all during that terrible day, with a Mr Frank remaining there to serve the wounded soldiers. The mayor himself, who was not named, was 'not quite up to our ideal of such an official'. Doffing his wooden sabots as he entered the room, the mayor's appearance shocked the sensibilities of these English gentlemen, though they found him in the end an 'intelligent, kind-hearted, and worthy fellow'.[16]

On to Bazeilles. Despite the foreshadowing tales he had encountered on the road, McMichael was unprepared for the destruction that he witnessed. Only five houses remained standing. All others were blackened and crumbling, gutted, unsafe to enter, and some of them still smouldering. 'I have neither the power nor heart to describe what we saw there . . . you must see it yourselves to realise it in all its horrid truth!'[17] Despite their attempts to prepare themselves, they were 'utterly bewildered' by what they saw. Swarms of children begged for food and money, which the travellers hastily disbursed.

Life in Bazeilles since September had been difficult. The weeks that followed the battle brought new horrors. As armies passed out of Bazeilles, they left a trail of disease behind: dysentery, typhus, and smallpox. Corpses lay in heaps, many unburied. Since the bodies could not be buried fast enough, villagers ended up cremating many of them in deep trenches dug in the shape of a cross. French and German soldiers were piled together in those trenches and left to burn. But many thousands lay in lines of putrid shallow graves extending for 10 miles or so. One report noted that 'Among the dead were many peasants, and even some women. How they came to be among the soldiers, no one knows; but there were their corpses.'[18]

Some 150 villagers died in the weeks and months that followed the battle, about one in every ten. Madame Oudart, the eighty-three-year-old kicked and dragged out of her house, died a few days later. M. Harbulot-Lambert, who had been tied to a staircase, was left in that condition for six days. He died of his wounds six weeks afterwards. Others left. The population declined from 2,048 in 1870 to 1,470 in 1875.

Those who remained had been traumatized by the ordeal. When McMichael and Ironmonger arrived, a few inhabitants came over to greet the travellers. They were pitiful, McMichael noted, but did not ask for alms. 'They walked by our side, showing us spots where deeds of blood had been done, and where the vengeance of their foe had reached its climax. I cannot venture to repeat all we heard.'[19] Emotional and mental strain manifested in 'violent commotions, poignant dramas of this time, [and] violently shook nervous systems. Madness, hysteria, neurasthenia, paralysis of all kinds were the consequence of all these tragic events.'[20] Others reported that people went mad and showed symptoms that later might have been called some kind of shell shock or PTSD, though they did not have a label to describe it at the time.

McMichael tried to sort through the stories and rumours that had been in circulation since early September. News of Bazeilles had travelled quickly and grew to exaggerated proportions. Europeans were shocked by the violence that had unfolded in that suburban village. A letter from the duc de Fitz-James (a Frenchman) published in *The Times* on 15 September claimed that only 300 of the 2,000 inhabitants had survived. Unsubstantiated reports (with basic errors, such as placing the battle on 2 September) reported that 'hundreds of families – fathers, mothers, and children – were ROASTED TO DEATH, while the combatants, encircled with fire, died fighting to the last.' An anonymous report recounted, 'I was told by the *curé* of the village, who was himself saved only by accident, that out of a population of over 3,000 souls, not more than a third were now living.'[21]

Bazeilles quickly entered the British popular imagination. In *Tales of the Franco-Prussian War by an Eye-Witness*, a cheap paperback of short dramatic stories, Bazeilles was the backdrop to a rather treacly story concerning a Bavarian officer and his engagement to a British woman. It repeats the account of both Bavarian excess and unwarranted French civilian fighting: 'two peasants and a woman even, found with gun in hand' who had shot at the soldiers from a cellar; and – a story not substantiated elsewhere – 'a priest was shot who fired on the soldiers from the church.'[22]

The Germans, too, struggled to come to terms with the events of 1 September. After the battle ended, they began courts martial to adjudicate the fate of arrested civilians. Overall, these findings tended to favour civilians. Joseph Steinberger served as a translator in one trial; he later stated that thirty-two French men and women had been tried, accused of firing on Germans. Although one man was sentenced to death, General von der Tann pardoned him. Steinberger stated, 'It had turned out that our soldiers, in their understandable fury, were much too quick with the accusation that this or that person had fired at them. Everyone who just had black fingers was arrested.'[23]

Tann himself attributed the suffering of civilians to the incidental fires and to the fighting with the naval infantry. He decried the 'exaggerations' and 'unjust accusations' that followed in the wake of the battle.[24] Like the French, the Bavarians who had fought in Bazeilles spent years unpacking their memories and coming to grips with their actions.

The French government did not open an official inquiry into Bazeilles. Nevertheless, French accounts testify to an animalization of the enemy and a willingness to treat them in ways contrary to their human dignity. French accounts characterized the German soldiers in Bazeilles as 'barbarian conquerors', 'ferocious beasts', or 'wild beasts' capable of 'horrors comparable to those of barbarian times'.[25] Yet using such animalistic language and moral condemnation served to make the violence less real, to obscure actions and the logic of their deployment. The actions of German soldiers were ambivalent: sometimes respectful, sometimes devoid of moral restraint.[26]

And what, then, did McMichael make of the events at Bazeilles? He was, poor soul, unable to contemplate, process, or adjudicate the atrocities:

> The burning of Bazeilles is matter of history, and whether justified by the usages of war or not, was certainly an act of retribution of the most fearful character . . . But apart from the merits of the case, which may never be understood, one thing is certain, that on that fatal day, were committed both by French and Bavarians, deeds of blood and murder that will stand through all time as a foul blot on the history of this nineteenth century.[27]

For McMichael, culpability remained murky, but the moral of the story was clear: the British public should continue to send aid to alleviate the suffering of civilians in Bazeilles and across France. This 'stream of benevolence must still flow on,' he wrote, 'and when we feel the least able to do all our hearts would prompt, we must carry the whole matter to One who is higher than we.'[28] His eye-witness testimony stood as a call to action for humanitarian aid.

McMichael's travels reflected a new impulse for international observers to take responsibility for the suffering of civilians during wartime. The most striking example of this phenomenon took place in Strasbourg during the period of the regular siege. On 10

September, a group of Swiss humanitarians arrived at the city gates with a request to lead women, children and the elderly out of there. It was the first international humanitarian intervention on behalf of civilians during wartime, a small but important moment in the development of modern ideas about warfare and the responsibility that civilians from afar bear for those caught in conflict. The historian Frédéric Piton recorded in his diary, 'The Swiss people are a great people. They alone did not abandon us . . . they alone extended a fraternal hand.'[29]

The Swiss extracted some 2,000 civilians from the city and took them to safety in Switzerland. Individuals and families registered with the Swiss for this assistance, and General Werder made the decision about who could stay and who could leave. While the rhetoric of the Swiss focused on women, children and the elderly, about 15 per cent of those who left were adult males at the head of a household, and another 5 per cent were men travelling alone. Those who left faced derision from the men who stayed. The departure lists favoured those with the means to support themselves when they reached Switzerland – the Swiss authorities had no interest in creating infrastructure to support refugees. As a result, those who left included doctors, professors, judges and others with resources. Werder redirected the German fire as civilians departed on the mornings of 15, 17, 19, 20, 21 and 22 September, but he did not allow a ceasefire.

The Swiss helped the people of Strasbourg for complex reasons. Swiss cities had a long and friendly relationship with Strasbourg. Zurich and Strasbourg had signed their first treaty of mutual assistance in 1474. A century later, they took common cause as Protestant cities facing threats from the Catholic cantons. Yet this particular intervention – assistance to civilians caught in a war between great powers – mobilized new understandings and tools. Humanitarianism became an expression of righting wrongs in the modern world. In an era when railroads and telegrams allowed for greater communication and access to the sites of suffering, the geographic scope of action widened. Humanitarian intervention reimagined the relationship between oneself and the rest of the world. Those with means now felt the need to act. Humanitarians believed the world could be a better place, a more civilized place, and that they could actively help make it happen. The Swiss who intervened were bourgeois activists who had the connections, drive and organizational skills to arrive at Werder's doorstep and gain entry. Humanitarianism also expressed a spiritual need: this act would atone for the suffering of innocents. It was an outgrowth of the valorization of sympathy that had occurred over the previous two centuries. The Swiss acted within a robust civil society that allowed them to intervene in the moment, as the conflict unfolded. They believed, too, that some people were victims whom the more fortunate must save. The objects of pity were not on the same moral plane as the actors who extended their aid. In this effort, the Swiss helped to create a humanitarian ethos that continues to reverberate.

Furthermore, the Swiss saw their humanitarian intervention as an investment in their own neutrality. Since the Reformation, Swiss cantons had increasingly seen themselves as nonaligned parties to European conflict. The growing tension between France and German states that erupted into war in 1870 became the new grounds on which to claim this neutral space. Given this longstanding commitment, the Swiss could gain the trust of both sides in delicate negotiations on behalf of the civilians of Strasbourg. In addition, Switzerland could burnish its reputation as having risen above the need for war and present an alternative to the rise of the bellicose nation-state. The municipal commissioner Antoine Zopff made the immediate connection between the Swiss intervention and the Red Cross: 'Switzerland . . . covered with its flag the humanitarian work undertaken in favour of soldiers wounded on the battlefield; today it gives the world a yet nobler example.'[30]

The Prussian commander at Strasbourg, August von Werder, agreed to the Swiss intervention for rather different reasons. He recognized that in early September, the people of Strasbourg had not yet received reliable news of the defeat at Sedan and the capture of Napoleon III. When Werder informed Uhrich of these events, the

French commander saw it as a ruse to trigger capitulation. Werder likely hoped that the Swiss could serve as trusted outsiders whose very neutrality would help the French inside Strasbourg understand their desperate situation.

The Swiss intervention served Prussian strategy, and yet it is undeniable that the Swiss succeeded in saving civilians' lives and alleviating their suffering. This act of generosity set the pattern for humanitarian intervention – noble and flawed – that has unfolded in times of modern war.

After visiting Bazeilles, McMichael and Ironmonger returned to Sedan before the gates closed at 6 p.m. and went to dine with a local banker named Ninnan, 'a whitehaired and venerable man', and his son, highly respected gentlemen to whom they had a letter of introduction. The son, André, was around thirty years of age, courteous, well-mannered, energetic and devoted to the people of Sedan.[31]

Over dinner, father and son related their own experiences of war. On the day of the battle, the two men had been standing at their window on an upper floor, watching the battle from afar. Suddenly, a shell burst through the window, passing between the two men. The father lost part of his ear, while the son received a blow to the chest. The shell passed through the room, destroying furniture and a painting hung in the hallway behind them. Despite their wealth, the family went without bread for three days following the battle. The banker's elderly sister, who lived in the countryside, spent two days and a night hiding in her garden.

Despite these challenges, McMichael emphasized André Ninnan's suave ability to rise above these circumstances and come to the aid of others. Ninnan marshalled his resources to assist with supplying warm, dry clothes at the onset of winter. Civilian men in leadership positions, like Ninnan, occupied an ambiguous status. They were the most likely to be victims of war's violence, but they could not admit their own suffering. For example, in Strasbourg the civilians killed and wounded by the bombardment were overwhelmingly adult males. Men were disproportionately harmed because they were more likely to be out in the open streets, but their own rhetoric repeated the old story that women and children were the primary victims of war. Auguste Schneegans, to take one example, argued that 'While the city thus perished, the walls of the fortress were intact; and while children agonized on all sides, hardly any soldiers were wounded on the ramparts.'[32] Civilian men of means tended to place victimhood status on women and children, and not on other men.

Civilian men stepped into the gap of assistance in this era prior to massive non-governmental organizations and international charities. They were supposed to be strong, to lead, to guide their communities and towns, yet they were not soldiers at a time when France did not have universal conscription (this changed in the wake of the war). In fact, despite their roles as mayors, doctors and civic leaders, these civilian men possessed few options to truly protect their wives, sisters and children.

Trapped within this gender bind, these men rarely acknowledged their own suffering. Nor did they see women as full partners in the wartime endeavour, typically relegating them to victim status or, at best, as selfless and docile caregivers. Observers worried about the fate of women and children did not see them as individuals with inner lives, but rather as foils to Prussian aggression, or, worse, as foolhardy victims, as described by a French doctor, Henri-Étienne Beaunis: 'Women and children . . . more imprudent and losing their heads more easily, lost the presence of mind necessary for saving themselves in time.'[33] Civilian men believed that women and children should have been protected from war, and the men's failure to protect them suggested that civilization itself was crumbling.

In a rare acknowledgement from a civilian man of these challenges and ambiguities, Schneegans, fearing death and feeling helpless to protect women and children, expressed his envy of warriors of previous times 'who, under the open sky, could fight a visible, tangible enemy, exposed like them! . . . They were not constrained by this yoke of impotence, that breaks the most robust courage and destroys the most valiant men.'[34] He distinguished between men like himself – journalists and civil servants who openly faced danger in the streets – and those who cowered in the cellars. When the Swiss humanitarians assisted in leading civilians out of besieged Strasbourg, the male leadership in the city felt a sense of relief, not only because their loved ones could leave for the relative safety of the countryside, but also because they would no longer feel the anguish of watching them suffer. The Swiss 'fraternal hand' that Piton had embraced extended to its male citizens. To women and children, the Swiss offered a paternal hand.

For a British observer like McMichael, all women and children fell into the category of victim, along with the peasants and working men felled by Prussian guns. Bourgeois civilian men, however, were his allies and co-leaders. McMichael was loathe to give these men the status of victimhood, even when they manifestly became targets of war.

Many French women, however, resisted the label of victim. They saw themselves as contributing to the cause of saving France and protecting fellow countrymen and women. Instead of fleeing the war, they intentionally engaged with it. The divide between home front and battleground blurred, and thousands of women became directly involved with the war. The sacrifices they were required to make could prove devastating and fatal, but for many women hardships strengthened their relationships with each other, bolstering their resolve for the national cause against the invading army.

In concrete terms, these women wanted to help soldiers physically and spiritually, and to protect other women who were victimized by war. Some performed the necessary but mundane tasks of knitting clothing or preparing compresses and linens. Others tried to console the families of soldiers by writing letters to mothers of sons who had died. In besieged Paris, women of means made several efforts to help those who could no longer afford food. Juliette Adam appealed to M. Cernuschi, a member of the *commission des subsistances* in the Government of National Defence, to think of 'the poor women . . . in the rain, in the cold, standing for half a day to get a meagre portion of meat.'[35]

Women of means also ran charities. The founders of the Société de secours aux victims de la guerre included the wives of republicans Jules Simon and Eugène Pelletan as well as André Léo, the woman who later used this pseudonym to argue for women's rights during the Commune. The women called for commitments from their compatriots for weekly donations of money, food, clothing and medical aid, which would be given to women, children and the elderly. The Société des écoles professionnelles Lemonnier, in five locations, provided space for the reception and distribution of donations. Hermione Quinet reported that women held a charity auction at the Ministry of Public Instruction for the benefit of war victims. The 'patriotic eloquence' of these women convinced their audience to pay 100 francs for a box of sardines.[36]

Not all assistance efforts consisted of outright charity. At least two groups of women aimed to form workshops, or *ateliers,* to provide work for women in need of a wage. These groups wanted to help women help themselves. The goal of the Association pour l'organisation du travail des femmes was to 'replace . . . the work of absent men by the work of women'.[37] This project may seem to anticipate the mass influx of women into the workplace during the Great War, which allowed combatant countries to manufacture immense quantities of arms and other battle necessities. However, for this smaller-scale project, the desire to help women as poor mothers raising the future of France overshadowed the national economic interest. Juliette Adam, listed as one of the *Dames protectrices et fondatrices*, explained that the goal was 'to find a way to give to each working woman ownership of her machine, thus to elevate the salary of women completely naturally'.[38] The Association was meant to work throughout Paris in conjunction with smaller organizations that women had created in a few *arrondissements*. In the 3rd *arrondissement*, a Société des Dames, attached to the Société de secours des vingt arrondissements, also aimed to help women find work during the siege. The extraordinary circumstances of war encouraged women to use their resources to help others, reproducing the gender role of charity-giver although with a republican and secular valence. These charities and *ateliers* also re-enforced the notion that only women, not men, should receive assistance.

A major avenue for women's participation in the war effort was voluntary service as nurses in mobile hospitals under the auspices of the Red Cross. By the end of the war, the Red Cross had raised 22 million francs and treated at least 110,000 soldiers in hospitals across France.

The International Committee of the Red Cross had been founded in 1863 by a group of Genevan philanthropists with a focus on care for sick and wounded soldiers. By 1864, twelve countries had signed the Geneva Convention, affirming neutrality for ambulances, hospitals and their work during international conflicts. That September, France had become the first country to ratify the Geneva Convention. The Franco-Prussian War was the first major conflict in which both parties had adopted it.

The Geneva Convention is a signature piece of international humanitarian law. With this landmark agreement, nations attempted to codify right action in war, making concrete, permanent, pre-existing laws to protect sick and wounded soldiers and those who cared for them. In previous centuries, the Just War tradition had, by contrast, established principles from which action could be derived, without setting concrete laws in advance. In the 1700s, pre-battle agreements to care for the wounded or bury the dead had only applied to the specific conflict at hand. International humanitarian law sought to mitigate the suffering of war through a standing agreement and was intended to reign in the fervour of nineteenth-century nationalist wars, as well as the Clausewitzian belief that the ends justify the means.

Each member nation created its own Red Cross organization. In France, the duc de Fezensac founded the nation's first one, the Société de Secours aux Blessés Militaires (SSBM) in 1866. At first, the organization did not grow beyond a small circle of Parisian high society. It held a few charity balls and had an exhibit at the Universal Exposition of 1867 but did not develop substantive materials or organization.

When the war began in 1870, civilians formed improvised hospitals in any buildings that could accommodate them to address the immediate needs on their doorstep. These spaces often became affiliated with the Red Cross. Hospitals cropped up throughout the war zone, in spaces donated and requisitioned. In Paris, under Juliette Adam's watch, the Music Conservatory of the 9th *arrondissement* was transformed into a hospital. Adam, the daughter of a doctor and granddaughter of a surgeon, knew anatomy and how to dress a wound. Even the Comédie-Française used its theatre as a hospital, staffed by nuns as well as actresses. (A scandal erupted when someone put a sheet over a statue of Voltaire to hide his anticlerical presence.) The actress Sarah Bernhardt, not yet an international celebrity, served as a nurse at the Théâtre de l'Odéon. In besieged cities like Strasbourg, smaller Red Cross hospitals were located throughout the city, to be closer to where injuries were likely to happen and because many organizations wanted to contribute to the effort.

This proximity put the hospitals in danger of bombardment, too. The Franco-Prussian War may have been the first major conflict in which both parties had adopted the Geneva Convention, but implementation was imperfect in practice. Many commanders did not trust the other side, or ignored the Convention, or did not know about it. Furthermore, it was difficult to respect Red Cross hospitals, which were small, imperfectly flagged, and hard to avoid given the relative inaccuracy of long-range weaponry. German and French newspapers alike complained that the other nation failed to uphold the Geneva Convention. Some grumbled that men sought the protection of the Red Cross armband with the intention of stealing from the dead and wounded on the battlefield.

The Red Cross welcomed both male and female volunteers, including members of female religious orders. Nursing wounded or sick soldiers reproduced women's traditional role as a caregiver, and it provided women with new opportunities for leadership and learning. Some women, like Baroness Ida de Crombrugghe of Belgium, were already active in the Red Cross, and the outbreak of war gave new meaning to their work. Crombrugghe followed the progression of the armies, nursing in Saarbrücken, Metz and Cambrai.

Other Red Cross volunteers, especially non-religious volunteers, came into conflict with professional medical staff almost immediately. While volunteers had noble intentions, many did not have the training or the supplies. Some volunteers were viewed as morally dubious. Many women volunteered for service, though not all were accepted. Crombrugghe screened her applicants and welcomed 'only women who were personally known to me or were particularly recommended'.[39] She wanted her nurses to live up to their image as virtuous servants. It was important that nurses minister to the spiritual recovery of their charges, as well as the physical.

Women found the experience of nursing together extremely rewarding. When Crombrugghe returned to her post after a brief trip back to Belgium, she wrote, 'The pleasure I experienced upon seeing my dear companions again, and the joy that they showed at my return, testified to the attachment cemented between us by the common exercise of charity.'[40] M. Vineuil told his wife that many volunteers he encountered in Parisian hospitals found the work gratifying. They told him that 'the suffering is horrible to see . . . but at least we are combating evil and suffering. And also, we are living for the first time as God wants us to live.'[41] For Juliette Adam, the ambulance became a source of female solidarity and empowerment, in which women from various classes chose to spend their time, rather than staying isolated at home, and talk over the siege, the war, the government and the news in rumour and newspapers.

Many nurses were inspired to serve out of religious conviction. Crombrugghe tried to encourage wounded soldiers to renew their faith, saving their souls as well as their bodies. She intervened in a ward that often had mocked the attempts of a chaplain to pray. Her request for tolerance from the soldiers made it possible for religious prayers to be said for those who wanted them. The common work of nursing sometimes placed service to the sick and wounded above religious differences. Coralie Cahen, a Jewish woman, led a hospital staffed by seven nuns. Although they recognized the differences between their faiths, the *religieuses* asked to call Cahen 'mother' out of respect and affection.

Nursing also encouraged some women to try to rise above national differences, an effort that did not go unchallenged. Crombrugghe was frustrated by the suspicions aroused in each town as her hospital arrived. First suspected of favouring the French, then the Prussians, Crombrugghe, a Belgian, insisted on her neutrality each time she was asked to show her papers. Upon her arrival at Cambrai, she wrote, 'It is distressing, especially for women, to have to establish their respectability by means of a legations seal.'[42]

French women also looked beyond national differences and cared for Prussians. In the Calvados, the countess of Montgommery risked her life to tend the wounded of both sides on the battlefield. Madame Vineuil cared for two sick German soldiers in her home and shared with them her photographs and stories about her sons. Daughter Berthe was shocked to see her mother chatting with 'the enemy', but her mother responded angrily, 'A sick man is no longer an enemy.'[43] Clearly, many women emphasized their roles as care-givers over their national identities. However, not all nurses could ignore the national defeat. The *ambulancières* of Metz left a memorial to the 7,203 French soldiers who died under their care. The inscriptions they chose, culled from the Bible and the words of Saint-Bernard and Saint-Francis de Sales, emphasized that soldiers did their duty and left an example to the nation 'of intrepidity and devotion'. The monument was meant to honour only the French, not the Prussian 'enemy'.[44]

Hospital work was not just a matter of being virtuous or patriotic. To treat wounded and sick men, supplies and medical skill were as necessary as honourable intentions. Women in hospitals were called on to be responsible contributors to intense situations of life and death. When Crombrugghe arrived in Metz, she was named *Infirmière-major*, a position which gave her the power to direct the other nurses as well as to request anything necessary for the service and security of the hospital. Crombrugghe also learned new treatments from doctors. For example, bathing soldiers suffering from typhoid fever in cold water reduced the mortality rate for that disease from 30 per cent to under 8 per cent.

Furthermore, female nurses were well aware of the war surrounding them. Crombrugghe believed she knew better than 'the authorities' how long Cambrai could hold out against the Prussian bombardment, based on her experience at Thionville. She reported in her journal that she expressed her confidence that Cambrai could hold out for at least eight more days. 'I made this remark to two visitors in our hospital this evening, who [had] seemed very alarmed. As I perceived that they felt a certain confidence in my knowledge of military science, I did my best to reassure them.'[45]

Nurses also helped mourners who came to the hospitals to find word of their sons or husbands. Often, they arrived too late to spend final moments with their loved ones and came only to recover their bodies. Crombrugghe recorded her encounter with a grieving widow in her diary:

> Two days ago, a young woman in mourning arrived at the hotel. She was certain that her husband had been killed at the battle of Spicheren, and she came to reclaim his body. She asked me to help her through the process. It was only after having had the remains of a number of victims exhumed and examining them herself that she recognized the body of the one she sought.[46]

Other mourners may not have been able to locate the remains of their loved ones. Crombrugghe reported that when a patient died, he would be thrown 'with the other cadavers on a cart, covered with a black flag; [the cart was] driven to one of the city cemeteries, where since September around six thousand French soldiers who died at Metz from wounds or illness, have been buried.'[47]

*

Coralie Cahen was widely celebrated for her contributions to volunteer nursing both during the war and afterwards, as a co-president of the Association des Dames Françaises, an organization of the French Red Cross. Her actions earned her a reputation that inspired hope and awe. 'When I despair to think that France has produced Maréchal Bazaine,' wrote one observer, 'I hold my head up again thinking of Mme Cahen.'[48]

The little known about Cahen before the Franco-Prussian War indicates that she spent the first half of her life (she lived from 1832 to 1899) in the comfort of one of the wealthiest Jewish families in Nancy, the daughter of Pierre Lévy and niece of the Paris banker Lazare Lévy-Bing. Coralie Lévy married Mayer Cahen, a doctor like his father Moïse, who was a prominent member of the Consistory of Paris. Brief biographies of Cahen do not elaborate on her activities before the war. Whether or not she engaged in volunteer work is unclear, although a footnote in *L'Univers Israélite* later mentioned her talent as a sculptor who 'has exhibited several times at the Salon under the pseudonym Karl Ivel'.[49]

The Franco-Prussian War was the watershed moment in Cahen's life. Just before the outbreak of war, her domestic existence was interrupted by the deaths of her husband and child. Perhaps in an effort to fill the loss, Cahen devoted herself to the war effort. She took the initiative on several projects and earned the respect and trust of journalists and politicians. Furthermore, she appears to have had knowledge about nursing learned from her husband before his death. She was not viewed simply as charitable by nature, but rather as a talented woman able to use her skills.

Over the course of what became known as the Terrible Year, Cahen was involved in several projects for the aid of French soldiers. First, she travelled to Metz to serve with the French Red Cross in a hospital for non-commissioned officers and soldiers. After the fall of Metz, Gambetta assigned Cahen to head an ambulance in Vendôme, where she worked with doctors and religious sisters from Sainte-Croix du Mans. Throughout the conflict Cahen cared for both French and German soldiers, but her support for the French cause was never in doubt. When the Prussians occupied Vendôme, she refused to allow them to replace the French flag with the German one, and they acceded to her, perhaps because she nursed Germans as well as French.

From the early months of fighting, journalists recognized Cahen's service to the war effort. Despite negative reports about some of the Red Cross's activities, Cahen stood out as an example of what was going right. Descriptions of Cahen and her actions evoked religious and heroic imagery. In *L'Univers Israélite*, her work in mobile hospitals was depicted as 'slow and arduous'.[50] In contrast with the obstacles she faced, Cahen's devotion was 'saintly' and the 'mysterious magic in her hands' could almost literally work miracles.[51]

Cahen's charity and her ability to overcome the challenges of a lone journey conferred on her, in the eyes of *L'Univers Israélite*, a heroic status. She embodied 'true heroism' and 'feared nothing: neither bullets, nor machine guns, nor the blood that she sees flowing'. Unlike male heroes, whose bravery might be due to physical prowess or skill, Cahen's heroism stemmed from her 'opposition to suffering'. Physically, Cahen was 'not extremely robust. She does not have the correct beauty of lines, but one reads on her face an infinite softness, steeped in courage. When she struggles against her emotions, when, to forget the tears that fill her eyes, she tries to smile, her face is filled with a radiant light.'[52] Her reward was the esteem and adoration of all who surrounded her.

Not all efforts enjoyed the same respect. Victoria, the wife of Crown Prince Friedrich Wilhelm and daughter of Queen Victoria, attempted to tend the sick in Berlin and Potsdam, but found her offers rejected. She then determined to travel to Hamburg to establish a hospital and inspect those on the Rhine. In this effort she succeeded, and subsequently she established – at her own expense – hospitals along the Rhine and in Frankfurt-am-Main. Her husband expressed delight at her success and the 'repeated expressions of the high respect my wife's quiet but strong and efficient activity evokes'.[53] The king, however, did not acknowledge this work, much to the disappointment of the crown prince. In fact, 'His Majesty, it seems, speaks disapprovingly of my wife's staying away from Berlin, and finds fault with all the children being with her, on the ground that in such times the Royal family should keep all together.'[54]

Civilians from across Europe insisted that they could shape the course of the Franco-Prussian War through their generosity, connections and willingness to put themselves in the centre of the conflict. Rather than view themselves as victims, women and men claimed the role of volunteer in a bid to temper the suffering of war. They aimed to protect both soldiers and other civilians in efforts that eschewed the dominant nationalist narrative. As the war continued into November, these efforts provided solace and meaning to volunteers with little else to provide comfort.

In his account of his travels to France and Belgium, McMichael evoked a sense of gratitude that Britain would not join the fight but exhorted his fellow countrymen to ameliorate the suffering of civilians and soldiers. Upon his return to England, he hastily published his account of his travels and arranged to read it to local audiences. Every time, in a communal expression of solidarity and loss, the British sang the hymn heard on the border between Belgium and France, between peace and war, 'The Sigh of the Exile'.

McMichael closed his report with a sentimental evocation of home, faith and family:

> Let us therefore, in our happy homes of England, remember those whose Christmas firesides have had many a vacant chair, and whose festive songs are changed into a wail for the dead – and let our cry go up unto Him who is the 'Father of the fatherless, and the Husband of the widow', and who, as the God of battles, can in His own good time, stay the murderous hand, and say to this seat of strife 'Peace be still'.[55]

15. *Suffering*

For the Bavarian soldiers in and around Orléans, the month of October had been one long wait. Some, of course, participated in Tann's continuing movements to clear the area of French forces. Tann took Chartres on 22 October and headed west toward Tours. By the end of October, he had cleared the German rear to Chartres and Orléans, but did not know where the French would attack – Le Mans? Tours? Bourges?

Dietrich von Lassberg was not part of Tann's actions. During this long month of inaction, he had been moved to Chécy, just outside Orléans. After weeks without news from home or about the wider war, Lassberg started to get restless. He could do only so much sightseeing in Orléans and even less in Chécy. Several times over the course of October, he met with his brother Rudolf, whom he had scarcely seen since Sedan. They visited a friend in the hospital. Still, violent death remained a possibility even during this slow period. He and Rudolf got tangled in a requisition skirmish that left two dead and eleven wounded.

The only bright spot came with the news of the fall of Metz on 27 October. Lassberg and his comrades celebrated in hopes that it augured the end of the war. It certainly freed up German forces: Moltke had two more armies available to counter the French provincial strategy. The First Army, now under General Edwin von Manteuffel, went north to attack the remaining fortresses – Verdun, Thionville, Montmédy, Mézières – and then moved west along the Oise against French forces in the north. The Second Army under Friedrich Karl set off for the Loire on 3 November, but not in time to affect the battle about to unfold.

For Gambetta, however, the fall of Metz only prompted the will to fight harder. Immediately after the fall of Orléans, he had replaced

Janvier 1871

A. Lancon

General de la Motte-Rouge with a commander from the old guard: General Louis d'Aurelle de Paladines, aristocratic, Catholic and Bonapartist. Aurelle detested republicans, and Freycinet and Gambetta kept giving him good reasons.

The first order of business was to restore discipline and morale. XV Corps, supplemented with new soldiers, including members of the Mobile Guard, appeared strong, but in reality it was divided and poorly trained with the *mobiles* (now referred to as the territorial divisions) electing their own officers and sometimes refusing to follow orders. Aurelle moved his army south of the Loire to Salbris and restored their confidence and their discipline by being present and punishing those who disrupted their orderly camp.

The GND planned to move these forces directly toward Paris to relieve it from the south. Freycinet crafted a plan for Aurelle to retake Orléans to establish a logistical base of operations closer to the capital. On 24 October, Freycinet visited Aurelle in Salbris and explained the plan: using the railway system, Aurelle was to move most of XV Corps to Tours to create the appearance that they were heading to Le Mans and thence to Paris.

In reality, Aurelle would move up the Loire to Blois where XVI Corps was located, and from there attack Orléans. The French would approach Orléans from two directions: all but one division of XV Corps would meet with the XVI at Blois and approach from the west, while the final division of XV Corps, under General Martin des Pallières, would approach Tann's rear from Gien, south-east of Orléans on the Loire. They would surround Tann's 50,000 men with their superior numbers of 120,000 men.

Like other plans hingeing on movement by rail, this one was much harder to pull off than it appeared on paper. The manoeuvre took three demoralizing days in the rain instead of a brisk thirty-six hours. Afterwards, Aurelle wanted a delay of a week before launching the attack – a week that saw the collapse of Metz. Relations between Gambetta and Aurelle, already strained by the former's insistence on civilian oversight, frayed even further after Gambetta's tactless announcement of Bazaine's surrender on 31 October. In his message to an army whose officers were largely Bonapartists, Gambetta referred to the 'corrupting power of Bonapartism' and to the 'treason of [France's] officers amid a national crisis'.[1]

Aurelle began to advance on 7 November, but the march went poorly, and his columns quickly became disorganized. He paused and pushed Freycinet to postpone the advance. Freycinet insisted, however. So, on 9 November, Aurelle continued ahead. Meanwhile, Tann got wind of the French advance and sought to avoid the trap. On the 8th, Tann marched out of Orléans with 110 guns and 20,000 men – including Lassberg – to take up positions at Coulmiers, about 12 miles west of Orléans and out of Pallières' reach.

Tann believed he could be victorious despite being so greatly outnumbered. After all, Aurelle's 70,000 troops were raw and untested. Instead, the French fought well and with confidence. Furthermore, the Government of National Defence had learned to make better use of their artillery than had the Second Empire. They also now used percussion fuses in their guns. The Bavarians experienced horrible shelling, trapped in Montpipeau Wood under a creeping barrage that splintered the trees around them and sent shards of wood through the air. Dietrich von Lassberg and his comrades were caught in the firestorm. 'Behind us in the forest, before us in the field, next to us in the trenches, over our heads, in brief, everywhere shells of all calibre exploded and showered us with explosive stuff, dirt, sod, and branches; it was a thunderstorm of the most appalling kind.'[2] He survived a close call from a shell.

Although the Bavarians held out most of the day, Tann decided he had to pull his exhausted troops back around 4 p.m. The French held their ground. The next morning Aurelle realized that he had won the first French victory of the war. The French marched into Orléans on 10 November to the sound of the city bells. Tann retreated for two days through a blizzard – first snow, then rain.

From her home in the Creuse, George Sand could not trust the news that France had recaptured Orléans. Rumours spread that 'the Mobile Guard has fought well, the city defended itself bravely. Let's hope that's all true! If we can fight, honour commands us to fight again, but I don't believe, myself, that we can fight for more. We are too disorganized . . . everyone is suspicious, accusatory, hating each other in silence.'[3]

Yet, for a brief moment, the French experienced the hope of victory and the will to keep fighting. The recapture of Orléans suggested that the GND's strategy to march on Paris with its hastily raised armies just might work.

For Lassberg, the battle had personally devastating consequences. On 10 November, he learned that his brother had been badly wounded in the head. As Lassberg sought more information he ran into his fellow Bavarian Karl Tanera, who informed him that in fact Rudolf had been killed outright. Lassberg immediately thought of his mother, waiting in Munich for news. That night, he recalled, 'I could hardly imagine that I would never see him again in this life.'[4] The next day, he took up the weary task of writing home with the terrible news. In the following weeks, Lassberg recorded very little of his grief. Twice, as the coda to long days of soldiering, he simply catalogued the receipt of letters from home addressed to Rudolf, sent prior to their knowledge of his death.

During the course of the war, soldiers on both sides experienced immense suffering and loss. On the French side, 136,000 soldiers were killed in action, declared missing, or died of their wounds; an additional 131,000 were wounded and 339,000 fell sick. In Metz alone, 35,000 died of typhus and dysentery. On the German side, there were 117,000 casualties, of whom 17,000 died in action and 11,000 died later from their wounds. In addition, 475,000 Germans fell sick, with 14,904 dying, largely from typhoid fever and dysentery (the sources are not always clear whether typhus or typhoid fever were present). For every wounded man, there were four sick men. Out of the 375,000 French prisoners, 156,000 fell ill and 17,000 died. Only 278 German soldiers died of smallpox – a major victory thanks to compulsory vaccination. But smallpox vaccination was inconsistent among French soldiers, and 1,963 died of the disease. Furthermore, French prisoners spread smallpox among the German civilian population. Doctors and volunteer nurses in Paris and across the country attempted to treat soldiers and civilians for disease, wounds and, to a small degree, psychological trauma. They were particularly stunned by the damage done to bodies by shrapnel and long-range rifles, and sought new medical treatments to address these new kinds of wounds.

The most significant pre-war strides to support soldiers' health had come in the form of immunization: more Prussian soldiers died in battle than due to disease. Hygiene, however, remained compromised in most settings. In 1870, soap was not yet standard issue to soldiers. Soldiers did not always use latrines, clean clothing could not be assumed, lice were rampant, and disease remained common.

The Germans had recent military medical experience, having just fought Denmark and Austria, and they had built up their medical expertise by conscripting medical students who then became doctors in the army reserve. They therefore had a higher calibre of doctors in their armies compared with other countries, which had to recruit them at a later stage in their careers. Doctors were organized by a Berlin-based central committee, and the Germans boasted one doctor for every 290 mobilized men. At the outset of the war, the German armies had 3,853 physicians and increased that number to 5,548, along with almost 6,000 hospital attendants and 3,000 nurses. Each German corps had three medical detachments with a total of 21 doctors and some 450 stretcher-bearers, a dozen small field hospitals (with 30 men staffing them, including 5 doctors). By contrast, the French started the war with 1,020 surgeons and had one doctor for every 740 men. German health care included both the military medical service and volunteers, which caused a constant friction. The twenty-five-year-old Friedrich Nietzsche served as a volunteer hospital attendant (and contracted both diphtheria and dysentery).

In addition, medical help came from Britain, Belgium, the Netherlands, Italy, Russia and, especially, Switzerland. The Committee of the British National Society sent ten doctors and five nurses (later increased to sixty-two and sixteen, respectively), split equally between the French and German armies. Each surgeon had £1 per day to support patients in military hospitals. The Irishman William MacCormac, surgeon-in-chief to the Anglo-American Ambulance, served in Metz, Paris and Sedan.

Not surprisingly, the presence of doctors from non-combatant countries brought some friction. The Prussian crown prince protested, 'It is very annoying how most of the English doctors and ambulance men who come here, in the first place, can speak no German, and moreover, pay no heed to the orders of the Physicians-in-Charge, but insist on acting independently, a thing that will never do.'[5] It was a rare complaint. Abbé Emmanuel Domenech attributed to these foreign doctors a decline in death rates among the wounded from 30–50 per cent down to 10 per cent.

From the beginning of the war, it was clear that new weaponry created more damaging wounds. The French Chassepot had a small entry wound and 'with its gyration scooped at its exit a trumpet-like mouth'.[6] The *mitrailleuse* killed quickly and indiscriminately. Shells and shrapnel led to horrific wounds.

Soldiers witnessed their fallen comrades on the battlefield. The sight of so many dead and wounded deeply moved them. In a letter home on 21 January 1871, H. Rosenthal wrote,

> When I once more consider the very high number of dead and wounded, when I shudder thinking about the pools of blood that we had to cross on the battlefield, when I remember all the moaning and crying, all my liveliness and all my willingness to remain in this horrible world pass away.[7]

Another soldier, in a letter published on 16 August in the *Coburger Zeitung*, wrote of his shock at seeing for the first time 'wounded, some of them horribly mutilated, moaning dreadfully'.[8] Traversing a battlefield after the fighting has ended, one soldiers wrote, 'is the most difficult thing you can ever experience and worse than the battle itself'.[9]

In his diary, one veteran of the battle of Wörth tried to see past the suffering. 'With every step you saw new misery,' he recorded, 'but in war and in danger you become hardened. Although you do everything to ease the situation of an unfortunate comrade, all the misery passes by more quickly than in other times and there is a good side to it.'[10] It was not clear what this good side could be. The English correspondent Archibald Forbes described the wounded at Sedan:

> We saw where MacMahon lay wounded and also how full the town was of troops. They were swarming, densely packed, everywhere. Of the wounded, some were in churches, the houses, public buildings, and others lying unheeded and jostled in the courtyards: the dead were everywhere – in the gutters trampled on by the living, in the swampy margins of the moat, littering the narrow way through the glacis and the fortifications, lying some of them on the steps of the church, the sight was one never to be forgotten.[11]

Ad hoc treatment occurred on the battlefield as well. Prussian soldiers each had a first-aid kit, but other expediencies could be used. During the fighting at Orléans, a wounded man asked Lassberg to cut off his finger, which was hanging by a thread. He complied 'not without the creeps' (*nicht ohne Grausen*) and threw the finger away. The man wrapped up his hand and ran off to join his comrades.[12]

In rear areas, sick and wounded men were sent behind the lines back to Germany or to the French southern provinces. At first, the French had to improvise its railroad evacuation system. Freycinet developed instructions that directed a wounded soldier along a series of lines from the front to the south. A soldier wounded around Orléans might follow Line 5, which passed through the Massif Central, stopping in Saint-Étienne and Clermont-Ferrand, then heading to the Mediterranean coast. The German system included special open-plan railway carriages instead of wagons divided into compartments. One reporter enthused, 'If it were not presumptuous, you would (almost) wish to be wounded once to enjoy the good of this institution. With [these trains] humanity experiences a real triumph.'[13]

Wounded soldiers arriving at a hospital underwent brutal triage. Henri-Étienne Beaunis, a surgeon at the Military Hospital in Strasbourg, published an account of one particularly difficult day in early September:

> I lifted the cover thrown over the first wounded man; it's an artilleryman; his right leg had been almost detached by a shell burst; it is next to him, clad still in the standard-issue boot, and holding on only by a shred of flesh; I had him taken up to the operating room to finish the amputation. The second was a young *mobile*, almost a child; his skull had been crushed in, his face bloody, his eyes dull; at his temple an open wound at the bottom of which his brain rose with each respiratory movement; the projectile is in the cerebral substance; he will die; the chaplain, kneeling at his stretcher, hastily administers [last rites]. The third is dead; do not even look at his wound; time is pressing. This one's chest has been shot through with a bullet, he is hardly breathing, let's move on: nothing to be done. What is that one rasping in the corner? I look: his thigh is crushed; the projectile entered from the rear deeply into the pelvis; this is not a wound, it is something shapeless and without name, a mix of pulsating muscles, loops of still-living intestines, shreds of fabric, pieces of straw and dung, the hint of bones.[14]

The men selected for surgery often faced amputation. Some doctors favoured a conservative approach, while others used amputation regularly to save lives and to provide decisive action in an arena where surgeons had little control over anything else. 'Amputate, always amputate,' recalled Beaunis.[15] Because the Germans had a larger and better-organized medical corps, they were able to give more attention to wounded men and therefore were less inclined to quickly move to amputate.

Use of the latest antiseptic techniques was mixed in 1870. Louis Pasteur's work on germ theory had reached the English surgeon Joseph Lister by 1865, and Lister's antiseptic theories had been published in the *Lancet* in 1867. By 1870, Lister's experiments in antiseptic surgery had lowered the percentage of deaths following amputation from 50 per cent to 15 per cent. On the German side, surgeons used carbolic acid spray to sterilize their operating areas and tools. The French, however, made little use of Lister's antiseptic techniques. When French doctors spoke of hygiene, they referred to preventing overcrowding in the wards and maintaining medical supplies, but they did not discuss sterilization. Linens, chloroform, quinine and trained doctors all ran in short supply as the war wore on. Death rates for amputations among the French reached 75 per cent (10,000 out of 13,000 cases, including fingers and toes).

Soldiers also suffered from shock due to devastating wounds caused by modern artillery. François Poncet, who directed Strasbourg's Military Health Service School, described the situation:

> A man hit by a voluminous burst, having his two legs blown off or crushed, falls struck down, annihilated . . . His face has a mortal pallor, his features are contracted, immobile, his eyes closed or haggard, fixed, sickly; saliva stains [his] beard . . .[His] chest is cold, or covered with a viscous sweat (as are the temples). The extremities are . . . insensible and cold. The pulse is light, slow, spindly . . . It is the image of agony or death.[16]

All Poncet could do to counter the risk of shock was to provide hot water and alcohol infusions and wrap the man in blankets with warm bricks. Surgeons could not amputate if a wounded man lay in shock, but in those cases in any event the man risked losing too much blood to live.

Head trauma posed additional challenges. The large size and relatively slow velocity of bullets during the Franco-Prussian War made head wounds so destructive that it was difficult for medical researchers to do detailed studies of brain injury.

After surgery, wounded men convalesced in hospitals for weeks at a time. During his travels to the Continent, McMichael visited temporary hospitals scattered across the convents and aristocratic homes of Brussels, which treated about 500 wounded men – both French and German – at the cost of 1,000 francs per day paid for by the Belgian Red Cross committee. Concerned civilians in Russia, Italy and Switzerland packed up linens, bandages, pillows, clothing, mattresses, shoes, wine, potatoes, books and dressings and shipped them to ambulances in Brussels. 'All nationality was evidently forgotten in the effort to relieve our common humanity,' McMichael reported. 'French and Germans were cared for alike, and the gratitude that beamed from many a countenance told how tenderly they were nursed.'[17] At the Hôtel de Grunne, the residence of an Austrian count in Belgium, Ironmonger and McMichael were moved to tears by the sight of maimed and sick soldiers. 'Here were several French officers, some of noble birth, who at our entrance rose as well as their maimed limbs would allow; and, besides these, a number of Prussian, Bavarian, and French soldiers of every rank.'[18]

These were no simple injuries:

> Some there were whose faces told of the passage of a bullet through both cheeks, and others whom the shell or cannon ball had deprived of a limb. One poor fellow, whose countenance I shall not soon forget, held out to us the stumps of his two arms, both hands having been carried away by a shell at the battle of Beaumont. His look was piteous, and seemed to say 'What shall I do?' We were glad to learn that a pair of mechanical arms was to be supplied to him.[19]

They also encountered 'a young Bavarian who had lost a leg, he was only twenty years of age, and had a comparatively happy face. *His* trouble seemed to sit lightly on him, but *our* thoughts travelled to the home he had left, where, perhaps, was an aged mother sorrowing for her boy.'[20] Patients who suffered from septicaemia and pyaemia might convalesce for ten to forty days and form friendships with the doctors who treated them. When these patients did not recover, the sadness and loss hit their caregivers even harder.

McMichael was stunned by the wounds he witnessed in the hospitals, 'representing every possible injury which modern instruments of war can inflict on poor human nature'.[21] Men suffered from amputated calves, thighs and arms, and from blindness and disfigurement. And yet – in a description that surely under-emphasized acute suffering and mental anguish – they endured through their suffering and could even be cheerful. One young man displayed the bone fragment that had been removed from his own body as a sort of trophy, in a grim separation of self into two parts. To while away the hours of convalescence, the men occupied themselves with dominoes, chess and sketching, and gratefully accepted the cigars brought by visitors.

McMichael emphasized that rumours the Prussians had been mistreated in Brussels were unfounded; rather, any difference in treatment vis-à-vis French soldiers was due to differences in diet. The Belgian diet was similar to that of the French, and the Prussians were simply not accustomed to it. McMichael was eager to dispel rumours of mistreatment by demonstrating that any less-than-perfect situation could be explained rationally by resources and logistics, not by national rancour or prejudice.

As for their reception of English visitors, the French soldiers were excited to learn of the visitors' nationality, because they had been picked up on the battlefield by members of an English Ambulance. In general, both the French and the Germans were positive toward them. The only problem was McMichael's friend's overcoat. It happened to be fashioned with a similar cut and colour to those of the Prussian Army, and as they walked through the makeshift wards his friend was sometimes mistaken for a Prussian.

In Red Cross hospitals as well as in the private letters of soldiers, the national distinction between French and German sick and wounded melted away. Similarly, Germans donated funds to help both wounded Germans and French prisoners of war. The press, however, told a different story. The German National Liberal press distinguished the suffering of German soldiers as symbolic of unification. In the words of the historian Christine Krüger, the press claimed 'that the blood lost by the German soldiers would be the fertilizer for an abundant national harvest or the firm "cement" (*Kitt/Blutkitt*) for the newly built nation.'[22] The French press, for its part, adopted the metaphor of the 'amputation' of Alsace and Lorraine.

Apart from this metaphorical use of German suffering, German newspapers rarely described fighting and the level of violence in combat. When they published engravings depicting battle scenes, these illustrations minimized the destructive capacity of modern weapons on the human body. For readers at home, it appeared that the dangers of warfare could be contained. This impression was bolstered by real improvements in medical care, well documented in the press, that reduced death rates among the wounded.

While minimizing the suffering inflicted by bullets and shrapnel, the German press devoted disproportional attention to the suffering attributed to the 9,000 *Turcos* serving in the French Army. The North African colonial soldiers were characterized as 'beasts' driven by instinct instead of rationality. Journalists openly published rumours that *Turcos* engaged in the mutilation of wounded and dead soldiers. After Sedan, journalists turned their focus to the *francs-tireurs* and the dangers of partisan fighting, including accusations that partisans also mutilated the bodies of German wounded and dead soldiers.

The press moreover shaped the narrative of the future of warfare, given the destructive capabilities of modern weaponry. In the German press, the National Liberal majority argued that the technological development of weaponry would in fact humanize war. An observer in the *Schwäbischer Merkur*, the newspaper of the National Liberals in Württemberg, wrote,

> If under the impression of the murderous fights at Metz you came to the conclusion that the modern perfection of weapons, the needle-gun and the Chassepot, the *mitrailleuses* and the breach-loading artillery, made the battles bloodier than they had been in the past, you are mistaken . . . No, despite all the horror, the casualty numbers decrease while the benefits for the fatherland grow.[23]

The democratic press, however, feared that these new weapons would lead to unimaginable destruction. The Württemberg *Beobatcher* of 31 August predicted:

> This slaughter of thousands . . . has grown into a monster, the hunger of which it will be impossible to satisfy. Our weapons are now so sophisticated that, in regard to their potential for destruction, they leave almost nothing to be desired, but nonetheless they will again be improved considerably. Our projectiles, shrapnel shells, *mitrailleuses* and needle guns already devour so much human flesh that the forces of the biggest nations hardly permit us to wage war for longer than four weeks without completely incapacitating each other. What will happen, if there are further improvements and if with our speed of manoeuvre the war will consume at least a third more flesh than it already does?[24]

Evidence of mental trauma from 1870 remains elusive and rare. Authors who wished to convey their suffering or that of others described the suffering of the moment itself, not any lingering effects. For example, a man buried in rubble for four days in Strasbourg recalled, 'What passed through my head during the first hour of being trapped, I do not know how to describe; I passed from mute rages to a general despondency. Little by little, I came back, because I must say that I had completely lost reason.' Over time, he slowly recovered his focus and recalled a kerosene lamp that he had brought down to the cellar, and slowly managed to dig his way out. Later, he did not mention ongoing mental trauma, only the financial hardship of losing his home and shop.[25]

In the early 1870s, however, some professionals began to argue that the war had caused long-term psychological trauma. Ludger Lunier, the French Inspector General for psychiatric services, claimed that war trauma was related to 18 per cent of male admissions (civilians and soldiers) and 13 per cent of female admissions to asylums in the twelve months from 1 July 1870. These traumas included invasion, losing a loved one, surviving a siege, and political upheaval, including the Paris Commune.

Beaunis also identified nervous symptoms among women (and only women) in Strasbourg, including 'Palpitations, fainting, insomnia, nightmares, slight fever, gastralgia, etc.,' and sometimes 'mental alienation'. He attributed these symptoms to the experience of the siege, notably 'This state of anxiety and perpetual anguish, this alternating rest and noise, hope and discouragement, this ever-present impending fire, produced, especially in certain women, a nervous state that sometimes came close to madness.'[26] Some doctors later called this disease *maladie des caves*, 'cellar sickness'. François Poncet also worried about psychological damage, what he called *le délire moral*, a hallucination stemming from overly strong emotions. But he did not describe somatic ailments that did not have an obvious cause.

These hints that war could cause mental trauma were a continuation of the early nineteenth-century psychiatry that held that situational factors – such as war – could be the source of mental disorders. This ran counter to the emerging focus at the end of the century on hereditary degeneracy as the cause of mental disorders and anticipated a renewed interest in traumatic disorders in war, notably the notion of 'shell shock' that arose out of the trenches of the Great War.

After besieged cities fell the armies moved on, but civilians and the sick and wounded remained. In occupied Metz, after ten weeks of siege, 43,000 sick and wounded (out of a population of 200,000) were scattered in hospitals, ambulances and the homes of individuals. The Prussian army now used the train station as a warehouse for straw, which was piled in waiting rooms and the back offices, and on which wounded Prussian soldiers reclined.

McMichael and his travelling companions arrived in Metz in early November to bear witness to the city's fate. The city had little hotel space. After six attempts, the travellers begged for shelter at the Hôtel de Commerce and were welcome to sleep on the floor of the dining room.

McMichael was appalled at what he saw. In the city streets, 'confusion reigned supreme' among the soldiers and piles of military equipment, rail wagons, tents and straw. 'The population seemed just awaking out of a dream, and rubbing their eyes, while the Germans were hard at work, reducing the chaos to something like order.' Thousands of sick and wounded lay in the streets. French soldiers begged from door to door with 'a demented look about them, which seems present with me to this very day; and it will indeed be wonderful if many of them do not end their days in a mad-house; an opinion in which I am not singular.' Whole buildings had been filled with captured Chassepots, many broken and rusting on the ground, next to piles of rotting leather pouches and belts, and every once in a while, a drum from the French Imperial Guard with its skins knocked off, 'suggesting the exclamation "How are the mighty fallen!" '[27]

General von Kummer was the occupying general. As was typical in this war, he promised protection to those citizens who posed no threat to the occupiers and imposed discipline on his own soldiers. The inhabitants were required to provide lodging for the occupiers and firewood for the soldiers. The women of Metz, according to McMichael, encouraged the defenders of their city and ministered 'as only women can minister, to the needs of the wounded, starving, or fever-stricken soldiery'.[28]

Back at the Hôtel de Commerce, the travellers sat for their evening meal. 'Fever and dysentery were fearfully prevalent, and my appetite was not at all sharpened by seeing on the dinner table in the evening, a row of black bottles filled with disinfecting fluid!'[29] At least these unappetizing bottles suggested an attempt to act on the new understanding of germs as the agents of illness.

The travellers did not stay long in Metz. The dining room was prepared for their sleep at midnight, with three on the floor and one on the sofa. They rose at 4 a.m. to take the five o'clock train – with no breakfast – to get out of the city before illness could take them. The 300-mile train ride to Brussels was filled with many delays, and they did not want to stop for meals, so they arrived at half past ten, having appealed to fellow passengers for some bread and sausage.

The women of Metz received many accolades. On 10 November, the *Voeu National* printed one letter although the editor viewed it as a hoax, and despite his admonition that 'the time is not particularly well chosen for thinking of marriage. Mythologically speaking, Mars has always driven off love, even conjugal love.' Nevertheless, the paper printed the letter:

> A captain of a cavalry regiment who is in vigorous health, and forty-five years of age, who has had many medals awarded him, who possesses property in the south of France, of the value of 50,000 francs, and has a brother who has received the kind care of the ladies of Metz (whose devotion he admires) desires to marry a young lady or widow of Metz over twenty-five years of age. Address by way of Luxembourg to the undersigned initials, 'Post Office, Toulouse'.[30]

Thousands of French soldiers had left Metz as prisoners of war, joining their comrades from Sedan, Strasbourg and fallen fortresses across the country. The Franco-Prussian War was the first European conflict in which a nation housed thousands of prisoners of war. The surrender of 83,000 men at Sedan is the most famous capture of prisoners, but it made up a relatively small percentage of the total taken. The Germans imprisoned up to 723,500 French soldiers for some portion of the war, including 373,000 held for several months in the German states.

Prisoners of war during the Franco-Prussian conflict were not protected by international agreement, although the Prussian army issued regulations regarding their treatment in July 1870. The vast majority of the prisoners were military personnel, not civilians.

Many did not return home until months after the armistice, if they returned at all. About 17,000 prisoners died, accounting for about one in eight of all military deaths on the French side.

Conditions for prisoners of war could be severe, even before their arrival at camps and fortresses. Sylvain-Paul Olivier, a soldier in the 100th infantry regiment, was captured in early August and marched to Wittenberg along with over a thousand other prisoners. Food was a constant concern. Prisoners were not allowed to take anything out of their sacks and ate hard bread, 'black like carbon'.[31] Nights were worse. Olivier wrote, 'You always have nightmares when you sleep [. . .]. You shiver, you're cold and always have an empty stomach.'[32] Prisoners travelling by train fared no better. One observer described the state of prisoners passing through Lorraine: 'Our unhappy prisoners arrived almost without shoes, without underclothes, showing their naked chests under their tattered tunics, poorly fed or not fed at all, piled into half-open wagons in the middle of the most bitter cold of December and January . . . In the morning they would find some dead.'[33] In Orléans after the battle of Loigny in December, 6,000 French prisoners were packed into the cathedral.

One observer sympathetic to France was unable to detect any intentional cruelty of the Germans toward their captives, only the unintended cruelty of being overwhelmed with tens of thousands of prisoners for whom they had not garnered food and supplies, who were on foot and bedraggled and slow in front of their Prussians guards on horseback. Perhaps these prosaic failings and not a moral one explained the reports back home of prisoners' mistreatment.

Yet McMichael saw with his own eyes the devastating result of this lack of supplies. In Saarlouis in Prussia, he encountered a train of cattle-cars containing French prisoners heading into Germany.

> Our hearts sickened at the sight. There they were, stowed together like oxen, and eagerly devouring bread and fruit given to them by some women at the station. Their wasted and shivering frames told

> of the privations they had endured, and how unfit they were for the long and bitter journey that was before them. In justice to the Prussians it should be stated that the prisoners were, I believe, convoyed, as far as the rolling-stock of the railway would permit, in covered carriages, and that cattle-trucks were only used when the supply of better conveyances failed.[34]

Captured soldiers threw away their letters and the book with their regimental description, so that if they were to escape from their capture they would not have any identification. They lost, then, any connection with loved ones and their regimental companions. McMichael recorded that 'Thousands of letters had been picked up, and we succeeded in getting a few.'[35]

The passage of so many prisoners of war through France was a new experience requiring improvised responses. The working women of Nancy threw their spare morsels of bread to passing soldiers and gave them their handkerchiefs. Committees of women in Nancy and other cities in the north-east gathered food to pass to the prisoners as they went through the train station. The hand-over was not always easy to accomplish. The German commandant of Nancy only allowed a few women into the station when prisoners passed through, an insufficient number to reach convoys of 1,500 men. Sometimes the trains did not stop at all. Even given the opportunity to approach the trains, passing food and clothing to the prisoners inside rail cars was tricky:

> [The women] tried to attach the [bread and bottles of wine] to the end of long poles and to hold them above the cars, so that our soldiers could untie them as they passed. They also tried to lower [the packages] with string when the train entered the station; but all this only worked by halves, because often blows from rifle butts broke the bottles or the poles; other times, the glass hit against the wagon and broke.[36]

After several tries, an old woman came up with the idea of wrapping bottles in bread and meat, so they could be thrown up and into the trains more easily. This method appeared to work, but the author commented, 'Too bad for the guy who got it on the head.'[37] German soldiers keeping guard over the French prisoners are nearly absent in these accounts, though the reference to 'blows from rifle butts' raises the question of who was sabotaging these efforts.

The prisoners eventually arrived in one of at least 249 sites, 7 in Switzerland, 6 in occupied France, 3 in Alsace-Lorraine, 7 in Belgium, and 226 in Germany, going all the way up to Tilsit where, in 1807, Napoleon I had imposed a treaty annexing half Prussia's territory and population. Conditions in prison varied. Olivier, in Wittenberg, was able to work for 1–1.25 francs a day, most of which went directly to pay for food, which he found to be decent. Later transferred to Bonneberg, in Saxony, Olivier found the inhabitants generally friendly, 'for as they say, they are not Prussians, they are Saxons.'[38] Other reports were not as positive. A twenty-seven-year-old volunteer from the Mediterranean town of Bédarieux wrote, 'With the money that we have we are often not even free to provide ourselves with necessary supplies.'[39] Another observer wrote of the prisoners in Berlin, 'Their food is atrocious, many only eat dry bread! Their clothes are now just rags.'[40] For a few observers, the treatment of prisoners of war only confirmed the 'brutality, the cruel carelessness, the absence of generosity even in victory' of the German character.[41]

The prisoner of war camps also contributed to the spread of typhoid fever, dysentery and, especially, smallpox. The camps were a key factor in the diffusion of smallpox during the epidemic of the early 1870s that killed 500,000 Europeans, including 176,977 German civilians. Disease spreads easily in wartime as military personnel from diverse backgrounds are assembled and deployed in areas to which they are not acclimatized, exposed to diseases to which they have little or no acquired immunity, and then come in contact with civilians who are in the same boat. All these populations suffered from weakened immunity due to malnourishment, fatigue, mental stress, trauma and exposure, compounded by unsanitary conditions, enforced population concentration and crowding, lack of medical care, and a general collapse of normal rules of behaviour.

Charities sprang up to help prisoners of war to fill the need that government could not or would not address during the war crisis. Of primary concern to the charities was the facilitation of communication between prisoners and their families. Imprisoned officers sometimes had permission to be accompanied by their families, but the vast majority of prisoners were not so lucky. The International Committee of the Red Cross published lists of prisoners of war held in Germany or German-occupied France. Activists on behalf of the prisoners, including rabbis and journalists, gathered letters and mailed them, or passed general news about the prisoners to their communities. The women of Nancy sometimes slipped a piece of paper and pencil to the soldiers passing through on trains. The prisoners wrote the names and addresses of their parents down and returned the paper to the civilians so that word could be sent that they were alive.

Individuals and organizations also sent packages to ease the hunger and cold. The International Committee of the Red Cross in Basel, Switzerland, co-ordinated the distribution of packages sent both by individuals and by local committees of the Red Cross. The committee of Montpellier, for instance, sent thirty-three barrels of wine and nearly five thousand clothing items over the course of the winter, especially shoes for soldiers about to march home again. Not all of the aid sent could reach particular soldiers. Three hundred and forty-two packages sent by the Red Cross were sent back because they could not find the recipient, and there was no guarantee that packages reached the intended hands. As autumn turned into winter, prisoners of war faced a long, cold wait for the war to come to an end.

In the last days of November, the French attempted two major thrusts: north toward Paris from the Loire and a breakout from Paris.

The timing, as it happened, was perfect, but it was not a co-ordinated strategy. The two operations relied on untrained, untested men of varying levels of enthusiasm, and they unfolded 70 miles apart, separated by hundreds of thousands of Germans. Their most rapid and trusted communications came by carrier pigeon. In the end, the French suffered yet more setbacks and established a new set of myths to help them grapple with their ongoing suffering.

In mid-November, the French disagreed on how to leverage their success at Coulmiers and the recapture of Orléans. Freycinet and Gambetta wanted to advance on Paris in co-ordination with a sortie from the capital, whereas Aurelle believed that such an advance was impossible given that the German Second Army under Friedrich Karl was heading their way from Metz. Freycinet and Gambetta agreed on 12 November that for the time being Aurelle could fortify his base of operations in Orléans, building trenches and warehouses. More men were still arriving, some 200,000 in total in three new corps: the XVII at Vendôme, XVIII at Gien, and XX Corps at Châteaudun. But while Freycinet eagerly awaited battle, Aurelle knew the soldiers were not ready. They remained under-supplied and overstretched. 'Two nights without sleep, two days without eating,' recorded a *zouave* in late November.[42]

For their part, the Prussians, admittedly, were satisfied to see the Bavarians fail at Coulmiers. Tann was sent to be a corps commander under a new Army Section with additional detachments from Metz (the Bavarian I Corps, Prussian III, IX and X) and placed under the command of Friedrich Franz, grand duke of Mecklenburg-Schwerin. This Army Section moved west from Chartres in the direction of Le Mans.

The German Second Army's role now shifted. Instead of marching on Tours, it was to defend the road from Orléans to Paris. This was a challenging assignment for Friedrich Karl because French detachments could harass these defenders anywhere along the line and then disappear. It was a demoralizing few weeks; supplies ran so short that boots were not replaced, and the French main force failed to materialize.

Finally, Moltke realized that the French had not in fact shifted away from the Loire. On 22 November, he placed Friedrich Karl as commander-in-chief of the Loire theatre, including Mecklenburg's Army Section. They disagreed about the aims at this point. Moltke wanted to protect the German siege lines around Paris and guard against Aurelle's expected attack, so he wanted to make an anticipatory frontal attack to push him back. Friedrich Karl wanted to destroy Aurelle's Army of the Loire, a strategy that would have involved an envelopment rather than a frontal attack. This kind of success might have ended the war in November.

Two days later, however, the French made their own move. On 24 November, after two weeks in Orléans, Aurelle grudgingly advanced, obeying Freycinet's order, with the main force at the centre: the XV and XVI Corps, who had been victorious at Coulmiers and now straddled the road from Orléans to Paris. The newly formed XVIII and XX Corps supported Aurelle on his right.

On the 28th, the French right met with forward members of Friedrich Karl's III and X Corps at Beaune-la-Rolande, about 30 miles north-east of Orléans. The French XVIII and XX Corps – about 50,000 men – converged against the Hanoverians of General Voigts-Rhetz's X Corps, who held a strong defensive position. Despite the greater French numbers and strong enthusiasm, German discipline and guns defended the village in a day of exceptionally hard fighting. The French came wave after wave into the streets of the village and were beaten back by the men of the 38th Brigade, who were, in the historian Dennis Showalter's words, 'weavers and factory workers, not the farm boys so prized in the Prussian system . . . stunted by malnutrition, stooped by labour' yet steady and disciplined.[43] The XVIII Corps was delayed in arriving, and, at the end of the day, the French had to break off the attack. Beaune-la-Rolande proved that German infantry could hold out as well as its artillery. This was a victory of steely, well-trained Germans against raw French, of professionals against reservists. The thrill of victory at Coulmiers was not repeated.

*

Meanwhile in Paris, Trochu and Ducrot continued to prepare for a breakout toward the west, originally planned for 15 November. It was postponed on the 14th by a rising of the level of the Seine and by news via a pigeon from Tours of Aurelle's victory at Coulmiers and recapture of Orléans. This news led the press in Paris to call for a breakout to the south, to meet Aurelle's forces around the Forest of Fontainebleau. Trochu did not believe that Aurelle could in fact stride forward with alacrity, but his ministers did. The GND therefore ordered a plan for a breakout toward the south-east.

Ducrot was informed of this change on the 20th. In short order, he was obliged to scrap his plan and develop a new breakout across the Marne at Champigny, move 400 guns through Paris's narrow streets, transport 80,000 men and their supplies by rail and by foot, re-deploy 54 pontoon bridges, and do all of this with the utmost secrecy to preserve the element of surprise. It was a great logistical feat. To lighten the burden, Ducrot cut back on baggage, supplies, even blankets, and took it upon himself to write detailed plans that stifled agility or initiative. He wrote in his Orders of the Day, 'As for myself, I have made up my mind, and I swear before you and before the entire nation: I shall only re-enter Paris dead or victorious.'[44]

Trochu had tried to alert the GND at Tours to the details of this sortie on 26 November, but the balloon blew north to Norway and the message did not reach its destination until the 30th. Freycinet called a council of war late that day. The possibility of a rapid thrust coming to the aid of this sortie might just provide the opening the French needed. By this time, the breakout from Paris was already (supposedly) twenty-four hours under way and required immediate support from the Loire theatre. Freycinet ordered Aurelle to advance some 170,000 men in an attack toward Pithiviers: the XV and XVI came from the west, and the XVIII and XX from the east, and from there, they were to march toward the Fontainbleau Forest to meet the advance coming southward from Paris.

Aurelle disagreed. He had no reserves behind his thin lines; the Orléans Forest forced a difficult manoeuvre on the right, and the

XX did not yet have the equipment to allow for an advance. But Freycinet insisted. First, General Antoine Chanzy's XVI Corps, positioned left of the Orléans Forest, needed to attack north in order to protect Aurelle's flank. They marched forward on 1 December and met the I Bavarian Corps at Villepion.

The French fought well against demoralized Bavarians. The Bavarians had by this time lost 21,000 men to illness and 7,000 casualties in battle, with replacements slow to arrive and officers spread thin. Dietrich von Lassberg, like many of his comrades, had lost his enthusiasm for the fight and wondered what he was doing so far from home. On 26 November, after nearly two weeks on the march, he reported,

> Some had scarcely any boots on their feet, some walked in wooden shoes, some in women's shoes, and others even in slippers, or they had wrapped their feet in a piece of leather or material. Blankets in all colors and sizes, as well as pieces of French uniforms – especially that practical grey-blue chasseur coat with a hood, which almost every soldier and officer up to the rank of general had – served against the wet cold and for protection at night in often very makeshift quarters. Our faces were pale and haggard, and morale sank because of the enormous strains and the continuous marches, which almost went in circles without seriously encountering the enemy . . . Through sickness our ranks dwindled in an alarming manner, and it was no rarity for 15, even 20 men from a company to be left behind because of exhaustion, who would then drag themselves along again on a wagon or on foot at night.[45]

The enthusiasm of July and the boredom of October had worn down into depression and gloom.

The last day of November was the first real day of winter at the end of a month of marches day and night. In their low morale, the Bavarians failed to fortify the villages they held and only survived due to their artillery. After a day of falling back, their final stand at the chateau of Villepion was beaten back by an assault led by

Admiral Jean Jauréguiberry. It was the Army of the Loire's second victory.

That same day, Gambetta received news that a breakout from Paris had taken Épinay. He assumed the news referred to Épinay-sur-Orge, some 12 miles south of Paris, which would have been a real success. He issued an exultant proclamation:

> The genius of France, for the moment veiled, is appearing anew! The Prussians can now judge the difference between a despot who fights to satisfy his whims and a People in Arms determined not to perish . . . France and the universe will never forget that Paris first set the example, taught this policy and thus founded its moral supremacy in remaining faithful to the heroic spirit of the revolution. Long live Paris! Long live France! Long live the one, indivisible Republic![46]

This elation did not last long. Gambetta was mistaken. The message he had received referred to Épinay-sur-Seine, north of Paris near Saint-Denis, a minor success in the wrong direction. In fact, the breakout from Paris was stalled. Ducrot's attack was supposed to begin on 29 November but it was delayed by a day due to flooding on the Marne that necessitated additional pontoon bridges. Rail movements, diversionary attacks and the French soldiers' red trousers revealed their intentions. With an extra day of warning, the German Royal Guard and the XII Saxon Corps could move into position to meet them.

Inside Paris, however, civilians awaited news of the sortie. Juliette Adam heard the sound of the *tambour* from her window at dawn. A friend had witnessed Ducrot's departure from the Place de l'Opéra with his soldiers, and Adam breathlessly awaited the results of the latest attempt to break out of Paris. Ducrot's 70,000 men crossed the Marne on 30 November and made their way east toward Champigny-sur-Marne. The French proved that they could mount a successful large-scale attack from Paris. But the German line of fire proved impenetrable. In the day's fighting, the French did not even break through the first line of the Germans, though they had managed to take Champigny and rattle them.

The next day, 1 December, was a day of truce as the two sides buried their dead. On 2 December the Germans counter-attacked, but they could not recapture the positions the French had taken and prepared for a French attack the next day. Ducrot, however, was not ready to push his men further. They were exhausted and cold, with no blankets and no cooked food for days in temperatures below freezing. On the morning of 4 December, under cover of mist, Ducrot ordered his troops back across the Marne and into Paris, with 12,000 fewer men than they had had a few days earlier. It was a battle of attrition in which the Germans, too, were stretched to the limit. Ducrot blinked first.

On the Loire, Gambetta sought to capitalize on the successes at Coulmiers and Villepion. Expectations ran high that now the tide would finally turn. In the early dawn on 2 December, Chanzy moved men from his XVI Corps forward from Villepion against Mecklenberg's positions, which stretched from the village of Loigny to the château of Goury, about 18 miles north-north-west of Orléans. The two sides had a nearly even match of numbers – about 35,000 Bavarians and Prussians from Mecklenburg's detachment against 45,000 French. At first, Chanzy had some success driving back the Bavarians, but it did not last. In a long day of fighting, the Germans in turn pushed Chanzy back. By early afternoon, the French centre began to fold, and the Bavarians retook Loigny.

The battle of Loigny became known for one final desperate charge led by General Gaston de Sonis that, in an ironic twist, placed the sacrifice of Catholic soldiers at the heart of the republican People's War. As twilight fell, the Catholic monarchist Sonis decided to try to reclaim the village. Sonis' XVII Corps had become dispersed, and he had only about 700 men at his disposal: the first battalion of the Volontaires de l'Ouest along with men from the *franc-tireur* battalions of Tours and Blidah and the Mobile Guard of the Côtes-du-Nord.

The Volontaires de l'Ouest were no ordinary volunteer formation. Until just a few months earlier, a substantial core of the men, along with their commander Colonel Athanase de Charette, had served as *zouaves* defending the Pope against the encroaching Kingdom of Italy. They pulled out of Rome due to the war in France. On 20 September, Italian troops besieged Rome, and Pius IX lost his temporal power beyond the Vatican. The international band of papal *zouaves*, volunteers who had defended the Pope since 1860, now became prisoners and were repatriated to their home countries. In France, the Volontaires de l'Ouest, formed from a nucleus of *zouaves*, were fortified by additional volunteers from the strongly Catholic west of France. They claimed to offer France the hope of regeneration, without the stain of defeat, as true patriots rooted in Catholic values. This claim put the Volontaires distinctly at odds with the very secular GND, particularly with Gambetta's exuberant insistence on the success of the People in Arms, which had angered many of his conservative, Catholic generals, including Aurelle.

It was this band of fervent, faith-driven soldiers, then, that Sonis led into a desperate counterattack to take Loigny. Under the standard of the Sacred Heart with the motto 'Heart of Jesus, Save France', they cried '*Vive la France! Vive Pie IX!*' It was in vain. After having been briefly held, Loigny was abandoned by the end of the afternoon, and the French retreated so quickly that they left most of their wounded on the field.[47] Two-thirds of Sonis' men fell. Charette was wounded and captured. Sonis fell on the battlefield, his knee shattered. He survived the frigid night, he reported, through a vision of Notre-Dame de Lourdes. He later recovered from an amputated leg.

Yet the story of Loigny lived on, with its soldiers cast as unbeaten and unbowed. Distinct from all the suffering that soldiers had endured on both sides of the conflict, the soldiers at Loigny claimed that their physical pain would lead to a renewed and purified France. The story of Loigny was repeated in the Catholic press as well as in sermons, biographies and memoirs as a key moment in the development of a revived Catholic nationalism that emphasized emotions, physical pain and the miraculous. Lieutenant Colonel Albiousse, who became commander in Charette's absence, articulated the *zouave* understanding of the battle:

> The war which we undergo is a war of expiation and God had already chosen from amongst us the most noble and pure victims . . . It was by an act of faith that France was born on the battlefield of Tolbiac; it is by an act of faith that she will be saved . . . with the help of God and for the *patrie*, let us remain here what we were at Rome, the worthy sons of the eldest daughter of the Church.[48]

Altogether, the French lost 7,000 casualties at Loigny. Over the following two days, Aurelle's men panicked. Despite fighting bravely on 3 December to hold their line against Friedrich Karl, they disintegrated in the cold and snow. Aurelle finally received permission to retreat on the afternoon of the 4th and fell back south of Orléans to save the army from total collapse. He lost 18,000 as prisoners and 2,000 casualties that day.

Loigny spelled the end of Aurelle's Army of the Loire. The Germans cut the army into two unco-ordinated parts, but did not destroy it completely: XVI, XVII and XXI Corps remained north of the Loire under Chanzy, and XV, XVIII and XX Corps south of the Loire under Marshal Bourbaki. Aurelle was relieved of command and was not replaced.

Mecklenburg led his Germans into Orléans after midnight on 4–5 December and held a review in the central square in front of a statue of Joan of Arc. The Germans, too, had suffered large casualties due to the *mitrailleuse* but kept moving forward. North, middle and south Germans all fought together for this victory.

The twin setbacks at Loigny and at Champigny both fell on 2 December, a date of significance for the Bonapartist legacy and one of infamy for the republicans: the anniversaries of the crowning of Napoleon I as emperor, the battle of Austerlitz and, almost fifty years later, of Louis-Napoleon's dismantling of the Second Republic and declaration of himself as Napoleon III. If the republic had been successful in battle, 2 December 1870 might have salved these bitter memories, but instead it proved another day of disappointment.

As soldiers tramped through the snow, the war seemed like another Russian campaign, never ending and doomed to fail. In Paris, however, Juliette Adam greeted the rumours of the second fall of Orléans with scepticism. After all, how many French soldiers were really in Orléans at this point? And did Moltke really think that Paris would surrender based on that news? She vowed to hold on.

16. *Christmas*

After Loigny, what hope did France still have? Despite their setbacks, the French continued to gather new recruits and to hold ground in the north (under General Louis Faidherbe), west near Le Mans (Chanzy), and east in the Vosges (Bourbaki). And they held Paris. At the same time, the Germans felt overstretched. In addition to the forces massing around Paris, they sent armies and detachments across northern France, extending as far as Dijon, Orléans and Dieppe. The Loire campaign was no longer just a part of the siege of Paris; it was its own arena. The resources that were released by the fall of Metz certainly helped, but a month later these men too felt tired and demoralized. It was just possible that between the armies of Chanzy, Faidherbe and Bourbaki, and the irregular *francs-tireurs* causing continuous anxiety, the French could convince the Germans to conclude a peace that did not include the devastating annexations Bismarck had been insisting upon.

Yet in December's cold and darkness, the circumstances for civilians continued to worsen. Troop movements expanding into the west, north and east spread disease exacerbated by privation. A twenty-three-year-old French *mobile* named Roger de Mauni stayed in a farmhouse where a woman there refused to come to the fire and stayed huddled in a corner weeping and shivering: 'The poor woman of the house did not dare, in spite of my entreaties, to come near the fire. She spends her days shivering and weeping in a dark corner . . . Her husband has lost an arm and her sons are little children. The sight of this family fills one with sorrow.'[1]

Soldierly discipline began to tatter in the winter months. The Bavarian Hoesslin wrote to his sister that

> we are like . . . a mobile corps that spreads misery and distress wherever it goes. The bitterness of our soldiers has reached such a high degree that the inhabitants of the affected villages really suffer under it . . . In peacetime we never would have thought that people's lives would be thus treated. But I do not want to get carried away by these thoughts.[2]

On 2 December, the crown prince stated, 'General von der Tann himself admits that he can no longer take responsibility for the cohesion of his corps.'[3]

In late December and early January, the French-held city of Péronne experienced widespread destruction and fires as a result of German bombardment: dozens of houses, the hospital and the church, notably the belfry, which one observer described as 'a spectacle of a beauty both sinister and majestic at the same time, that involuntarily recalled to an obsessed spirit the image of the capture of Moscow and of the Kremlin in flames'.[4] A witness reported that 'enemy soldiers, atop the surrounding hills, danced, in the light of an immense fire, an infernal dance, and howling patriotic songs and defiant cries that the wind carried to our ramparts.'[5]

Fires continued to plague villages. In the Sarthe, the village of Sougé-le-Ganelon lost fifty-three houses or buildings to a fire set in retaliation for isolated shots. Sougé sits on a hill and served as a visible warning to the surrounding towns. In the Eure-et-Loir, about forty communes or villages, 10 per cent of the department, were affected by fire during the course of the war.

From the valley of the Seine to Cotentin, Normandy was occupied for a long and difficult winter. Étrépagny (Eure) partially burned after a night of combat on 29 November, the fire consuming bakehouses, storehouses and woodsheds. The Germans briefly occupied the village, taking care to break the fire pumps before they departed. A month later, according to a witness, 'a thick smoke emanated still here and there from the rubble buried in the snow.'[6] According to another observer, Saxons slaughtered agricultural horses in the middle of the street with bayonets to the stomach 'with a savagery that would have astonished the Bavarians themselves'.[7]

Gambetta was clear-sighted in his understanding of the challenging situation. He engaged in a double discourse: one in public, in which he sought to keep up spirits and galvanize energy, whatever situation he and France faced, and another in private that grappled with France's precarious situation. In a revealing telegram to Favre dated 5 December, Gambetta presented the war as a duty. 'I have no illusions,' he wrote,

> but I tell you that in the terrible circumstances in which fortune has carried us to power, the least that we owe to our country . . . to our ideals . . . to posterity and to history . . . is to carry the glorious flag of the French Republic for as long, as high and as firmly as we can, and to fall along with it, never to rise again, if in the end it must perish.[8]

Despite this messianic defence of the republican ideal, Gambetta had no interest in becoming a martyr. After the twin disappointments at Paris and Loigny, the French government was no longer safe in Tours. It moved south-west to Bordeaux, the magisterial port city on the Garonne, which became the national capital on 8 December.

The city in which the GND prepared for this final stage of the war had become a strong supporter of the new regime. Back in September, Bordeaux had celebrated the fall of Napoleon III. Citizens overturned his equestrian statue and removed imperial eagles on the customs house and stock exchange. Clubs held daily pro-democracy meetings. As in many departments, local republicans created a defence committee and sought to acquire arms. Unlike many departments, the Gironde had access to the sea, and Bordeaux enjoyed a long-standing relationship with Britain that made it easier to arm its men. On 9 September, the city of Bordeaux reallocated 1.5 million francs intended to build a museum and pay for construction work on the Church of Saint-Louis. Those funds now financed military equipment in the city and across the rest of the Gironde. The department formed five regiments, of three battalions each, which were deployed by mid-December, an exceptionally early date in comparison with other departments. At one point, 2,000 soldiers slept outside in the snow, awaiting departure.

The arrival of the Government of National Defence required a reconfiguration of civic buildings and hotels. Freycinet occupied the ground floor of the Hôtel de Ville. The prefect requisitioned the annexes of the Grand Théâtre to house the GND's massive telegraph services, which sent some 100,000 telegrams between September and January. This operation required large spaces and tolerance for noise.

For the first few weeks, the GND ran without Gambetta's presence as he made a tour of the armies in the field. At first, Freycinet clashed with members of the older guard, including Adolphe Crémieux and Admiral Fourichon. The elder statesman Adolphe Thiers also headed to Bordeaux, to develop his own influence in the capital and to prepare for the impending peace.

When Gambetta arrived, he needed to establish his authority. The day after his arrival on 29 December, Gambetta delivered a speech from the prefectorial balcony in which he contrasted Bordeaux with Tours. 'The Government subsisted [in Tours] on the enervating action of this population inclined toward a traditional sluggishness . . . Here [in Bordeaux], among your active populations, who ally with the love of progress the moderation and prudence that the habits of business inspire, the Government will find itself fortified.'[9]

Although accused of being a dictator, Gambetta spoke in favour of pluralism and dissent. Yet, he continued, elections were impossible given that thirty departments were occupied, men were mobilized away from their voting locations and communications with Paris remained limited. The urgent need to defend the country was the priority. Rather than seek terms after the second fall of

Orléans, Gambetta prepared to launch additional offensives. Yet this hope was increasingly small.

Freycinet recalled with pleasure the work in Bordeaux at Gambetta's side. In addition to their work meetings, they often lunched together at Gambetta's lodgings for an hour of distraction between the heavy labours at hand. 'The conversation hardly ever lagged,' he later reminisced, 'all hierarchy disappeared, each of us spoke freely.' And what was the topic of conversation? The war, of course. 'The conduct of the principal actors was appreciated with much verve; the government itself did not escape from satirical remarks and we commented without great respect on the telegrams of Jules Favre or of Trochu.'[10]

As winter fell, France continued to call up new soldiers. George Sand recorded the departure of local men for the front:

> The whole town accompanied them. They are very decided, very patriotic, very proud. We embrace each other, we hold back our tears. Where will they go? What will become of them? They don't know, they are ready for anything. There is a surge of hope and devotion. We believe that salvation is still possible. I don't know why my hope is weak and of short duration.[11]

Yet after the second fall of Orléans, efforts to raise forces slowed. Local officials and potential conscripts were less inclined to heed the GND's rallying cries, and those already recruited deserted in greater numbers. Not surprisingly, the French experienced a steady drop in volunteers, from 17,000 in October to 10,000 in November, then 5,700 in December and 4,000 in January.

The month of December proved to be particularly cold, well below freezing each night, with French soldiers continuing their practice of bivouacking in tents. Regimental workshops that normally provided clothes, munitions and other equipment could no longer meet the demand. Each night, some men froze to death.

When the temperature rose above freezing, the snow melted into interminable mud. Soldiers in Paris had a much better material situation than those in the provinces, as they had more regular provisions and were spared constant long, exposed marches.

The GND armed its new recruits with supplies coming in from the south-west and via the Atlantic ports. France held the sea – Prussia's fleet was one-tenth the size of France's – and so could access arms from Britain and the United States. It was a mixed blessing, as rusted surplus rifles, eighteen types of them, required different calibres of ammunition. The commanding general of Lyons wrote on 19 December, 'The question of armament is a true calamity. Currently there are some *mobilisés* who require Enfield cartridges, and others Springfield, and others another make. Where in the devil will I find all that? I don't have a single one, and these troops are facing the enemy.'[12]

Lack of munitions meant lack of training. Many soldiers had never used their rifles prior to entering battle. One *conseiller générale* from the Manche wrote this alarming message to Gambetta at the end of December: 'the mobilized soldiers from Ille-et-Vilaine and the Côtes-du-Nord . . . have not shot . . . a single round since they were mobilized. It is urgent that they shoot at least five or ten rounds in target practice before seeing the Prussians.'[13]

The winter of 1870 saw the start of large private armament factories in France, in the service of national military operations. Private industry started supporting the war effort in December, along with imports from Britain. The two largest private companies, Schneider and Forges et Chantiers de la Méditerranée, both produced cannon. Industrial workers were exempt from conscription.

Meanwhile, the Germans continued to take strongholds and release more of their soldiers to fight elsewhere. In November, Verdun, Neuf-Brisach, Thionville and La Fère had fallen. Phalsbourg fell on 12 December and Montmédy just two days later. The crown prince noted smugly, 'it's for all the world as if we took a tablespoonful of fortresses every two days.'[14]

*

After the second fall of Orléans, the large Army of the Loire had broken into two smaller armies: Chanzy commanding the one north of the Loire (XVI and XVII Corps) and Bourbaki commanding those to the south (XV, XVIII and XX Corps). For a few days, Gambetta did not realize that Ducrot had been defeated in his attempted sortie from Paris – he found out on 6 December – so at first, he ordered Bourbaki to concentrate on Gien and attack north toward Fontainbleau, while Chanzy would retake Orléans. Both Bourbaki and Chanzy thought this move was crazy. Their men were too tired, wet and cold for such an operation. Gambetta accepted their protest. On 7 December, Bourbaki withdrew south to Bourges and eventually moved east to pursue a new strategy away from the Loire theatre. Chanzy tried to regroup on the Loire before Beaugency, 18 miles south-west of Orléans.

Moltke did not want France to have a 100,000-man army in the field as a lever during peace negotiations. The Germans had not completely destroyed France at Orléans, and Moltke wanted it to happen now. He therefore encouraged Friedrich Karl to pursue Bourbaki at Bourges, and Mecklenburg, now returned to an independent command, to advance south-west. Mecklenburg and Chanzy met in a hard, fierce battle at Beaugency on 8–9 December. Eventually, Mecklenburg broke off the fighting. He had only 24,000 men against Chanzy's 100,000.

After Beaugency, Chanzy's troops were exhausted and, as the GND departed for Bordeaux, they no longer needed to defend Tours. Chanzy simply wanted to maintain a French army in the field. He recognized that if the Germans destroyed his army, the country would have no further defences. He retreated west to Vendôme and hoped to remain there, but Mecklenburg's forces were massing, and Chanzy's men were too cold and miserable to make a stand. On 16 December, Chanzy therefore moved his army further west toward Le Mans, a railroad junction connected to Paris, Nantes and Brest, to rest and re-equip itself.

This was a tough slog for Chanzy's men through slushy snow. French peasants had little interest in helping with supplies (the

Germans, at least, could sometimes pay for their requisitions). Chanzy had no hope of co-ordinating with Bourbaki, either. The final 45 miles from Vendôme to Le Mans were slow and demoralizing as they confronted hills, high hedges and twisting lanes. Through this march, however, Chanzy proved himself to be competent, confident and willing to work with the army he had, instead of bemoaning the ideal he might have wanted. He knew that most of the men were not regulars and would not be able to fight like regulars, so he did not push them beyond their capacities. At the same time, he did not despair or give up on them. For the next seven weeks, he patiently led his armies through an unbroken retreat across inhospitable land and in cold winter weather, while he himself suffered from malarial fever. Freycinet admired Chanzy's character. 'Firm without haughtiness, brave without recklessness, cold, methodical, not allowing himself to be swept away by illusions but nevertheless equipped with that dose of confidence necessary for great enterprise,' Chanzy inspired his soldiers and his superiors alike.[15]

Luckily for Chanzy and his men, the Germans under Friedrich Karl and Mecklenburg were equally exhausted and slowed by icy roads and hilly country, with *francs-tireurs* at their backs. They had not rested much since Coulmiers a month earlier. They lacked boots and instead used wooden clogs stuffed with straw. The Bavarian Karl Tanera noted on 11 December that his brigade had shrunk from 192 officers to 40 officers, 20 of whom were replacements. The men dwindled from 7,000 to 2,124, of whom 500 were replacements. They were filthy and undisciplined, and their uniforms were disintegrating.

By 17 December Moltke formally called off the pursuit of Chanzy. Despite the lack of much success by Aurelle, Ducrot, Chanzy and Bourbaki, the French showed no sign of calling for peace and French armies remained in the field. These armies remained a distraction from Moltke's main focus on Paris. The Prussian commander-in-chief was not in a hurry to bombard the capital, but he believed that Paris would need to fall for the war to end. He determined in mid-December to allow his armies to pursue the French armies in the field only so far. They were to prevent the French from gaining strength but were not to further stretch their own supplies and men. The German armies were to stay concentrated and send detachments to deal with *francs-tireurs* as needed: the First Army at Beauvais (with detachments at Saint-Quentin, Amiens and Rouen); Mecklenburg's Section at Chartres and Dreux to focus on the west; the Second Army at Orléans (with detachments at Blois and Gien); Dietrich von Zastrow's VII Corps at Châtillon; and General von Werder's XIV Corps in the Saône valley. The point, for Moltke, was not to occupy all of France while besieging Paris – he did not have the men, of course – but rather to keep the newly formed French armies off balance and the irregulars in check.

On the plains of Picardy and Artois, a new French Army of the North formed from newly called-up men who managed to arrive from the occupied north-east, as well as officers who had escaped at Metz or even from Germany. General Louis Faidherbe took command of these forces. Like Chanzy, Faidherbe, a native of Lille and the former governor of Senegal, had been serving in Algeria when the war began. He, too, suffered from fever and cold as he returned to the metropole. He did not think the French had any chance of victory – in this he differed from Chanzy – but he did enjoy the confidence of the republicans and he enforced discipline in his soldiers.

Faidherbe understood his position well. The Army of the North, with Lille as its political centre, was isolated from the rest of France due to the Germans surrounding Paris and beyond. The north could communicate with Bordeaux only by semaphore or by telegraph via England and Le Havre. Faidherbe would not lead France to victory. However, he could serve as an important distraction and annoyance to the Germans.

Already, after the fall of Metz, General von Manteuffel's First Army (I, VII and VIII Corps) had been sent to take small fortresses in the north and contend with the growing Army of the North. On

24 November, two of Manteuffel's corps, I and VIII, met with the Army of the North at Viller-Bretonneux, just east of Amiens. As a result, the French could not advance south toward Beauvais. Instead, they pulled back to the fortresses of Arras and Lille. Manteuffel did not pursue them. Rouen was occupied without a fight on 5 December. The French soldiers from Rouen moved west to Le Havre, but Manteuffel did not have enough men to send after them. The Germans could only stretch so far.

Like every other French commander after Sedan, Faidherbe wanted more time to train his soldiers, but he recognized that he did not have it. So, under orders from Gambetta to possibly meet up with Ducrot's supposed breakout at Saint-Denis, he moved on 9 December, despite the dark and the snow. He captured the fortress at Ham, cutting rail access between Rheims and Amiens.

From Ham, Faidherbe attempted to move east but was blocked at La Fère. He therefore moved west along the Somme toward Amiens. On 23 December, he waged a successful defensive battle about 5 miles north-east of the city to keep up morale. Still, he did not take the city and could not hold ground on cold exposed hills. Faidherbe fell back to Arras.

By the end of December, Gambetta and Freycinet had shifted their strategic focus to Bourbaki's army in the east. From their other main provincial forces – Chanzy's in the west and Faidherbe's in the north – however, they still needed distractions to tie up German troops. Faidherbe advanced on Bapaume on 3 January. He might have taken the town the following day, but again faced exhaustion – he could not push his men further. Faidherbe's final battle came on 18–19 January at Saint-Quentin. With 3,000 casualties and 11,000 missing (mostly made prisoner), Faidherbe lost a third of his army. He sent the rest to the fortresses in the north where they remained until the armistice was signed.

Meanwhile, upon arrival in Le Mans, Chanzy began making plans for an attack. Freycinet and Gambetta, now focused on a new strategy in the east, had the rare experience of trying to convince a general to postpone an advance. Yet Chanzy's position remained precarious. Although he held Le Mans for several weeks in December, it was only because Moltke had held back Prince Friedrich Karl and Mecklenburg due to issues with their supplies. Once these logistical challenges were worked out, on New Year's Day 1871, Moltke ordered Friedrich Karl to sweep westward to defeat Chanzy at Le Mans. Mecklenburg was leading on the right (a newly named XIII Corps made up of the 22nd and 17th divisions), with Friedrich Karl on the left (with X, IX and III Corps). The German advance in early January, along cold, twisting roads, proved to be just as challenging as the French retreat had been in December.

Chanzy held a strong position. He had fortified the plateau he occupied, and the Sarthe river covered his flank and rear. Chanzy added to his men twenty-two battalions of National Guards from Brittany. These men were poorly trained and had muzzle-loading guns left over from the American Civil War, with snow-soaked ammunition of the wrong calibre and defective, rusted firing mechanisms. The Germans attacked on 10 January but could not break through. Battle resumed the next day and this time the French could not hold against the German attack. Chanzy's forces suffered 25,000 dead and wounded and 50,000 cold, wet and exhausted deserters. By 12 January, the Germans occupied Le Mans and demanded 2 million francs and shelter for 40,000 soldiers.

After the battle fell apart, Chanzy's remaining men headed further north and west, first to Alençon to plan an advance on Paris, and then, on Gambetta's instructions, west to Laval to plan yet another advance.

Germans far from home on Christmas Eve 1870 struggled to grapple with the ongoing war as they missed their traditional warm family togetherness. Soldiers decorated trees in the forests where they were encamped with candles and makeshift ornaments. The crown prince's thoughts turned to his wife and children as well as to the widows and orphans who were in mourning during this festive season. He prayed that once the war was over, they might look back and find that it had ushered in an era of lasting peace. That evening, he organized a Christmas raffle in which each of the eighty members of his staff brought two small presents to share along with punch, pepper cakes, nuts and apples to celebrate the occasion under a Christmas tree, with much laughter and amusement at their gifts: pincushions, riding-satchels, toiletries and even a pocket revolver.

Dietrich von Lassberg found the gulf between Christmas past and Christmas present too wide to bridge with trinkets. He had returned to Orléans after having assisted with transporting another group of French prisoners. He had wanted to ride to the location of Rudolf's death now that he had returned to the area, but had had to move on before he got the chance.

As the holiday approached, Lassberg thought back to his initial entry in his daily war journal: 'War! War with France!' he had written with joy, not understanding the sorrow and misery the conflict would bring. He had now learned the 'shadow side and horror' of war, and suffered an incalculable loss.[16] On 18 December, he had received a stack of twenty-three letters, the first ones he had received from family after they had learned of Rudolf's death. In his journal he recorded an unusual mark to signal his unspoken distress: '—'.[17]

Without Rudolf, Lassberg found no joy. On Christmas Eve, he sat in silence around the campfire, homesick and reflective, drinking hot grog out of a tin cup with his comrade Walter. Their monosyllabic exchange belied the deep longing underneath, as they dreamed of their kin back home, gathered beneath the Christmas tree eating bratwurst soup and smoked meats. It was a Christmas Eve he would never forget.

17. *Winter Theatre*

In Paris, Christmas day appeared particularly bleak. As the journalist Francisque Sarcey recounted,

> No one had the heart to amuse himself. With what melancholy bitterness one remembers the sparkling quality of Paris, of our Paris, in those days that led up to the 1st of January? What animation on our boulevards and streets! How the carriages rolled joyously by the thousand along the macadam! What gaiety in the lights in the windows of department stores decorated for this holiday![1]

An anonymous municipal worker blamed the Prussians for their miserable holiday:

> You are the reason that the most beautiful and happiest day of Paris is spent in an immense and needy sadness, made worse by the cold. All the houses seem destined for sleep, with the exception of a few lights here and there that seem to want to prolong the holiday, but they make no noises. The joyous conversations and the singing are replaced by rare and almost silent muttering.[2]

By Christmas, Paris had been under siege for three months with little communication from the outside. The revolutionary *journée* of 31 October lay in the past. Civilians suffered from long queues for food, the use of horse and rat meat, the outbreak of illness and the daily search for fuel in a particularly cold winter. Parisians who strayed too close to the ramparts risked being shot by Germans as 'marauders'.[3]

The siege stretched the limits of Parisians' endurance. Across the city, people weighed the burden of sacrifice against the possibility

LA

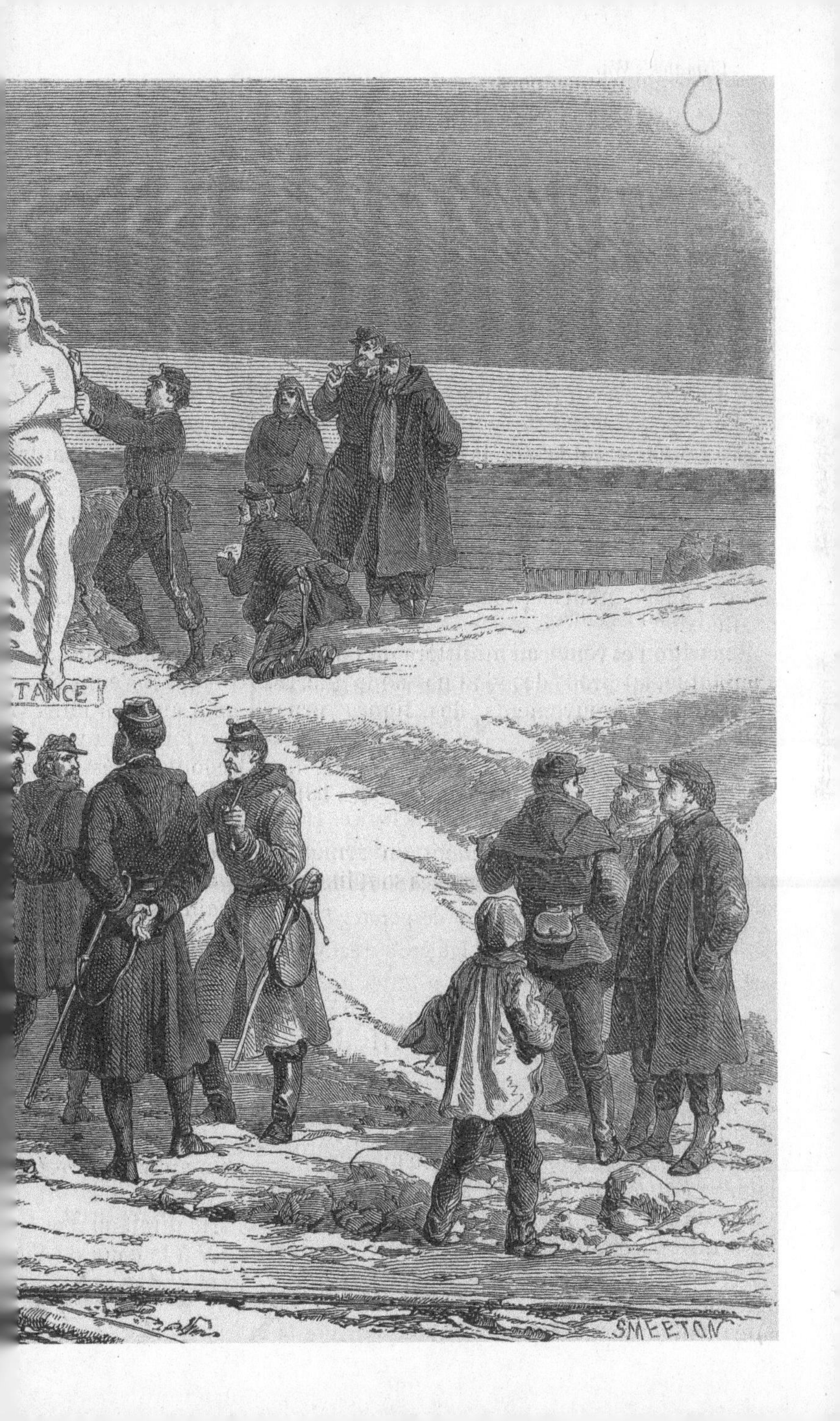
TANCE
SMEETON

of victory. Juliette Adam's haberdasher told her, 'Madame, all of this is nothing if France wins; but, if we must see France defeated and make ourselves bankrupt at the end of the siege, we will go mad!'[4] Parisians stayed motivated by focusing their anger on the Prussians and on the failures of the GND.

The siege of Paris did not produce any real heroes who performed memorable acts that either succeeded in liberation or symbolized dashed hopes. Instead, Parisians invented heroism for themselves through their writing and observations. They made symbolic women, allegories of Paris and the nation, into their heroes, in contrast with their disappointment in failed male politicians. And they made themselves the heroes of their own story. In writing and in art, reference was always to the 'defence' of Paris, not to its 'defeat' or 'suffering', even as the quest for provisions grew in importance and the winter claimed an increasing number of lives.

On 8 December, heavy snow fell on the all-artist Seventh Company of the Nineteenth Battalion of the National Guard, stationed at Bastion 84 on the edge of the 13th *arrondissement*. The next day, in the space of two or three hours, Jean-Alexandre-Joseph Falguière, thirty-nine years old and the 1859 winner of the Prix de Rome, created a snow sculpture of a muscular female nude, seated on a cannon with arms crossed in defiance. *La Résistance*, both strong and vulnerable, caught the imagination of the Parisian press. This ephemeral allegory of Paris exhorted its citizens to maintain their fortitude as the winter grew desperate. The very act of sculpting in snow, the harnessing of Falguière's creativity and skill and defiance, captured Parisian imagination. After it melted, Adam recorded, it remained 'sculpted in their hearts'.[5]

The winter of 1870 felt unusually cold, dark and isolating. Coal became scarce by late October, so Parisians cut down trees along the boulevards to keep warm. The Seine froze over for three weeks straight. By December, gas was rationed to support the balloon service. Three out of four gas lamps stayed dark, and oil lamps replaced gas-lit streets.

The gloomy streets shocked Parisians, especially the well-to-do, who felt keenly the disappearance of open cafés, theatres and illuminated windows. 'This lugubrious city . . . is it still Paris?' asked *Le Gaulois*.[6] Paris had fallen back in time to the medieval city, one in which the stars became visible at night. The small nubs of diminished gaslights, wrote Théophile Gautier, 'spot the darkness with scanty red dots, the reflection of which lengthens and melts in the river like a gout of blood'.[7] The sad state of Parisian boulevard life contrasted with the bright, stark use of electric searchlights, a new feature of the militarized landscape.

In December, Parisians held more than double the number of burials than in normal times. In January, the number of deaths climbed to four times the monthly average: almost 20,000 registered burials. Officials worked to honour the dead, even as the collective numbers strained resources. Since the eighteenth century, the city had developed its capacity to track and properly bury all corpses, including those of individuals who, in the expanding, anonymizing city, did not have friends or family on hand to mourn them. For a generation, impoverished Parisians had had the right to be buried without cost in a common grave in a municipal cemetery, each individual spaced apart and marked with an identifying cross.

'For a besieged city,' wrote a customs agent, 'the greatest suffering is the inability to know what is happening beyond its walls, what are its friends and its enemies doing, whether it's been forgotten, if there is a world beyond the lines that surround it.'[8] The rare appearance of a letter from the outside caused celebration. Juliette Adam rejoiced on 20 December when she heard from her daughter Alice and her parents for the first time since her visit in September. They had moved to Jersey and were alive! Adam learned this news from a letter written by a Mme de Pierreclos, who lived in Mâcon. This letter was sent to New York and returned to France in a double envelope, and somehow made its way to Adam at the post office on avenue Joséphine. Adam was not sure how it had arrived, but she suspected the American ambassador might have been behind it. The American Embassy in Paris enjoyed a special dispensation on

Tuesdays to exchange sealed correspondence and packages through the lines.

The siege of Paris is primarily remembered as a food crisis. Most people lacked vegetables and ate cats, dogs and horses. Men could acquire rations through their service in the National Guard, while women and children suffered and waited in long queues seeking bread and milk.

Paris did not suffer more than other besieged cities, but it was the largest population to be besieged and bombarded, with 2 million people in the city during the siege, including approximately 230,000 refugees and 200,000 provincial soldiers. City administrators had started to stock Paris for a siege in August, but there was not a unified food administration until 26 September.

The government tended toward a liberal political economy, and so did not immediately move to ration food and firewood. As a result, the gap between rich and poor widened. Meat was taxed from mid-October and rationed at the end of that month (50 grams, or 1½ ounces, per person per day, later reduced to 30 grams or 1 ounce), and could not be sold except by municipal butchers' shops. Certain butchers' shops specialized in cats and dogs. Horses were requisitioned for food in mid-December. Bread was not rationed until late in the siege. Flour was requisitioned in December and bread rationing began on 19 January, limiting each person to 10½ ounces daily of very poor-quality bread sold at specific bakeries in their neighbourhood.

In late November, the French negotiated an opportunity for foreigners to depart. Soon thereafter, about 200 British, Americans and Swiss left via Créteil, a small fraction of the approximately 1,500 Americans, 40,000 Belgians, 30,000 Swiss and 5,000 Britons in the capital city. By the end of November, with no sign that the Prussians would allow provisions to be sent to the city, British humanitarians began to stockpile supplies in warehouses in English harbours so that they could be ready to distribute once the siege came to an end.

Inside the city, the daily subsidy to wives of National Guardsmen was raised from 1.50 francs to 2.25 francs at the end of November, but this amount could not make up for the dramatic rise in food prices. Butter sold at eight times the pre-war price, milk at three times, eggs at fourteen times and potatoes at ten times. Cheese, butter, beef and lamb disappeared early, followed by vegetables and milk. One man documented the dearth of fresh food for sale in the central marketplace:

> I've just come from les Halles: there are a good number of vendors, but little merchandise and in what a state! The few vegetables that one can find there are ripped up from the gardens between the forts and the ramparts of the city: half-rotten or half-dried out vegetables, and everything is selling despite the prices. Because in a few days there will be no more green vegetables.[9]

Strange food and Parisian ingenuity in making it palatable became a frequent subject of ironic or humorous images, including those by the cartoonist Cham with the captions 'The danger of eating a mouse is that your cat may run in after it' and 'The line for rat meat', which appeared in *Le Charivari* on 1 and 8 December. The latter image, depicting a cross-section of Parisians on their hands and knees before a sewer grate, is, in the immortal words of the art historian Hollis Clayson, 'a classic of the rat cuisine genre'.[10]

An anonymous English woman wrote on 4 November, 'I made up my mind at last yesterday to eat horse, and think I have got over my disquiet; I was really too hungry . . . I am favoured by the milkman – only soon he will have to kill his cows, as there is no forage.'[11] Nearly every line of the letter discussed food, food prices and interactions about acquiring food. 'I am very well,' she concluded, 'and my impression is that I am not a woman, but a horse. I only require food, and then I am as well as possible.'[12]

Only the very rich maintained a high quality of life. In early December, sugar and cake flour were first rationed. By the end of the month, recorded Juliette Adam, hosts seeking to hold a dinner party resorted to potlucks, 'a kind of picnic' in which each friend supplies a different comestible that they have been able to procure.[13] Zoo animals – yaks, zebras and the two famous elephants – were reserved for the well-to-do. Rats populated the press as a necessary cuisine, but in reality the rodents were less frequently eaten (they were difficult to prepare, typically as pâté or salmis). The claim to have eaten rat during the siege served as a badge of honour for the well-off. To celebrate the new year, Adam managed to procure at the English butcher a morsel of Castor the elephant. The flesh, she reported as 'appetizing, pink, firm, with a fine grain and little flecks of the purest white'. She invited Louis Blanc and his brother Charles to dine on Castor, to their great interest and with much discussion on the flavour and merits.[14]

Hermione Quinet, a Romanian-born author and translator who married the historian Edgar Quinet, depended upon her unnamed servant to secure food. The couple had moved to Paris immediately after 4 September, ending Edgar Quinet's eighteen years of exile during the Second Empire. While her husband wrote political tracts and newspaper columns, Quinet oversaw the household. As a wealthy woman, Quinet could afford to employ a servant in all but the most desperate times. Nevertheless, procuring food frequently became a challenge. Women helped each other, exchanging information informally about the possibilities of securing a tin of sardines or the new way to cook rice. Through the generosity of her female friends, Quinet was sometimes able to serve rabbit at her table. Making the meal palatable was another question. Newspapers like *Le Temps* included advice on the back page on 'Consumption of Rat Meat – Precautions to Take' and 'Preparation of Horse Meat – 8 Recipes'.[15] Even with these suggestions, Quinet found it difficult to make the meat tender without using too much precious fuel.

For working women, the situation became much more desperate. Frequently, observers invoked the image of the working-class Parisian woman as a stoic patriot with just a hint of the sans-culotte. The image of Parisians, especially women, lining up to wait for food is the dominant artistic representation of the siege. Nevertheless, before the Commune, republicans did not see these women as threatening. They were described as merely waiting in orderly lines for bread, not breaking down doors. According to Quinet, impoverished women supported the national cause whole-heartedly. Through 'their long hours waiting in the streets, with their children in their arms, to wait for a ration of black bread', their only fear, it was said, was 'capitulation'.[16]

Ignoring the unrest against the Republic on 31 October, Quinet insisted not only on the patriotism of working women, but also on their support for the Republic: 'women have stared down [famine] as boldly as the Red Spectre.'[17] Quinet emphasized that the sacrifices were worth the chance to return to Paris under a republic, 'the only time of true liberty France has ever known.'[18] Women were bound to make sacrifices without complaining. Quinet was told by her servant that in the queue outside the baker's one morning, a woman had grumbled about the wait. 'Think about our soldiers on the battlefield,' replied the servant. 'They also have their feet in the snow, but it's not bread they're waiting for.' The rest of the crowd agreed.[19] This incident, illustrating the tenacity of Parisian women during the final week of the war, was anticipated in a cartoon by Cham in *Le Charivari*. A poor woman holding a baby refuses alms offered by a well-dressed man, gesturing at a cannon mouth, and saying, 'Thanks, I'm not hungry! As long as there is one Prussian in France, here is the mouth you should feed!'[20]

By focusing on women's queuing for food as noble and virtuous, artists obscured the other actions that women undertook during the siege, including nursing, attending and speaking at political clubs and neighbourhood meetings, working as *cantinières* and participating in the 31 October uprising. This diminution of women's activities therefore also masks the crisis in manhood, in which military impotence and failure did not lend themselves to the recognition of female strength. Adam reported a rare story of male civilian powerlessness. On Christmas Eve, she witnessed a man falling down on rue de la Banque. She asked the police agents who picked him up, is he a drunk? No, came the response, he is suffering from cold and hunger. He's a seller of horse whips. Since horses had been requisitioned for food, nobody had a need for his wares. Adam bought the man's horse whips and gave them to the police agents, who returned them to the man when she turned her back to preserve a modicum of his pride.

By the end of November, some theatres reopened, and Parisians were eager to attend. By then, witnessing theatrical performances seemed patriotic rather than frivolous. Parisians flocked to watch re-enactments of the fall of the Second Empire and to bond with their fellow citizens in this now-political venue. Theatres donated their proceeds to the war cause. Male actors who had enlisted in the National Guard sometimes performed in uniform. Henri-Polydore Maubant delivered a monologue from *Le Cid* in this way. Alternatively, they performed in street clothes, as their costumes and sets remained in safe storage. Beards also identified men as members of the military.

The stand-out event of the winter was a reading of Victor Hugo's *Les Châtiments*, a collection of poems criticizing Louis-Napoleon Bonaparte. First written in 1853 in the wake of the *coup d'état*, the collection sold 20,000 copies during the course of the siege. Hugo had gone into exile in 1851 and did not return to France until September 1870 (despite an amnesty having been granted in 1859), settling in Paris just before it was cut off by the Prussians. The civic authorities decided to stage a reading of the work at the Opéra on rue Le Peletier, free and open to the public, on 28 November. Tickets were distributed first-come, first-served by each *arrondissement*, with each allotment proportional to its population. Juliette Adam attended the reading, where she debated the characteristics of the revolutions of 1848 versus 1870 with Louis Blanc, a leader in the provisional government during the hopeful days of the Second Republic. That winter, many Parisian poets published works in Hugo's style and odes to Parisian resistance and experiences during the siege, often set to the music of the 'Marseillaise'.

The presentation of *Les Chatîments* looked back at the Second Empire's early injustices. Parisians grappled now with the new

Government of National Defence that seemed unable to manage the invasion and its consequences for civilians and unwilling to fully embrace the direct engagement of the people in military and political life. Within the ranks of the National Guard, anger at the GND grew deeper after the insurrection of 31 October and the failed sortie of 30 November: why were they suffering from hunger, cold, depression, inaction, defeat? The lack of discipline worsened as some members of the National Guard took to vandalism and disorder and abandoned their posts – sometimes in their hundreds.

In December, the press did not let up in their attacks on the GND. Rumours abounded that the GND deliberately held back the war effort and that reactionaries wanted a Prussian victory so that they could restore the monarchy. *Le Réveil* accused Trochu of having 'led Parisians to famine in order to force them to open the doors to the Prussians'.[21]

Neighbourhood clubs met nightly to discuss the situation. There was little else to do, and the meeting movement of the previous two years had prepared the groundwork for this kind of sociability. Clubs became a source of neighbourhood identity, where place of residence consolidated as the primary collective political identity. Speakers referred to the 'citizens' of Montmartre, Belleville, or La Villette, and the conflict was increasingly conceptualized as one of the neighbourhood against the state. At the 10 November meeting in the 20th *arrondissement*, a speaker identified as 'citizen Gaillard *fils*' called on 'the citizens of Belleville to refuse to let themselves be defeated'. The speaker went on to call on his fellow neighbours to sign a letter and take it to the Hôtel de Ville 'to demand the liberation of the prisoners' – the mayor and deputies of Belleville, arrested after 31 October for their participation in seizing the Hôtel de Ville. 'If the government refuses, that will demonstrate that it has declared war on Belleville, and we will know what to do. (Thunderous applause.)'[22]

Clubs discussed far-fetched plans for success using novel tactics. In the 9 December meeting of the Club Démocratique des Batignolles, participants discussed the efficacy of an incendiary substance known as 'Greek fire' as it had been used by the Byzantine Greeks to attack naval vessels and reportedly ignited on contact with water. One speaker, Delescluze, a future martyr of the Commune, argued that the plan required directing 'high-caliber fire-pumps at the Prussians to get them wet'.[23]

More seriously, in the clubs speeches increasingly criticized the wealthy for hoarding food. At the club Favié on 15 January, an informant wrote,

> People participated in an animated discussion concerning the bread rationing that had begun that morning in the [20th] arrondissement and the women in particular distinguished themselves with the vehemence of their complaints. In some groups it was said that the people at the Hôtel de Ville are indulging themselves freely; they eat as much meat as they please, they and the rich folk who support them; they keep hams in their cellars and have wild parties in the restaurants, accompanied by young ladies. Since they are not subject to rationing, the comfortable make patriotic speeches about 'fighting to the end' [*la guerre à outrance*] at the expense of our stomachs. But we, we who have nothing left but bread, can we live on a pound or even 100 grams of bread a day? They want us to die of hunger so they can be rid of Belleville, which threatens them even more than the Prussians do.[24]

The socio-economic dimension rankled, but it was generally not yet understood in a Marxist framework. Most people in the city shared in the suffering from privation, including the class most usually targeted by the working class: shopkeepers and small employers. Furthermore, the issues at hand were the lack of food and firewood, along with the military frustrations and daily danger, not a Marxist focus on wage work. The struggle focused on the state, not on capital. In addition, most lists of demands formulated by clubs included a provision for establishing a democratically elected municipal council.

On the right, too, critics of the GND called for elections out of the conviction that the country would not support a republican government and in hope of a more conservative future regime. At the end of November, the *Paris-Journal* wrote, 'For heaven's sake, [we need] a national assembly, with or without an armistice, with or without resupplying; let us eat the soles of our boots if we must, to give France a true government instead of orators who are accidentally in charge.'[25]

By the end of December, military setbacks elsewhere had led to the arrival of two more Prussian armies outside Paris. The GND was forced to recognize internally that surrender was imminent. Inside the city, however, calls for a sortie led by the National Guard grew louder. Determined to demonstrate to Parisians his willingness to take the offensive, Trochu authorized one more attempt at a breakout on 21 December. This time he looked toward Picardy since the Army of the North under Faidherbe was active and large, and the way forward crossed a large broad plain that provided less cover to the Germans from French artillery. Trochu attacked on the 21st with the aim of taking Le Bourget, the village that the French had briefly captured at the end of October. The troops had high morale as they arrived at Le Bourget, but soon found themselves facing intense German shellfire from a distant line, with no infantry in sight to shoot at. The French quickly fell into disarray, unable to capture the village or to dig into the frozen ground to besiege it. The men had no fuel, and the ground was so icy they could not even set up tents. They had lost their fight.

After Le Bourget, Trochu was ready to resign, but who would replace him? Ducrot clearly opposed the Liberals and believed they were heading to defeat; Vinoy, who gamely suggested a massed attack on an unspecified point, was too tied to the imperial regime. Trochu stayed on.

That winter, Bismarck also worried about the other Great Powers intervening in the war through a diplomatic conference set to take place regarding Russia. In 1856, the Treaty of Paris at the end of the Crimean War had prohibited Russian warships in the Black Sea.

The conflict in 1870 provided an opening for the Russian foreign minister, Alexander Gorchakov, to declare in a circular dated 31 October that Russia no longer considered itself bound by that clause. Bismarck had previously made it clear that he would support such a move, and he reinforced this support in the autumn of 1870. The British insisted on a diplomatic conference, one that France should attend as a signatory of the Treaty of Paris. Bismarck sought to avoid this, because such a situation would open the door for the other Great Powers to seek a negotiated end to the conflict between Prussia and France. He cut communications with Paris to prevent Jules Favre from receiving an invitation until it was too late, and so the French were not able to attend and the conference went nowhere.

Meanwhile at Versailles, Bismarck and Moltke, both exhausted by their heavy responsibilities, continued to dispute the preparations for the bombardment. Moltke insisted he needed more time, given the limitations of rail transport to the Paris region. He had only a single line of track to work with, and that ended a full 15 miles short of the German lines. Moltke would have preferred to fight all the armies in the provinces and then shell Paris and occupy it. However, Roon, the minister of war, agreed with Bismarck that the preparations needed to accelerate. Moltke finally agreed to prepare for a bombardment to appease the political demands, but one that would not commit German soldiers to an assault.

A 17 December council of war, from which Bismarck was excluded, determined that the bombardment would begin as soon as the Germans had a ten-day supply of shells, at five hundred per gun. An experimental bombardment of the Avron plateau, Trochu's easternmost stronghold just outside Rosny, took place on 27 December. Within two days, Trochu withdrew from the plateau. After this success the Germans bombarded forts to the east and south – Nogent, Noisy, Rosny; Montrouge, Vanves and Issy. King Wilhelm ordered the bombardment of the city proper to begin on 4 January. It was postponed due to fog until the following day.

The crown prince continued to disagree with the decision,

calling it a 'folly' and a 'wretched bombardment'.[26] Given the lack of materiel in place and the ease with which the French could disrupt the transportation of supplies and ammunition, 'the Parisians will just laugh at us, and if famine does not eventually force them to surrender . . . I fully expect that at the sound of the first shot the spirit of resistance will flare up again more hotly than ever.'[27]

Friedrich Wilhelm was well aware that public opinion across Europe was turning against Germany:

> We are no longer looked upon as the innocent sufferers of wrong, but rather as the arrogant victors, no longer content with the conquest of the foe, but fain to bring about his utter ruin. No more do the French appear in the eyes of neutrals as a mendacious, contemptible nation, but as the heroic-hearted people that against overwhelming odds is defending its dearest possessions in honourable fight.[28]

The bombardment of civilians, including children, would only exacerbate this image.

In the British press, indeed, pro-France sentiment had steadily grown. Many Britons sympathized with the suffering of the French population, which they learned about from first-hand reports such as the one published by McMichael, as well as reports from members of the diplomatic corps, military counsellors who witnessed the conflict and war correspondents. Germany now appeared exploitative and greedy. France, meanwhile, was no longer in a position to threaten Belgium and Luxembourg, and had declared itself a republic. Even the illustrated *Graphic* newspaper, which favoured the Germans, began to incorporate themes of depression and humiliation in its portrayals of the French.

The *Illustrated London News*, however, continually reminded readers that the French had brought this situation on themselves by electing Louis-Napoleon Bonaparte as president and then supporting his empire. While sympathetic to the plight of Parisians, the paper could not help but note in a 21 January piece that the Germans had the right to destroy the city:

> As we have said before, when the true story of this *siège* shall be told, most abundantly will be justified the sympathy now felt for the Parisians by such of us as nevertheless believe that no choice is left to the Emperor of Germany as to finishing the work that has been forced upon him.[29]

Britain never saw its interests touched closely enough to intervene in the conflict. When it came to the new balance of power on the Continent, it was clear that Britain in any event did not have the military capacity to intervene. A young Horatio Kitchener, who had just completed his studies at the royal military academy at Woolwich, entered service with a mobile hospital unit and witnessed the battle of Laval. He convinced his superiors to allow him to ascend in a French balloon to study the movements of German soldiers. This action was caught by the British press, and the young officer was brought before his military commander. He did not lose his commission but received a warning for having imperilled his country's neutrality.

On the evening of 5 January, German gunners redirected their shells toward the centre of Paris, not for direct military purposes but to immiserate the population and incline them toward peace. Every night for three weeks, at around 10 p.m., the bombardment began and lasted for four or five hours, with 200–500 rounds each night. The bombardment sent over between 6,000 and 7,000 shells in total. The range was incredible. A gun on Châtillon heights could send a shell to Île Saint-Louis some 5 miles away. Dietrich von Lassberg, now stationed 10 miles south-east of Paris at Montgeron, witnessed the bombardment from afar.

> At night especially the bombardment offered a grand drama; for hours we sat sometimes at the windows or went outside . . . and watched the flashes from the German or the French batteries . . [that] lit up the whole horizon, and [we] took pleasure in the majestic thunder of the heavy artillery and in every fire that arose on the enemy side.[30]

By day, thick clouds of smoke covered the view.

Many Parisians sought refuge in their cellars. One observer, Francisque de Biotière, marvelled at the perfect order of living spaces in the cellars, each one separated from the other with white sheets. A few mattresses, a table, a lamp completed the scene. Two large stoves stood at either end of the cellar, which ravenously burned chairs, tables and armoires. In an aristocratic cellar, wrote Biotière, the concierge kept a careful watch over her renters. The most well-to-do brought down furniture, carpets, linens and precious objects to give the scene the air of a *salle de réception*. A satirical newspaper, *La Cave*, facetiously offered to deliver goods to basements. The curé of Saint-Sulpice won praise from a British observer as he 'kept his calm when a bomb interrupted mass, begging the faithful to depart quietly and walking up and down the aisle like a sea captain pacing his deck in the midst of a tempest'.[31]

Still, the bombardment did not cause serious damage. Despite their great range, the German guns were unable to send projectiles beyond the Seine, and so the Right Bank remained unscathed. Most shells landed in open spaces. The Invalides and the Panthéon made easy targets. Still, damage to buildings – the Sorbonne, the Church of Saint-Sulpice, the Panthéon, the Invalides and the Convent of the Sacred Heart – was mostly superficial and symbolically fortifying. The bombardment did cause fires to break out, which gave the Germans hope: houses, wooden construction sites, the wine entrepôt, the Grenelle slaughterhouse. In total, about 1,500 buildings were damaged.

Yet Parisians fixed the damage as quickly as possible. Trochu particularly protested at the accidental bombing of hospitals, including la Pitié, la Salpêtrière, le Val-de-Grace and Necker. The damage to hospitals garnered some sympathy for France internationally, including in the United States, and the Germans came under pressure to explain their strategy of targeting civilians, especially unarmed women and children. Bismarck responded by publishing an open letter in January 1871 defending the siege of Paris by decrying the *francs-tireurs* for what he viewed as illegitimate engagement.

The bombardment of Paris caused distress far beyond its damage to the city and its inhabitants. Deaths were reported daily in *Le Temps* and recorded in the diaries of Adam and Quinet. Wrote Adam, 'One mother, returning to her house, found only the shreds of her two children.'[32] This attack on children, innocents killed in their own home, made it clear that nobody was safe from modern warfare. The randomness of bombardment meant that at any moment a shell or bomb could destroy a house and kill those inside. The shells greatly disturbed Adam, who found she could scarcely write and left off keeping her diary for nearly a week. She had six days of horrible headaches in which she could not read, write, or listen to anyone.

Even from afar, George Sand found it unbearable to hear about the bombardment. Among her family, 'we don't speak of it,' for 'there are some pains that do not allow any space for reflection and that no words could ever express.'[33] When the temperature warmed, Sand thought of Parisians: 'the weather is nice, they are suffering less in Paris.'[34]

In mid-January, Trochu reported 189 civilian casualties, including 45 women and 21 children. As in Strasbourg, civilian men were more likely to be killed or wounded than civilian women but reports rarely mentioned that civilian men were part of the casualties. In total, around 100 Parisians were killed and fewer than 300 were injured. Meanwhile, 3,000–4,000 Parisians died of cold and hunger each week in January.

Once it had begun, the crown prince expected impatience from those who thought that bombardment would yield an immediate surrender. 'Now will the wiseacres of Berlin be triumphant indeed and expect the capitulation to come about at latest this evening. Only what will they say, if in a fortnight's time everything still remains *in statu quo?*'[35]

From his vantage point south-west of the city, the crown prince surveyed the results. Forts Issy and Vanves suffered, the barracks on the western side of Montrouge burned, and smoke rose from various locations across Paris. The thought of children and civilians caught in the bombardment pained him, but he felt trapped. 'Considering my personal aversion to war, it is a veritable cross for me to be forced under present conditions to carry out this painful obligation. But in this war of giants there is no duty I can shirk.' His only consolation lay in wishful thinking about the future: 'May its results at any rate be such that the true blessings of peace in all directions, progress and full development of all that can only thrive in times of quiet and good order, may grow out of it.'[36]

With this intensive firing, the German guns began to wear out. They simply could not withstand constant use, round after round, night after night. Some guns had to be taken out of service, and others exploded without warning.

While the bombardment of the city centre garnered the most attention, the primary target of the bombardment remained the outer forts – Issy, Vanves, Montrouge – which, despite a vigorous defence, could not hold on for long. Within three days of each targeted bombardment, the Germans could come in closer and therefore expand their range. By 21 January, Saint-Denis was under fire and its inhabitants fled into Paris.

Contrary to the Germans' expectation, Parisians did not agree to surrender; they demanded another sortie. Far from convincing them to capitulate, the bombardment solidified for many the resolve to hold on. At the same time, for many radical Parisians, the bombardment provided additional evidence that the GND did not have their best interests in mind. On the first night of the bombardment, 5 January, the Central Committee of the Twenty Arrondissements, which had been quiet in recent months, put up its second 'red poster' calling for an all-out attack on the Prussians:

> Will the great People of '89, who destroyed Bastilles and overturned thrones, wait in despair for cold and famine to freeze the last drop of blood in its heart, whose every beat is counted by the enemy? No! The population of Paris will never accept this misery and this shame. It knows that there is still time, that decisive steps can be taken to ensure the ability of working people to live, and to fight.[37]

The poster explicitly blamed the GND for this situation. 'The government has given its measure. It is killing us.'[38]

By January, even the moderate republican press had turned on the GND. On 6 January, *Le Siècle* called for the government to 'speak with serious and firm language and reveal its plan, if it has one'. On the 19th, the same newspaper wrote that it 'would like not to believe much in treason, but it believes in foolishness and incapacity'.[39]

For Parisians, the siege was a tragedy in which the very courage and solidarity of the National Guards and their supporters prolonged their own misery without success, in which the new Republic could not win the hearts of the people it claimed to represent. It was a romance in which the common person could become the hero of the story, refusing to give in to unjust systems of oppression, unlike the crown prince who remained trapped in perpetuating violence that he did not condone. It was a farce in which the endless parade to and from the barricades achieved nothing, a futile recursion of National Guard actions from previous revolutionary eras. It was an absurdist happening, too, in which 'perseverance against obviously insurmountable obstacles can form the basis of rebellion or revolution'.[40] But the one thing the siege was not was a comedy, in which the world turned upside down is restored in the end with a marriage and a happy ending. No *deus ex machina* intervened to save Paris.

In Versailles, a very different historical drama was about to unfold: the declaration of the German Empire. The series of conflicts that came to be known as the wars of German unification were not wars of conquest but rather Prussian demonstrations of strength. The 1866 war against Austria had established conclusively that the Habsburgs would not be the dominant force in a Greater Germany. Out of that war, the creation of the North German Confederation, led by Prussia, had decreased the number of sovereign German states from thirty-nine to six (including Prussia and Austria). And while the war against France resulted in the annexation of French territory into a united German Empire, territorial gain was not the main purpose or locus of conflict. The war instead made clear to the leaders of the four south German states of Baden, the Grand Duchy of Hesse, Württemberg and Bavaria the advantages of joining with the stronger grouping led by Prussia. The incorporation of the south German states occurred through diplomacy and negotiation, rather than through outright annexation. The wars legitimized the idea of a new, unified Germany. But the unification of the German Empire was not inevitable, and pulling it off required astute diplomacy, the navigation of parliaments and princes, and just-in-time pageantry.

After 1866, Bismarck viewed the unification of the remaining few German states under Prussia as inexorable and something that he could shape, but he did not have a precise timetable by which it would occur. As early as the Ems dispatch that helped to trigger the current conflict, he framed the war as a national struggle rather than as a war between monarchs. Still, as the war unfolded in August, Bismarck did not want to appear to apply any pressure on the other states beyond hinting that Alsace might serve as a common part of a future yet-to-be-determined Germany.

After Sedan, negotiations began in earnest. Baden was easy: as early as 2 September, Karlsruhe sent a request, from Minister-President Jolly to Bismarck, calling for the creation of a 'German Reich'. In Bavaria, the victory at Sedan convinced King Ludwig and his ministers that change was coming, but they still hoped for a new, looser German confederation to replace the North German Confederation. Bismarck, for his part, sought to incorporate the south German states in such a way as to continue and strengthen the terms of the North German Confederation.

At the end of September, Bismarck responded to Baden with a request that it join the North German Confederation. Delegations from Baden and from Württemberg soon arrived in Versailles, followed by representatives from Bavaria and Hesse. The four sovereign states had their own complicated relationships and rivalries, and so did not present a common front in their negotiations with Bismarck. Instead, the Prussian was able to play them off against each other and did not have to make the same concessions to each of them.

Bavaria remained the most difficult, willing to accept 'Reich and Kaiser' but demanding an equal voice in foreign policy, its own separate army except in war, its own military budget, and the right to veto constitutional changes. Bismarck countered by isolating Bavaria, accelerating negotiations with the other three states, and using his press propaganda to boost pressure. By 8 November, Bavaria was ready to give up on a loose confederation and instead negotiate on the terms of unification.

With so many players, each decision led to new complications. 'First endless difficulties of every sort and kind,' wrote the crown prince, 'then, when you think you have at last gained your object, a perfectly eel-like nimbleness in slipping out of the conclusions already arrived at.'[41] The king of Württemberg caused delays by demanding the same concessions Bavaria had achieved. In this he was not successful, but in the end each state won special considerations. Bavaria retained the right to regulate its own railroad, and Bavaria and Württemberg could maintain their own postal and telegraph systems, with only limited regulation by the Second Reich. Baden could tax its domestic beer and spirits. The Württemberg king could retain the ceremonial rights of a commander-in-chief, without any actual authority. The Bavarian king had additional command of the army – the Kaiser commanded the Bavarian army only at the declaration of war, and thereafter it was commanded independently by the Bavarian king, who also could appoint the officers and commanders of the fortresses in Bavaria. Bavaria also held the symbolic right to have a delegate at peace negotiations (a right exercised in 1917 at the conference of Brest-Litovsk).

In the end, however, Bismarck succeeded in expanding the governmental system of the North German Confederation to this new Germany. Each state signed its treaties between 15 and 25 November.

Two more issues remained. First, the name of this new unified German state and the title that King Wilhelm would assume as its leader. Second, ratification of these agreements in each state, including in the Reichstag of the North German Confederation in Berlin.

For Bismarck, the new title was crucial. The other kings would more readily accept the leadership of an emperor (*Kaiser*) than of the king of Prussia. He faced opposition from Wilhelm himself, who did not want to accept a title that had in previous centuries been seen as that of the oppressor of Prussia (that is, the Habsburgs of Austria). Therefore, in the midst of his negotiations with Bavaria, Bismarck suggested to King Ludwig that if he were to propose to Wilhelm that he should use the terms 'Emperor and Empire', Ludwig would find Bavaria's demands would be met. Ludwig furthermore would receive an annual income of 300,000 marks to his personal account. On 2 December, Ludwig signed a missive known as the 'Kaiser letter' – penned in fact by Bismarck – that offered Wilhelm the crown of emperor. Although Wilhelm continued to grouse, he accepted that the decision had been made. 'I thank God that the sixty-five years' interregnum is over,' wrote the crown prince. 'May our House, in due recognition of the task laid upon it, know how, not only on battle-fields, but also in the paths of peace, duly appreciating the needs of the age we live in, to pave the way for a liberal development of the German Empire!'[42]

The Reichstag in Berlin also needed to ratify each treaty and the revisions to the constitution of the North German Confederation. Naturally, representatives on the Left objected, calling for an all-German parliament to draft a new constitution. This measure failed. They put forward amendments to guarantee civil rights and compensation for deputies. Again, they failed. August Bebel, a socialist, called for a republic. Bismarck again called in all his tricks to get the measure accepting the agreements to pass, 195 votes to 32, on 9 December. On the following day the constitutional changes were also accepted, with the inclusion of the words 'Emperor' and 'Empire'. Finally, the Reichstag voted to send a delegation to Versailles entreating the king to accept the imperial crown.

Wilhelm would not accept this delegation until all of the sovereigns had confirmed their acceptance. The king still had not accepted 'Kaiser and Reich', nor had most of the sovereigns, but Bismarck had presented him with another fait accompli from the Reichstag. As in other cases when Wilhelm opposed Bismarck's plans, Wilhelm declined actually to stop his minister, but he did expect Bismarck to make things feel unavoidable. He received the deputies of the Reichstag on 18 December, an event the crown prince experienced with great relief on behalf of 'all German-thinking people'.[43]

In December, the states of Baden and Hesse ratified their respective treaties, and Württemberg passed theirs after a victory of the German Party at the election of 5 December. Bavaria, however, did not start the debate until 11 January, and passed it – after threats from Bismarck about how bad it would be for Bavaria to conclude a separate peace with France – with the required two-thirds majority on 21 January with a margin of two.

Meanwhile, preparations for the ceremony on 18 January went apace. As late as the 15th, the crown prince fretted that arrangements for the ceremony had not yet been settled 'as to title, escutcheon, armorial bearings, etc.' but explained with relief that a velvet Imperial Eagle would be decorated with gold brocade to create a new escutcheon. He further recorded his own discomfort with the new designation that he himself would bear – 'Imperial Highness'. Still, he gamely arranged to provide his own officers with banners to populate the palace's Hall of Mirrors for the ceremony.[44]

The day before the ceremony, the king held a sitting with Bismarck, the crown prince and the minister of the household, Alexander von Schleinitz. A three-hour debate over the final issues ensued: would Wilhelm be called the Emperor of Germany or the German Emperor? The Bavarian plenipotentiaries had rejected 'Emperor of Germany', and Bismarck – without having consulted Wilhelm – agreed to 'German Emperor', reducing the German lands to an adjective devoid of much meaning. Wilhelm was aghast, but Bismarck was adamant. The Bavarians would baulk at any change now, and besides, could Wilhelm really claim to control the entire territory of Germany, which for many included Austria? In the end, Wilhelm and the crown prince had to resign themselves to the styling of 'We, Wilhelm, by the grace of God German Emperor, King of Prussia', consoling themselves that in common language, 'of Germany' would likely come into use.[45] But Wilhelm's temper did not improve.

The crown prince greeted the morning of 18 January with a quiet acceptance. 'From now on,' he recognized,

> my duties and my wife's will have become twice as heavy, important, and responsible, but I welcome the increased burden, because I shrink from no difficulty, because I feel sure I have no lack of fresh courage to set about the work fearlessly and steadfastly, and lastly because I am convinced it was not for nothing it came about that between the ages of thirty and forty I have been again and again called upon to make the most weighty decisions, and, looking the dangers connected with them fairly in the face, to carry them to completion.[46]

In the Hall of Mirrors, fires lit in every fireplace barely warmed the frigid gallery. Yet the formal recognition of this moment seemed at times oddly muted. The court chamberlain simply stated in his official notification, 'The ceremony of installation will be held in the Hall of Mirrors at the Palace of Versailles at midday twelve o'clock, a short prayer and after that the proclamation.'[47]

The crown prince arrived in a carriage behind his mounted military gendarmes, though he refused to allow cannon salvoes that would disturb and dishonour the many wounded around the palace and grounds. He wore his dress tunic, helmet, sash and decorations, but retained his high boots. The Hall of Mirrors filled with royal dignitaries, officers and non-commissioned officers, all men who had spent the previous six months in service to the crown and country, sent as delegates from the various corps representing German nations soon to be incorporated into one empire. Each man wore the Iron Cross. A choir of singers offered 'Sei Lob und Ehr' after which a prayer – a rather clumsy and tactless criticism of Louis XIV – echoed beneath the ceiling on which the Sun King had had his successes glorified.

After the *Te Deum*, the king proceeded to a platform and summoned the ensigns of two regiments forward with their shot-up and tattered colours. The king offered a brief address to the German sovereigns, after which Bismarck in a cold and business-like remark delivered the address 'to the German people', in which a reference to Wilhelm as the 'Enlarger of the Empire' caused a ripple of emotion through the otherwise silent crowd.

Finally, the moment of high drama arrived. The grand duke of Baden approached the crown in solemn yet natural dignity, and 'with his uplifted right hand, cried in a loud voice: "Long live His Imperial Majesty the Emperor Wilhelm I!" '[48] The room erupted in a loud hurrah repeated six times, with flags and standards waving above. The crown prince knelt to kiss his father's hand. Wilhelm raised him up and they embraced. 'My feelings I cannot describe,' wrote the crown prince, 'all quite understood them; even among the flag-bearers I remarked unmistakable signs of emotion.'[49]

One by one, the princes offered their congratulations in a crush of men and medals. As Wilhelm left the assemblage, not pausing to greet Bismarck, the crown prince signalled the band to play the 'Hohenfriedberger March'. The kaiser sent a letter to his wife in Berlin to vent his feelings. 'I am just back from the "Emperor" act! I cannot tell you what nervous emotion I have been in during these last few days, partly because of the high responsibility I have now to undertake, partly and above all to see the Prussian title supplanted!'[50] Prince Otto of Bavaria wrote to his brother, 'I cannot begin to describe to you how infinitely and agonizingly painful I found the scene . . . It was all so cold, so proud, so glossy, so strutting and boastful and heartless and empty.'[51]

For Lassberg, the day passed like any other day. The next day, the Bavarians had a special celebration in honour of the occasion that was interrupted by the last French sortie from Paris.

With the ceremony and ratifications complete, the question

remained whether Germans living in these lands would embrace the new titles. Later that day, the first time that the crown prince was addressed as 'Imperial Highness', he startled with emotion. On 22 January, the first Sunday following the ceremony in the Hall of Mirrors, the prayer service offered in the palace chapel gave thanks to Wilhelm as 'Emperor and King'. The crown prince felt relief that 'people are beginning to take the externals of the Imperial question in earnest'.[52] This brief statement confided in the crown prince's diary reveals the fragility of the declaration of empire. While it is doubtful that a German chaplain serving in the Palace of Versailles that winter could have failed to adopt the imperial title, the shakiness of this symbolic assertion was entrusted to the hearts of Germans across central Europe who would use the name, or not.

Creating Germans out of such diverse sovereignties was another matter altogether. With his new title, 'Crown Prince of the German Empire, Crown Prince of Prussia', Friedrich Wilhelm felt himself 'for the first time a true "German"' with no distinction between himself and a Bavarian, Badenese, or Hessian. Still, he carefully recorded for posterity, 'by no means do I therefore propose to concern myself in the internal affairs of the several countries, or to wish in any way to deprive them of their individual privileges and peculiarities.'[53] Lassberg kept silent on the issue.

18. *Last Stands*

At the start of 1871, both sides longed to end the conflict, but faced the same challenges: the French refused to admit they would have to accept a loss of territory, and the Germans would not negotiate anything less. Neither side wanted this protracted conflict to lead other European powers to take advantage.

The GND, still divided internally by politics and generation, became increasingly unpopular. The far Left continued to stand in opposition to a moderate government that refused to call elections. The Right saw in Gambetta a nascent republican dictator, a concern that grew after he dissolved the departmental *conseils généraux* – elected under the Empire – on 24 December.

Despite their vast resources, neither side could move quickly enough to fundamentally alter the chessboard. They lacked the administrative capacity and the moral authority to harness all labour and industry to the war effort. In terms of manpower, however, the French seemed to have an endless supply. They kept sending fresh troops even if they were not well trained or equipped, whereas the Germans had to continue fielding the same, tired soldiers. Between September and January, the GND mobilized some half a million men, including twelve new corps. The French had still not exhausted all their resources, as they probably had about 470,000 men not yet mobilized, as well as the married men aged twenty-one to forty and the new class of 1871.

In January, peasant communities began to worry about the growing season as the enemy took requisitions, including seed for sowing in early 1871. Yet while some areas were ready to admit defeat, many French remained angry at the Prussians and vowed to keep fighting. The prefect of the Gers reported on 21 January that 'nowhere does anyone signal to me the desire to negotiate or make peace. It seems, on the contrary, that war to the extreme is willingly accepted, even by the peasants . . . My personal conviction is that if we were to win any victory, the country would be disposed to do anything that we asked of it.'[1] As late as 23 January, a village in Maine-et-Loire resisted invasion with arms, pitchforks and scythes. France maintained additional strengths too. Due to French naval power, French commerce remained strong, and its overseas colonies were not threatened. French credit was respected, and France could import weapons without difficulty. Brest, Bordeaux and Marseilles brimmed with armaments and activity.

Yet the Germans could easily see cracks in the French resolve. The raw troops were already exhausted and had experienced too many failures. On 3 January, a French officer surrendered himself and his company to the forces at Versailles. The crown prince recorded, 'His men declared they could not put up anymore either with the bad, scanty rations or the insults superiors heap upon them as if they were dirt.'[2]

Throughout January, besieged cities continued to fall: Mézières, Rocroy, Péronne and Longwy. Only Bitche and Belfort held out. Bitche had been encircled in early August. By September, it had been partly burned to the ground, but it nevertheless held on. Belfort submitted to seventy days of bombardment, which killed and wounded three hundred of the town's four thousand inhabitants.

By January, the war cost the French about 10 million francs per day, which the GND financed through debt. But the improvised financing of the war stretched France thin. The country had 337 million francs in expenses and 123 million in receipts – a deficit of 214 million francs. The GND had managed a successful loan effort at the end of October, which raised 250 million francs on the French and British markets, but by January the government sustained the war through advances from the Banque de France. Prussia financed the war through loans and public subscriptions, which it intended to pay off using a French war indemnity.

For many, the war dragged on with seemingly endless monotony. Yet in a short span of days in mid-January, a series of emotional

VINS

NOUVEAUTES

dramas unfolded in a constellation of specific localities that brought the war to a climax. From a tiny western village to the streets of Paris to a mountain pass on the Swiss border, the war between France and the German states sounded its final, terrible toll.

Gambetta continued to place faith in raising armies in the countryside to relieve Paris or to serve as a diversion for the Germans surrounding the capital. Until mid-December, he still envisioned that Bourbaki would either distract the Germans from Chanzy's forces or would eventually head north from Bourges and attack the besiegers of Paris via Gien and Montargis.

Only in mid-December did the strategy of an eastern offensive begin to emerge, with the aim of cutting off communication with Germany. For the first time, Gambetta began to imagine that the war might continue even after Paris fell. In late December – when Friedrich Karl temporarily returned to Orléans instead of going after Chanzy, and with Ducrot remaining trapped in Paris – Freycinet crafted a new plan. He sent his assistant, a civil engineer named de Serres, to explain. Bourbaki was now to move XVIII and XX Corps to the Saône valley, leaving XV Corps to cover Bourges. With other forces – Camille Crémer's in Beaune, Garibaldi's and the garrison at Besançon – Bourbaki was to assemble 110,000 men who could recapture Dijon, relieve Belfort and Langres, and then head north to cut the German communications, possibly in combination with Faidherbe coming from the north.

It was an audacious plan and Gambetta and Bourbaki both agreed to it. The large numbers involved seemed to make the case. If the soldiers and staff officers had been more experienced – and had been led by a more talented and determined commander – it might have been successful. After all, the Germans were overextended as they pursued the new French provincial forces, with their weak point in the east: the flank protected by XIV Corps, mostly from Baden, commanded by August von Werder.

Bourbaki's two corps left Bourges on 20 December and soon encountered their usual problems. It was challenging to move the two corps via the rail system in the winter and expect that same rail line to also have the capacity to supply the men consistently. Troops waited on platforms for days and then became stuck in cattle trucks as lines were clogged by trucks and breakdowns. De Serres showed the ability to adjust and improvise with great energy despite his lack of experience with campaign logistics. Even so, he could not complete this impossible task. Once the French corps arrived in the east, it was not clear which pieces of the operation to perform in which order and just how Garibaldi's men fitted into the chain of command. With Gambetta in Lyons, de Serres with Bourbaki, and Freycinet in Bordeaux, the civilian leadership lacked co-ordination.

Bourbaki himself hindered the plan through his pessimism and failure of imagination. The general believed his first task was to relieve Belfort, which had been under siege since October. Its updated defences had managed to resist the half-hearted, weak German siege by eleven reserve battalions, making Belfort a welcome topic for a French press hungry for good news. The city was not close to capitulating, and relieving the city was not going to win any strategic advantage. Nevertheless, Bourbaki was sent to relieve Belfort as a grand gesture.

By the time the French were able to advance on 30 December, Freycinet feared that the Germans had enough intelligence and time to crush Bourbaki, so Freycinet now also wanted to send the XV Corps from the Loire valley. This change caused more delay and confusion. In fact, Moltke had not yet perceived the threat from Bourbaki.

That changed after 5 January. Bourbaki managed to push Werder out of Dijon without a battle and pursued him north-east to Vesoul, on the road to Belfort. Moltke responded by creating a new Army of the South under General von Manteuffel for the purpose of finding and destroying Bourbaki's Army of the East. This force included Werder's XIV Corps as well as VII and II Corps from Lorraine and Paris. Under Manteuffel, in contrast to the French, the Germans were given their general objectives and instructions and then told to figure it out for themselves.

Despite the momentum after Dijon, Bourbaki did not press forward. Rather than attack, he made the unlikely claim that he would manoeuvre Werder out of France and similarly relieve the siege of Belfort also via manoeuvre. Of course, Bourbaki's hesitancy ultimately was because his soldiers were disorganized and had few supplies. They were cold and scrounging for food. Meanwhile, the French general acted a bit like Bazaine at Metz, hopelessly and passively unable to grapple with the events unfolding around him. Between 10 and 13 January, he and his men moved a mere 5 miles along the Vesoul–Belfort road. Despite an encounter at Villersexel on the 9th, Bourbaki could not prevent Werder from digging in on the Lisaine river to stop the French advance.

They met at Héricourt on 15–17 January. The French outnumbered the Germans 110,000 to 40,000, but they were tired, hungry and poorly led. It was intensely cold on the night of the 15th and, unlike the Germans, the French had not cleared the forest roads of snow. Nevertheless, the French broke through near Héricourt on the 16th, but Bourbaki did not pursue the opportunity. Instead, he fell back to defend his section of the Belfort–Besançon railroad. When a younger officer begged him to move forward, Bourbaki replied, 'I'm twenty years too old. Generals should be your age.'[3]

Héricourt left six thousand more French dead or wounded for nothing. Anticipating the growing strength of Manteuffel's Army of the South – and perhaps seeking an excuse to withdraw – Bourbaki fell back to Besançon. It was too late. By 21 January, Manteuffel took Dôle and cut Bourbaki off from the rest of France. He no longer had access to roads or rail lines, only to rivers and a German army of 140,000. His supplies dwindled as the shoes of his men fell apart.

The only way out was toward Switzerland. Whereas MacMahon in a similar position had stood to fight at Sedan rather than fold and retreat into Belgium, Bourbaki recognized the hopelessness of his situation. On 24 January, in consultation with his corps commanders, he ordered a move into the Jura toward Pontarlier. Freycinet could not believe it: 'Haven't you made a mistake about the name?' he wired.

> Do you really mean Pontarlier? Pontarlier, near Switzerland? If that is really your objective, have you envisaged the consequences? What will you live on? You will certainly die of hunger. You will be forced to capitulate or to cross into Switzerland . . . at all costs you must break out. Otherwise you are lost.[4]

Freycinet was correct, but Bourbaki knew that his soldiers could fight no longer. Bourbaki wired back to Freycinet the same day: 'If this plan does not suit you I really would not know what to do; believe me, it is a martyrdom to exercise the command at this moment . . . If you think that one of my corps commanders could do better than I, do not hesitate to replace me . . . the task is beyond my strength.'[5] He tried to hold out for two more days as the Germans closed in. Growing increasingly despondent and exhausted at the destruction of his army and the disavowal of his leaders, on 26 January Bourbaki ordered his men toward Pontalier.

After delivering this order, Bourbaki retired to his room, where his associates had gathered. He pulled the curtains on his bed, lay down, and placed a revolver against his temple, held steady with his left hand. He pulled the trigger.

At the sound of the detonation, Bourbaki's associates ran to the bed and opened the curtains. They found him with his face bloodied and left hand burned, but alive and conscious. The bullet had flattened against his skull and run under his skin, but he suffered no skull fracture and no damage to his brain. He later wrote, 'Not having been fortunate enough to receive a bullet in the glorious circumstances of my little Lucien [his nephew, killed at the château of Ladonchamp near Metz], I wanted to be otherwise finished with life.'[6] Bourbaki nevertheless survived after a long recuperation.

Freycinet had already decided to replace Bourbaki with General Justin Clinchant, who now simply had to march to Pontarlier. There was not much army left to command.

Even at this late stage, the war touched the lives of villagers who came in its path. Pontmain in 1871 was a tiny, isolated hamlet some

200 miles west of Paris, too small to be considered its own commune. It had reached its peak over four centuries earlier, before the English burned it to the ground during the Hundred Years War. For years, the inhabitants had reportedly believed that 'When Paris burns, Pontmain will rise again.'[7] The prophecy seemed to come true in the spring of 1871.

On the evening of 17 January, the Prussian army was just a day's march from Pontmain, approaching the departmental capital, Laval. It appeared that Pontmain would soon be occupied or become a battlefield, and experience the requisitions, destruction, disease and death that the war had already brought to so many other villages. Thirty-eight men from Pontmain (about 8 per cent of the total population) already served in the army, including a young man named Auguste Barbedette.

Auguste's twelve-year-old brother Eugène was doing his chores outside when suddenly he saw a vision of a woman floating above the yard. Young, clad in blue and surrounded by stars, the woman smiled down on him. Another brother, ten-year-old José, soon joined Eugène in watching the woman in awe.

The brothers called for their parents and other villagers, including the nuns who taught the village children and the long-time local priest, Michel Guérin. None of the adults could see the woman, but a few other children said they did. They realized that it was the Virgin Mary, who then wrote out a message for them in the sky: 'But pray, my children; God will hear your prayers soon. My son may be touched.'[8] After about two and a half hours, during which the villagers prayed and sang, the vision disappeared.

Nineteenth-century Europe saw a revival of Marian sightings, most famously at Lourdes, typically with young children as the visionaries in the context of poverty or insecurity. Mary often warned of national or societal failings. The anthropologists Victor and Edith Turner explain that Mary appeared as 'compassionate, tender, a little capricious perhaps, vulnerable to suffering, infinitely maternal and understanding, and inclined rather to grieve at than to punish the sins of the world'.[9] Although nineteenth-century pilgrimages had been viewed as anti-modern and out of place in the industrialized, secularized era, historians in recent decades have reinterpreted than as a modern response to a changing world. Pilgrimages were not detached events hidden inside a bubble of reaction but integrated into and adapted to the modern world through its use of the media, transportation and medical knowledge.

In France, Marian shrines evolved from local sites of devotion into regional and national pilgrimage centres. The rise of evangelical devotion, the sacralization of the image of women, and the spread of railways and cheap publications fuelled this change. Lourdes (1858) became, and remains, the most famous French pilgrimage site, while smaller pilgrimages occurred at over one thousand sites.

The 'terrible year' of 1870–71, however, was particularly portentous for French Catholics, who experienced three disasters: the fall of France, the French army's abandonment of Rome to secular Italian forces, and the anti-clerical Paris Commune. Pilgrims to Pontmain began to visit almost immediately, starting with five hundred pilgrims from Landivy (Mayenne) on 26 January.

In Pontmain, Mary's words 'But pray, my children; God will hear your prayers soon. My son may be touched' were widely interpreted to hold two promises: first, the end of the war with Prussia, and second, the end to all war and trouble in France. The first responded to fear about the present, and the second expressed hope for the future.

Anxiety was certainly high in the month of January 1871. Accounts of the vision did not fail to place it in the context of the war and Auguste's service in the army. Some authors attributed the vision to a Mass held at the same time in Paris at Notre-Dame des Victoires. Both Eugène and José Barbedette reported that they had prayed intensely for the end of the war, especially since Auguste had gone to fight in September. 'I prayed,' said Eugène, 'to prevent my brother from getting badly hit, for peace, the departure of the Prussians, and the return of tranquillity.'[10] José later described the 'path of the cross' that they performed 'every day since the outbreak of hostilities, but with still more zeal since Auguste had left us.'[11]

The positive, calming effects of the vision had been immediate. An often-repeated vignette tells that a villager named Joseph Babin, who had been travelling, returned to Pontmain during the vision and reported the arrival of the Prussians in Laval. The villagers, in the midst of prayer, responded, 'even if they were entering the village, we would not be afraid,' and Babin joined in the prayers.[12] Sister Timothy, one of the teaching nuns, wrote that she felt better because of the vision, and Abbé Guérin reported that the mood of the hamlet improved.

Furthermore, the end of the war occurred almost immediately after the vision. The Prussians outside Laval halted their advance and withdrew from the area. The armistice was signed eleven days later. All thirty-eight soldiers from Pontmain who participated in the war returned unharmed, including Auguste Barbedette. The worldly explanation for the halt of the German invasion maintains that German headquarters wanted to end the war as soon as possible. But many authors agreed with Bishop Wicart's official judgement:

> The very day when these astonishing events occurred at Pontmain, the Prussian army pushed its advanced troops right up to the gates of Laval; and the next day, two kilometres from the city, the last cannon shots (at least, the last for our area) were heard of this terrible war that flooded the soil with blood and covered our unfortunate *patrie* with so many ruins. Three days later the enemy troops [. . .] began to fall back into the Maine-et-Loire and the Sarthe. Finally, the belligerent parties concluded an armistice and signed the preliminaries of peace on 28 January. [. . .] We cite these facts and these dates, without drawing any conclusions. But there is nobody who, when comparing them with the events of Pontmain, is not struck by the exact concordance of the words with [. . .] the decisive circumstances that immediately followed the event itself.[13]

An account of the second anniversary of the vision, in 1873, published in *La Semaine Religieuse de Laval*, linked the date of the vision, 17 January, with that of the retreat, 20 January: 'We have an obligation not to separate these two dates, which we will perpetually solemnize each year.'[14]

In Poitiers, a similar story unfolded, but with a slight twist. Poitiers, like Pontmain, was under threat of a Prussian invasion, and was believed to have been saved through holy intervention. In this case, it was St Radegund who interceded. While Mary held the promise of France's unique glory, Radegund symbolized reconciliation between the French and the Germans. Born a Thuringian princess in the sixth century, Radegund married Lothar of the Franks. Putting aside doubts about the direct continuity between Thuringians and Germans, and Franks and French, not to mention the fact that Radegund ran away from her husband to found a convent, Bishop Pie of Poitiers invoked the saint as a figure of peace. Believers prayed to St Radegund not for glory, conquest, or revenge, but for an honourable peace. St Radegund both made France stronger and brought together nations.

In this same week in January, the clashes between *francs-tireurs* and German occupiers reached a climax at the village of Fontenoy-sur-Moselle. The Chasseurs des Vosges had formed in mid-November and were recognized as a unit by the Ministry of the Interior on 14 November. It regrouped members of the Army of the East and of the Rhine, volunteers from Alsace and Lorraine, forest guides and members of the National Guard. They were led by Captain Jacques Bernard, formerly in service in North Africa, Italy and Mexico, and Lieutenant Henry Coumès, who had studied at Saint-Cyr and, as an officer of the 93rd Regiment of the Line, had been wounded at Saint-Privat.

The Chasseurs des Vosges and other detachments in the area formed a camp just north of Lamarche, a commune located about midway between Dijon and Nancy. A palisade surrounded the camp, and the forest road was defended by a blockhouse, embankments and trenches. On 20 December, the GND ordered the Chasseurs to undertake a mission against the rail lines, but nothing could be done until gunpowder was issued to them. On 15–17 January, gunpowder now in hand, military leaders in the Vosges met at the camp to determine a target. After much discussion, the group could not agree, and so they settled on two potential railroad targets about 50 miles to the north, near Toul: either the bridge over the Moselle near Fontenoy, or the tunnel at Foug. The leadership decided to send expeditionary columns north and decide which target to pursue once they could assess local conditions.

On 18 January at 5 p.m., the first columns left the camp and marched north, in smaller groups to avoid attracting attention. They included four companies of the Chasseurs des Vosges – about three hundred men under Bernard and Coumès – two small companies of *francs-tireurs* totalling forty men (one company colourfully called the *Partisans de la mort*, and the other more prosaically the *Francs-tireurs de la Meuse*), and eight hundred men of the 4th battalion of the *mobiles* of the National Guard in reserve. Each man carried three packets of cartridges, a bit of bread and biscuit, and a ration of lard. The transport brought with it 1,000 pounds of gunpowder.

After two days on the march, the *francs-tireurs* approached Toul. At an encampment west of Colombey-les-Belles, they finally had to decide on which target to pursue. Fontenoy was a modest village of five hundred inhabitants that had been occupied by a detachment of fifty Prussians since September. The Prussians held the rail station and kept watch over the tracks. Two sentinels stood on the bridge day and night, half a mile from the station, but Fontenoy seemed to have less surveillance than Foug. The Chasseurs des Vosges took the fateful decision to head east to Fontenoy.

At 2 a.m. on 21 January, the column left its encampment and headed north, keeping silent to avoid detection by the Germans stationed in and around Toul. After a long day with little rest, they arrived at 7 p.m. at the château of Pierre-la-Treiche for a brief halt.

They silently set off again at 1 a.m. on the 22nd. They crossed the Moselle with difficulty using two large boats signalled to them by a woodsman who worked in the château. Two boatmen helped, not hesitating to wade into the frigid water to push the boats through the fog. In groups of forty, they arrived on the other side, along with several of their horses.

At 5 a.m., the Chasseurs des Vosges silently passed through Fontenoy. A German-speaking non-commissioned officer, Josué Dreyfus (who had escaped from Phalsbourg), approached the sentinel outside the station and, being prevented from passing, struck him down with a sabre blow to the head. The men rushed in, engaged in hand-to-hand combat, and took the station and thirteen Prussians, seven of whom were wounded. They cut the telegraph lines and headed west toward the bridge. After wounding the two guards there, two men proceeded to lay the gunpowder sacks.

Just then, the men could hear a train arriving from Toul. They feared a derailment due to damaged tracks. With half a mile to spare, the train stopped and turned back, the driver having noticed that the train signals were wrong and that the station lamps had been lit. The men continued their work to lay the gunpowder. In their haste, one man dropped a lantern onto the gunpowder sacks, but a quick-moving captain managed to blow it out. At 7 a.m., the gunpowder in place, the fuses set, the men hurried away before three explosions blew a 100-foot gash in the bridge. The men were unharmed. They departed with their six non-wounded prisoners and, after two days on the march, returned to their camp with no losses for the entire expedition.

The Prussians reacted with fury. This attack aroused all the fears of partisan resistance that the Germans had been living with for the past four months. It came out of nowhere in a sector that had seemed quiet, and it caused real damage. No one was safe. Although the Chasseurs des Vosges came from miles away and had no contact with Fontenoy, the Prussians blamed the population for the sabotage. The 57th Infantry Regiment sacked the village and set it on fire. The conflagration lasted for four days. In the end, only the church and four of the village's fifty-five houses remained standing. The Prussians took twenty-three civilian hostages. All the inhabitants suffered in the weeks to come without shelter from the cold and snow. The Germans sent a photographer to capture the destruction, placing their soldiers in artful locations to make the effect all the more shocking. They even went so far, it was said, as to destroy one of the few standing buildings to create a more striking image of the disaster.

Furthermore, on 23 January the governor general of Lorraine, von Bonin, imposed a 10-million-franc fine on Lorraine. Although the fine was never raised, since the armistice occurred just a few days later, it revealed the depths of the Prussians' displeasure and issued a warning to others who considered acts of sabotage. Despite the fact that the *francs-tireurs* wore a basic uniform of military caps and brown shirts, the Germans refused to recognize them as an organized military unit distinct from civilian resistance. Instead, they assumed that civilians must have been involved in the actions of partisans or did not care to make a distinction between the two.

To rebuild the bridge, the Prussians requisitioned five hundred men in nearby Nancy. None of them showed up to work. The occupiers then resorted to more punitive tactics. They shut down factories and workshops and prohibited paying the unemployed workers. After a concert on Place Stanislas, they blocked the exits from the massive square and, having allowed women and children to leave, requisitioned 250 men of all ages and professions to spend seventeen days working to clear the debris from Fontenoy.

The destruction of the bridge, however, did little to change the course of the war. The Germans already had access to supplies via a northern rail line through Mézières. If this attack had occurred three months earlier, it might have caused serious problems for the German supply chain, perhaps a total collapse for some time. But by late January, it came too late. The battle of Buzenval on 19 January had sealed the fate of Paris.

★

Gambetta felt increasingly embattled but continued to insist that the opposition to him and his policies was rooted in ill-placed politics rather than war-weariness. In early January, he wrote to Jules Favre:

> At bottom France is growing more and more attached to the Republican regime. The mass of the people, even in the countryside, understand, under the pressure of unfolding events, that it is the Republicans . . . who are the true patriots, the true defenders of the nation and of the rights of man and of the citizen . . . We shall prolong the struggle to the point of extermination [*jusqu'à l'extermination*], we shall ensure that there cannot be found in France a man or an Assembly to adhere to the victory of force.[15]

For Gambetta, surrender would betray the honour of France and threaten the longed-for establishment of a lasting republic. In his eyes the conflict pitted the forces of Bonapartism against the republicanism of the people. Negative press, allowed because of 'extreme liberty' under the GND, could only be understood as the lingering nefarious influence of Bonapartism. Evoking the 1789 Declaration of the Rights of Man and of the Citizen and the struggle for liberty, Gambetta equated true patriotism with the continuation of the conflict. He called for an attack from Mont Valérien against the defences at the Gennevilliers peninsula and thence to Versailles – on the Germans' strongest point.

Trochu and Ducrot recognized the futility of this plan immediately. Trochu did not want to pursue a doomed sortie except as a last resort. The Council of Ministers furthermore ordered this operation to start on the night of 18–19 January, two days earlier than Trochu believed was possible. No matter. The attack was an attempt to convince the clubs and radicals in Paris that the French position was hopeless and that it was time to prepare to surrender. On 15 January the ministers discussed surrender seriously. Favre had started sharing information with the mayors of the twenty *arrondissements* so that they too would be implicated in the GND's decisions.

At dawn on 19 January, 90,000 men, including 42,000 National Guardsmen, advanced from Mont Valérien. It was the *sortie en masse* that the clubs had long demanded and the first time in its history that the National Guard had fought a foreign enemy. They met the Germans on a 4-mile front extending south-west from Bougival to Saint-Cloud, at the base of a peninsula formed by the Seine, cutting through the village of Buzenval. If the French had broken through, they could have headed toward Versailles and ruined the celebrations of the nascent German Empire.

The French plan called for three simultaneous attacks at 6 a.m., but it proved difficult to get all 90,000 men in position. While the French recognized that it would take all night to move them over just two bridges, they did not account for the fact that the approaches to these bridges had been barricaded, allowing only a narrow passage, and were blocked by private vehicles used as mobile hospitals. Recent heavy rain slowed their progress even further. At six o'clock none of the columns was ready, and Trochu himself was not yet in place to give the signal. By seven, two columns were in position, one of them too close to German guns as the sky began to lighten. The fortress commandant therefore gave the signal to attack.

The men moved with *élan* at first, but their advance was checked at every turn, the National Guard lost its discipline, and they had no reserves. Trochu arrived at Mont Valérien and showed courage as he watched his soldiers defend themselves well against counter-attacks. Nevertheless, by the evening, he had to call the order to retreat. They were able to do so skilfully, without the Germans becoming aware of it, though their rear was full of confusion with supply wagons, ambulances and guns blocking their way. The long winter night under a bright moon allowed them to clear the battlefield by 6 a.m. the next day. The French had suffered 4,000 casualties and the Germans, 700. In Versailles, just two days after the declaration of the German Empire, the Hall of Mirrors was transformed into a hospital for wounded soldiers.

*

After the battle of Buzenval, officials in Paris's Hôtel de Ville adopted a new practice. They photographed unidentified corpses before they were buried, to assist family and friends in locating the remains of their loved ones. On 20 January, 250 bodies arrived at the morgue. The officials took an inventory of their belongings before delivering them to Père Lachaise cemetery. Prior to their interment, a police official named Gustave Macé had them photographed, individually or in groups. This practice was later adopted during the Paris Commune by the Bureau of Information, resulting in one of the most famous and terrible images of the period: twelve Communards in a double line of coffins.

Juliette Adam despaired at 'Yet another enterprise solemnly prepared, maladroitly conducted, miserably terminated.' With the same phrase, she noted, 'we could write the military history of the siege.'[16] Everyone felt the strain of a possible surrender. 'We all have a fever,' wrote Adam. 'We are making [an] extravagant project of deliverance. My nephew tells me that the idea of capitulation makes him crazy, that he has lost the ability to sleep, that at Fort Rosny the sailors and the artillerymen of the National guard, himself included, swear that they will never surrender.'[17] The ideals of 4 September now crumbled.

The battle of Buzenval ended the notion that an enthusiastic People's Army could defeat a modern military. Nevertheless, Favre and Gambetta remained frustrated. Their plans to distract Moltke in the provinces appeared to be working. If the Prussians had sent 200,000 from Paris west to encounter Chanzy, and 100,000 east to deal with Bourbaki, why not keep going from Paris? The answer came in a telegram with the news of Chanzy's defeat at Le Mans and 10,000 new prisoners. Nobody was left to relieve Paris. Favre himself now recognized the need to surrender.

Favre and Trochu therefore met with the mayors of Paris on 20 January. The mayors still could not accept capitulation after so much sacrifice. They called for another *sortie torrentielle* and Trochu's resignation. Trochu would not resign; he wanted the government to ask for his dismissal. Instead, the government got rid of the position of governor of Paris, convinced Trochu to stay on as President of the Council, and, after Ducrot refused it, gave command of the armies to Vinoy, the Paris garrison commander.

The GND now faced one final obstacle to concluding a peace: the potential uprising of the people of Paris. Vinoy was tasked with quelling any action in the streets, to be the General Cavaignac of 1870. He was happy to do this. The moment came on 22 January. Unlike on 31 October, revolutionary leaders including Blanqui were present from the beginning of the unrest; some of them had been liberated from prison by the crowd the previous evening. On the morning of the 22nd, members of revolutionary battalions of the National Guard crowded at the Hôtel de Ville, which was defended by *mobiles* from Brittany. Shots broke out between these two armed groups in the early afternoon – it is unclear who shot first. It was the bloodiest confrontation in Paris since the start of the war, leaving five dead and eighteen wounded, including a number of bystanders. It was the first time that Parisians had fired on Parisians during the siege. By the following evening, the authorities had arrested revolutionaries, shut down clubs and suppressed newspapers, including *Le Réveil* and *Le Combat*, and the city regained calm.

Meanwhile, the government was meeting in session in the Hôtel de Ville and learned that the flour supply would last for only two more days. Favre prepared for the painful task of asking the Germans for surrender.

The renewed possibility of negotiations sharpened internal power struggles for both sides. On the German side, Bismarck and Moltke continued to jockey for position, including control over the peace negotiations to come. The crown prince attempted to reconcile Bismarck and Moltke but failed. On 14 January, Moltke wrote a memo to the king regarding his ideas for post-bombardment operations as well as his expectation to lead negotiations for the surrender of Paris. Bismarck learned of this memo and wrote one of his own the same day, and another on 19 January, making clear his belief that Moltke had overstepped his authority into politics and diplomacy, insisting that Wilhelm clarify that he, Bismarck, should be made a party to any negotiations between Paris and Versailles.

The newly declared emperor, despite his military leanings, sided with Bismarck. In the following days, as Favre showed his desire to enter into talks, Wilhelm made it clear to Moltke that Moltke could not enter any discussion with the French without first assuring, via Wilhelm, Bismarck's involvement, or at least that Bismarck should be informed of the conversation. He also forbade any additional military operations without first consulting Bismarck and allowing the chancellor the opportunity to make his own views known. This decision paved the way, on the German side, for the negotiations that began on 23 January.

On the French side, Favre acted without the knowledge and approval of the government delegation in Bordeaux. In fact, Gambetta planned to continue the war after the fall of Paris. On 22 January, Gambetta wrote to Favre, 'whatever may be the effect of stupor and sadness that follows the fall of this heroic capital, I believe we will be able to respond that, resting on public sentiment and with certain decisions regarding political measures that will be necessary, we will be able to get through this formidable eventuality.'[18]

Favre was more ready to face the facts. He sent the comte d'Hérisson to seek a meeting and arrange a brief ceasefire. D'Hérisson returned to Paris and collected Favre late in the day on the 23rd. They crossed the Seine in a leaky boat on a moonless night, the red firelight from the palace of Saint-Cloud gleaming on the water's surface. Favre and Bismarck met in the house where the latter was staying. Favre had little guidance from Paris other than to find out what terms might be available. That evening, Bismarck did not reveal to others the nature of his conversation with Favre, but as he left the room, he whistled a hunting call that signalled the end of the chase.

Favre and Bismarck met again on the 24th and 25th. Both men sought a quick end to the conflict. Bismarck had previously kept open lines of communication with a representative of Empress

Eugénie as a possible path to securing an armistice, but at this point he made clear he would pursue peace with Favre and the GND. Favre did not deny that the city was starving and that an uprising had resulted in the dismissal of Trochu as governor. 'Favre could not hide a feeling of something like horror at the thought of a return to Paris,' reported the crown prince, 'and appears to have developed a perfectly wolfish hunger at the supper provided by Count Bismarck.'[19] French troops at outposts who heard why Favre was driving to Versailles reportedly broke into dancing the cancan on the bridge of Sèvres.

With the authorization of the cabinet in Paris, Favre tried his best to secure an honourable armistice. Bismarck held all the cards. After three days of negotiations, Favre and Bismarck signed a three-week armistice early on 26 January, to take effect on the 28th. France would pay an immediate indemnity of 200 million francs. The forts and walls of Paris would be handed over to the Germans, including 2,000 cannon and 177,000 rifles. The Germans would help to re-supply the city. Officers could keep their swords, and no Germans would set foot in Paris at this point. In addition, Bismarck agreed not to disarm the National Guard, convinced by Favre's argument that it would be impossible to do so without sparking a civil war.

As a cornerstone of the negotiations, Favre agreed that France would hold elections by 19 February and convene a National Assembly in Bordeaux – far from Paris – that would either ratify or reject the armistice. If they rejected it and hostilities continued, Prussia would be all the stronger. In a typically Paris-centric position, the armistice was linked to the fall of Paris. While the capital was spared a lengthy occupation, the occupying forces in the provinces stayed in their positions, with a 6-mile demarcation line separating them from the French forces.

The armistice and the capitulation of Paris were signed only by Bismarck and Favre, which underscored that these were political documents, not military ones. The requisite military convention was signed on 28 January by Moltke, Bismarck and Theophil von Podbielski (the quartermaster general) and by Favre, General

Valdan (called to perform this unwelcome task following Trochu's resignation) and a staff officer.

On the evening of the 28th, Dietrich von Lassberg and his Bavarian comrades stayed up to await midnight. They could see from afar the firing of each cannon. They sat, tense, waiting for the clock hands to reach twelve o'clock. The guns fell instantly silent. No spark or sound reached across the darkness. Then, from numerous batteries, Lassberg heard the sound of the soldiers' jubilation. With joy and thanks, they cried, 'God be praised, the war is over!'[20]

One final, sputtering corner of combat remained. Moltke, with Bismarck's support, had insisted on keeping eastern France out of the armistice, since there was still an active resistance. Favre did not agree, but he was not in a position to negotiate. For reasons that are unclear, when Favre telegraphed Gambetta to inform him of the armistice, he failed to tell the GND in Bordeaux that military operations would continue in the departments of the Jura, the Côte d'Or and the Doubs. On the night of 29 January, Clinchant – who had taken over the Army of the East from Bourbaki – learned of the armistice signed at Versailles, but he was not informed that the eastern departments had been excluded from the ceasefire. Manteuffel, however, learned about the exception, and on 30 January he continued his manoeuvres to prevent a French escape. Clinchant refused to surrender his men as prisoners. After officially learning on 31 January that the armistice had not applied to the east, Clinchant concluded a convention with the Swiss to allow some 80,000 men to escape across the border at Les Verrières on 1 February while a handful of reservists fought off a German advance at La Cluse, 4 miles beyond Pontarlier. The French left all their arms in a pile at the side of the road. The war was over.

19. *From Armistice to Peace*

Preparations for the national elections unfolded in haste and confusion. With just a week and a half between the armistice and the elections due on 8 February, hastily assembled committees determined their lists of candidates, sometimes without consulting the men in question and certainly without allowing them the chance to formulate and communicate their views. In occupied areas, the Germans did not allow postal communications, so German soldiers put up information about the elections on walls and public boards. There was no clarity over who was leading the country at this point, and no political organization.

As late as 31 January, some areas had not yet received news of the armistice. In many others, the armistice felt temporary with the threat that hostilities could recommence. George Sand had no patience for those who cursed Favre for having signed the armistice:

> Unhappy agitators! May the disaster, shame, and despair of the country muffle you, if you have a conscience! . . . As for me, it is beyond my strength to contemplate it any longer, and I swear that in this moment I am irritated against those who reproach our government for having given way before the horror of your suffering.[1]

It was a period of high uncertainty all around. It was difficult to keep order in Paris, where Parisians went into the neutral zone to seek food and some menaced German shopkeepers in the city, even if they had lived there for decades.

Within the French military, General Chanzy was ready to keep fighting once the armistice expired. He made plans to move his army to the south bank of the Loire, and from there force the Germans into a long stand-off that he imagined would exhaust them into better peace terms. This project was not likely to succeed and, indeed, would only have angered the Germans more. For their part, Moltke and his generals prepared to destroy the French forces if fighting resumed. These preparations have often been interpreted as Moltke's preference to continue the fight to fully ruin the French military. However, it may be that he was simply pessimistic about the French ability to accept the armistice – that once Paris fell, he might need to put it under martial law, crush provincial resistance and demand a heavy war indemnity. The historian Dennis Showalter raises the possibility that, even though he never said it, Moltke may have been relieved that Favre requested a ceasefire. After all, Moltke understood that an army can never fully destroy an enemy in practice and that France could inflict serious damage even in defeat.

Moltke and Bismarck both had reason to worry that the armistice might prove to be temporary. Gambetta, who had not taken part in concluding the armistice, interpreted it as a temporary measure that should allow for the election of politicians who would continue the fight. He made plans to raise another new army and worked to redefine the election so that a majority would favour the continuation of the war. On 31 January, Gambetta and three members of the Government Delegation in Bordeaux issued decrees that prohibited anyone with any official connection to the Second Empire from standing for election. Jules Simon, who had already been dispatched from Paris to assure Gambetta's co-operation, arrived soon after and demanded the nullification of these decrees. Simon could have used his plenary powers to overrule Gambetta, but as a subtle politician he instead notified Paris and called for additional members of the Government to come from the capital to out-vote Gambetta and his supporters.

Bismarck was furious. Gambetta's insistence on this limited election threatened to undo the negotiations ending the war. Under pressure from Bismarck, and eager to secure an end to the conflict, Favre and leaders in Paris met and a majority now agreed to defy Gambetta's decrees. In a public announcement, they declared them annulled and called for his resignation and, as Simon had requested,

RUE DE
DEMENAGEMENTS
POUR TOUS PAYS

N

sent three members of the Paris Cabinet to Bordeaux. Gambetta still dug in, demanding 'an Assembly that is truly national and republican, desiring peace, if peace assures our honor, but capable also of waging war, ready for anything rather than lend a hand in the murder of France'.[2] But even within Bordeaux, Gambetta had lost his standing. The local press and the city elites had become distanced from him, worked on by Thiers and tired of the war. Outnumbered, he finally resigned on the morning of 6 February.

The elections of 8 February took place under strained and confused circumstances. The results did not reveal a clear picture of French ideological preferences, because the election was clearly tied to the end of the war. Voters were asked, in essence, whether or not to resume hostilities. They overwhelmingly voted for peace in the form of local conservative leaders. Peasants are often accused of reverting to a vote for their local notable, as uncritical electors, but they were also voting in concert with a rational reading of the situation. The return of the gentry and the aristocracy to political power signified a return to peace, not necessarily support for conservatives. Still, it cannot be denied that republicans were not popular in 1871, especially outside the major cities. Gambetta's bravado and Parisian radicalism had failed to instil broad trust in leadership emerging from the people.

The Bonapartists, with their leader still imprisoned in the German Empire, proved to be even less popular. Out of 676 deputies elected, 400 were monarchists and 200 were republicans. Only about thirty were Bonapartists. In terms of specific leaders, the electorate's preferences were clear. Thiers, who had opposed the war to begin with and had tried to make peace in the autumn, was elected in twenty-six departments, and Gambetta in nine (French deputies could be elected in multiple departments but serve only in one). Freycinet was not elected, not even in his adopted department of the Tarn-et-Garonne. He stayed in Bordeaux, disappointed and exhausted. Trochu declined to run for election to the National Assembly and retired to Brittany.

*

The French Provisional Government assembled at the Grand Théâtre in Bordeaux on 12 February. On the following day, Favre submitted the resignation of the members of the Government of National Defence. On 17 February, a great debate opened when Émile Keller, a representative from the Haut-Rhin in Alsace, speaking on behalf of some members of the republican Left, demanded that the assembly refuse to agree to give up Alsace and Lorraine unless a plebiscite supported the annexation. Thiers stood firmly in opposition to this idea: 'Either war or peace. This is serious. There's no room for childishness when it's a matter either of the fate of two very important provinces or the fate of the country as a whole.'[3] The Assembly appointed a committee to study Keller's proposal, which determined that they expressed sympathy with it but did not endorse it. The Assembly agreed to place its trust in the negotiators and, furthermore, made Thiers head of the government with the title *chef du pouvoir exécutif*. On 19 February, Thiers and his new foreign minister, Jules Favre, left Bordeaux and arrived at Versailles two days later.

With only a few days left before the armistice expired, even with a short extension from 24 February to the 26th, the two sides were only able to determine the Preliminaries of Peace. Thiers hoped to negotiate the same terms he had negotiated in October and November, but the situation had changed. In France, those who demanded war to the last extremity were silenced after the elections of 8 February. In the German Empire, however, voices still clamoured for harsh terms for the French. The peace treaty reflected this continued push for exacting measures, largely supported by Moltke.

The most important question involved the fate of Alsace and northern Lorraine, including Metz. This had been brewing since the capture of Strasbourg in September, and the issue of Lorraine grew more pressing after the fall of Metz at the end of October. Not everyone in the German states agreed on the annexation of Alsace and Lorraine. Industrialists raised concerns about competition with a region so tightly integrated with France, particularly the Alsatian textile industry. Social Democrats and others on the Left opposed the annexation on both practical and moral grounds.

Still, German support for annexation grew louder, at least in many political circles and in Bismarck's well-controlled press. As the conflict wore on, the press more and more (with Bismarck's encouragement) presented annexation as righting a historic wrong. In the south German states, annexation justified their participation in the conflict. For Bismarck, the public call for annexation also provided him with one more argument against intervention from third parties, especially from Britain as its public opinion shifted against Germany. Bismarck made clear that the nationalist call for annexation meant that Germans would fight for just, defensible borders. Britain did not have the interest or the military power to oppose them.

The fortress city of Metz, however, remained a source of disagreement within the German camp. Bismarck questioned the wisdom of keeping Metz, with a largely French-speaking population. He anticipated that it would be hard to incorporate the city into the German Empire. Instead, Bismarck would have been happy to take Luxembourg, or a greater war indemnity, or an overseas possession such as Saigon.

But the emperor and Moltke both insisted on Metz, a hard-won prize that for the soldiers would be a humiliation to hand back to France. Furthermore, incorporating Metz into the western border of the German Empire would help guard against a future conflict with France and would make certain the French understood that they had been defeated. Thiers and Favre could do little to prevent the inclusion of Metz in the annexation.

Thiers succeeded, however, in saving Belfort. Still holding out after the ceasefire, the city had ended the fight on the orders of the French War Ministry on 15 February. Thiers threatened to resign over the annexation of Belfort, which would have left Bismarck to risk uncertainty in French leadership. Thiers won. Moltke did not oppose this decision. After all, given its particular location, Belfort would not be the opening gambit in a future war with France and so it was less risky to leave in the hands of the French.

Thiers also negotiated the initial amount of the war indemnity down from 6 billion to 5 billion francs and set limited terms for the German triumphal march into Paris. French troops, except for 40,000 remaining in Paris, were to withdraw south of the Loire. The National Assembly ratified the treaty on 1 March by a vote of 546 to 107. Gambetta resigned his seat in the National Assembly and decamped for Spain. Émile Küss, the mayor of Strasbourg and a member of the Assembly, died from the stress on that same day.

On the day that the Assembly considered the Preliminaries of Peace, 30,000 German soldiers marched into Paris via the racecourse at Longchamp and the avenue de Neuilly, toward the Arc de Triomphe. The streets were empty and the canals frozen. By agreement, the Germans limited their triumphant march to the north-east neighbourhoods between the Seine, the avenue de Ternes and the rue du Faubourg Saint-Honoré, far from the revolutionary neighbourhoods of the east. Prussian soldiers had permission to visit the Louvre, a low point for the staff who had worked hard to protect the collection from bombardment.

Though shops remained closed, and posters reminded Parisians to avoid making trouble with the Germans, many came out into the streets anyway, making jokes, some jeering and throwing stones, and others preventing any friendly exchanges with the enemy, who wore a leaf or a sprig of greenery in their caps. The crown prince reported, 'A crowd of such onlookers fell upon an individual who accepted a cigar from one of our officers, elsewhere the proprietor of a café was threatened for giving a drink to one of our men, and more instance of the same sort.'[4]

The Germans had planned to rotate groups of 30,000 men into Paris each day, to allow more soldiers the opportunity to see the city that they had encircled for so many months. Bordeaux disrupted this plan. The Assembly signed the Preliminaries of Peace more quickly than anticipated, and the Germans had agreed to vacate the capital once they were ratified. The Assembly's swift work brought the plans for a three-day triumph to a quick conclusion. Dietrich von Lassberg – whose Bavarian regiment had been slated to enter Paris on 2 March – was deeply disappointed and angry. From his perspective, he had fought hard and suffered much during the previous six months and deserved this moment of celebration.

The state of peace came into effect on 3 March. At this point, the German troops were no longer supposed to demand requisitions, whether in cash or in kind. Still, some Germans took supplies anyway and tried to continue to collect taxes already claimed on mayors, until a convention on the 16th relieved mayors of payment for any arrears, taxes, or demands. The foot-dragging had paid off, as the head of the municipal commission of Vic-sur-Aisne noted in a letter: 'We must congratulate ourselves . . . on having shown a mediocre eagerness to pay.'[5] In April 1871, requisitions finally came to an end as the French government assumed the responsibility of paying for the occupying German soldiers.

With the preliminaries signed, the Germans made plans to return home. The crown prince left Versailles on 7 March and expected to never set foot in France again. He returned to a series of celebrations, banquets and parades as he made his way across Germany and rejoined his beloved family at Potsdam.

The new French government under Thiers soon faced two serious revolts. In Algeria, the Mokrani Revolt that began on 16 March posed the most severe challenge to French colonial claims since the conquest of the country in 1830. Some 150,000 of the Kabyle people rose in a widespread revolt to reclaim self-rule that included some 250 tribes, about a third of the population. The French army crushed the revolt and allocated confiscated land to Alsatian and Lorrainer settlers seeking a new life away from the German Empire.

In Paris, less than three weeks after the Germans left the capital, the city erupted in the event known as the Paris Commune. The series of revolutionary days that punctuated the course of the war – 4 September, 31 October and 22 January – built on decades of frustration against a centralized state. Favre may have surrendered Paris, but Parisians did not surrender. Angered at the capitulation, dismayed by the terms of the Preliminaries of Peace and the German triumphal march, Parisians continued to be suspicious of the government in Bordeaux and its motivations. Particularly in the neighbourhoods that had been active in club life in opposition to the Government of National Defence, the siege mentality and the reality of armed members of the National Guard continued into March. The National Assembly lifted the moratorium on rents, debts and pawned materials, leaving many threatened with eviction and the loss of their few possessions. The Government limited pay for National Guardsmen to only those who could demonstrate need, and it voted to move the capital to Versailles instead of Paris.

Then on 18 March, in yet another symbolic blow against Parisian independence, Thiers sent troops to remove the cannon that the National Guard had placed on the hills of Paris in February. Some soldiers fraternized with Parisians as they awaited horses to help them complete the task. At the end of the day, as tensions mounted, two French generals were killed. Parisians soon declared a new government, independent of the National Assembly and Thiers, led by an elected municipal council seated at the Hôtel de Ville. They sought to negotiate local rule with Thiers, not fully appreciating that their declaration would lead to civil war. Thiers built up his army and prepared to take back the city by force.

The Germans allowed the French to have 80,000 soldiers north of the Loire (instead of the 40,000 originally agreed) and left Versailles a week earlier than originally planned to allow the French Government and Assembly to move there from Bordeaux.

On 21 May, the Versailles army entered Paris and began a period of street fighting known as the 'Bloody Week' that left thousands dead, many summarily executed with little evidence that they were actively engaged in rebellion. Some Communards set fires, which destroyed the Tuileries Palace and the Hôtel de Ville, and others executed prisoners, including the archbishop of Paris. Many thousands more were taken prisoner. German soldiers watched the progress of the Versailles troops by noting when the tricolour flag waved on the Arc de Triomphe, whereas the red flag of the

Commune continued to wave on the Panthéon. Fifty-nine German inhabitants of Paris are recorded as having fought on the barricades. On 28 May, the resistance came to an end.

The Commune reflected social conflicts that pre-dated the war and which the siege and club movement had exacerbated. Contrary to perception at the time, the Communards did not simply react in anger to the disappointment of the capitulation after so many months of sacrifice. Furthermore, *pace* Marx, the Commune's primary social conflict did not rest on class distinctions between the industrial, liberal bourgeoisie and the proletariat. Instead, the Commune's basic social units were rooted in Parisian neighbourhood groups that had come to view the state as the enemy – first the centralized Second Empire, and, later, the Government of National Defence.

The Commune also obliged the Germans to linger in France until order had been restored, which the soldiers and Bismarck resented. Bismarck felt that the trust he had placed in Thiers and Favre to make the French support the peace had been misplaced (and maybe this helps to explain a widely held assumption that the Commune was primarily a protest against the end of the war). Now Bismarck was the hardliner, while Moltke and the General Staff moderated their demands, so long as they could return the soldiers home.

In this context, the negotiations for the final peace treaty in Brussels broke off between Favre and Bismarck's representative, General von Fabrice, and had to be resumed with Bismarck in person on 6 May in Frankfurt-am-Main. Bismarck now insisted on maintaining 50,000 soldiers in six departments of France until the final payment of the war indemnity could be made. The parties agreed to an aggressive payment schedule of 500 million francs due a month after the establishment of governmental authority in Paris, 500 million due in May 1872, and 3 billion francs due on 2 March 1874, with 5 per cent annual interest.

Given the high war indemnity, Bismarck did not press hard for compensation for individual Germans who had been expelled from France. Instead, he focused on the negotiations over the inhabitants of the conquered territories in Alsace and parts of Lorraine. In a striking move, the Germans allowed the inhabitants of Alsace-Lorraine to retain French nationality, so long as they made a formal declaration and moved their residence to France by 1 October 1872. Rather than simply transferring the population into the hands of the victors – as happened commonly up until the nineteenth century – or undertaking a policy of ethnic cleansing, as occurred with brutal regularity in the twentieth century, individual families (led by the male head of household) could determine their nationality. Article 2 of the treaty fixed in place the notion that national borders ought to coincide with historic or emotional attachment to a nation. This article assumed that, for many, attachment to the nation would trump attachment to the region. Yet it allowed for individual families to make this determination for themselves, rather than imposing it by forcibly uprooting peoples deemed dangerous to the new order or holding a vote in which the majority would determine the choice for all. In a stunning concession to peaceful integration (in their own interests of empire-building), Germany allowed Alsatians and Lorrainers to decline integration into the new Empire. In this singular case, nationality was determined by both place of origin and choice.

Implementation entailed the creation of a new bureaucracy to verify citizenship and adjudicate particular situations. Questions arose immediately: did a family from annexed Colmar but who had earlier moved to Rennes need to make a declaration? Would a person born in French Nancy but living in annexed Metz automatically become German? Could a French woman who had married a German declare herself French? A Convention issued in December 1871 clarified that anyone born in Alsace or annexed Lorraine, and no others, would automatically assume German citizenship unless they made a declaration and moved to France. Out of bureaucratic necessity, place of birth became the starting point for this process. Following the patriarchal French legal code, married women and children depended on their husbands and fathers to determine their nationalities. Altogether, about 130,000 individuals, about 8.5 per cent of the population of Alsace and annexed Lorraine, chose to emigrate to France between the summer of 1870 and the deadline of October 1872. France lost 1.6 million inhabitants as part of the annexation, many of whom were young men who then served in the German army.

Finally, the Treaty of Frankfurt expanded the French circle around Belfort in exchange for some territory between Luxembourg and Metz. The Treaty of Frankfurt was not as harsh as the Treaty of Tilsit that the French imposed on Prussia in 1807. The Prussians did not attempt to interfere in France's politics, did not limit the size of the French army or destroy the French navy, and did not dismantle France's overseas possessions. France remained a Great Power. Favre and Bismarck signed the Treaty of Frankfurt on 10 May and exchanged the ratifications of their respective governments on the 21st.

In the months that followed, the National Assembly convened a Commission of Invaded Departments to assess the cost of requisitions, pillaging and damages caused by the war. In total, the commission estimated damages to civilians at 690 million francs. After lengthy debate – including protests from areas that had not been invaded and did not want to pay for it – a law passed on 6 September 1871 provided 100 million francs to the war-damaged departments and 6 million to Paris, and a second law, in April 1873, allocated 120 million francs to the departments and 140 million to Paris. The department of the Seine received nearly the entire amount of their claims, whitewashing the facts of the siege and Paris Commune to create the Belle Époque. The rest of the country's departments were allocated only a quarter of their requests.

Dietrich von Lassberg's march home began on 6 June. Unlike the voyage west, when the rail system whisked him toward the border, he undertook the trip home entirely on foot. He glimpsed the Rhine and the Black Forest on 2 July. Although he had technically passed into German territory much earlier, this moment felt to him like a true homecoming. He marched into Munich on 16 July, in a triumphal parade, the day before the anniversary of his mobilization. Finally, late that afternoon, he returned to his mother's house in a bitter-sweet homecoming. He had been part of a victory against France, but Bavaria was no longer an independent country. At Bazeilles, he had come to see the humanity of his enemies, yet he had participated in one of the most violent attacks on civilians of the entire conflict. Two brothers had left; only one returned.

20. *Settling Accounts*

In the months and years after the signing of the Treaty of Frankfurt, those whose lives had been shaped and destroyed by the Franco-Prussian War engaged in a deep settling of accounts. Both France and Germany re-founded themselves in the wake of the war. Despite national elections, France's political future remained uncertain. Bavarian soldiers came to terms with their new status as subjects in the unified German Empire. All sides mourned their dead in public and solemn ceremonies.

The occupation of French territory continued until the French fully repaid the 5-billion-franc war indemnity. During that time, contact between German soldiers and French civilians became infrequent and remained largely peaceful. German soldiers built barracks and lived separately from the French population, limiting their daily contact and potential for conflict. French authorities had oversight of elections, the press and the gendarmerie. Both sides punished their own people for rare violent encounters, to keep the peace and enforce the rule of law.

Thanks to French loan offerings in June 1871 and July 1872, the French government was able to raise funds rapidly, both domestically and internationally. The July 1871 loan raised 3.498 billion francs, the largest loan transaction of the nineteenth century. With this success, France negotiated an earlier end to the occupation. In Nancy, now a French frontier city on the border with the expanded German Empire, 4,000 inhabitants watched in silence on 1 August 1873 as the Germans departed. Only when the French flag flew over the balcony of City Hall did the citizens of Nancy allow themselves to cheer. Four days later, French soldiers arrived. The final German soldiers marched out of France on 16 September 1873. In gratitude, the citizens of Nancy built a statue of Thiers in 1879.

Meanwhile, French prisoners of war made their way back home. Over the course of the war, 373,000 French prisoners had been sent to the German states. The exchange of prisoners began after the signing of the Preliminaries of Peace on 26 February. The process for those held in Germany was accelerated so that they could be used to crush the Commune in Paris. While the final wounded soldiers were sent home by August 1871, some soldiers had been held back for bad behaviour or for trying to escape. As late as February 1872, around 200 remained on German soil. The Red Cross nurse Coralie Cahen made three trips to Germany in 1872 to visit, nurse and account for French prisoners of war held in sixty-six different fortresses. During these trips, Cahen became the link between the prisoners and their families in France, whom she visited and wrote to, so they would know if their sons and husbands were alive. In Berlin, Cahen was given access to the files of 59,000 prisoners, the details of which she reported to Paris.

Unlike the homecoming accorded to soldiers returning in victory from Italy and Crimea under Napoleon III, the prisoners of war coming from Germany symbolized disorder and disgrace. As the prisoners returned home, they were a living reminder of the defeat. One inhabitant of Lunéville in north-east France reflected in 1873:

> One of the most distressing spectacles imposed on our hospitable city was the return of our unhappy prisoners that peace had returned to their homes. Sad debris of the misfortune of our army, the glorious defeated, many of whom came to expire before our eyes, these soldiers died leaving their imprint on our soil![1]

In its final report, the Strasbourg Aid Committee concluded, 'May an era of justice finally open up for the world, and may future times no longer see the return of these acts, whose bloody trace we would like to see erased from the book of humanity!'[2] Instead of a new era of peace, however, Europe headed toward a period of warfare more terrible than ever before.

For many after the war, the question of primary importance was, how did Germany win so decisively? Moltke succeeded not because of brilliant leadership on the battlefield – whether his or that of his subordinates. The German armies did little in terms of manoeuvre, and their tactics often led to bloodbaths. Their strategic directions were solid, but not surprising. The Germans had better cannon, but the French had better rifles. Instead, the Germans won because they were better organized, had a better military education and had more manpower, especially in the early stages of the war. The Germans had a plan for invading France, whereas Napoleon III had no concrete proposals for how he might successfully engage the Prussian army. The French army of the Second Empire fought well but had strikingly weary and incompetent commanders, all reporting to an exhausted and enervated Napoleon III. The republican army had some better commanders, but the new troops themselves were swept aside by experienced German soldiers, who now had the inestimable advantage of recent successful combat. Militaries across the Continent learned the lesson that they should raise a well-trained nation-at-arms, capable of being swiftly mobilized and concentrated on enemy borders.

In the years that followed, armies across Europe emulated the Prussians' example. They expanded conscription, developed their General Staffs, professionalized military education, and engaged in war games. They focused on logistics, including the use of railroads, telegraphs and medical staff. Mobilization and concentration plans became rapid and large scale. Armies across Europe built fortress complexes on the model of Metz. The French Séré de Rivières system, constructed between 1874 and 1910, included 166 forts and cost 6 billion francs. As each national army sought the upper hand, the potential for destruction of human life in a deadlocked war expanded accordingly.

The expansion of military service to include most, if not all, young men shaped armies and the social fabric for decades to come. Over time, France adopted near-universal conscription in order to remake its army and instil a sense of duty and self-sacrifice in its male citizens. The French eliminated the practice of allowing conscripted men to buy their way out of service in 1873, and they introduced universal conscription and a one- to three-year military service term in 1889. The French army meanwhile phased out its use of female *cantinières*. The Third Republic was heavily committed to its military, though the radical Left pushed to reduce the length of obligatory service. Charles de Freycinet, who later served as prime minister four times between 1880 and 1892, believed in the character-shaping experience of military service. He argued in his 1871 history of the war, in which he justified his own role and decisions, 'Let us teach our children that to defend the fatherland is not a burden but a duty, a duty like that of defending one's family and home that, in consequence, is close, direct, and personal, the performance of which no one has the right to avoid.'[3] He later expressed a faith in the education learned in the barracks, including the virtues of hierarchical authority, as cement for the social order.

The Imperial German Army also built upon the legacy of 1864–71 with a focus on using maximum force to decisively achieve a limited objective. Germany, no longer seeking to expand in Europe, sought to contain conflict. To contain conflict required speed in terms of mobilization and concentration, which had been the hallmarks of Prussian victories in 1866 and 1870. So, preparation remained paramount, along with the need for the military to retain its autonomy from the rest of government.

At the same time, the tactical lessons of the war were not always easy to discern, and this failure to learn from 1870 contributed to greater carnage later. The French Chassepot rifles, coupled with their tactical discipline, should have stopped the Prussians in their tracks (and they often did). The Prussians had suffered enormously from the French rifles, with more than twice the number of casualties at Gravelotte alone than in the entire Austro-Prussian War. Yet Prussian artillery helped the infantry to break through and was often the decisive factor in key battles.

Despite this experience, a pervasive narrative held that the moral action of attacking soldiers would be the key to victory. The Germans were lucky that the French repeatedly failed to counter-attack at moments when they might have secured victory. If the French had done so and demonstrated definitively that the fierce *élan* of any infantry attack would simply lead to carnage, perhaps Europeans would have learned this lesson and avoided the destruction of the Great War. The Prussian Guards' successful counterattack at Le Bourget on 30 October, in which they used widely spaced smaller units, advancing piecemeal and on their own initiative, was also forgotten.

At the conclusion of the war, the German Empire now unquestionably ranked as the strongest continental power. Unlike Napoleon I at the start of the century, Bismarck had worked to ensure that German hegemony was achieved through general consent across Europe. In the medium term, the war led to a lasting continental peace. Bismarck had successfully limited the conflict to the two main belligerents, both on the battlefield and diplomatically. He also managed to prevent Moltke from prolonging the war or from trying to utterly destroy France, which would have likely brought Russia and possibly Great Britain and Austria–Hungary into the fighting.

That said, Bismarck's system assured and relied on continued antagonism with France. He knew that France could not forgive Germany for the defeat. Bismarck succeeded in his aim to damage France so that it took Prussia's place as the weakest of the Great Powers, but this transition also meant coping with long-standing grievances right on its border. The Franco-Prussian War not only created Germany, but also destroyed independent nations: Bavaria, Württemberg, Baden and the Grand Duchy of Hesse. Without these states, no buffer separated France and Germany.

It would be a mistake, however, to assume that the Franco-Prussian War created a direct line to the Franco-German conflict at the heart of the Great War or the alliance system that brought most major European countries into combat with each other in 1914. In the decades after the war, Bismarck's diplomacy worked against such a conflict. Neither the French nor the Germans had an interest in stoking mutual resentment. Most French politicians saw revenge on the German Empire as a low priority, even though the loss of Alsace-Lorraine was taught in schools and indicated on maps. Bismarck himself did not seek a new war with France.

Instead, the German chancellor focused on reining in the ambitions of Russia and Austria–Hungary as they turned to the south and east. Bismarck pulled back German expansion of its navy and overseas possessions to help ensure that Britain would remain neutral, even though the balance of power now had a very different pattern than it had had previously in the nineteenth century. For their part, Britain's political leaders were not interested in challenging German military dominance on land. From 1871, it was twenty years until the Franco-Russian alliance of 1894, and another ten years until Britain joined the other two to form the Triple Entente in 1904, and a further decade until these alliances helped to guide the decision-making of national leaders in the wake of the unexpected crisis over the assassination of Archduke Franz Ferdinand. It was only in these later years that the Germans created hubristic strategies designed to generate a knock-out blow in the event of encirclement due to these new alliances.

None of this was yet apparent in late January 1871. At that time, Crown Prince Friedrich Wilhelm reflected on the burden placed on his own son, the future Wilhelm II, who later led Germany into the disastrous Great War. On the occasion of Wilhelm's twelfth birthday, he wrote, 'May he grow up a good, upright, true, and trusty man, one who delights in all that is good and beautiful . . . It is truly a disquieting thought to realize how many hopes are even now set on this boy's head.'[4]

Wilhelm of Prussia returned to Berlin in March as the German emperor, and German soldiers enjoyed parades and triumphal arches. Yet the war had surprising negative consequences for the Second Reich. Bismarck now had to create stability out of the forces that had brought Germany together – nationalism, militarism and authoritarianism. He did so by exploiting the natural faults in a parliamentary system rather than allowing them to become part of the democratic process, by keeping parties and individuals divided and antagonistic, hardening differences into fractures. The Reichstag had limited power and heavily favoured large landholders. The chancellor was responsible to the emperor, not to the Reichstag. Its budgetary oversight did not include spending by the emperor, who retained wide-ranging emergency powers. The Reichstag could not even propose legislation or exert control over foreign affairs or the military. Military conservatives – the new emperor and the *Junkers* – now controlled the German state and a class of militarists saw Germany's expansion through military action and colonial conquest as crucial to the perpetuation of the German state. After Sedan, many German liberals forgave Bismarck for going over the head of the Reichstag to fund the military.

The French ability to repay the war indemnity ahead of schedule boosted German financial speculation and led to a subsequent bursting of the resulting bubble that undermined trust in liberalism, encouraged anti-Semitism, and deepened a sense of guilt and shame for having indulged in such excessive speculation, contrary to the traditional Lutheran and Prussian sense of moderation. Furthermore, the annexation of Alsace and Lorraine posed challenges to Germany that were never fully resolved. Germany could never decide how to relate to or incorporate the new province with the rest of Germany.

The unification of Germany also raised questions about the purpose of nationalism once its primary objective had been met. It seemed unlikely that German unity would lead the new Empire to cast a more benevolent gaze on other similarly struggling claimants to national status. As one observer questioned in 1870,

> And when German unity is complete, are we to suppose that the swords will be forthwith beaten into ploughshares, and will Germany give free play to those nationalities different from her own, towards which she has hitherto exhibited anything but a tolerant spirit? Will she aid the Pole, and the Magyar, and the Czech, and the Croat, and the Servian [*sic*], and the Roumanian, each in their

several attempts to found separate and independent nationalities? I suspect not.'[5]

Indeed, nationalism showed no sign of abating in the aftermath of 1870. The crown prince reported on disturbing anti-French sentiment in Berlin. Boasting of bringing France to its knees, he declared, 'seems to me to be as petty and narrow-minded as can possibly be but is regarded as patriotism'. Instead, he declared, 'it would really and truly be better for our countrymen if they rejoiced at our great successes in a quiet, dignified way, at the same time recognizing the fine persistency of the French in their devotion to their cause of their country.'[6] He heard news from Berlin, however, that 'an implacable hatred of the French dominates our countrymen there, instead of the sympathy and gentle, forgiving spirit, especially among the educated classes, that should find expression in view of the calamities of our opponents.'[7]

The German army and the victory at Sedan now became the primary symbol of the unified German Empire. Germany was united by the military system, there is no doubt, and the public generally accepted this situation. An 1898 *Berliner Illustrierte Zeitung* poll of readers revealed that they believed the nineteenth century's greatest thinker to be Helmuth von Moltke. Military experience was synonymous with participation in the nation and in the identification as German. The war had gone so smoothly, and was fought almost entirely in France, that there was no backlash and no attempt to demilitarize. The conflict had been so short that it did not even afford women the chance to rise in status as the workers, mothers and national keepers of the home front. German veterans, however, did not particularly foment war, as they did not want to repeat their experiences or see the next generation share in their glory. In the German Empire, soldierly virtue and the characteristics of a good citizen were intertwined. Many soldiers drafted into the barracks saw an increase in their quality of life, though they did socialize distinctly from civilians, and engaged in talk, drink and sexual activity that could not be tolerated in civilian life.

Dennis Showalter argues that the wars of unification were too cheaply won, and that the very ease with which Germany unified may have haunted the Second Reich. Without a founding moment of shared sacrifice, the state itself had won the war, not the people of Germany.[8] The war did not create larger than life public heroes – it was too short to allow them to emerge.

In the aftermath of Sedan, the crown prince recognized the dangerous precedents this war could unleash. 'When at last the War is over,' he wondered,

> will a different spirit from that shown heretofore prevail among the several nations, grow to yet wilder proportions? I build upon the deep seriousness with which our German people entered into the struggle, and which is still preserved, for it was no mood of levity that urged us to the fray, and thus I hope a revulsion of feeling will not fail to appear.

Perhaps the German people could be counted on to restrain themselves from the passions of war. Such a hope rested, he believed, on the leadership of the country – on himself and on his son, the future Wilhelm II – developing society to contain and better direct the emotions of the people. Otherwise, 'in the succeeding period of spiritual stagnation . . . the passions that have been unchained [will] come to the front again and lead to the most lamentable errors.'[9]

Contrary to the hopes of the crown prince, who died prematurely during his first year as emperor, in Germany the nation saw its unification as rooted in military prowess and therefore believed its future strength would rest in continued military strength, backed by great stories of the heroic recent past. Military leaders continued to maintain a leading role in politics and society, ignoring the good luck and moderate politics that made their successes possible and lasting. In the end, Germany's victory in 1870–71 was disastrous both for Germany and for the rest of the world.

*

France, too, undertook a political realignment and engaged in soul-searching about the meaning of the war. The conflict cost France 12 billion francs, not counting the 5-billion-franc war indemnity. Yet France steamed back, established a long-lasting republic, increased its literacy rates, and expanded its paved roads, railroads, banks, public health efforts, industry and pride in being French.

In spring 1871, it was not yet clear that France would establish a republic. With the Orléanist Thiers as chief executive of the provisional government, a majority monarchist National Assembly, and the recent repression of the radical Left during the Paris Commune, the establishment of a republic was not assured. Legitimists hoped for a restoration of the monarchy. However, the royal heir, the comte de Chambord, helpfully refused any compromise and therefore lost any chance he might have had at the throne. Still, after the fall of Thiers, executive power rested with the reactionary soldier Marshal MacMahon.

Nevertheless, over time, the long development of republican civil society supported the establishment of republican political institutions, notably the presidency and the Chamber of Deputies. Men like Léon Gambetta came to the fore. These politicians avoided the romantic and revolutionary view of republicanism – which had failed in 1848 and 1871 – and instead focused on pragmatic steps and alliance-building to create a republican consensus, however incomplete and contentious. The new middle class of businessmen and professionals embodied by Gambetta – the son of a grocer who became a lawyer and statesman – made common cause with the small-landholding peasantry and lower-middle-class shopkeepers, teachers and craftsmen to provide material improvement. This was not a revolutionary cause but a rather conservative one. The middle-class men who served at the national political level in the early Third Republic created a social compact with the rural and small-towns-people, to the exclusion of women, labour and colonial subjects. The Third Republic shifted from conservative to moderate to radical by 1899. For all its shortcomings – a weak presidency, a revolving door of ministers, a series of high-profile divisive scandals – it survived to and through the Great War, unlike the German Empire. The Third Republic only ended in 1940, after France's invasion by the Nazis.

Part of the French republican strategy lay in successfully convincing the public that blame for the war should entirely rest with the ill-prepared and authoritarian Second Empire. In the 1870s, republicans campaigned on the peaceful, conservative goals of the republic while emphasizing the dangers of personal rule embodied by Bonapartist adventurers. War, they argued, no longer served to liberate oppressed populations, but instead brought ruin. Napoleon III had brought war and destruction, and the republic now claimed the mantle of peace. France would recover from the war through the successful installation of republican political institutions. These accounts all contributed to the generally accepted view during the early 1870s that the loss of the Franco-Prussian War was due to the incompetence or imprudence of the French government and military leadership, and that ordinary citizens and soldiers had done the best they could in the war effort.

Some French authors, however, argued that the French national character had declined and required regeneration. The painter Henri Regnault, shortly before his death at Buzenval on 19 January, wrote of the need to abandon Romantic individualism for the sake of the common good:

> We have lost many men; we must replace them with even better and stronger ones. We must learn a lesson from this. Don't let easy pleasures make us soft. The life of the solitary self is no longer allowed. There was a time, not long ago, for belief in nothing other than pleasure and all the wicked passions. Egotism must flee and take with it that fatal vainglorious scorn for everything that was honest and good. Today the Republic requires of everyone a pure life, honorable, serious, and we must pay everything for the *patrie*, and even above the *patrie* to free humanity, the tribute of our body and soul.[10]

Similarly, the historian Albert Sorel wrote in 1875, 'It is against ourselves that we must undertake a true and fruitful revenge for the disasters of 1871.'[11] Too much pleasure-seeking, too little science, and a lack of discipline and duty had diluted France's ability to wage a successful war. For many, the decline in religious observance and spirituality had weakened France's moral fibre and ability to make sacrifices. For some, insufficient faith had led to the war as a punishment from God.

By the 1880s, as republican institutions became more firmly established, the narrative of blame shifted from the Empire to themselves. Increasing numbers of citizens believed that they were responsible for preparing the nation for future armed conflict. In the 1880s, the French Red Cross expanded from the makeshift, improvised organization it was in 1870 to an established force. Red Cross committees trained nurses and gathered stockpiles of linens and medical equipment. The Red Cross was not envisioned as a neutral organization so much as a nationalistic one that would serve French soldiers under the banner of the Geneva Convention. Thousands of French men and women joined committees across the country, responding to the call of the Red Cross activist Dr Pierre Bouloumié at a conference in 1886: 'We must have the courage to say that not everyone did his duty, all his duty, in 1870, and that is precisely because no one was prepared.'[12] Instead of relying on the French state, the Red Cross furthered the idea that all citizens had the responsibility of preparing for the next war.

In the same period, young French men trained their bodies for future military service through private clubs and school-based organizations. Shooting societies, which included older men as well, helped youths become accustomed to weaponry and sharpen their skills. No longer would men arrive on the field of battle without having handled ammunition. These training societies aimed to overcome the fears of degeneracy that had plagued France at the turn of the last century. The Third Republic supported these efforts and, in contrast with the Second Empire, encouraged the placement of guns in the hands of citizens. Gymnastics societies inculcated the discipline to follow whistled orders while in uniform. The preferred gymnastics display of the era featured dozens of young men performing synchronous athletic feats rather than individual acts of skill. National events such as the annual Fête Fédérale Française brought together gymnastics clubs from across the country in a celebration of masculine strength. The 1892 Fête brought 125 gymnastics societies to Nancy, now a border city, and provided a venue for demonstrating France's new alliance with Russia when the tsar's cousin paid a visit. The Fête catalogue proudly declared, 'France, said to be panicky, is calm; France, said to be torn apart, is united; France, said to be isolated, is supported.'[13]

Policy-makers emphasized the role of women in addressing French weakness. The images and experiences of women became part of a national discussion about the regeneration of France. The experience of the Franco-Prussian War encouraged women to think of themselves as redeemers of France. Despite the wide variety of actions undertaken by women during the war itself – such as the participation in combat by female *francs-tireurs* – afterwards, many narratives reproduced the stereotype that women needed protection, as the guardians of the French nation who raised the next generation. It was an exceptional honour, that went against the dominant narrative, for Marie-Julienne Jarrethout to be awarded the *Légion d'honneur* in 1880 for her combat service. She was the only French *cantinière* to receive this distinction.

The private sphere became a matter of public interest. In a typical statement, the author Joseph Turquan wrote that women 'make men out of children . . . Therefore, the power and the glory of a country actually depend on women.'[14] In order to ensure that women would be able to raise physically and morally healthy children, several laws protecting women and encouraging them to become mothers were passed between 1874 and 1919, including the regulation of wet-nursing, the eight-hour workday and restrictions on when and where women could work. Women were in need of protection, not just for their own sakes, but so that they could watch over the new nation. Some of the experiences of women during the

Franco-Prussian War, particularly charity operations and family decisions protecting women and children, anticipated the concerns that led to pro-natalist legislation.

For many thousands who had lost their sons, husbands and brothers, the proper mourning of the dead remained a central issue in the 1870s and beyond. Thousands of soldiers had been buried in the immediate vicinity of the battlefields, on farmland and hillsides, in communal cemeteries or in mass graves on private property. Most graves were marked, and few bodies were unclaimed or lost. These temporary resting places remained on the landscape until the late 1870s. In keeping with a provision in the Treaty of Frankfurt, the French government undertook a project to oversee the maintenance of the tombs of soldiers. The republican French government viewed the care of the tombs of fallen soldiers, including respect for the remains of German soldiers, as paramount. In 1873, the French passed a law to plan to exhume and rebury the remains of soldiers on consolidated gravesites that the French government would maintain and protect (under French law, bodies could not be exhumed and reburied until five years had passed). This project laid to rest 87,396 French and German soldiers who had died during or soon after a battle.

For many French, however, the tombs project did not pay sufficient homage to the soldiers who had died. Across the country, and especially in areas that had been particularly marked by the conflict, local organizations arose to build monuments and hold ceremonies in honour of the soldiers. These practices extended beyond individual mourning to include community gatherings and, in some cases, yearly events that continued for decades.

The annual ceremony on 16 August at Mars-la-Tour drew thousands of visitors through to the early 1900s. Mars-la-Tour, a village of some 800 inhabitants, lay on the French side of the new border that cut through the road between Verdun and Metz. Vionville and Rezonville, which had seen much of the fighting on 16 August, had become German. The uncertain conclusion to the battle that had taken place that day – two days before the battle at Gravelotte (also incorporated into the German Empire) and two weeks before Sedan – became the locus of French national mourning and frustration at Bazaine's handling of the war during those crucial days. The commemorative event arose in the 1870s with the establishment of an annual Funeral Mass, followed by a procession to the crypt of fallen soldiers just outside the village. A secular monument was erected on top of the crypt, decorated with allegories of France and images of children destined to avenge this wrong. The local priest, Joseph Faller, decorated the parish church with war memorabilia, flags, plaques and ex-votos, shells, portraits and arms, creating a unique commemorative church. The speeches and sermons at Mars-la-Tour focused on the suffering of the men who died and their eternal rewards, rather than on the politics of blame or the shortcomings of Bazaine.

The ceremony grew in popularity as the decades passed, drawing an estimated 30,000 visitors in 1908 and in 1910. Crowds engaged in battlefield tourism, taking pictures at the border crossing and listening in vain to unamplified speeches before enjoying a picnic. Despite these holiday trappings, the anniversary held emotional significance for many. A speaker in 1900 broke off in emotion. 'Excuse me,' he continued. 'If I paused, it is because I am thinking how thirty years ago, at the exact hour that I am speaking, I fell myself, hit by a Prussian shell!'[15] By the twentieth century, the political conflict between the republicans and the Bonapartists had subsided and it was now seen to be poor taste to blame the Second Empire for the loss of Alsace and parts of Lorraine. Throughout this period, French and German officers were expected to keep their distance from each other at the anniversary events, but no major incidents arose at the border.

Meanwhile, a new commemorative group emerged, the Souvenir Français, which created a culture of commemoration around the turn of the twentieth century. Founded in 1887 by Alsatians who had opted for France, the Souvenir Français co-ordinated local commemorative efforts into a national network that promoted French glory and aimed to transmit the memory of past sacrifices to a new generation through the creation of plaques, monuments, the placement of wreaths and holding of ceremonies. By 1907, it boasted 800 local committees worldwide.

The Franco-Prussian War also inspired religious pilgrimages within France, and their popularity increased throughout the early Third Republic. Pilgrimages addressed the hope that public prayer and ritual could expiate the sins of the nation, particularly the Revolution and the Paris Commune.

After the sacrifice of the Volontaires de l'Ouest, Loigny became a site of memory and pilgrimage for faithful French Catholics. Accounts of the battle in religious weeklies emphasized the expiatory power of the suffering and pain of the soldiers who had died in the charge. General de Sonis exemplified this tradition with his words following the amputation of his leg due to wounds sustained at Loigny: 'I love to be broken, consumed, destroyed by you . . . Let me be crucified, but crucified by you!'[16] Despite the fact that the battle had ended in defeat, Loigny symbolized the restoration of French greatness and the expiation of French sins, particularly the sin of Napoleon III in betraying France's mission to serve the Catholic Church. Loigny welcomed 350 pilgrims in 1901, organized by the Union provinciale de la jeunesse catholique de l'Orléannais.

Similarly, in Pontmain, perhaps 100,000 pilgrims made the trip in 1871, including General Charette and former *zouaves* and members of the Volontaires de l'Ouest. By early 1872, the bishop of Laval, Joseph Wicart, pronounced the vision a miracle and four local children as visionaries. He organized a national pilgrimage to Pontmain on 23 September 1873, which was repeated each year and regularly attracted tens of thousands of pilgrims. Over a thirty-year period, Wicart oversaw the construction of a basilica in Pontmain, which he linked to the cult of the Sacred Heart and the construction of the Sacre-Coeur de Montmartre in Paris, which was constructed with the explicit aim of expiating the 'sin' of the Commune. In 1873, Revered Father Félix delivered an oft-quoted sermon proclaiming,

'Pontmain is especially the pilgrimage of the future, when France, having returned to Christianity, powerful and glorious, will see the realization of Mary's promises.'[17] The pilgrimage would bring an end to France's long fall.

As in the case of Mars-la-Tour, fear of invasion and hope for French glory in the future were important components in the meaning of the pilgrimage during its early decades. These villages became centres of hope for a Catholic, unified, powerful France, fully restored after being laid low during the Franco-Prussian War.

When German veterans – whether Bavarians or Prussians, Württembergers or Badanese – recalled their time in France, they recognized that they had participated in a historic moment, the foundation of their unified nation. The war was a major event in their lives, perhaps the defining moment. Some knew from this war the kind of man that they were and the limits to which they could be tested.

In the German Empire, public memory was largely defined by veterans' associations, which thrived in the 1870s and beyond. These largely social groups aided their members in the years prior to the founding of Bismarck's welfare state. Sedan Day, a de facto holiday celebrating the crucial victory, was never fully embraced across German society. Bourgeois liberals and their civil associations drove the commemoration of Sedan Day to bolster the project of national unity, but workers, Catholics and Social Democrats could not see themselves in this holiday.

German war memorials only rarely depicted the suffering and death of soldiers. These memorials glorified the German achievements of 1870–71 using images such as men on horseback poised for battle. Inscriptions celebrated the victory and called on the youth to follow in the glorious footsteps of the men who came before. They listed the names of the dead as heroes, not as victims.

Similarly, German school textbooks avoided accounts of suffering and instead exhorted students to emulate the courage of the men who died for Germany. One textbook, for example, described that the French '*mitrailleuses* creakingly fired their lethal bullets ten times a minute from twenty-five or more barrels almost simultaneously and knocked many German fighters to the ground, but the Germans could not be frightened off by this.'[18] Usually, however, German textbooks focused on military leaders, strategy and the course of the war, and relegated soldiers' experiences to brief colour commentary. Nor did partisan warfare play a large role.

As part of the trend of celebrating the victorious soldiers and denying their suffering, German war invalids came to be seen as a symbol of failure. In the absence of sufficient social care for invalid veterans, they became encoded as criminals and a menace to German society. Precise numbers are difficult to confirm since there was not an agreed-upon definition of invalid; some reports claimed over 40,000. Few wanted to look upon the deformed bodies of invalids or consider their sacrifices as worthy of national conversation and support. Fewer men were missing limbs compared with veterans of the Great War because survival rates for amputations were so low. Instead, the sick and weak could not work and depended on charity to survive. In the immediate aftermath, French reparations were used to support invalids, but this was a relatively small and short-lived amount. Only later, in a spate of war writing published in the 1890s, did some veterans, including Dietrich von Lassberg, include more detail on the suffering of soldiers.

Civilian suffering remained largely ignored. Reminders of civilian suffering are rare, including in towns and villages that experienced months of occupation during the conflict. Châteaudun provides a striking exception. Antonin Mercié's 1897 monument to the memory of the defence of Châteaudun, which stands at the edge of the heights overlooking the Loir, commemorates the events of 18 October while also according a special place to the fires at nearby Varize and Civry. It is dominated by a *franc-tireur* in nondescript uniform taking aim, while a female figure representing Châteaudun wilts below. She is wounded and barefoot, her hair blown forward to block her face, her dress bedraggled and torn, yet still her crown clings to her head. A dying Mobile Guardsman falls backward, one hand across his forehead and the other stretched toward the sky. 'Châteaudun was worthy of the *patrie*' reads an inscription on the base, now barely legible. The first stones for this monument were set in a ceremony on 18 October 1894, at which Abbé Saignes – the former chaplain for the *francs-tireurs* of Paris – stated:

> If the memory of 1870 saddens us because it recalls the bloody period of the war and the misfortunes of Châteaudun, it is another memory that should make us rejoice, despite everything, that is the one of a duty nobly accomplished and of the glory in which this valiant city was covered by its chivalrous resistance to the German invasion.[19]

Bazeilles, however, has little to mark its horrific experiences. Unlike the Belgian atrocities of 1914, the actions at Bazeilles never had an official French inquiry. It would have been possible for the Government of National Defence to open such an inquiry, as they did with regard to actions at Metz and Strasbourg. Other towns were honoured for their suffering. Châteaudun received an official note of distinction from the Delegation in Tours and signed by Gambetta on 20 October 1870, and in 1877 received the *Légion d'honneur*. Bazeilles did not receive similar recognition from the GND, since to recognize its martyrization would have brought attention to the imperial army's courage in facing overwhelming circumstances at Sedan. It would furthermore recognize that there had been some civilian resistance to the invasion prior to 4 September, contrary to the republican claim that the population did not rise up to defend the Second Empire.

In Bazeilles, a monument to those who died was inaugurated on 23 November 1875. Yet even in that context, the memories of 1 September 1870 remained buried. The mayor of Bazeilles, M. de Fiennes, spoke: 'If I were to allow myself to remember, I would trace for you an appalling tableau, I would recount for you horrible scenes, I would evoke before you lamentable days. – No, let us remain silent, let us stifle all the sobs we hold in our souls.'[20] The monument recognizes both the naval infantry and the civilians (and this is unusual, even unique, for the era), but records only twenty-seven civilian names. The families of thirteen of the victims did not want their relatives' names listed. It was only in the 1890s, just as French republicans began to reassess the war, that they also began to recognize the suffering of Bazeilles. The village received the *Légion d'honneur* in 1900.

The Franco-Prussian War did not create the atrocities of the World Wars, but it made them more thinkable and created their possibility. During the war, it was possible to imagine civilians as the direct targets of bombardment and to see them as national enemies who must be identified by the state and forcibly moved. Civilians came to be seen as groups bound up and identified with their national status (though Article 2 of the Treaty of Frankfurt allowed for individual decision-making, as French-born Alsatians and Lorrainers could opt for French citizenship if they moved to France). The French expelled Germans from Paris. (The few French in Germany were less targeted, as they were primarily unmarried women who did not threaten to become soldiers.) As the war dragged on, the Germans cared less and less about the villagers whose farms and houses had been destroyed and who became targets of increasing aggression. Instead, the Germans focused on the actions of *francs-tireurs*, exaggerating their danger. Therefore, civilians in arms, went the story, had to be treated without pity as outlaws of international conventions. The experience of Bazeilles in particular lodged two narratives in the imagination: for the Germans that of dangerous armed civilians, and for the French that of German atrocities. It thus paved the way for mutual distrust and atrocities in the early days of the Great War in 1914.

In the decades that followed the Franco-Prussian War, international jurists sought to understand the implications of the treatment of civilians during the war. They recognized that the expulsion of Germans from Paris had been the prerogative of France as a sovereign state, and not a breach of international law. After all, in 1870, the creation of positive international law extensive enough to protect civilians and limit the sovereignty of nations was in an early stage. Yet jurists also judged the expulsion to be overly harsh and to have left German denizens too short a period of time to leave. Jurists also deplored the frequent disregard of the Geneva Convention on the treatment of sick and wounded soldiers.

Despite these readings of the war, jurists were unable to craft concrete protections for civilians during wartime. International humanitarian law and military custom continued to leave the question of civilian rights to protection unanswered. The public emphasis that military necessity could drive the treatment of civilians became a simplified truth that allowed the possibility of harsh reprisals, and the ambivalence toward civilians hardened into a ruthlessness and deep suspicion. Humanitarian aid for civilians in conflict remained spotty and improvised. By the Great War, population politics and national security trumped individual rights and civil liberties. In 1914, civilians in Belgium and northern France paid dearly for this assumption of guilt.

And yet, one far-sighted and hopeful writer saw in this conflict the seeds of a future peace that honours our common humanity. George Sand reflected, 'War will never be an instrument of life because it is the science of destruction; to believe that we can suppress it is not utopian. The realization of the dream of the alliance of the peoples is not so far off as we believe. It will be perhaps the work of the twentieth century.'[21]

Bibliography

Archives Départementales, Bas-Rhin, 14 M 1
Archives Départementales, Hérault, Ph 28, 3 R 88, 8 R 29
Archives Diocésains, Laval, PC 586
Archives Municipales, Nancy, (m) H 4–7 guerre 1870–71
Archives Nationales, F 19 5562
Archives de la Ville et de la Communauté de Strasbourg [AVCUS], 272 MW 84
L'Avenir National
Le Bulletin des lois
Le Charivari
L'Éclair
Le Figaro
L'Impartial de l'Est
Kölnische Zeitung
L'Univers Israélite
Volks-Zeitung (Berlin)
Reuters Telegrams, Private Secretary's Office, Simla

Accampo, Elinor A., 'Gender, social policy, and the formation of the Third Republic: an introduction', in Elinor A. Accampo, Rachel G. Fuchs and Mary Lynn Stewart, *Gender and the Politics of Social Reform in France, 1870–1914* (Baltimore: Johns Hopkins University Press, 1995).

Adam, Juliette, *Mes illusions et nos souffrances pendant le siège de Paris* (Paris: A. Lemerre, 1906).

Adriance, Thomas J., *The Last Gaiter Button: A Study of the Mobilization and Concentration of the French Army in the War of 1870* (New York: Greenwood Press, 1987).

Agulhon, Maurice, *Marianne into Battle: Republican Imagery and Symbolism in France, 1789–1880*, trans. Janet Lloyd (Cambridge: Cambridge University Press, 1981).

Anonymous, *Apparition de la Sainte Vierge à Pont-main 17 janvier 1871* (Rennes: Oberthar et fils, 1875).

Anonymous, *Notre-Dame de Pontmain* (Abbéville: C. Paillart, 1896).

Anonymous, 'Souvenirs – à mes enfants'. AVCUS, 272 MW 84.

Anonymous, *Tales of the Franco-Prussian War by an Eye-Witness* (London: Charles H. Clarke, 1871).

Audoin-Rouzeau, Stéphane, *1870: La France dans la guerre* (Paris: Armand Colin, 1989).

Beaunis, H., *Impressions de campagne (1870–1871)* (Paris: Alcan et Berger-Levrault, 1887).

Berthelon, R. P., *Notre-Dame de Pontmain* (Paris: D. Dumoulin et Cie, 1891).

Bion, B. (Abbé), *Mais priez! . . .*, 3rd edn (Château-Chinon: Dudragne-Borget, 1877).

Biotière, Francisque de, *Paris dans les caves, épisode du siège 1870–71* (Paris: Librarie gauloise, 1872).

Bismarck, Otto von, *Reden, 1847–1869*, edited by Wilhelm Schüssler. Vol. 10 of *Bismarck: Die gesammelten Werke*, edited by Hermann von Petersdorff (Berlin: Otto Stolberg, 1924–1935). Trans. by Jeremiah Riemer on https://germanhistorydocs.ghi-dc.org.

Blackbourn, David, *Marpingen: Apparitions of the Virgin Mary in Bismarckian Germany* (Oxford: Clarendon Press, 1993).

Boissonnas, B. (Mme), *Une famille pendant la guerre 1870–1871*, 6th edn (Paris: J. Hetzel et Companie, 1875).

Bonhomme, Éric, 'Bordeaux et la Défense Nationale'. *Annales du Midi* 110, no. 223 (July 1998), 319–42.

Bonnel, Julien (Abbé), *Notre-Dame d'Espérance de Pontmain* (Laval: Chailland, 1884).

Botzenhart, Manfred, 'French prisoners of war in Germany, 1870–71', in Stig Förster and Jörg Nagler, eds., *On the Road to Total War: The American Civil War and the German Wars of Unification, 1861–1871* (Cambridge: Cambridge University Press, 1997), 587–96.

Bour, Charles, *Rapport sur le Concours pour le Monument à Élever à Lunéville aux Victimes de la Guerre de 1870–1871, Lu au Comité le 24 août 1873* (Lunéville: Chatelain, 1873).

Bourguinat, Nicolas and Gilles Vogt, *La guerre franco-allemande de 1870: Une histoire globale* (Paris: Flammarion, 2020).

Boutry, Philippe and Michel Cinquin, *Deux Pèlerinages au XIXe siècle: Ars et Paray-le-Monial* (Paris: Beauchesne, 1980).

Brennan, Brian, 'Piety and politics in nineteenth-century Poitiers: the cult of St Radegund', *Journal of Ecclesiastical History* 47, no. 1 (January 1996), 65–81.

Breuilly, John, 'Revolution to unification', in Breuilly, ed., *Nineteenth-Century Germany: Politics, Culture and Society 1780–1918* (New York: Oxford University Press, 2001), 138–56.

Brown, Howard G., *Mass Violence and the Self: From the French Wars of Religion to the Paris Commune* (Ithaca: Cornell University Press, 2018).

Caglioti, Daniela, 'Waging war on civilians: the expulsion of aliens in the Franco-Prussian War', *Past & Present* 221, no. 1 (November 2013), 161–95.

Cappé, G., *Souvenirs de 1870. La Mobile de Vitry* (Vitry-le-François, 1887).

Caron, Jean-Claude, *Les feux de la discorde: Conflits et incendies dans la France du XIXe siècle* (Paris: Hachette Littératures, 2006).

Cathal, J., *L'Occupation de Lunéville par les Allemands, 1870–1873* (Nancy: Berger-Levrault, 1913).

Chambers II, John Whiteclay, 'American views of conscription and the German nation in arms in the Franco-Prussian War', in Daniel Moran and Arthur Waldron, eds., *The People in Arms: Military Myth and National Mobilization since the French Revolution* (New York: Cambridge University Press, 2003).

Chapelle, Sandra and Odile Roynette, 'Tuer le temps: le journal d'August Castan pendant la guerre de 1870–1871', *Revue d'histoire du XIX siècle* 51 (December 2015), 157–68.

Cholvy, Gérard and Yves-Marie Hilaire, *Histoire Religieuse de la France Contemporaine*, 3 vols. (Toulouse: Privat, 1985).

Chrastil, Rachel, 'The French Red Cross, war readiness, and civil society, 1866–1914', *French Historical Studies* 31, no. 3 (Summer 2008), 445–76.

Chrastil, Rachel, *Organizing for War: France 1870–1914* (Baton Rouge: Louisiana State University Press, 2010).

Chrastil, Rachel, *The Siege of Strasbourg* (Cambridge, MA: Harvard University Press, 2014).

Claretie, Jules, *Histoire de la révolution de 1870–1871* (Paris: Aux bureaux du journal *L'Éclipse*, vol. 1, 1872).

Clayson, Hollis, *Paris in Despair: Art and Everyday Life under Siege (1870–71)* (Chicago: University of Chicago Press, 2002).

Confino, Alon, *The Nation as a Local Metaphor: Württemberg, Imperial Germany, and National Memory, 1871–1918* (Chapel Hill: University of North Carolina Press, 1997).

Corbin, Alain, *The Village of Cannibals: Rage and Murder in France, 1870*, trans. Arthur Goldhammer (Cambridge, MA: Harvard University Press, 1993).

Crombrugghe, Ida, Baronne de, *Journal d'une Infirmière pendant La Guerre de 1870–71*, 3rd edn (Paris: Henri Plon, 1871).

Dauphinot, Simon, *Souvenirs du Maire de Reims pendant la Guerre Franco-Allemande* (Rheims: L. Michaud, 1904).

Delteil, Frank, 'Les Protestants et la campagne en faveur de la paix en 1870', *Bulletin de la Société de l'Histoire du Protestantisme Français* 117 (Jan.–Feb.–Mar. 1971), 136–50.

Fischbach, Gustave, *Le siège de Strasbourg: Strasbourg avant, pendant, et après le siège* (Strasbourg: L'Imprimerie Alsacienne, 1897).

Flach, Jacques, *Strasbourg après le bombardement: 2 octobre 1870–30 septembre 1872; Rapport sur les travaux du Comité de Secours Strasbourgeois pour les Victimes du Bombardement* (Strasbourg: Fischbach, 1873).

Foss, Colin, *The Culture of War: Literature of the Siege of Paris, 1870–1871* (Liverpool: Liverpool University Press, 2020).

Frederick III, *The War Diary of the Emperor Frederick III, 1870–1871*, trans. and ed. A. R. Allinson (2006 reprint edn; originally published New York: F. A. Stokes, 1926).

Freycinet, Charles de, *Souvenirs, 1848–1878* (Paris: Delagrave, 1912).

Gould, Roger V., *Insurgent Identities: Class, Community, and Protest in Paris from 1848 to the Commune* (Chicago: University of Chicago Press, 1995).

Goutière-Vernolle, E., *Les Fêtes de Nancy, 5, 6, et 7 juin 1892: ouvrage orné de trente planches hors texte* (Nancy: Crépin-Leblond, 1892).

Gullickson, Gay L., *Unruly Women of Paris: Images of the Commune* (Ithaca: Cornell University Press, 1996).

Guyot, P., *Les femmes du peuple de Nancy et les prisonniers français* (Nancy: N. Collin, 1872).

Harris, Ruth, *Lourdes: Body and Spirit in the Secular Age* (London: Penguin Press, 1999).

Hazareesingh, Sudhir, *The Saint-Napoleon* (Cambridge, MA: Harvard University Press, 2004).

Horne, John, 'Defining the enemy: war, law and the levée en masse and guerrilla warfare from 1870 to 1945', in Daniel Moran and Arthur Waldron, eds., *People in Arms: Military Myth and National Mobilization since the French Revolution* (New York: Cambridge University Press, 2002).

Howard, Michael, *The Franco-Prussian War: The German Invasion of France, 1870–1871* (New York: Macmillan, 1961).

Isambert, Gustave, *Documents publics pour servir à l'histoire de la guerre de 1870–1871. IX, Combat et incendie de Châteaudun (18 octobre 1870): avec notes et pièces justificatives* (Paris: A. Lacroix, Verboeckhoven et cie, 1871).

Koehler, Peter, 'Eduard Hitzig's experiences in the Franco-Prussian War (1870–1871): the case of Joseph Masseau', *Journal of the History of the Neurosciences* 21, no. 3 (2012), 250–62.

König, Mareike, 'Les immigrés allemands à Paris 1870/71: entre expulsion, naturalisation et lutte sur les barricades', *Migrance* 35 (2010), 60–70.

Krüger, Christine G., 'German suffering in the Franco-German War, 1870/71', *German History* 29 (Sept. 2011), 404–22.

Kselman, Thomas A., *Miracles and Prophecies in Nineteenth-Century France* (New Brunswick, NJ: Rutgers University Press, 1983).

Lacroix, Louis, *Journal d'un Habitant de Nancy pendant l'Invasion de 1870–1871* (Nancy: Vagner, 1873).

Landon, Melville D., *The Franco-Prussian War in a Nutshell, A Daily Diary of Diplomacy, Battles, and War Literature* (New York: G. W. Carleton & Co., 1871).

Lardemelle, Général de, *Le Général Comte de Geslin* (Nancy: A. Crépin-Leblond, 1911).

Lassberg, Dietrich von, *Mein Kriegstagebuch aus dem deutsch-französischen Kriege 1870–71* (Munich and Berlin: R. Oldenbourg, 1906).

Laurentin, R. and A. Durand, *Pontmain: Histoire Authentique*, 3 vols. (Paris: Apostolat des Éditions, 1970).

Le Verrier, Lucille, *Journal d'une jeune fille: Second Empire* (Cadeilhan, France: Edition Zulma, 1994).

Ledeuil, Édouard, *Campagne de 1870–1871: Châteaudun 18 octobre 1870* (Paris: A. Sagnier, 1871).

Lefebvre, Pierre, 'The unsuccessful suicide of General Bourbaki', *Histoire des Sciences Médicales* 32, no. 1 (March 1998), 11–15.

L'Huillier, Fernand, 'L'attitude politique de Mgr Raess entre 1859 et 1879', *Études alsaciennes* (1947), 251.

Lix, Tony, *Á Paris et en Province* (Tours: Mame, 1889).

Lobb, S., *Thoughts on the War and on European Policy by a Positivist* (Calcutta: Thacker, Spink, and Co., 1870).

Lumière, [Ernest], *Châteaudun* (Châteaudun: H. Lecesne, 1870).

Lunier, Ludger, *De l'influence des grandes commotions politiques et sociales sur le développement des maladies mentales: Mouvement de l'aliénation mentale en France pendant les années 1869 à 1873* (Paris: F. Savy, 1874).

MacCraig, Charles Neilson, *Defensive Warfare Lawful: A Sermon Preached to the 10th Argyle Artillery Volunteers on the 14th August 1870 by the Rev. Charles Neilson MacCraig, Honorary Chaplain, with Reflections on the Franco-Prussian War* (Glasgow: George Gallie & Son, 1870).

McMichael, J. W., *Sedan, Bazeilles, & Metz: Being an Account of a Visit to Those Places in November, 1870, during the Franco-Prussian War* (London: C. A. Bartleet, 1871).

McPherson, James M., *Battle Cry of Freedom: The Civil War Era* (New York: Oxford University Press, 1988).

Marcère, *Exécution de la Loi du 4 avril 1873 Relative aux Tombes des Militaires Morts pendant la Guerre de 1870–1871* (Paris: Imprimerie Nationale, 1878).

Marrus, Michael R., 'Cultures on the move: pilgrims and pilgrimages in nineteenth-century France', *Stanford French Review* 1, no. 2 (Fall 1977), 205–20.

Martin, Michèle, 'Conflictual imaginaries: Victorian illustrated periodicals and the Franco-Prussian War (1870–1871)', *Victorian Periodicals Review* 36, no. 1 (Spring 2003), 41–58.

Martin, Paul, *Guerre de 1870. Batailles sur la Lauter, la Sauer et la Sarre. Wissembourg-Reichshoffen-Forbach* (Paris: Administration du Spectateur Militaire, 1891).

Mehrkens, Heidi, 'L'occupation militaire de 1870–1871 vue par les Anglais', in Jean-François Chanet, Annie Crépin and Christian Windler, eds., *Le temps des hommes doubles. Les arrangements face à l'occupation, de la Révolution française à la guerre de 1870* (Rennes: Presses universitaires de Rennes, 2013).

Merriman, John, *A History of Modern Europe*, 4th edn (New York: W. W. Norton & Company, 2019).

Micale, Mark S. and Paul Lerner, 'Trauma, psychiatry, and history: a conceptual and historiographical introduction', in Micale and Lerner, eds., *Traumatic Pasts: History, Psychiatry, and Trauma in the Modern Age, 1870—1930* (New York: Cambridge University Press, 2001).

Mitchell, Allan, *The Divided Path: The German Influence on Social Reform in France after 1870* (Chapel Hill: University of North Carolina Press, 1991).

Moltke, Helmuth von, *Correspondance militaire du Maréchal de Moltke*, vol. 2, *Guerre de 1870–71* (Paris: H. Charles-Lauvauzelle, n.d., ca. 1900).

Montarlot, Paul, *Journal de l'invasion: Châteaudun (4 septembre 1870–11 mars 1871)* (Châteaudun: Pouillier-Vaudecraine, 1871).

Nord, Philip, *The Republican Moment: Struggles for Democracy in Nineteenth-Century France* (Cambridge, MA: Harvard University Press, 1998).

Orr, Andrew, *Women and the French Army During the World Wars, 1914–1940* (Bloomington: Indiana University Press, 2017).

Parisot, Guillaume, 'De la négotiation comme instrument d'occupation pacifiée et d'exploitation économique efficace pendant la guerre de 1870–1871', in Jean-François Chanet, Annie Crépin and Christian Windler, eds., *Le temps des hommes doubles. Les arrangements face à l'occupation, de la Révolution française à la guerre de 1870* (Rennes: Presses universitaires de Rennes, 2013).

Pflanze, Otto, *Bismarck and the Development of Germany. The Period of Unification, 1815–1871* (Princeton: Princeton University Press, 1963).

Piton, Frédéric, *Siège de Strasbourg: Journal d'un assiégé* (Paris: Schlaeber, 1900).

Poncet, François, *Hôpital militaire, service de la 1re division de blesses, siège de Strasbourg (1870)* (Montpellier: Boehm et fils, 1872).

Przybylski, Stéphane, *Atlas de la guerre de 1870–71* (Metz: Éditions des Paraiges, 2014).

Quinet, Hermione, *Paris: Journal du Siège* (Paris: E. Dentu, 1873).

Rambaud, Alfred, 'La Lorraine sous le Régime Prussien', *Revue des Deux Mondes*, 1 May 1871.

Raymond-Signouret, P., *Souvenirs du bombardement et de la capitulation de Strasbourg* (Bayonne: P. Cazals, 1872).

Reichard, Max, *Aus den Tagen der Belagerung Strassburgs* (Bielefeld & Leipzig: Velhagen & Klasing, 1873).

Reuss, Rodolphe, 'Chronique strasbourgeoise de la guerre franco-allemande du 16 juillet au 24 août 1870', in Jean Rott, ed., *Le siège de Strasbourg en 1870:*

Conférence et chronique strasbourgeoise juillet–août 1870 (Strasbourg: Librairie Istra, 1971).

Roth, François, *La guerre de 70* (Paris: Fayard, 1990).

Roynette, Odile, 'Le village de la mort. Les "atrocités allemands" en 1870', in Anne-Emmanuelle Demartini et Dominique Kalifa, eds., *Imaginaire et sensibilités au XIXe siècle: études pour Alain Corbin* (Paris: Creaphis, 2005), 257–68.

Sand, George, *Journal d'un voyageur pendant la guerre* (Paris: M. Lévy frères, 1871).

Sand, George, *Correspondance*, vol. 22, ed. Georges Lubin (Paris: Garnier, 1987).

Schneegans, A[uguste], *La guerre en Alsace: Strasbourg* (Neuchâtel: J. Sandoz, 1871).

Schneegans, A[uguste], *Strasbourg! Quarante jours de bombardement par un refugié strasbourgeois* (Neuchâtel: J. Sandoz, 1871).

Showalter, Dennis, *The Wars of German Unification*, 2nd edn (London: Bloomsbury, 2015).

Simpson, Martin, 'From *Zouaves Pontificaux* to the *Volontaires de l'Ouest*: Catholic volunteers and the French nation, 1860–1910', *Canadian Journal of History* 53, no. 1 (2018), 1–29.

Smallman-Raynor, Matthew and Andrew D. Cliff, 'The geographical transmission of smallpox in the Franco-Prussian War: prisoner of war camps and their impact upon epidemic diffusion processes in the civil settlement system of Prussia 1870–71', *Medical History*, 46, no. 2 (April 2002), 241–64.

Sorel, Albert, *Histoire diplomatique de la guerre franco-allemande*, 2 vols. (Paris: Plon, 1875).

Stoneman, Mark R., 'The Bavarian army and French civilians in the war of 1870–1871: a cultural interpretation', *War in History* 8, no. 3 (July 2001), 271–93.

Trailles, Henry and Paul de, *Les femmes de France pendant la guerre et les deux sièges de Paris* (Paris: Polo, 1872).

Truesdell, Matthew, *Spectacular Politics: Louis-Napoléon Bonaparte and the* Fête Impériale, *1849–1870* (New York: Oxford University Press, 1997).

Turner, Victor and Edith Turner, *Image and Pilgrimage in Christian Culture: Anthropological Perspectives* (New York: Columbia University Press, 1978).

Turquan, Joseph, *Les femmes de France pendant l'invasion, 1870–1871* (Paris: Berger-Levrault, 1893).

Uhrich, Jean-Jacques-Alexis, *Documents relatifs au siège de Strasbourg* (Paris: Dentu, 1872).

Union des Femmes de France, *Conférence à Lyon, le 13 avril 1886* (Paris: Coopération Typographique, 1886).

Walser, Hans H., 'Die Aerzte und der Krieg am Beispiel des deutsch-französischen Krieges von 1870/71', *Clio Medica* 2, no. 2 (June 1967), 103–20.

Wawro, Geoffrey, *The Franco-Prussian War: The German Conquest of France in 1870–1871* (New York: Cambridge University Press, 2003).

Wetzel, David, *A Duel of Giants: Bismarck, Napoleon III, and the Origins of the Franco-Prussian War* (Madison: University of Wisconsin Press, 2001).

Wetzel, David, *A Duel of Nations: Germany, France, and the Diplomacy of the War of 1870–1871* (Madison: University of Wisconsin Press, 2012).

Zaidman, Pierre-Henri, 'Les Chasseurs des Vosges et L'Expédition de Fontenoy: 18–22 janvier 1871', *Gavroche: revue d'histoire populaire* 23, no. 138 (November 2004), 24–31.

Zeys, Louise, *Une Fille de la Vraie Alsace: Marie-Antoinette Lix, Lieutenant de Uhlans Polonais, Lieutenant de Francs-Tireurs* (Paris: Plon, 1931).

Notes

1. Declaration

1 'War! War with France!' Lassberg, *Mein Kriegstagebuch*, 17 July, 1.
2 'The great questions' Bismarck, *Reden*, 139–40.
3 'fearful solemnity' Quoted and translated in Landon, *Franco-Prussian War in a Nutshell*, 39.
4 'war to the knife' Quoted and translated in Landon, *Franco-Prussian War in a Nutshell*, 40.
5 'amazement has changed to joy' Quoted and translated in Landon, *Franco-Prussian War in a Nutshell*, 41.
6 'pride and tranquility' Quoted and translated in Landon, *Franco-Prussian War in a Nutshell*, 47.
7 'stormy enthusiasm' Quoted and translated in Landon, *Franco-Prussian War in a Nutshell*, 47.
8 'amid cheers for Germany' Quoted in Landon, *Franco-Prussian War in a Nutshell*, 59.
9 'went their own way' Lehmann's *Die Mobilmachung*, quoted and translated in Howard, *Franco-Prussian War*, 59–60.
10 'By manifesting a readiness' Quoted and translated in Landon, *Franco-Prussian War in a Nutshell*, 51.
11 'a big, unknown' Lassberg, *Mein Kriegstagebuch*, 23 July, 4.
12 'despite the joy of the advance' Lassberg, *Mein Kriegstagebuch*, 23 July, 4.
13 'quite, quite difficult' Lassberg, *Mein Kriegstagebuch*, 24 July, 4.
14 'the most onerous of responsibilities' Frederick III, *War Diary*, 16 July, 7.
15 'all Germany has risen like one man' Frederick III, *War Diary*, 17 July, 8.
16 'the enthusiasm of France' Quoted in Audoin-Rouzeau, *1870*, 51.
17 'vast surging crowds' Quoted and translated in Landon, *Franco-Prussian War in a Nutshell*, 39.
18 'Is it out of the mouth of this "babe and suckling"' Quoted and translated in Landon, *Franco-Prussian War in a Nutshell*, 39.
19 'everyone is on the task' Quoted in Audoin-Rouzeau, *1870*, 38.
20 'What enthusiasm' Beaunis, *Impressions de campagne*, 10–11.
21 'Tracts' Reichard, *Belagerung Strassburgs*, 6.

22 'there are nevertheless' Anonymous, 'Souvenirs – à mes enfants', 1.
23 'all these handsome men' Anonymous, 'Souvenirs – à mes enfants', 3.
24 Landon, *Franco-Prussian War in a Nutshell*, 49, 51.
25 'Announced that Russia joined Prussia' Reuters Telegrams, Private Secretary's Office, Simla.
26 'monster demonstration' Reuters Telegrams, Private Secretary's Office, Simla, 25 July 1870.
27 'by the fact of' Anonymous, *Tales of the Franco-Prussian War*, 1–2.
28 'How long is Humanity to suffer' Lobb, *Thoughts*, 1. This article originally appeared in the *Bengalee* on 23 July 1870.
29 'Ollivier declares' Reuters Telegrams, Private Secretary's Office, Simla, 28 July 1870.
30 'whereby all, regardless of rank, wealth, or position' Quoted in Chambers, 'American views of conscription', 87.
31 'Not one [telegram] came from Napoleon' Quoted in Landon, *Franco-Prussian War in a Nutshell*, 43.
32 'They will no longer be able to make a coat cheaper in Europe than in this country' Quoted in Landon, *Franco-Prussian War in a Nutshell*, 16 July, 48.
33 'An infinity' Quoted in Caglioti, 'Waging war on civilians', 164.
34 'very difficult, as well as responsible and embarrassing' Quoted in Caglioti, 'Waging war on civilians', 168.
35 'modern and more humane' Quoted in Caglioti, 'Waging war on civilians', 169.
36 'all the well-established principles of public law' Quoted in Caglioti, 'Waging war on civilians', 170–71.

2. Mobilization

1 'The present war' Quoted in Wawro, *Franco-Prussian War*, 84.
2 'We are ready, very ready!' Adriance, *Last Gaiter Button*, 3.
3 'Little by little' Quoted in Audoin-Rouzeau, *1870*, 83.
4 'Am in Belfort' Quoted in Adriance, *Last Gaiter Button*, 15.
5 'As we have neither materiel nor personnel' Quoted in Audoin-Rouzeau, *1870*, 85.
6 'most agreeable' Quoted in Audoin-Rouzeau, *1870*, 91.
7 'If . . . we had to depart for Prussia' Quoted in Audoin-Rouzeau, *1870*, 89.
8 'As we pass through, we're acclaimed' Quoted in Audoin-Rouzeau, *1870*, 89.
9 'Let war not scare you' Quoted in Audoin-Rouzeau, *1870*, 90.
10 'who holds in his hand' Quoted in Audoin-Rouzeau, *1870*, 90.

11 'The call of the Mobile Guard caused a certain emotion' Quoted in Audoin-Rouzeau, *1870*, 52.
12 'When young men came to the price of true sacrifices' Quoted in Audoin-Rouzeau, *1870*, 52.
13 '*Un! deux! trois! merde!*' Quoted in Adriance, *Last Gaiter Button*, 78.
14 '*A Paris!*' Quoted in Wawro, *Franco-Prussian War*, 76.
15 'The imperial government has denied the French people' Quoted in Roynette, 'Village de la mort', 268.
16 'every man between the age of twenty and thirty-eight' Quoted and translated in Wawro, *Franco-Prussian War*, 80.
17 'I am pained by the realization' Quoted and translated in Wawro, *Franco-Prussian War*, 83.
18 'We didn't belong there anymore' Lassberg, *Mein Kriegstagebuch*, 25 July, 4–5.
19 'packed like sheep' Quoted and translated in Wawro, *Franco-Prussian War*, 84.
20 '*Ei, komme se denn endlich?*' Quoted and translated in Wawro, *Franco-Prussian War*, 66.
21 'we hope to come into battle' Lassberg, *Mein Kriegstagebuch*, 4 August, 9.
22 'Which of us will come back?' Frederick III, *War Diary*, 24 July, 10.
23 'but I must not let my thoughts dwell' Frederick III, *War Diary*, 26 July, 11.
24 'the thought of sharing the same pang of parting' Frederick III, *War Diary*, 26 July, 11.
25 'Who would ever before have dreamed' Frederick III, *War Diary*, 26 July, 11–12.
26 'The Prussian point of view must be entirely abandoned' Frederick III, *War Diary*, 30 July, 17.
27 'I can never again look upon' Frederick III, *War Diary*, 30 July, 17.
28 'Men's minds could not be better attuned' Frederick III, *War Diary*, 30 July, 17.
29 'Thus then we stand at the beginning of a historical world crisis!' Frederick III, *War Diary*, 1 August, 20.

3. Concentration and Command

1 'Why not? Everything is ready' Quoted and translated in Adriance, *Last Gaiter Button*, 13.
2 'Railroads are the weakest things in war' Quoted in McPherson, *Battle Cry of Freedom*, 515.
3 'You cannot conceive the difficulty' Quoted in Wawro, *Franco-Prussian War*, 74–5.

4 'I have the honour of requesting' Quoted in Audoin-Rouzeau, *1870*, 85.
5 'With each passing day' Quoted and translated in Wawro, *Franco-Prussian War*, 86.
6 'To my People' Quoted and translated in Landon, *Franco-Prussian War in a Nutshell*, 79.
7 'His judgment and activity had been affected' Quoted and translated in Howard, *Franco-Prussian War*, 61.
8 'shall hardly be in a position' Frederick III, *War Diary*, 24 July, 10.
9 'will power and self-assertion' Showalter, *Wars of German Unification*, 238.
10 'Whatever may be the road' Quoted in Howard, *Franco-Prussian War*, 78.
11 'Our army has taken the offensive' Quoted and translated in Howard, *Franco-Prussian War*, 82.
12 'One praises the conduct of the Emperor' Quoted in Audoin-Rouzeau, *1870*, 94.
13 'inaugurated a new epoch of history' Quoted and translated in Wawro, *Franco-Prussian War*, 91.

4. Combat

1 'One thing is certain' Quoted and translated in Wawro, *Franco-Prussian War*, 99.
2 'The Bavarians have decisively defeated' Quoted and translated in Wawro, *Franco-Prussian War*, 105.
3 'Our fellows behaved' Frederick III, *War Diary*, 4 August, 25.
4 'dying and severely wounded men' Frederick III, *War Diary*, 4 August, 26.
5 'veritable savages' Frederick III, *War Diary*, 28, 42, 46.
6 'I saw the corpse' Quoted and translated in Wawro, *Franco-Prussian War*, 104–5.
7 'hurried to Bitscher Gate' Quoted and translated in Stoneman, 'Bavarian army', 279.
8 'We are not waging war against the peaceful inhabitants' Quoted and translated in Stoneman, 'Bavarian army', 272–3.
9 'We had to cover a part of yesterday's battlefield' Frederick III, *War Diary*, 5 August, 29.
10 'full of blood, dirt and filth' Lassberg, *Mein Kriegstagebuch*, 5 August, 11.
11 'meaning we had to take it' Lassberg, *Mein Kriegstagebuch*, 5 August, 12.
12 'Today we will also be there' Lassberg, *Mein Kriegstagebuch*, 6 August, 13.
13 'it is a really eerie sound' Lassberg, *Mein Kriegstagebuch*, 6 August, 14.

14 'Greetings, Lassberg!' Lassberg, *Mein Kriegstagebuch*, 6 August, 15.
15 'forward, ever forward' Lassberg, *Mein Kriegstagebuch*, 6 August, 17.
16 'What a very strange feeling it was' Lassberg, *Mein Kriegstagebuch*, 6 August, 18.
17 'We had become' Lassberg, *Mein Kriegstagebuch*, 6 August, 18.
18 'So that was our first day of battle!' Lassberg, *Mein Kriegstagebuch*, 6 August, 21.
19 'The Bavarian troops were terribly slow' Frederick III, *War Diary*, 6 August, 31.
20 'a deep stillness reigned' Frederick III, *War Diary*, 6 August, 37.
21 'I have lost a battle' Quoted in Howard, *Franco-Prussian War*, 117.

5. Retreat

1 'No, there is no announcement of victory' Quoted in Freycinet, *Souvenirs*, 102.
2 'Marshal MacMahon has lost a battle' Quoted in Martin, *Guerre de 1870*, 259.
3 'France has been compromised by your imbecility!' Quoted in Wawro, *Franco-Prussian War*, 140.
4 'in the presence of a nation in arms' Quoted in Howard, *Franco-Prussian War*, 122.
5 'If France sustains another defeat' Quoted in Wawro, *Franco-Prussian War*, 141.
6 'the physiognomy of the region' Quoted in Audoin-Rouzeau, *1870*, 138.
7 'Finally, at eleven at night' Quoted in Audoin-Rouzeau, *1870*, 101.
8 'I don't know what we're doing' Quoted in Audoin-Rouzeau, *1870*, 107.
9 'I am not even yet master' Frederick III, *War Diary*, 10–12 August, 51.
10 'I begin to believe' Frederick III, *War Diary*, 14 August, 55.
11 'no Prussians in Bar yet' Quoted in Audoin-Rouzeau, *1870*, 132.
12 'Great emotion everywhere' Quoted in Audoin-Rouzeau, *1870*, 132.
13 'I cannot but think' Quoted in Mehrkens, 'L'occupation militaire de 1870–1871', 98n54.
14 'The soldiers are not inclined to be harsh' Quoted in Mehrkens, 'L'occupation militaire de 1870–1871,' 98n55.
15 'and when newsboys' Quoted in Martin, 'Conflictual imaginaries', 47.
16 'Some are getting ready' Quoted in Martin, 'Conflictual imaginaries', 48–9.
17 'Government have been forced' Reuters Telegrams, Private Secretary's Office, Simla, 9 August 1870.
18 'The function discharged by the Correspondent' Quoted in Mehrkens, 'L'occupation militaire de 1870–1871', 93.
19 'numbers of Englishmen' Frederick III, *War Diary*, 23 August, 69.
20 'does not imply neutrality' MacCraig, *Defensive Warfare Lawful*, 19.

21 'See France full of folly and vanity' MacCraig, *Defensive Warfare Lawful*, 17.
22 'a playground' MacCraig, *Defensive Warfare Lawful*, 17.
23 'the thunderbolt' MacCraig, *Defensive Warfare Lawful*, 18.
24 'No talk, no bluster' MacCraig, *Defensive Warfare Lawful*, 18.
25 'prayer' MacCraig, *Defensive Warfare Lawful*, 18.
26 'Had a Protestant element existed' MacCraig, *Defensive Warfare Lawful*, 19.
27 'revolutionary horrors' MacCraig, *Defensive Warfare Lawful*, 19.
28 'We should seize the opportunity' Quoted in Mehrkens, 'L'occupation militaire de 1870–1871', 96n48.
29 'I am shocked by the misery' Quoted in Wawro, *Franco-Prussian War*, 145.
30 'Knapsacks were emptied out' Quoted in Wawro, *Franco-Prussian War*, 147.

6. *Turning Points*

1 'everyone was and felt free' Quoted in Hazareesingh, *Saint-Napoleon*, 219.
2 'Long live the army, which has saved us from anarchy' Quoted in Hazareesingh, *Saint-Napoleon*, 63.
3 'it is now not only the victory that is popular' Quoted in Hazareesingh, *Saint-Napoleon*, 65.
4 'We have to go back to 1814' Quoted in Hazareesingh, *Saint-Napoleon*, 65.
5 'We are supporting the struggle' Quoted in Hazareesingh, *Saint-Napoleon*, 66.
6 'Glory may well be transmitted' Quoted in Hazareesingh, *Saint-Napoleon*, 93.
7 'War has fled' Quoted in Hazareesingh, *Saint-Napoleon*, 73.
8 'On 15 August, after the Te Deum' Archives Départementales, Bas-Rhin, 14 M 1, letter (draft) Uhrich and Pron to clergy of Strasbourg, 12 August 1870.
9 'There are only two possible positions' Quoted in Fischbach, *Le siège de Strasbourg*, 86–7.
10 'blown to bits' Quoted in Corbin, *Village of Cannibals*, 54.
11 'they all have the attitude, faces, and demeanor of poor, uncivilized peasants' Quoted in Corbin, *Village of Cannibals*, 104.
12 'few decisions on the battlefield' Howard, *Franco-Prussian War*, 154.
13 'would wait for orders' Quoted in Wawro, *Franco-Prussian War*, 155.
14 'A bomb fell on the horse' Quoted in Audoin-Rouzeau, *1870*, 102.
15 'Everywhere, along the whole range' Quoted in Howard, *Franco-Prussian War*, 170.
16 'Picture to yourself . . . a continuous wall of smoke' Quoted in Howard, *Franco-Prussian War*, 172.
17 'the noise of explosions' Quoted in Howard, *Franco-Prussian War*, 174.

18 'like a hurricane' Quoted in Wawro, *Franco-Prussian War*, 176.
19 'You promised me a victory' Quoted in Howard, *Franco-Prussian War*, 176–8.
20 'The battles, the shooting' Quoted in Wawro, *Franco-Prussian War*, 186.

7. The Road to Sedan

1 'Our adversaries must now despair' Quoted in Wawro, *Franco-Prussian War*, 188.
2 'Our troops need severe discipline' Quoted in Wawro, *Franco-Prussian War*, 194.
3 'The Emperor Napoleon' Private Secretary's Office, Simla, 20 August 1870.
4 'I presume that the minister' Quoted in Howard, *Franco-Prussian War*, 187.
5 'Number of *mobiles* presently armed' Quoted in Audoin-Rouzeau, *1870*, 114.
6 'The King I found well' Frederick III, *War Diary*, 20 August, 64.
7 'In this very moment' Quoted in Howard, *Franco-Prussian War*, 192n3.
8 'The men steal' Quoted and translated in Stoneman, 'Bavarian army', 285.
9 'There is no choice' Quoted and translated in Stoneman, 'Bavarian army', 286.
10 'Here we live like God' Quoted and translated in Stoneman, 'Bavarian army', 288.
11 'In his house for breakfast' Quoted and translated in Stoneman, 'Bavarian army', 289.
12 'especially where no troops are stationed' Frederick III, *War Diary*, 21 August, 67.
13 'must be opposed' Frederick III, *War Diary*, 23 August, 70.
14 'in a cunning, cowardly fashion' Frederick III, *War Diary*, 28 August, 75.
15 'shouts of jubilation' Frederick III, *War Diary*, 24 August, 71–2.
16 'That was a frustrating day!' Lassberg, *Mein Kriegstagebuch*, 25 August, 37.
17 'Everybody, it seems, pilfers' Frederick III, *War Diary*, 29 August, 77.
18 'with the view of both relieving itself from the presence' Quoted in Caglioti, 'Waging war on civilians', 178.
19 'Since the breaking out of the war' Quoted in Caglioti, 'Waging war on civilians', 176.
20 'as it would be unfair to punish men' Quoted in Caglioti, 'Waging war on civilians', 186.
21 'The beauty of the scenery' Quoted in Howard, *Franco-Prussian War*, 203.
22 'an incalculable complication' Frederick III, *War Diary*, 27 August, 74.

8. Sedan and Bazeilles

1 'genteel suburb of Sedan' McMichael, *Sedan, Bazeilles, & Metz*, 19.
2 'a quite pretty, but today deserted and partially burning village' Lassberg, *Mein Kriegstagebuch*, 31 August, 47.
3 'Now we have them in a mousetrap' Quoted in Wawro, *Franco-Prussian War*, 211.
4 'We are inside a chamber pot' Quoted in Howard, *Franco-Prussian War*, 208.
5 'From the stone houses' Quoted and translated in Stoneman, 'Bavarian army', 276.
6 'deceitful' Quoted and translated in Stoneman, 'Bavarian army', 276.
7 'Everyone wanted to have his revenge here' Quoted and translated in Stoneman, 'Bavarian army', 277.
8 'The ground was so furrowed' Quoted in Roynette, 'Village de la mort', 261.
9 'This was just a single tableau' Lassberg, *Mein Kriegstagebuch*, 1 September, 55.
10 'Suddenly a man stepped out' Quoted in Wawro, *Franco-Prussian War*, 214.
11 'We need a victory' and 'You will be very lucky' Quoted in Howard, *Franco-Prussian War*, 211.
12 'watching the remains of their independence dwindling' Howard, *Franco-Prussian War*, 212.
13 'the poet's aphorism' Quoted and translated in Stoneman, 'Bavarian army', 280.
14 'Things really had to change' Quoted and translated in Stoneman, 'Bavarian army', 282.
15 'wounded on the forehead' Quoted in Roynette, 'Village de la mórt', 265.
16 'She was taken prisoner' Quoted in Roynette, 'Village de la mort', 265.
17 'Herr Major, they just shot at us!' Quoted and translated in Stoneman, 'Bavarian army', 277.
18 'The villain swore his innocence' Quoted and translated in Stoneman, 'Bavarian army', 277.
19 'The woman had achieved her purpose' Quoted and translated in Stoneman, 'Bavarian army', 278.
20 'And even in this bitter fight' Quoted and translated in Stoneman, 'Bavarian army', 282.
21 'struggling among five or six Bavarians' Quoted in Roynette, 'Village de la mort', 265–6.
22 'who with shotgun in hand' Quoted and translated in Stoneman, 'Bavarian army', 279.
23 'the widow P . . .' Quoted in Roynette, 'Village de la mort', 266.
24 'I was with the commander' Georg von Bismarck, quoted in Wawro, *Franco-Prussian War*, 227.

25 'with mathematical precision' Frederick III, *War Diary*, 1 September, 88.
26 'Your emperor has been taken prisoner' Quoted in Stoneman, 'Bavarian army', 277.
27 *'Ah! Les braves gens!'* Quoted in Howard, *Franco-Prussian War*, 215–16.
28 'running around unarmed' Frederick III, *War Diary*, 1 September, 89.
29 'Each man felt instinctively' Frederick III, *War Diary*, 1 September, 92.
30 'the Grand Duke of Saxe-Weimar' Frederick III, *War Diary*, 1 September, 92.
31 'Monsieur my brother' Quoted in Howard, *Franco-Prussian War*, 219.
32 'Calm and serious they stand' Lassberg, *Mein Kriegstagebuch*, 1 September, 58.
33 'One can rely on nothing in your country' Quoted in Howard, *Franco-Prussian War*, 221.
34 'The fortune of battle' Quoted in Howard, *Franco-Prussian War*, 221.
35 'It is now just a big smoky, burning dump' Lassberg, *Mein Kriegstagebuch*, 2 September, 77.
36 'German and French' Lassberg, *Mein Kriegstagebuch*, 2 September, 80.
37 'This is the dark side of war!' Lassberg, *Mein Kriegstagebuch*, 2 September, 80.
38 'It's Anton!' Lassberg, *Mein Kriegstagebuch*, 2 September, 82–3.
39 *'Die Weltgeschichte ist die Weltgericht!'* Frederick III, *War Diary*, 2 September, 95.
40 'When Napoleon saw me' Frederick III, *War Diary*, 2 September, 99.
41 'The troops have little food' Quoted in Audoin-Rouzeau, *1870*, 122.
42 'When I consider' Quoted and translated in Landon, *Franco-Prussian War in a Nutshell*, 225.

9. *New Beginnings*

1 'inhabitants of Cahors recoil' Quoted in Audoin-Rouzeau, *1870*, 139.
2 'It is very important' Quoted in Audoin-Rouzeau, *1870*, 141.
3 'received in profound silence' Reuters Telegrams, Private Secretary's Office, Simla, 5 September, 1870.
4 'To the French: A great misfortune has struck the *patrie*' Quoted in Audoin-Rouzeau, *1870*, 139.
5 'You see . . . the butcher of 2 December wants more blood' Quoted in Adam, *Mes illusions et nos souffrances*, 4 September, 17.
6 'The Republic, is neither a woman nor a divinity' Adam, *Mes illusions et nos souffrances*, 4 September, 23.
7 'with drawn swords' Landon, *Franco-Prussian War in a Nutshell*, 262.
8 'neither a clod of our earth' Quoted in Wawro, *Franco-Prussian War*, 235.
9 'traitors' Quoted in Audoin-Rouzeau, *1870*, 150.
10 'After having served' Quoted in Audoin-Rouzeau, *1870*, 152.

11 'If the Emperor hopes' Quoted in Landon, *Franco-Prussian War in a Nutshell*, 254.

12 'people had been petrified' Frederick III, *War Diary*, 12–14 September, 118–19.

13 'leaving him with only the poor refuge of death' Quoted in Landon, *Franco-Prussian War in a Nutshell*, 254.

14 'and a hundred wild brokers danced a weird *can-can*' Landon, *Franco-Prussian War in a Nutshell*, 254.

15 'Prussia's strongest supporters' Landon, *Franco-Prussian War in a Nutshell*, 69.

16 'Brethren: The struggle which French audacity forced upon you is closing' Quoted and translated in Landon, *Franco-Prussian War in a Nutshell*, 352.

17 'the sickening tales of slaughter' Lobb, *Thoughts*, 42. Originally published as a letter to the *Daily Examiner* on 20 September 1870, under the name of CIVIS.

18 'men who regard the needle-gun' Lobb, *Thoughts*, 54–5. Originally published as a letter to the *Daily Examiner* on 14 October 1870, under the name of CIVIS.

19 'Thousands of people throng the streets' Quoted in Landon, *Franco-Prussian War in a Nutshell*, 251.

20 'On the battle-fields of France' Quoted and translated in Landon, *Franco-Prussian War in a Nutshell*, 276.

21 'The German Government' Quoted in Howard, *Franco-Prussian War*, 231.

22 'I had hardly heard of the existence of this Order' Frederick III, *War Diary*, 7 September, 110.

23 'To-day a half-crazy Prince Max of Württemberg' Frederick III, *War Diary*, 25 September, 134.

24 'He spoke not a word' Lassberg, *Mein Kriegstagebuch*, 9 September, 96.

25 'simply and sincerely' Lassberg, *Mein Kriegstagebuch*, 9 September, 97.

26 'my previously mentioned Turco' Lassberg, *Mein Kriegstagebuch*, 9 September, 98; 'my often mentioned Black friend' 11 September, 101.

27 'What must the poor, good-natured "savage"' Lassberg, *Mein Kriegstagebuch*, 11 September, 101.

28 'I struggle, I use the ruses of a savage!' Adam, *Mes illusions et nos souffrances*, 10 September, 52.

29 'Madame . . . if you have the courage' Adam, *Mes illusions et nos souffrances*, 10 September, 53.

30 'our patriotic enthusiasm' Adam, *Mes illusions et nos souffrances*, 10 September, 55.

31 'At every window' Quoted in Howard, *Franco-Prussian War*, 322.

32 'at the sight of those gray beards' Quoted and translated in Clayson, *Paris in Despair*, 106.

33 'The darling children!' Adam, *Mes illusions et nos souffrances*, 6 September, 46.

10. *The Paris Strategy*

1 'will rather bury themselves in ruin' Reuters Telegrams, Private Secretary's Office, Simla, 26 September 1870.

2 'You may take the fortress, you will find the rampart' Quoted and translated in Landon, *Franco-Prussian War in a Nutshell*, 287.

3 'Paris was going to be besieged like a vulgar stronghold!' Freycinet, *Souvenirs*, 104.

4 'France is again mistress of herself' Quoted in Audoin-Rouzeau, *1870*, 154.

5 'The torpor of the Lozère country' Quoted in Howard, *Franco-Prussian War*, 235.

6 'If there is not enthusiasm' Quoted in Audoin-Rouzeau, *1870*, 155.

7 'thrown like a rubber ball over the walls' Adam, *Mes illusions et nos souffrances*, 10–11 October, 108.

8 'We must set all our resources to work' Quoted in Howard, *Franco-Prussian War*, 240.

9 'rather eccentric than intelligent' Landon, *Franco-Prussian War in a Nutshell*, 269.

10 'which seem made for energetic grasping' Landon, *Franco-Prussian War in a Nutshell*, 270.

11 'Eloquence, for M. Gambetta' Freycinet, *Souvenirs*, 161.

12 'to leap upward' Landon, *Franco-Prussian War in a Nutshell*, 270.

13 'There was authority even in his laugh' Quoted in Howard, *Franco-Prussian War*, 225.

14 'Didn't [I] have something better to do?' Freycinet, *Souvenirs*, 111.

15 'The principle of universal and obligatory conscription' Audoin-Rouzeau, *1870*, 186.

16 'To become soldiers' Quoted in Audoin-Rouzeau, *1870*, 202.

17 'Several days later' Quoted and translated in Clayson, *Paris in Despair*, 130.

18 'developed in me a powerful and strong love' Quoted in de Trailles, *Les femmes de France*, 192.

19 'The regular army is destroyed' Sand, *Journal*, 16 October, 110–11.

20 'You can improvise soldiers in a threatened location' Sand, *Journal*, 16 October, 111.

21 'Can willpower give us cannon?' Sand, *Journal*, 16 October, 112.

22 'But isn't the task beyond the strength of a single man?' Sand, *Journal*, 11 October, 102.

23 *'Boulen la Marianne'* Quoted and translated in Agulhon, *Marianne into Battle*, 144–6.

24 'I shudder to think' Frederick III, *War Diary*, 12–14 September, 118.

25 'The *mobiles* are brave' Sand, *Journal*, 16 October, 110.

26 'He was to offend [the Army] daily' Quoted in Howard, *Franco-Prussian War*, 242.
27 'It was such a beautiful moment' Lassberg, *Mein Kriegstagebuch*, 11 October, 140.
28 'the Bavarian Infantry fought very well' Frederick III, *War Diary*, 12 October, 153.

11. Choices

1 'like an oil stain' Quoted in Chapelle and Roynette, 'Tuer le temps: le journal d'Auguste Castan', 167.
2 'the population remains in ignorance' Quoted in Audoin-Rouzeau, *1870*, 268.
3 'Each commune is a prison' Quoted in Audoin-Rouzeau, *1870*, 268.
4 'One day we have killed in one fell swoop' Sand, *Journal*, 30 September, 71.
5 'We fall into the unknown' Sand, *Journal*, 8 October, 93.
6 'As I open my windows' Sand, *Journal*, 15 September, 3–4.
7 'for his life' *L'Avenir National*, 23 September, 1.
8 'your ruined families' *L'Avenir National*, 30 November, 1.
9 'Arthur! How are you, *ma chère*?' *Le Charivari*, 21 August, 3.
10 'if you had a wife and children' Boissonnas, *Une famille*, Berthe to André, 5 September, 6–7.
11 'Her child had been born six weeks before' Boissonnas, *Une famille*, Berthe to André, 12 October, 66–7.
12 'Nowadays [during the war] you have black ideas' Sand, *Journal*, 29 September, 63–4.
13 'they would condemn us to the shadows' Boissonnas, *Une famille*, Madame de Thieulin to Madame de Vineuil, 30 November, 171.
14 'Paris will probably be under siege' Boissonnas, *Une famille*, Berthe to André, 6 September, 9–10.
15 'distressing to only be a woman' Le Verrier, *Journal d'une jeune fille*, letter to the Marquise Blanche de Saffray, 14 August, 116.
16 'I am happy to be so young' Le Verrier, *Journal d'une jeune fille*, letter to Madame Marie Talabot, 8 November, 133.
17 'in hospitals, in workshops, in *cantines*' Quinet, *Paris*, 47.
18 'young men unknown to me' Piton, *Siège de Strasbourg*, 58–61.
19 'The [Republican] government still tries' Quoted and translated in Horne, 'Defining the enemy', 110
20 'Because several murders have been committed' Quoted and translated in Stoneman, 'Bavarian army', 274.

21 'As we were dressing' McMichael, *Sedan, Bazeilles, & Metz*, 23.
22 'best of their fruits' Quoted in Audoin-Rouzeau, *1870*, 215.
23 'with no gain' Isambert, *Documents*, 70.
24 'completely disavowed the disarmament' Quoted in Isambert, *Documents*, 72.
25 'duty as refraining from any discussion' Quoted in Isambert, *Documents*, 72.
26 'very young' Isambert, *Documents*, 85.
27 'the author does not explain' Isambert, *Documents*, 8n1.
28 'anywhere other than at the mayor's office' Lumière, *Châteaudun*, 3.
29 'ten who are entirely charred' Quoted in Caron, *Feux*, 119.
30 'submit to exigencies and exactions' Lumière, *Châteaudun*, 4.
31 'My fifteen Saxons were at heart' Montarlot, *Journal*, 83.
32 'The proper strategy consists' Quoted in Howard, *Franco-Prussian War*, 380.
33 'My task is not to simplify theirs' Boissonnas, *Une famille*, Berthe to André, 16 September, 25.
34 'At first we were forbidden' Quoted in Howard, *Franco-Prussian War*, 380.
35 'families are abandoned to the protection of God' Sand, *Correspondance*, letter to Edmond Plauchut, 29 December, no. 15288.
36 'useless' Quoted in Parisot, 'Négotiation', 290.
37 'Until now the population of Soissons' Quoted in Parisot, 'Négotiation', 281.
38 'Our duty is to wage war' Quoted in Parisot, 'Négotiation', 281.
39 'We aren't the police for the enemy' Quoted in Parisot, 'Négotiation', 286.
40 'the Mayor counts on the public-spiritedness' Quoted in Parisot, 'Négotiation', 285.
41 'Here and now' Quoted in Parisot, 'Négotiation', 297
42 'to make a man an excellent combat machine' Sand, *Journal*, 16 October, 113–14.
43 'No more heroes' Sand, *Journal*, 25 September, 30.
44 'who has the most courage' Sand, *Journal*, 25 September, 31.
45 'bronze age' Sand, *Journal*, 16 October, 116.
46 'exchange of projectiles' Sand, *Journal*, 25 September, 30.
47 'In the face of the burning fanaticism' Quoted and translated in Stoneman, 'Bavarian army', 283.
48 'roam the woodlands' Quoted and translated in Stoneman, 'Bavarian army', 286.
49 'We have bloodily revenged our many friends and comrades' Quoted and translated in Stoneman, 'Bavarian army', 288.
50 'Despite all victories' Frederick III, *War Diary*, 7 September, 110.
51 'staunch as his sword' Frederick III, *War Diary*, 7 September, 109.
52 'inflated rumours' Quoted in Chapelle and Roynette, 'Tuer le temps: le journal d'Auguste Castan', 167.
53 'our towns and villages' Quoted and translated in Krüger, 'German suffering', 414–15.

54 'Whoever got to see these *turcos*' Quoted and translated in Krüger, 'German suffering', 415 (*Christenbote*, 33, 14 August 1870, 240).
55 'of the savants, of the philosophers and artists' Sand, *Journal*, 16 October, 119–20.
56 'as though the half-century that has passed' Sand, *Journal*, 20 September, 20.
57 'In this war' Sand, *Journal*, 17 October, 121–2.
58 'We felt our voice break off' Reuss, 'Chronique strasbourgeoise', 56.
59 'If they are barbarians' Reuss, 'Chronique strasbourgeoise', 56.
60 'the indescribable immorality' Quoted and translated in Stoneman, 'Bavarian army', 288.
61 'racial war' Quoted and translated in Stoneman, 'Bavarian army', 289n79.
62 'All the sacrifices are demanded at the same time' Sand, *Journal*, 22 October, 132–3.

12. *Under Siege*

1 'we are completely unaware' Quoted in Audoin-Rouzeau, *1870*, 223.
2 'Our military obligations' Quoted in Howard, *Franco-Prussian War*, 269.
3 'a soldier of the Army of the Rhine' Quoted in Wawro, *Franco-Prussian War*, 250.
4 'horseflesh one franc per pound' McMichael, *Sedan, Bazeilles, & Metz*, 33.
5 'Here too we saw traces of the encampment of its late besiegers' McMichael, *Sedan, Bazeilles, & Metz*, 30.
6 'occupied first by the Prussians' McMichael, *Sedan, Bazeilles, & Metz*, 30.
7 'I saw some companions eat in one meal' Quoted in Audoin-Rouzeau, *1870*, 4 December, 221.
8 'They tell us that tomorrow' Quoted in Audoin-Rouzeau, *1870*, 222.
9 'It is not *we* who capitulate' Quoted in McMichael, *Sedan, Bazeilles, & Metz*, 35.
10 'Be calm, dear fellow citizens' McMichael, *Sedan, Bazeilles, & Metz*, 36.
11 'Day of mourning and desolation' Quoted in Audoin-Rouzeau, *1870*, 28 October, 225.
12 'No armistice! No peace!' Quoted in Audoin-Rouzeau, *1870*, 226.
13 'Such a crime' Quoted in Audoin-Rouzeau, *1870*, 227.
14 'pitiful production' Frederick III, *War Diary*, 5 November, 181.
15 'The population, a model of bravery' Quoted in Audoin-Rouzeau, *1870*, 216–17.
16 'The mission of Your Excellency' Moltke, *Correspondance militaire*, 283.
17 'military law condemns' *Bulletin des lois*, 1863/07-12, 919.
18 'so long as there remains a soldier' Archives Départementales du Bas-Rhin, 14 M 2, Uhrich and Baron Pron, proclamation, 10 August.
19 'Fear is not reasonable' Anonymous, 'Souvenirs – à mes enfants', 13.

20 'A flash illuminates a point' Raymond-Signouret, *Souvenirs du bombardement*, 126.
21 'It is a very burdensome and also dangerous task' Wickede, 'Kriegsfahrten', *Kölnische Zeitung*, 10 September 1870, 2.
22 'It will no longer' Reichard, *Belagerung Strassburgs*, 61.
23 'Thinking of our beautiful Library' Reuss, 'Chronique strasbourgeoise', 38.
24 'My walls remain standing' Uhrich, *Documents*, 45.
25 'in every group' Piton, *Siège de Strasbourg*, 91.
26 'I am not Saint-Leo' L'Huillier, 'L'attitude politique de Mgr Raess', 249.
27 'So terrible had been the terrors' Schneegans, *Strasbourg!*, 27.
28 'Never so many visits' Reuss, 'Chronique strasbourgeoise', 42–3.
29 'the real state of things' Schneegans, *Guerre en Alsace*, 162.
30 'Great emotion!' Reuss, 'Chronique strasbourgeoise', 40.
31 'did not dream of leaving' Reuss, 'Chronique strasbourgeoise', 41.
32 'Your father' Anonymous, 'Souvenirs – à mes enfants', 34.
33 'The maddest part' Frederick III, *War Diary*, 21 September, 129.
34 'To bury oneself' Schneegans, *Guerre en Alsace*, 277.
35 'Believe me' Uhrich, *Documents*, 122.
36 'we suddenly saw reappear' Schneegans, *Strasbourg!*, 52.
37 'We cried tears of rage and sadness' Schneegans, *Guerre en Alsace*, 294–5.
38 'the crown of German cities' 'Strassburg', *Volks-Zeitung* (Berlin), 29 September 1870, 1.
39 'They are polite' Piton, *Siège de Strasbourg*, 222–3.
40 'I had entered without a grey hair' Quoted in Raymond-Signouret, *Souvenirs du bombardement*, 129–31.
41 'the malicious joy' Piton, *Siège de Strasbourg*, 225–6.

13. *Autumn in Paris*

1 'Dear fellow citizens' Quoted and translated in Clayson, *Paris in Despair*, 91.
2 'Considering that the country is in mourning' Quoted and translated in Foss, *Culture of War*, 28.
3 'Sparta goes to bed' Quoted and translated in Clayson, *Paris in Despair*, 55.
4 'Paris, since its imprisonment' Adam, *Mes illusions et nos souffrances*, 1–2 October, 94.
5 'The very different aspect' Quoted and translated in Foss, *Culture of War*, 32.
6 'I can still see [. . .] the cobblestone courtyard' Quoted and translated in Foss, *Culture of War*, 173.
7 diarists could not plot the arc of their writing Foss, *Culture of War*, 74, 154–5.

8 'Until Sedan you even did us a favor' Quoted and translated in Clayson, *Paris in Despair*, 206.
9 'What an incorrigible Germanophobe you are' Quoted and translated in König, 'Immigrés allemands', 10.
10 'the triumph of the European revolution' Quoted in Audoin-Rouzeau, *1870*, 171.
11 'There are other *quartiers*' Quoted and translated in Gould, *Insurgent Identities*, 147.
12 'burlesque and derisory' Biotière, *Paris dans les caves*, 23.
13 '[Edmond] Adam asks Jules Favre' Adam, *Mes illusions et nos souffrances*, 15 October, 112.
14 'Batignolles is in a state of desolation' Quoted and translated in Clayson, *Paris in Despair*, 213.
15 'All men must go down!' Adam, *Mes illusions et nos souffrances*, 161.
16 'I'm doing everything in my power' Quoted and translated in Foss, *Culture of War*, 134.
17 'a comedy staged' Frederick III, *War Diary*, 6 November, 183.
18 'What humiliation! What shame!' Adam, *Mes illusions et nos souffrances*, 215.
19 'The armistice is rejected' Sand, *Journal*, 8 November, 178.
20 'half naked' Sand, *Journal*, 18 October, 122.
21 'For two days' Sand, *Journal*, 19 October, 123.
22 'fostered by the Crown Prince' Quoted in Howard, *Franco-Prussian War*, 354.
23 'I regret to hear from Berlin' Frederick III, *War Diary*, 31 October, 175.
24 'Yet surely it is the very first thing' Frederick III, *War Diary*, 31 October, 175.

14. Generosity

1 'If no considerations of mercy' Lobb, *Thoughts*, 42.
2 'all Englishmen' Lobb, *Thoughts*, 41.
3 'two brotherly peoples' Quoted in Delteil, 'Protestants', 141.
4 'Alas!' Quoted in Delteil, 'Protestants', 142.
5 'If we, the mothers' Quoted in Delteil, 'Protestants', 145.
6 'The peace must have a basis in justice' Quoted in Delteil, 'Protestants', 146.
7 'if there are women in France' Quoted in Delteil, 'Protestants', 148.
8 'galled and bleeding shoulders' McMichael, *Sedan, Bazeilles, & Metz*, 12.
9 'so questionable a character' McMichael, *Sedan, Bazeilles, & Metz*, 12.
10 'which were, one would hope, exaggerated' McMichael, *Sedan, Bazeilles, & Metz*, 14.

11 'a weapon in which he and all our fellow travellers firmly believed' McMichael, *Sedan, Bazeilles, & Metz*, 14.
12 'The old woman' McMichael, *Sedan, Bazeilles, & Metz*, 27.
13 'an unfriendly hand' McMichael, *Sedan, Bazeilles, & Metz*, 25.
14 'Much wanton damage was done here' McMichael, *Sedan, Bazeilles, & Metz*, 16.
15 'prostrate and paralysed' McMichael, *Sedan, Bazeilles, & Metz*, 24.
16 'not quite up to our ideal' McMichael, *Sedan, Bazeilles, & Metz*, 19.
17 'I have neither the power nor heart' McMichael, *Sedan, Bazeilles, & Metz*, 19.
18 'Among the dead were many peasants' Quoted in Landon, *Franco-Prussian War in a Nutshell*, 224.
19 'They walked by our side' McMichael, *Sedan, Bazeilles, & Metz*, 20.
20 'violent commotions' Quoted in Roynette, 'Village de la mort', 267.
21 'I was told by the *curé*' Quoted in Landon, *Franco-Prussian War in a Nutshell*, 223.
22 'two peasants and a woman even' Anonymous, *Tales of the Franco-Prussian War*, 75.
23 'It had turned out that our soldiers' Quoted and translated in Stoneman, 'Bavarian army', 282–3.
24 'exaggerations' Letter of General von der Tann, Nancy, 20 June 1871, reproduced in Clarétie, *Histoire de la révolution de 1870–1871*, 223.
25 'barbarian conquerors' Quoted in Roynette, 'Village de la mort', 264.
26 The actions of German soldiers were ambivalent Roynette, 'Village de la mort', 261.
27 'The burning of Bazeilles' McMichael, *Sedan, Bazeilles, & Metz*, 20.
28 'stream of benevolence' McMichael, *Sedan, Bazeilles, & Metz*, 39.
29 'The Swiss people' Piton, *Siège de Strasbourg*, 142–3.
30 'Switzerland' Quoted in Fischbach, *Siège de Strasbourg*, 274.
31 'a whitehaired and venerable man' McMichael, *Sedan, Bazeilles, & Metz*, 21.
32 'While the city thus perished' Schneegans, *Guerre en Alsace*, 147.
33 'Women and children' Beaunis, *Impressions de campagne*, 42.
34 'who, under the open sky' Schneegans, *Guerre en Alsace*, 145–6.
35 'the poor women . . . in the rain' Adam, *Mes illusions et nos souffrances*, 24 October, 131.
36 'patriotic eloquence' Quinet, *Paris*, 236.
37 'replace . . . the work of absent men' *Le Temps*, 14 November 1870, 4.
38 'to find a way to give to each working woman' Adam, *Mes illusions et nos souffrances*, 24 October, 130.
39 'only women who were personally known' Crombrugghe, *Journal d'une Infirmière*, 10.
40 'The pleasure I experienced' Crombrugghe, *Journal d'une Infirmière*, 64.

41 'the suffering is horrible to see' Boissonnas, *Une famille*, Father to Mother, 13 January, 279–80.
42 'It is distressing' Crombrugghe, *Journal d'une Infirmière*, 134–5.
43 'A sick man is no longer an enemy' Boissonnas, *Une famille*, Berthe to André, 3 January, 247–9.
44 'of intrepidity and devotion' Turquan, *Femmes de France*, 304.
45 'I made this remark to two visitors' Crombrugghe, *Journal d'une Infirmière*, 152.
46 'Two days ago, a young woman' Crombrugghe, *Journal d'une Infirmière*, 49.
47 'with the other cadavers' Crombrugghe, *Journal d'une Infirmière*, 90.
48 'When I despair to think that France has produced Maréchal Bazaine' Mézières, *Le Temps*, 30 August 1888, quoted in *L'Univers Israélite*, 16 September 1888, 9–10.
49 'has exhibited several times at the Salon' *L'Univers Israélite*, 16 September 1888, 9–10.
50 'slow and arduous' *L'Univers Israélite*, 1 September 1870, 14.
51 'saintly' *L'Univers Israélite*, 15 August 1870, 733; 'mysterious magic' *L'Univers Israélite*, 1 September 1870, 15.
52 'true heroism' *L'Univers Israélite*, 1 September 1870, 14–16.
53 'repeated expressions of the high respect' Frederick III, *War Diary*, 5 October, 147–8.
54 'His Majesty, it seems, speaks disapprovingly' Frederick III, *War Diary*, 23 October, 167.
55 'Let us therefore' McMichael, *Sedan, Bazeilles, & Metz*, 40.

15. *Suffering*

1 'corrupting power of Bonapartism' Quoted in Wawro, *Franco-Prussian War*, 266.
2 'Behind us in the forest' Lassberg, *Mein Kriegstagebuch*, 9 November, 173.
3 'the Mobile Guard has fought well' Sand, *Journal*, 10 November, 179–80.
4 'I could hardly imagine' Lassberg, *Mein Kriegstagebuch*, 10 November, 182.
5 'It is very annoying' Frederick III, *War Diary*, 9 November, 187.
6 'with its gyration' Quoted in Koehler, 'Eduard Hitzig's experiences', 252.
7 'When I once more consider' Quoted and translated in Krüger, 'German suffering', 406.
8 'wounded, some of them horribly mutilated' Quoted and translated in Krüger, 'German suffering', 407.

9 'is the most difficult thing' Quoted and translated in Krüger, 'German suffering', 407.
10 'With every step you saw new misery' Quoted and translated in Krüger, 'German suffering', 406.
11 'We saw where MacMahon lay wounded' Quoted in Koehler, 'Eduard Hitzig's experiences', 252.
12 'not without the creeps' Lassberg, *Mein Kriegstagebuch*, 10 October, 129.
13 'If it were not presumptuous' Quoted and translated in Krüger, 'German suffering', 411.
14 'I lifted the cover thrown over the first wounded man' Beaunis, *Impressions de campagne*, 47–8.
15 'Amputate, always amputate' Beaunis, *Impressions de campagne*, 46.
16 'A man hit by a voluminous burst' Poncet, *Hôpital militaire*, 62.
17 'All nationality was evidently forgotten' McMichael, *Sedan, Bazeilles, & Metz*, 8.
18 'Here were several French officers' McMichael, *Sedan, Bazeilles, & Metz*, 8.
19 'Some there were whose faces' McMichael, *Sedan, Bazeilles, & Metz*, 9.
20 'a young Bavarian who had lost a leg' McMichael, *Sedan, Bazeilles, & Metz*, 9.
21 'representing every possible injury' McMichael, *Sedan, Bazeilles, & Metz*, 10.
22 'that the blood lost by the German soldiers' Krüger, 'German suffering', 414.
23 'If under the impression of the murderous fights at Metz' Quoted and translated in Krüger, 'German suffering', 409.
24 'This slaughter of thousands' Quoted and translated in Krüger, 'German suffering', 408.
25 'What passed through my head' Raymond-Signouret, *Souvenirs du bombardement*, 129–31.
26 'Palpitations, fainting' Beaunis, *Impressions de campagne*, 44–5.
27 'confusion reigned supreme' McMichael, *Sedan, Bazeilles, & Metz*, 31–2.
28 'as only women can minister' McMichael, *Sedan, Bazeilles, & Metz*, 37.
29 'Fever and dysentery' McMichael, *Sedan, Bazeilles, & Metz*, 32.
30 'the time is not particularly well chosen' Quoted in McMichael, *Sedan, Bazeilles, & Metz*, 37–8.
31 'black like carbon' Archives Départementales [AD] Hérault, Ph 28 (formerly 1 J 825), Sylvain-Paul Olivier, 'Mémoires de la Campagne de Prusse de 1870 et 1871', unpublished, written in Bonneburg, 11 April 1871, 17, 22.
32 'You always have nightmares' AD Hérault, Ph 28, Olivier, 'Mémoires', 21.
33 'Our unhappy prisoners' Rambaud, 'Lorraine sous le Régime Prussien', 149.
34 'Our hearts sickened at the sight' McMichael, *Sedan, Bazeilles, & Metz*, 29.
35 'Thousands of letters' McMichael, *Sedan, Bazeilles, & Metz*, 27.
36 '[The women] tried to attach' Guyot, *Femmes du peuple*, 11–12.
37 'Too bad for the guy who got it on the head' Guyot, *Femmes du peuple*, 13.

38 'for as they say, they are not Prussians' AD Hérault, Ph 28, Olivier, 'Mémoires', 38–9.
39 'With the money that we have' AD Hérault, 3 R 88, letter of 14 April 1871, quoted by commissariat of police Bédarieux to prefect Hérault, 29 April 1871.
40 'Their food is atrocious' AD Hérault, 3 R 88, letter published in a Montpellier newspaper on 27 April 1871, addressed from Berlin to M. Saintpierre, president of the *Comité de recours pour les prisonniers*, cited by commissariat of police Bédarieux to prefect Hérault, 29 April 1871.
41 'brutality, the cruel carelessness' Rambaud, 'Lorraine sous le Régime Prussien', 149.
42 'Two nights' Quoted in Audoin-Rouzeau, *1870*, 249.
43 'weavers and factory workers' Showalter, *Wars of German Unification*, 296.
44 'As for myself, I have made up my mind' Quoted in Howard, *Franco-Prussian War*, 342.
45 'Some had scarcely any boots on their feet' Quoted and translated in Stoneman, 'Bavarian army', 287.
46 'The genius of France' Quoted in Howard, *Franco-Prussian War*, 310.
47 '*Vive la France! Vive Pie IX!*' Quoted in Audoin-Rouzeau, *1870*, 237.
48 'The war which we undergo is a war of expiation' Quoted and translated in Simpson, 'From *Zouaves Pontificaux*', 4.

16. *Christmas*

1 'The poor woman of the house' Quoted in Wawro, *Franco-Prussian War*, 287.
2 'we are like . . . a mobile corps that spreads misery' Quoted and translated in Stoneman, 'Bavarian army', 288.
3 'General von der Tann himself' Quoted and translated in Stoneman, 'Bavarian army', 288.
4 'a spectacle of a beauty' Quoted in Caron, *Feux*, 110.
5 'enemy soldiers, atop the surrounding hills' Quoted in Caron, *Feux*, 111.
6 'a thick smoke emanated' Quoted in Caron, *Feux*, 112.
7 'with a savagery' Quoted in Caron, *Feux*, 112.
8 'I have no illusions' Quoted in Audoin-Rouzeau, *1870*, 370n74.
9 'The Government subsisted [in Tours]' Quoted in Bonhomme, 'Bordeaux', 337.
10 'The conversation hardly ever lagged' Freycinet, *Souvenirs*, 162–3.
11 'The whole town accompanied them' Sand, *Journal*, 29 November, 186.

12 'The question of armament is a true calamity' Quoted in Audoin-Rouzeau, *1870*, 193.
13 'the mobilized soldiers from Ille-et-Vilaine' Quoted in Audoin-Rouzeau, *1870*, 193–4.
14 'it's for all the world' Frederick III, *War Diary*, 14 December, 223.
15 'Firm without haughtiness' Freycinet, *Souvenirs*, 212.
16 'shadow side and horror' Lassberg, *Mein Kriegstagebuch*, 18–23 December, 263.
17 '—' Lassberg, *Mein Kriegstagebuch*, 18–23 December, 263.

17. *Winter Theatre*

1 'No one had the heart to amuse himself' Quoted and translated in Clayson, *Paris in Despair*, 86.
2 'You are the reason' Quoted and translated in Foss, *Culture of War*, 128.
3 'marauders' Adam, *Mes illusions et nos souffrances*, 20 November, 230.
4 'Madame, all of this is nothing' Adam, *Mes illusions et nos souffrances*, 26 November, 240.
5 'sculpted in their hearts' Adam, *Mes illusions et nos souffrances*, 272.
6 'This lugubrious city' Quoted and translated in Clayson, *Paris in Despair*, 53.
7 'spot the darkness with scanty red dots' Quoted and translated in Clayson, *Paris in Despair*, 54.
8 'For a besieged city' Quoted in Audoin-Rouzeau, *1870*, 276.
9 'I've just come from les Halles' Quoted and translated in Foss, *Culture of War*, 148.
10 'a classic of the rat cuisine genre' Clayson, *Paris in Despair*, 168.
11 'I made up my mind at last yesterday to eat horse' Quoted in Landon, *Franco-Prussian War in a Nutshell*, 404.
12 'I am very well' Quoted in Landon, *Franco-Prussian War in a Nutshell*, 405.
13 'a kind of picnic' Adam, *Mes illusions et nos souffrances*, 23 December, 284.
14 'appetizing, pink, firm' Adam, *Mes illusions et nos souffrances*, 1 January 1871, 294.
15 'Consumption of Rat Meat – Precautions to Take' *Le Temps*, 20 and 23 December 1870.
16 'their long hours waiting in the streets' Quinet, *Paris*, 11 February 1871, 337.
17 'women have stared down' Quinet, *Paris*, 11 November, 161.
18 'the only time of true liberty' Quinet, *Paris*, 11 February, 338.
19 'Think about our soldiers on the battlefield' Quinet, *Paris*, 22 January, 294.
20 'Thanks, I'm not hungry!' *Le Charivari*, 4 September 1870, 3.

21 'led Parisians to famine' Quoted in Audoin-Rouzeau, *1870*, 279.
22 'the citizens of Belleville' Quoted and translated in Gould, *Insurgent Identities*, 147.
23 'high-caliber fire-pumps' Quoted and translated in Gould, *Insurgent Identities*, 138, 138n22.
24 'People participated in an animated discussion' Quoted and translated in Gould, *Insurgent Identities*, 138–9.
25 'For heaven's sake' Quoted in Audoin-Rouzeau, *1870*, 281.
26 'folly' and a 'wretched bombardment': Frederick III, *War Diary*, 31 December, 239.
27 'the Parisians will just laugh at us' Frederick III, *War Diary*, 1 January 1871, 244.
28 'We are no longer looked upon as the innocent sufferers' Frederick III, *War Diary*, 31 December, 240.
29 'As we have said before' Quoted in Martin, 'Conflictual imaginaries', 53.
30 'At night especially the bombardment' Lassberg, *Mein Kriegstagebuch*, 4 January–9 March 1871, 277.
31 'kept his calm' Quoted in Wetzel, *Duel of Nations*, 180.
32 'One mother, returning to her house' Adam, *Mes illusions et nos souffrances*, 7–8 January, 306.
33 'we don't speak of it' Sand, *Journal*, 18 January 1871, 240.
34 'the weather is nice' Sand, *Journal*, 20 January, 256.
35 'Now will the wiseacres' Frederick III, *War Diary*, 5 January, 248.
36 'Considering my personal aversion to war' Frederick III, *War Diary*, 8 January, 253.
37 'Will the great People of '89' Quoted and translated in Gould, *Insurgent Identities*, 155.
38 'The government has given its measure' Quoted in Audoin-Rouzeau, *1870*, 280.
39 'speak with serious and firm language' Quoted in Audoin-Rouzeau, *1870*, 281.
40 'perseverance against obviously insurmountable obstacles' Foss, *Culture of War*, 216.
41 'First endless difficulties of every sort and kind' Frederick III, *War Diary*, 17 November, 194.
42 'I thank God' Frederick III, *War Diary*, 3 December, 212.
43 'all German-thinking people' Frederick III, *War Diary*, 18 December, 225–6.
44 'as to title, escutcheon, armorial bearings' Frederick III, *War Diary*, 15 January, 261.
45 'We, Wilhelm, by the grace of God' Frederick III, *War Diary*, 17 January, 266.
46 'From now on' Frederick III, *War Diary*, 18 January, 269.
47 'The ceremony of installation' Frederick III, *War Diary*, 18 January, 270–71.

48 'with his uplifted right hand' Frederick III, *War Diary*, 18 January, 272.
49 'My feelings I cannot describe' Frederick III, *War Diary*, 18 January, 273.
50 'I am just back from the "Emperor" act!' Quoted in Frederick III, *War Diary*, 279n3.
51 'I cannot begin to describe to you' Quoted in Wawro, *Franco-Prussian War*, 282.
52 'people are beginning' Frederick III, *War Diary*, 22 January, 279.
53 'for the first time a true "German"' Frederick III, *War Diary*, 23 January, 281.

18. *Last Stands*

1 'nowhere does anyone signal' Quoted in Audoin-Rouzeau, *1870*, 287–8.
2 'His men declared' Frederick III, *War Diary*, 3 January, 246.
3 'I'm twenty years too old' Quoted in Wawro, *Franco-Prussian War*, 295.
4 'Haven't you made a mistake' Quoted in Howard, *Franco-Prussian War*, 427.
5 'If this plan does not suit you' Quoted in Howard, *Franco-Prussian War*, 429.
6 'Not having been fortunate enough' Quoted in Lefebvre, 'Unsuccessful suicide of Bourbaki', 12.
7 'When Paris burns' Berthelon, *Notre-Dame de Pontmain*, 10.
8 'But pray, my children' Laurentin and Durand, *Pontmain*, vol. 1, 154.
9 'compassionate, tender, a little capricious' Turner and Turner, *Image and Pilgrimage*, 161.
10 'I prayed' Quoted in Bion, *Mais priez!*, 31–2.
11 'path of the cross' Archives Diocésains, Laval [AdioL], PC 586, R. P. Joseph Barbadette, *Récit d'un Voyant*, 1891, 30.
12 'even if they were entering the village' AdioL, PC 586, R. P. Joseph Barbadette, *Récit d'un Voyant*, 1891, 144.
13 'The very day' Archives Nationales, F 19 5562, Wicart, Bishop of Laval, *Lettre Pastorale de Monseigneur l'Évêque de Laval Portant Jugement sur l'Apparition qui a eu Lieu à Pontmain le 17 janvier 1871* (Laval: Typographie Mary-Beauchêne, 1872), 1231–2.
14 'We have an obligation not to separate these two dates' AdioL, PC 408, 'Second Anniversaire de l'Apparition', 244.
15 'At bottom France is growing' Quoted in Howard, *Franco-Prussian War*, 373.
16 'Yet another enterprise' Adam, *Mes illusions et nos souffrances*, 20 January, 315.
17 'We all have a fever' Adam, *Mes illusions et nos souffrances*, 23 January, 323.
18 'whatever may be the effect' Quoted in Audoin-Rouzeau, *1870*, 199.
19 'Favre could not hide' Frederick III, *War Diary*, 24 January, 281.
20 'God be praised, the war is over!' Lassberg, *Mein Kriegstagebuch*, 28 January, 283.

19. *From Armistice to Peace*

1 'Unhappy agitators!' Sand, *Journal*, 29 January, 267–8.
2 'an Assembly that is truly national' Quoted in Wetzel, *Duel of Nations*, 197.
3 'Either war or peace' Quoted in Howard, *Franco-Prussian War*, 446.
4 'A crowd of such onlookers' Frederick III, *War Diary*, 1 March, 321.
5 'We must congratulate ourselves' Quoted in Parisot, 'Négotiation', 295.

20. *Settlings Accounts*

1 'One of the most distressing spectacles' Bour, *Rapport sur le Concours pour le Monument*, 3.
2 'May an era of justice' Flach, *Strasbourg après le bombardement*, 88.
3 'Let us teach our children' Quoted in Horne, 'Defining the enemy', 111.
4 'May he grow up a good, upright, true, and trusty man' Frederick III, *War Diary*, 27 January, 285.
5 'And when German unity' Lobb, *Thoughts*, 43.
6 'seems to me to be as petty' Frederick III, *War Diary*, 16 January, 263.
7 'an implacable hatred' Frederick III, *War Diary*, 24 January, 282.
8 Showalter, *Wars of German Unification*, 342–3.
9 'in the succeeding period' Frederick III, *War Diary*, 7 September, 110.
10 'We have lost many men' Quoted and translated in Clayson, *Paris in Despair*, 266.
11 'It is against ourselves' Sorel, *Histoire Diplomatique*, vol. 2, 371.
12 'We must have the courage' Bouloumié, speech in Union des Femmes de France, *Conférence à Lyon*, 25.
13 'France, said to be panicky' Goutière-Vernolle, *Fêtes de Nancy*, ix–x.
14 'make men out of children' Turquan, *Femmes de France*, 155.
15 'Excuse me' 'Cérémonie Patriotique de Mars-la-Tour', *L'Impartial de l'Est*, 18 August 1900.
16 'I love to be broken' Quoted and translated in Simpson, 'From *Zouaves Pontificaux*', 27.
17 'Pontmain is especially the pilgrimage of the future' Archives Diocésains, Laval, PC 442, 'Diocèse de Laval', 743.
18 '*mitrailleuses* creakingly fired' Quoted and translated in Krüger, 'German suffering', 418.
19 'If the memory of 1870' Placard near the monument at Châteaudun.
20 'If I were to allow myself to remember' Quoted in Roynette, 'Village de la mort', 268.
21 'War will never be an instrument of life' Sand, *Journal*, 16 October, 114–15.

List of Illustrations

Index

ALLEN LANE
an imprint of
PENGUIN BOOKS

Also Published

Naomi Klein, *Doppelganger: A Trip Into the Mirror World*

Ludovic Slimak, *The Naked Neanderthal*

Camilla Nord, *The Balanced Brain: The Science of Mental Health*

John Gray, *The New Leviathans: Thoughts After Liberalism*

Michèle Lamont, *Seeing Others: How to Redefine Worth in a Divided World*

Henry Farrell and Abraham Newman, *Underground Empire: How America Weaponized the World Economy*

Yascha Mounk, *The Identity Trap: A Story of Ideas and Power in Our Time*

Kehinde Andrews, *The Psychosis of Whiteness: Surviving the Insanity of a Racist World*

Ian Johnson, *Sparks: China's Underground Historians and Their Battle for the Future*

Diarmuid Hester , *Nothing Ever Just Disappears: Seven Hidden Histories*

David Sumpter, *Four Ways of Thinking: Statistical, Interactive, Chaotic and Complex*

Philip Gold, *Breaking Through Depression: New Treatments and Discoveries for Healing*

Wolfram Eilenberger, *The Visionaries: Arendt, Beauvoir, Rand, Weil and the Salvation of Philosophy*

Giorgio Parisi, *In a Flight of Starlings: The Wonder of Complex Systems*

Klaus-Michael Bogdal, *Europe and the Roma: A History of Fascination and Fear*

Robin Lane Fox, *Homer and His Iliad*

Jessica Rawson, *Life and Afterlife in Ancient China*

Julian Jackson, *France on Trial: The Case of Marshal Pétain*

Wesley Lowery, *American Whitelash: The Resurgence of Racial Violence in Our Time*

Rachel Chrastil, *Bismarck's War: The Franco-Prussian War and the Making of Modern Europe*

Lucy Jones, *Matrescence: On the Metamorphosis of Pregnancy, Childbirth and Motherhood*

Peter Turchin, *End Times: Elites, Counter-Elites and the Path of Political Disintegration*

Paul McCartney, *1964: Eyes of the Storm*

Theresa MacPhail, *Allergic: How Our Immune System Reacts to a Changing World*

John Romer, *A History of Ancient Egypt, Volume 3: From the Shepherd Kings to the End of the Theban Monarchy*

John Rapley and Peter Heather, *Why Empires Fall: Rome, America and the Future of the West*

Scott Shapiro, *Fancy Bear Goes Phishing: The Dark History of the Information Age, in Five Extraordinary Hacks*

Elizabeth-Jane Burnett, *Twelve Words for Moss*

Serhii Plokhy, *The Russo-Ukranian War*

Martin Daunton, *The Economic Government of the World: 1933-2023*

Martyn Rady, *The Middle Kingdoms: A New History of Central Europe*

Michio Kaku, *Quantum Supremacy: How Quantum Computers will Unlock the Mysteries of Science – And Address Humanity's Biggest Challenges*

Andy Clark, *The Experience Machine: How Our Minds Predict and Shape Reality*

Monica Potts, *The Forgotten Girls: An American Story*

Christopher Clark, *Revolutionary Spring: Fighting for a New World 1848-1849*

Daniel Chandler, *Free and Equal: What Would a Fair Society Look Like?*

Jonathan Rosen, *Best Minds: A Story of Friendship, Madness, and the Tragedy of Good Intentions*

Nigel Townson, *The Penguin History of Modern Spain: 1898 to the Present*

Katja Hoyer, *Beyond the Wall: East Germany, 1949-1990*

Quinn Slobodian, *Crack-Up Capitalism: Market Radicals and the Dream of a World Without Democracy*

Clare Carlisle, *The Marriage Question: George Eliot's Double Life*

Matthew Desmond, *Poverty, by America*

Sara Ahmed, *The Feminist Killjoy Handbook*

Bernard Wasserstein, *A Small Town in Ukraine: The place we came from, the place we went back to*

Mariana Mazzucato and Rosie Collington, *The Big Con: How the Consultancy Industry Weakens our Businesses, Infantilizes our Governments and Warps our Economies*

Carlo Rovelli, *Anaximander: And the Nature of Science*

Bernie Sanders, *It's OK To Be Angry About Capitalism*

Martin Wolf, *The Crisis of Democractic Capitalism*

David Graeber, *Pirate Enlightenment, or the Real Libertalia*

Leonard Susskind and Andre Cabannes, *General Relativity: The Theoretical Minimum*

Dacher Keltner, *Awe: The Transformative Power of Everyday Wonder*

William D. Cohan, *Power Failure: The Rise and Fall of General Electric*

John Barton, *The Word: On the Translation of the Bible*

Ryan Gingeras, *The Last Days of the Ottoman Empire*

Greta Thunberg, *The Climate Book*

Peter Heather, *Christendom: The Triumph of a Religion*

Christopher de Hamel, *The Posthumous Papers of the Manuscripts Club*

Ha-Joon Chang, *Edible Economics: A Hungry Economist Explains the World*

Anand Giridharadas, *The Persuaders: Winning Hearts and Minds in a Divided Age*

Nicola Rollock, *The Racial Code: Tales of Resistance and Survival*

Peter H. Wilson, *Iron and Blood: A Military History of German-speaking Peoples since 1500*

Ian Kershaw, *Personality and Power: Builders and Destroyers of Modern Europe*

Alison Bashford, *An Intimate History of Evolution: The Story of the Huxley Family*

Lawrence Freedman, *Command: The Politics of Military Operations from Korea to Ukraine*

Richard Niven, *Second City: Birmingham and the Forging of Modern Britain*

Hakim Adi, *African and Caribbean People in Britain: A History*

Jordan Peterson, *24 Rules For Life: The Box Set*

Gaia Vince, *Nomad Century: How to Survive the Climate Upheaval*

Keith Fisher, *A Pipeline Runs Through It: The Story of Oil from Ancient Times to the First World War*

Christoph Keller, *Every Cripple a Superhero*

Roberto Calasso, *The Tablet of Destinies*

Jennifer Jacquet, *The Playbook: How to Deny Science, Sell Lies, and Make a Killing in the Corporate World*

Frank Close, *Elusive: How Peter Higgs Solved the Mystery of Mass*

Edward Chancellor, *The Price of Time: The Real Story of Interest*

Antonio Padilla, *Fantastic Numbers and Where to Find Them: A Cosmic Quest from Zero to Infinity*

Henry Kissinger, *Leadership: Six Studies in World Strategy*

Chris Patten, *The Hong Kong Diaries*

Lindsey Fitzharris, *The Facemaker: One Surgeon's Battle to Mend the Disfigured Soldiers of World War 1*

George Monbiot, *Regenesis: Feeding the World without Devouring the Planet*

Caroline Knowles, *Serious Money: Walking Plutocratic London*

Serhii Plokhy, *Atoms and Ashes: From Bikini Atoll to Fukushima*

Dominic Lieven, *In the Shadow of the Gods: The Emperor in World History*

Scott Hershovitz, *Nasty, Brutish, and Short: Adventures in Philosophy with Kids*

Bill Gates, *How to Prevent the Next Pandemic*

Emma Smith, *Portable Magic: A History of Books and their Readers*

Kris Manjapra, *Black Ghost of Empire: The Long Death of Slavery and the Failure of Emancipation*

Andrew Scull, *Desperate Remedies: Psychiatry and the Mysteries of Mental Illness*

James Bridle, *Ways of Being: Beyond Human Intelligence*

Eugene Linden, *Fire and Flood: A People's History of Climate Change, from 1979 to the Present*

Cathy O'Neil, *The Shame Machine: Who Profits in the New Age of Humiliation*

Peter Hennessy, *A Duty of Care: Britain Before and After Covid*

Gerd Gigerenzer, *How to Stay Smart in a Smart World: Why Human Intelligence Still Beats Algorithms*

Halik Kochanski, *Resistance: The Undergroud War in Europe, 1939-1945*

Joseph Sassoon, *The Global Merchants: The Enterprise and Extravagance of the Sassoon Dynasty*